Frederick George Lee, John Purchas

The Directorium Anglicanum

Being a Manual of Directions for the Right Celebration of the Holy... Second Edition

Frederick George Lee, John Purchas

The Directorium Anglicanum
Being a Manual of Directions for the Right Celebration of the Holy... Second Edition

ISBN/EAN: 9783744767835

Printed in Europe, USA, Canada, Australia, Japan

Cover: Foto ©Lupo / pixelio.de

More available books at **www.hansebooks.com**

THE · HOLY · EUCHARIST ·

THE
Directorium Anglicanum;

BEING A MANUAL OF DIRECTIONS FOR THE
RIGHT CELEBRATION OF THE
HOLY COMMUNION,
FOR THE SAYING OF MATINS AND EVENSONG, AND FOR THE
PERFORMANCE OF OTHER RITES AND
CEREMONIES OF THE
CHURCH,

According to the Ancient Use of the Church of England.

WITH PLAN OF CHANCEL AND ILLUSTRATIONS OF "SUCH ORNAMENTS OF THE CHURCH, AND OF
THE MINISTERS THEREOF, AT ALL TIMES OF THEIR MINISTRATION, (AS) SHALL BE
RETAINED, AND BE IN USE AS WERE IN THIS CHURCH OF ENGLAND,
BY THE AUTHORITY OF PARLIAMENT, IN THE SECOND
YEAR OF THE REIGN OF KING EDWARD
THE SIXTH."

SECOND EDITION, REVISED.

EDITED BY

THE REV. FREDERICK GEORGE LEE, D C.L.

F. S. A. LOND. AND SCOT.; CHAPLAIN TO THE RIGHT HON.
THE EARL OF MORTON; ETC. ETC.

LONDON·
THOMAS BOSWORTH, 215, REGENT STREET.
1865.

"Let this Sacrament be in such wise done and ministered .... as the good Fathers in the Primitive Church frequented it."—*Homil.* b. ii.

"Here you have an Order for Prayer and for the Reading of Holy Scripture much agreeable to the mind and purpose of the Old Fathers."—*Prayer Book.*

"Whosoever, through his private judgment, willingly and purposely, doth openly break the Traditions and Ceremonies of THE CHURCH, which be not repugnant to the word of GOD, and be ordained and approved by common authority, ought to be rebuked openly."—*Art.* XXXIV.

TO THE ARCHBISHOPS AND BISHOPS

IN VISIBLE COMMUNION

WITH THE SEE OF CANTERBURY

THIS MANUAL

IS WITH EVERY FEELING OF PROFOUND RESPECT

MOST HUMBLY DEDICATED.

Extract from a Charge delivered to the Clergy of New Zealand, September 23, 1847. By George Augustus, Lord Bishop of New Zealand. London: Rivingtons, 1849.

"The care of sacred things is not an idolatry of inanimate matter, but a recognition of the unseen GOD, to whose service they have been dedicated. It has been deemed worthy of record in the Gospel that CHRIST, when He had ended His reading, closed the book, and delivered it to the minister, to be, no doubt, deposited in the proper place, to be preserved from injury and desecration. No event ever happened on earth more awful than the Resurrection, yet it was a work not unworthy of the care of the angels, even at that solemn season to lay the linen clothes by themselves, and to wrap together the napkin that was about the head in a place by itself. Even the linen cloth which had touched the most holy sin-offering was holy in the sight of those heavenly ministers."

Preface.

HE attention given to the decent and orderly performance of Divine Service in the Englifh Church by Priefts trained in the moft oppofite fchools of theology, and the number of new churches built with all the requirements for Catholic ritual, edifices carefully adapted for the celebration of the moft Holy Euchariſt, for the recitation of Matins and Evenfong, and for the other Rites and Ceremonies of the Church, are cheering figns, and efpecially fo when we fee that in cathedral nave and country miffion the Gofpel is being preached to the poor with affectionate warmth and Apoftolic energy. The balance of loving fervice towards our Bleffed LORD is accurately adjufted. Love and Faith keep a right proportion in things pertaining to CHRIST on the one hand, and to His poor members on the other. They lavifh their beft—their "alabafter box of ointment very precious"—on the Houfe and Worfhip of Almighty GOD, and yet ever remember that "the poor fhall never ceafe out of the land." The poor "are always with us," and we muft earneftly call them into His Church to hear the glad tidings which our Bleffed LORD JESUS CHRIST ſtill preaches by His Priefts to "the common people." CHRIST is ftill prefent in His Church, "verily and indeed," in the Sacrament of the Altar, Very GOD and very man, the centre of all Chriftian Worfhip. At fuch a time, and in fuch a hopeful afpect of the Church in this land, no apprehenfion can be felt, in publifhing the prefent Manual, of a charge of overexalting "the mint, and anife, and cummin," of Ritual and Ceremonial, and of unduly depreffing "the weightier matters of the law, judgment, mercy, and faith," feeing that by preaching the word the maffes are being "drawn by the cords of a man" into our churches, and by our ritual are being taught to feel "the beauty of holinefs," and to "worfhip GOD and report that GOD is in us of a truth."

The afpect of the prefent time favourable for the publication of a Manual of Directions for the Clergy.

Preface.

It has been sometimes alleged that the Rubrics of the Book of Common Prayer are in themselves a full and complete guide for the Priest in performing Divine Service, and also (with the Canons of 1603) for "the ornaments of the church and of the ministers thereof." The Canons of 1603 and their bearing upon the Rubrics will be disposed of subsequently.* In regard to the "ornaments," it is patent to every one that we are remanded back to a *stated period* in which the aforesaid "ornaments" were in use in this Church of England by authority of Parliament, viz. the second† year of the reign of Edward the Sixth.

As to the Rubrics being a complete code of ritual directions, the experience of every parish Priest attests that they are insufficient. Nor is any slight thrown upon our Service Book or upon its Revisers by this admission. The Rubrics *are* perfectly sufficient for the guidance of any clergyman moderately acquainted with the traditions of Catholic ritual and the real and ancient Use of the English Church. The Prayer Book was never meant to be a complete Directory; and in this respect it exactly follows the rule adopted by the old English Service Books, and also by the modern Roman Missal. The ancient rubrical directions were equally scanty and curt as our own, and yet they were quite sufficient, for, besides the traditional interpretation and the living commentary of daily practice, the Priest had *other written* directions for his guide which we unfortunately do not possess; in fact, in most churches the Priest was dependent on those other guides almost exclusively: the Missals being well nigh devoid of Rubrics. The printed Missals, which had such interpolations and additions as tended to make the rubrical directions more

sidenotes: The Rubrics of the Book of Common Prayer never were intended for a complete *Directorium*. Neither were those of the ancient English and modern Roman Missal. The Priest in ancient times had a Manual of Directions supplemental to the Service Book.

---

* See *infra*, p. xx, note *.

† "The Statute and the Rubric prove the SECOND YEAR was ultimately selected to regulate the ornaments; in all probability because the majority of the reviewers (of 1559) or the Parliament, or both, felt that while there were *important* distinctions between the ornaments of the *first* year and those of the *second* (as I have already shown¹), the standard of ornaments had, after the latter date, been reduced much lower than was consistent with the Ritual which they themselves wished to settle in the Church of England. Yet, in all this, there is no allusion whatever to Edward's First *Book*—an allusion most natural, if that *Book*, and not the second *Year*, had been in the minds of the various witnesses, more especially as the Secretary Cecil's questions had drawn the especial attention of the Reviewers to Edward's two Books, and had referred to the later Book as taking away Ceremonies" (not *Ornaments*) "the propriety of restoring which they were to consider." Perry's Lawful Church Ornaments, pp. 128, 129.

¹ Perry, pp. 23-39; 50, 51-62; 76-79; 109-114.

complete (naturally in the fewest words), had without doubt the *imprimatur* of the Bishops and Archbishops ere they were issued.

That the Rubrics of the Prayer Book were not at all designed to be, so to speak, a "Ceremonial according to the English rite," will be apparent from the following extract from the portion of the Preface added at the final revision:—"Most of the alterations were made, either first, for the *better direction* of them that are to officiate in any part of Divine Service: which is chiefly done in the Calendars *and Rubrics*." As the Rubrics in the former book, that of 1604, are thus declared to be insufficient guidance for the clergy of 1662 —insufficient from the disuse of the Service Book of the Church, which had been superseded by the "Directory for the Publique Worship of GOD in the three Kingdomes," from the desuetude of Catholic practices, and from the ignorance of the ancient ecclesiastical traditions, consequent thereupon—the present Book has additional and fuller rubrical directions, but still not sufficient to meet every case and each requirement, for that was not the intention of the Revisers, but to amplify them for "the better direction of them that are to officiate." Testimony of the Preface of the Book of Common Prayer.

Such a Manual as the clergy had for the better understanding and interpretation of the Rubrics of the Missal and other Office Books, and such a guide as Catholic tradition and knowledge of the old English Service Books afforded to the first Revisers of those books, and to the officiating Priests of that day, is now attempted to be given in the present volume. That such a work is necessary is only too well known to every clergyman. The recently-ordained Deacon and Priest have had generally no *official* training or example. The college chapel, and only too often the cathedral of the diocese, have with some favoured exceptions, worthy of all honour, been rather beacons to warn them off the rocks of irreverent slovenliness and ritual irregularity, than stars to guide them how to offer, or to assist in offering, acceptable Sacrifices in the Church of GOD. They have thus been forced to follow the mode of "conforming to the Liturgy," as practised in some church which most approves itself to their partially-informed instincts, the selection probably being made from circumstances of proximity or from something else equally accidental. The *Directorium Anglicanum* puts the Priest of the nineteenth century on a par with the Priest of the sixteenth as to ritual knowledge. The need of such learning.

The argument for a ritual is not within the scope of these remarks. We *have* a ritual, and must use it, whether we like it or not. It behoves us to use it aright, and not curtail and mar its fair proportion. Every part of the Church muſt have a ritual, and as there is but one Catholic Church, ſo the ritual of every portion thereof will have a family likeneſs, and be one in ſpirit, though diverſe in details. Ritual and Ceremonial are the hieroglyphics of the Catholic religion, a language underſtanded of the faithful, a kind of parable in action, for as of old when He walked upon this earth, our bleſſed LORD, ſtill preſent in His Divine and human nature in the Holy Euchariſt on the altars of His Church, ſtill ſpiritually preſent at the Common Prayers, does not ſpeak unto us "without a parable." But as our LORD's "viſage was marred more than any man, and His form more than the ſons of men," ſo has it fared, at leaſt in His Church in this land, with the aſpect of His worſhip on earth. For the laſt three hundred years, brief but brilliant periods excepted, our ritual has loſt all unity or ſignificance of expreſſion. We have treated "The Book of Common Prayer and Adminiſtration of the Sacraments, and other Rites and Ceremonies of the Church" much as if it were ſimply a collection of ſundry Forms of Prayer, overlooking the fact that beſides theſe there are acts to be done, and functions to be performed. And theſe* have been done infrequently, not to ſay imperfectly.

<small>Ritual and Ceremonial.</small>

<small>Book of Common Prayer not a Collection of forms of Prayer merely, but of functions to be performed.</small>

The old Puritan idea of Divine Service is confeſſion of ſin, prayer to GOD, and interceſſion for our wants, bodily and ſpiritual. Another theological ſchool, more perhaps in vogue, looks upon praiſe as the great element of worſhip—praiſe, that is, apart from *Euchariſtia*, itſelf, in one ſenſe, a mighty Act of Praiſe. Hence one Prieſt with his form-of-prayer theory affects a bald, chilling, and apparently indevout worſhip, whilſt another laviſhes all the ſplendour of his ritual upon his forms of prayer which are ſaid in choir; and both depreſs, by defective teaching and a maimed ritual, the diſtinctive Service of Chriſtianity. Matins and Evenſong are performed with a ſevere ſimplicity by the one, in an ornate manner by the other. Both ſchools have elements of truth in them, both err after the ſame manner, viz. in undue exaltation of the Church's ordinary Office, and in depreciation of the Sacramental ſyſtem —at leaſt the celebration of the Holy Euchariſt is not with them the centre of Chriſtian Worſhip. Yet ſurely the Communion Service is ſomething more than a mere form of prayer in the opinion of even the laxeſt ſchool of theology. The Zuinglian will admit it to be an acted ſermon. If in

<small>Both ſchools fall ſhort of Catholic truth.</small>

---

* E. g. the Sacraments of Baptiſm and the Holy Euchariſt.

Preface. ix

the dreary eighteenth century a periodical writer* could recommend a Prieſt to preach the ſermons of other divines in order to give more attention to a handſome elocution and an effective delivery; ſurely the ſame pains ought to be beſtowed on the performance of the acted ſermon of the Church. Even the Calviniſt will concede the Liturgy to be an Act, a miniſterial Act, and not a bare form of Prayer. But the Catholic Prieſt, who knows that this action is done in the Perſon of CHRIST, who knows his office to be to perpetuate on the altars of the Church Militant on earth the ſame Sacrifice which the Great High Prieſt conſummated once on the Croſs and perpetuates, not repeats, before the Mercy-ſeat in Heaven, will reverently handle ſuch tremendous myſteries, will be greatly careful that no diſhonour be thoughtleſsly done unto his LORD, WHO vouchſafes to be preſent on our altars. How delicately will he approach even before conſecration the elements which are thus to be ſo ſupernaturally honoured. How will he be exceeding urgent to do all things well as to *matter* and *form*, as to veſtment and ritual, whether in his own perſon or by his aſſiſtants, in this wondrous Service. And if in the Sacrament of the altar ſome things ſtrike the eye as graceful and beautiful, it is well; but this is not their object. The one aim is to offer the Holy Sacrifice in a worthy manner to Almighty GOD.

<small>The doctrine of the Church.</small>

<small>The Catholic Prieſt and the Holy Euchariſt.</small>

The order of the Offices in the Prayer Book has been adhered to in the DIRECTORIUM with this exception, that the directions for celebrating the Holy Euchariſt, as being the centre of all Chriſtian Worſhip, have been placed firſt. The Book of Common Prayer naturally puts the Ordinary Office before the Liturgy proper, as the Holy Euchariſt is generally ſuppoſed to be preceded† by the recitation of the Divine Office. But in a work which interprets rubrics, and explains, however inadequately, the theory of Chriſtian Worſhip, it ſeemed fitting to commence with what was in the earlieſt ages of Chriſtianity the *only* diſtinctive Chriſtian Worſhip,‡ and from which the Ordinary Office is an offshoot, a *radius*, not a ſubſtitute for it under any circumſtances. To theſe conſiderations it may be added that there is one Book

<small>The arrangement of Services in *Directorium Anglicanum*.</small>

---

* Addiſon, in the Spectator (No. 106).
† See Principles of Divine Service. Introd. to Part II. p. 116, note f.
‡ In regard to the Worſhip of the Early Church, the "Breaking of Bread" (Acts ii. 42) is believed to be the real and only *characteriſtic Chriſtian* Worſhip, and the "Prayers" to be at that time the Hour-Services of the Temple, which paſſed, on its deſtruction, into the adoption of ſimilar Services by the Chriſtian Church.

b

Preface.

of Holy Scripture—the Apocalypſe—which reveals to us the Ritual of Heaven. That Ritual is the normal form of the worſhip of the Chriſtian Church. The full ſcope and burden of the Epiſtle to the Hebrews is this, that the law was a ſhadow of good things to come, and not the very image of the things, that in the law we have but a copy (ὑπόδειγμα), but that in the Goſpel we have the object itſelf as in a mirror, the very image, (αὐτὴ ἡ εἰκών), the expreſs image or ſtamp. The Jewiſh Ritual was therefore a type or ſhadow of the Ritual of Heaven, which would be hereafter; not as then exiſting, at leaſt in the form it was to aſſume in the fulneſs of time. If the Jewiſh ritual had been a copy or pattern of things exiſting in Heaven at that time, it would have been an image thereof, not a ſhadow or type. But "coming events caſt their ſhadows before," and, it is written with reverence, the Worſhip of Heaven, always objective, became amplified, and, ſo to ſpeak, *ocularly objective*, (as GOD could be ſeen of man), when the Hypoſtatic Union took place; when bone of our bone, fleſh of our fleſh, was worſhipped by the Angelic hoſt in the Seſſion of the Incarnate Word in His glorified Humanity at the Right Hand of GOD the FATHER Almighty. Moſes was admoniſhed when he was about to make the tabernacle; "for ſee, ſaith He, that thou make all things according to the pattern ſhowed to thee in the Mount." The Jewiſh ritual was the ſhadow caſt upon earth from the throne of GOD of the Worſhip which was to be in heaven after the Incarnation and Aſcenſion of the GOD-MAN, our LORD JESUS CHRIST, WHO pleads before the throne His Sacrifice, at once the Victim, the "Lamb as it had been ſlain," and High Prieſt. The Ritual of Heaven is objective, and the principal worſhip of the Church on earth is equally ſo by reaſon of its being identical with the Normal and Apocalyptic ritual, and thus containing a great action, even the perpetuation of the Sacrifice made on the Croſs, in an unbloody manner on the altar. Not that this great action, the moſt marvellous condeſcenſion of the CREATOR to the creature ſince the Sacrifice, never to be repeated, was once offered on Calvary, excludes common prayer; not ſo, the prayers of the faithful form an appendage to the Holy Sacrifice of the altar. The Church in Heaven and on earth is indeed one, and the Holy Euchariſt* as a Sacrifice is all one with the Memorial made by our High Prieſt Himſelf in the very Sanctuary of Heaven, where He is both Prieſt,

marginal notes: The Jewiſh ritual a type of the Worſhip of heaven after the Hypoſtatic Union. The ritual of heaven always *objective*, became more intenſely ſo at the Aſcenſion of the Incarnate Word, viz. *ocularly objective* for ever.

---

* See Keble on Euchariſtical Adoration, p. 72.

after the order of Melchisedec, and Offering, by the perpetual presentation of His Body and Blood; therefore the Ritual of Heaven and earth must be one,—one, that is, in intention and signification, though under different conditions as to its expression.

A rationale has been given of Matins and Evensong, because the recitation of the Divine Office has been very grievously misunderstood. Matins and Evensong are the only Forms of Prayer without an action, and though not subjective, (for they are Common Prayers to ONE spiritually present); they form from their Eucharistic analogy the only permissible Divine Service without celebration of the Holy Communion, the only *Dry Service*, so to speak, which is not an unreality.

As to the Service to be used on Sundays and Holydays if there is no Communion, it will be observed that in the earlier pages of this work it is spoken of as *missa sicca*; in the latter part [following Mr. Freeman] as the Proanaphoral Service. Though our awful preference for a form of prayer, extracted from the order for the Administration of the Sacrament of the Holy Eucharist, to the Celebration itself, renders the name of the mediæval corruption really applicable, yet doubtless the latter term is the correct one.

No rationale has been given of the Communion Service, nor of Holy Baptism, nor of the Sacramental and Occasional Offices. These functions involve actions; and acts speak for themselves: but very minute Rubrical Directions are given, and much matter illustrative of what may be called "the secret history" of the Services will be found in the notes.

Nowhere is the Catholic spirit of the Prayer Book more plainly set forth, or in a more marked manner than in the Preface of 1662, which precedes the statement "Concerning the Service of the Church,"* and "Of Ceremonies, why some be abolished and some retained,"† and in those documents themselves. And yet these important statements have never had the attention bestowed‡ upon them even by some of the most approved ritualists of the day, which their very great value commands. *The importance of the Preface of 1662 as a document declarative of the Catholic spirit of the Book of Common Prayer.*

It has been truly said that the statement "Concerning the Service of the Church" "is the most authoritative exposition anywhere to be found of

---

* The original Preface in the Book of 1549.

† First inserted after the Preface in the Book of 1552. In the First Book (1549) it is placed after the Service for the First Day of Lent (Commination Service).

‡ Thus Mr. Procter, in his "History of the Book of Common Prayer," omits all mention of this part of the Book.

the principles of the English Church, and of the relation in which she desires to stand towards other branches of the Church Catholic."*

The *Directorium Anglicanum* has been based upon the principles laid down in these unmistakable and authoritative manifestos of the spirit, usage, and ritual of the Church of England. A key is given in the Preface of 1662 to the then alterations.

<small>This Manual based on the principles embodied in that Preface.</small>

"If any man, who shall desire a more particular account of the several Alterations in any part of the Liturgy, shall take pains to compare the present Book with the former; we doubt not but the reason of the change may readily appear." If the comparison of our present Service Book with its predecessors be needful for a perfect understanding of the Rubrics, it follows as a corollary that equally necessary is it to institute a comparison with the rubrical directions in the pre-reformation Service Books, (of which our Prayer Book is a revised collection), especially in an age in which the careful performance of Divine Worship is a happy characteristic, and yet in which, from the laxity of former times, the old Catholic uses and traditions, which were *household words* to the revisers of 1549, and which were familiar to those of 1661, are in some sort lost sight of. Hence this attempt to read our Rubrics by the light of the pre-reformation Service Books and ancient ecclesiastical customs: and not only have the old English Missal and Breviary rubrics been so used in putting together the *Directorium*, but also the most ancient Liturgies, agreeable with the King's warrant for the Conference at the Savoy, 25th of March, 1661. The terms of the commission, which are very important, are "To† advise upon and renew the said Book of Common Prayer, *comparing the same with the most ancient Liturgies* which have been used in the Church, in the primitive and purest times." It is, therefore, reasonable to refer to the Liturgies which the revisers of 1661 were to look to for a guide in their review of the Ritual. And that such a course was expedient for them, and is so for us in order that we may rightly understand their alterations, and indeed the whole spirit of the Prayer Book, is also evident from the language of the Homily,‡ that the Holy Sacrament of the altar should be " in such wise done and administered as the good Fathers of the Primitive Church frequented it;" as well as from the injunction§ that preachers

---

* "The Prayer Book; and how to use it." Churchman's Library, p. 4.
† Card. Hist. Conf. p. 300.
‡ Homil. b. ii.
§ "But chiefly they (the preachers) shall take heed that they teach nothing in their preaching, which they would have the people religiously to observe and believe, but that which is

in their sermons were to follow the consent of the Catholic Fathers and Doctors.

The ancient Liturgies, the mediæval Service Books, the present Uses of the East and West, have all been consulted to throw light upon and to interpret the Rubrics of our own Service Book in the *Directorium*, on the principle recognized by the last Revisers in their rejection of such proposed alterations* "as were either of dangerous consequence (as secretly striking at some established doctrine or laudable practice of the Church of England, or *indeed of the whole Catholic Church* of CHRIST) or else of no consequence at all, but utterly frivolous and vain."

Ritualism is a science as well as theology, and is in point of fact closely connected therewith, seeing that Divine Service is composed of rites and ceremonies, which involve Ritual and Ceremonial in their performance, and as Liturgies contain and are conservators of doctrine, so the Rubrics—enjoining a certain amount of Ritual and Ceremonial, and supposing and permitting a greater development of it than is laid down *nominatim*—are the very language of dogma. Divine Service is also compacted of "Christian persons," i.e. bodies *redeemed* by the SAVIOUR, and which therefore owe Him a dignified and honourable homage by prostration, and gestures of adoration, humility, and the like. Ritualism a science.

The religious use and the science of Ceremonial and Ritual are fully recognized in the Preface to the Book of Common Prayer. In the statement, "Of ceremonies, why some be abolished and some retained," Ritual and Ceremonial are distinctly accepted as "pertaining to edification," not† only as serving "to a decent order and godly discipline," but also as "apt to stir up the dull mind of man to the remembrance of his duty to GOD by some notable and special signification." The religious use and science of Ceremonial and Ritual recognized in the Book of Common Prayer.

The Preface authoritatively declares that Ritual and Ceremonial conduce to "edification," thus recognizing their theological use. What this consists of it may be well to state categorically. The science of Ritual and Ceremonial has a theological and a sacramental function. But the province of each function is intertwined with that of the other so as to be inseparable.

---

agreeable to the doctrine of the Old Testament and the New, and that which the Catholic Fathers and ancient Bishops have gathered out of that doctrine." Liber quorundam canonum disciplinæ Ecclesiæ Anglicanæ. Anno 1571.

* The Preface, Book of Common Prayer.

† But a preference is given to what is ancient in comparison with what is new.

Preface.

The primary use of Ritual and Ceremonial is founded on the claims of Almighty GOD upon the homage and love of His creatures. Hence it is that His Priest performs all Divine offices (and especially the celebration of the Holy Eucharist) with a minute and reverend care, perfectly without respect to the presence of worshippers, or to their absence. It is this that prompts him to use "the best member that he has" to the praise and glory of GOD, "Who made man's mouth;" a function which must edify both Priest and people. But He who made man's mouth, "made the eye" also, and seeing that we possess material bodies and are not simply spirits, which we shall only be in the intermediate state, He has been pleased to teach us in His Church through the visual organ, whilst we are praising Him with our lips out of the fulness of our hearts. Nor is this edification of the soul through the *medium* of the corporal eye, this *objectivity* in Divine Service, a mere concession to human weakness and infirmity, seeing that in the Church above we shall worship before the throne with spiritual bodies, and that the Divine ritual, as has been shown,* is of a purely objective character.

<small>Primary use of Ritual and Ceremonial.</small>

The ends to which Ritual and Ceremonial minister may be thus classified:—

I. They are the safeguards of Sacraments—that they may "be rightly and duly administered," and not endangered either in respect of "matter" or "form" by the chances of negligence or indevotion.

II. They are the expressions of doctrine, and witnesses to the Sacramental system of the Catholic religion.

III. They are habitual and minute acts of love to Him "Who so loved us," for love is shown not only in "the doing of some great thing," in the performance of some august rite in the very Presence of GOD, but also in an affectionate, reverent, and pious care in even the smallest details of the Service of the Sanctuary—marks of love to our Blessed LORD in the performance of Divine Service generally, and of dread and binding obligation in whatsoever concerns the essence of the Sacraments.

IV. They are securities for respect by promoting GOD'S glory in the eyes of men, and also in serving to put the Priest in remembrance of Him Whom he serves and Whose he is. This consideration has caused the giving of *directions* for the sacrifty as well as the sanctuary; for as the sanctity of a church is not a quality inherent in the worshippers according to the old Puritan idea, but in the building itself, the

<small>Directions needed for the sacrifty as well as the sanctuary.</small>

---

* See pp. ix, x.

Preface.   xv

consecrated House of God; so the rules which guide the Priest and choir, when out of sight of the faithful, will be as religiously observed as the rubrics and traditional usages which govern their actions and deportment when in their presence. All clergymen probably kneel down in the sacristy and say a prayer before vesting, and also pray whilst putting on the vestments. It seems desirable for us to use the same form of prayer, and *that* form appears most to commend itself which was used by the ancient clergy of England. Hence the selection of prayers for the sacristy which will be found in this Manual. Prayers for the Priest whilst vesting.

Thus it is evident that Ritual and Ceremonial tend to the "edification" of the Church, are "apt to stir up the dull mind of man to the remembrance of his duty to God by some notable signification," and conduce to the maintenance of "a decent order and godly discipline."

It is now proper to state the *statutable* authority of the "Ornaments of the Church and of the Ministers thereof." The Rubric before the "Order for Morning Prayer daily throughout the year," which regulate the "ornaments," directs that such ornaments "shall be retained and be in use as were in this Church of England by the authority of Parliament, in the second year of King Edward the Sixth." The authority of Parliament in the second year evidently refers to the statute of 25 Henry VIII. c. 19, § 7, which expressly enacts, "That such canons, constitutions, ordinances, and synodals provincial, being already made, which be not contrariant or repugnant to the laws, statutes, and customs of this realm, nor to the damage or hurt of the King's prerogative royal, *shall now still be used and executed as they were before the passing of this Act*, till such time as they be viewed, searched, or otherwise ordered and determined by the two and thirty persons authorized by the Act,* or the more part of them, according to the tenor, form, and effect of this present Act;"—an undertaking which was never accomplished, and therefore the ancient canons and provincial constitutions have still the force of statute law, subject to the limitations provided by the aforesaid Act of Parliament. It is, moreover, to be borne in mind that there is no statute of the second year of Edward VI. which contains any enactments respecting the Ornaments of the Church, and even the First Prayer Book of Edward VI. (which was authorized by the statute of the 2nd and 3rd of Edward VI. c. 1, but the use of which was not enjoined till the Feast of Pentecost then next coming, in other words till the *third* year The *statutable* authority of the "Ornaments of the Church and of the Ministers thereof."

---

* The 35 of Henry VIII. c. 16, § 2, renewed this for life.

of that King's reign, though it is doubtless *supplemental* to the old canons and constitutions of the Church of England," by the authority of Parliament in the second year of Edward VI.) does not describe the "Ornaments" of the Church, although it gives some directions for the Priest and his assistants for the celebration of the Holy Communion, thus following the order of the Missal, as of course the new Book, ostensibly a revised form of the old "Use," would not deviate from the accustomed arrangement, viz. that the Rubrics of the Missal were not, except *incidentally*, the direction for the ornaments and utensils of Divine Service. The old English Missals mention *nominatim* in an incidental manner nearly the same* *instrumenta* as the First Book of Edward VI.† does, whilst the modern Roman Missal specifies by name even a smaller number of utensils and ornaments, those of the minister not being mentioned at all.‡ It has been a *vexata quæstio* with some whether the first

<small>Ornaments named in the Ordinary and Canon of the Mass.</small>

---

* The York use prescribes *nominatim* precisely the same things; the Sarum, Bangor, and Hereford uses are rather more full in this respect.

† Elizabeth's Book (1559) only mentions the ornaments of the *minister* in the Rubric which governs this department of Divine Service. But this book was Edward's *second* book (1552) REVISED, and the rubric relating to "ornaments" was the *revised* rubric of that second book, the essential difference being—that now the minister was ordered to *use* the very ornaments which that second book had bidden him to disuse; but that rubric made no mention of the ornaments of the church, neither therefore did this.¹ However, Act 1 Eliz. c. 2, § 25, provides "that *such ornaments of the church* and of the ministers thereof shall be retained and be in use, as were in the Church of England by authority of Parliament, in the second year of the reign of King Edward VI." Our own rubric is the rubric of Elizabeth's and James' Books expanded in phraseology, taken from the Act of Elizabeth, and thus makes mention of both the ornaments of the church and of the ministers.

‡ In the Roman Missal the "ornaments of the ministers" are mentioned only in the

---

¹ "If it be thought strange that at a time, when both the ornaments of the church and of the minister had been under consideration, a distinct notice should be taken, in the rubric, of the latter and not of the former; it seems sufficient to say—that (1) like *both* of Edward's Books Elizabeth's Prayer Book was following the order of the old Missals in giving some direction for the habits of the Priest and his assistants at the celebration of the Holy Communion, though, like them, it did not prescribe the ornaments of the church; (2) that at a time when the marked tendency of the reforming party was as much (if not more) to cast off the *vestments* of the clergy as the ornaments of the church, it is not at all surprising that this order should have been distinctly put before them: the ornaments of the *Church* did not depend upon the parochial or the cathedral clergy: they existed in the churches, and the clergy had no *personal* power or authority to remove them, even if they disliked them: but they certainly had the power (and perhaps would claim the *authority*) to dispense with the use of a *personal* ornament. Moreover, the known anti-ceremonial tendencies of those whom the new reign had brought back to England (not to mention the anti-ritual party which had remained, and who now had hopes from the Queen) was in itself a reason for preventing them from casting aside their Ecclesiastical Vestments, as they were likely to do, and as it will be seen they soon attempted. It was of more consequence that 'the minister' should use the proper vestment, than even that the *church* should be correctly adorned: the likeliest way to secure this was by a rubric such as the one in question: merely to print the Act of Parliament at the beginning of the book, without drawing attention to this provision of it, would in all likelihood have been simply nugatory; for but few probably would think it needful to be read." Perry's Lawful Church Ornaments, pp. 132, 133.

Rubric in the Book of Common Prayer which regulates the ornaments of the church and of the ministers, refers to the ancient laws of the English Church, which have the force of statute law by virtue of 25 Henry VIII, or to the First Book of Edward VI. The present Manual was compiled in the belief that the "authority of Parliament" in the Rubric was intended to apply only to those ancient canons and provincial constitutions made statutable by the Act of Parliament alluded to; but subsequent investigation of the subject has induced the editor to modify that opinion thus far, viz. that the Rubric refers not only to the canon law, but also that it includes the First Book (of 1549). And this conclusion is grounded on the express reference in the Act of 5 and 6 Edward VI. c. 1, § 5, authorizing the Second Book (of 1552), which speaks of the Act of the 2 and 3 Edward VI, authorizing the First Book (of 1549, the *third* year), as the Act "made in the *second year* of the King's Majesty's reign." It is, therefore, reasonable to take the Rubric to refer primarily to the older canons and constitutions "which be not contrariant or repugnant to the laws and statutes of this realm, &c." to our present Book, and also to the First Book (of 1549), containing the reformed Missal, Breviary, and other Offices, with whose structure the ornaments ordered by the ancient canon law were to be in harmony.

The recent Judgment of the Judicial Committee of Her Majesty's most honourable Privy Council in the case of the churches of SS. Paul and Barnabas, in the Appeal Liddell *v.* Westerton, delivered March 21st, 1857, has decided that the First Book of Edward VI. *is* referred to in the rubric; the question of Parliamentary sanction given to the old canons and provincial constitutions was not entered into, and was only referred to collaterally. Bishop Cosin, one of the chief of the Revisers of 1661, in several passages of his *Notes** assumes that Edward's First Book is included as *part* of the authority of Parliament in Edward's second year, but he nowhere treats it as the *exclusive* authority. In addition to the ancient canon law and the book of 1549 he also cites the Injunctions of 1547† as a *supplemental* authority for altar lights. Now, though the First Book of Edward VI. was never *intended* to

<small>The First Book of Edward *part* of the authority of Parliament in second year.

The Injunctions of 1547 retain and order the lights on the altar at celebration of Holy Communion, as authorized by the old English Canons and</small>

Rubricæ generales Missalis [xix. *De qualitate paramentorum*]. In the First Book of Edward VI. they are mentioned in the third Rubric before "the Supper of the LORD, commonly called the Mass," in the first Rubric after the Collects, printed at the conclusion of the Mass, and in "Certain Notes" at the end of the book.

* See Cosin's Works, vol. v. pp. 227-30, 232, 233, 305, 436, 438, 440.

† *Ibid.* p. 231.

xviii   Preface.

<small>Provincial Constitutions.</small> be our complete directory for the ornaments either of the ministers or of the church, yet it contains *nominatim* the Eu-
<small>Edward's First Book gives nominatim the *Eucharistic vestments*.</small> charistic vestments: while the Injunctions of 1547 order the lights on the altar, and the inventories* of church goods (taken in 1552) in the Record Office, at Carlton Ride, prove
<small>The Inventories at Carlton Ride give lists of crosses, &c.</small> that they were retained by the Injunctions of 1547, and were in use by the authority of Parliament during the second year, and beyond it. These inventories give copious lists of crosses,
<small>No practical difference whether we appeal to the old canons or not, as Edward's Injunctions and First Book, together with the Carlton Ride Inventories, give all that is needed as far as ritual is concerned.</small> candlesticks, altar cloths and linen, vestments, frames for stone altars, lecterns, &c. &c. Therefore it makes no *practical* difference, however interesting as a recondite *legal* question, whether we go to the old canons and provincial constitutions *and* to Edward's Injunctions and First Book, or to the Injunctions and First Book alone (with the Carlton Ride Inventories) as authority for Lawful Church Ornaments.

But that the Book of 1549 was not referred to solely as the guide for "ornaments"—(it does not mention *any* church ornaments, though it does some utensils, *instrumenta*, used in Divine Service), will be *quite evident* from the following remarkable passage in Cosin's *Notes*,—"But† what the ornaments of the church and the ministers are not here specified;" (the Eucharistic vestments *are* specified in the rubrics of Edward's First Book; Cosin must, therefore, have been referring *to other ornaments* of the minister in use by authority of Parliament in the second year), "and they are so unknown to many, that by most they are neglected. Wherefore it were requisite that those ornaments used in the second year of King Edward, should be here particularly named and set forth, that there might be no difference about them." Now, if in Edward's First Book *all* "the ornaments of the church and of the ministers" were set forth *nominatim*, it would have been needless to specify what they were in a Rubric promulgated for that purpose, for there could be no possible difference of opinion upon this point. In addition to this, Mr. Perry (to whose labours the present writer is much indebted) in his learned and thoroughly exhaustive volume on "Lawful Church Ornaments," cites Archdeacon Robert Booth's (of Durham) Articles of Inquiry,‡ *circa* 1710-20, in which the provincial constitutions are referred to *throughout*, and spoken of as ecclesiastical laws

---

* Mr. Chambers, in his "Strictures Legal and Historical," gives an analysis of these Inventories of the Ornaments which remained in 1552, in 415 churches; only *eight* of the number being of an earlier date, viz. 1549.
† See Cosin's Works, vol. v. p. 507.   ‡ Lawful Church Ornaments, p. 459.

Preface.   xix

now in force. Thus the *ftatutable* authority of the ancient canon law seems perfectly clear, and Edward's Firft Book has been pronounced by the Court of Final Appeal to be the ftatutable authority for ornaments, and is to be regarded, as referred to in the Rubric "by the authority of Parliament in the fecond year of Edward VI," as the reformed exponent of the old canons and provincial conftitutions.

To fum up—firftly—the Rubric remands us back to the old canons and conftitutions, paffed before the Reformation, to fuch of which it gives ftatutable authority, as are not "contrariant or repugnant" to fubfequent enactments on the fubject; and fecondly, to Edward's Firft Book, as has been fhown at pp. xvi. xvii. and determined by the Privy Council; and thirdly, to the Injunctions of 1547, which were in force by authority of Parliament in the fecond year.

Bifhop Cofin thought it convenient (fee *fupra*, p. xviii.) that an inventory of the ornaments, *inftrumenta*, veftments, &c. of Edward's celebrated fecond year fhould be drawn up. For it is not every parifh Prieft who is familiar with the ancient canon law; and in Cofin's time, even the rubrics of Edward's Firft Book, which, with the Injunction of 1547, ordering and retaining the two altar-lights, give all that is effential as far as ritual is concerned, were not acceffible to the body of the clergy as they are now in reprints and other publications. Following out the fuggeftion of this eminent ritualift and divine, worthy of all attention from us as coming from the leading revifer of 1661, fuch an inventory is now for the firft time fupplied by the *Directorium Anglicanum*. Bp. Cofin thought that a lift of ornaments of the fecond year fhould be given. His fuggeftion carried out in the prefent Manual.

The ornaments of the Second Year muft be fought for in that portion of the ancient Englifh Canons and Provincial Conftitutions which relates to Ornament, Ritual, and Ceremonial, with the following limitations, viz. fuch ornaments, &c. as were abolifhed *before* the fecond year of Edward VI. and all fuch as are inconfiftent with the ftructure of the Book of Common Prayer. A complete lift of the titles of the feveral conftitutions and canons bearing upon the fubject is given at p. 466, in Mr. Perry's valuable work fo often referred to in this preface, and the whole of this portion of the ancient canon law is printed at length with its later *practical* modifications, and the ftatutable refiduum is thereby plainly fhown. Thus the ritualift, the parifh Prieft, and the inquiring churchwarden,* can fee at a glance

---

* "It will be feen by a comparifon of what each is to provide, that the parifhioners were and *are* refponfible for whatever was or *is effential to* Divine Service; the Prieft for 'other decent

what the ornaments* of the Second Year really are from the lift at p. 491, and alfo the canons and conftitutions which order them, duly docketed as "unrepealed," "partly repealed," "unrepealed, but obfolete," "wholly repealed,"—as the cafe may be. Befides this, the inventories† of church goods in the Record Office, at Carlton Ride, eftablifh the fact of thefe ornaments, in addition to his liability to maintain' the principal chancel. This, then, feems a diftinct anfwer to the prevalent notion, no lefs than to fome deliberate ftatements which are to be met with, to the effect, that the clergyman has nothing whatever to do *with ordering the ornaments of the church*. So far is this from being true, that the canon fays he '**MAY BE COMPELLED**' by the ordinary to find them." Lawful Church Ornaments, p. 488.

* A difficulty exifts in the minds of fome in reconciling the canons of 1603 with the rubric which governs the veftments. The XXIVth Canon orders copes to be worn in cathedral churches by thofe that adminifter the Sacrament of the LORD's Supper; and the LVIIIth Canon directs "minifters reading Divine Service and *adminiftering the Sacraments* to wear hoods." This would prefcribe a *quafi* Euchariftic veftment in cathedrals, but no fpecial Euchariftic veftment for parifh churches. It fhould, however, be remembered that the Canons of 1603 (which though never confirmed by Parliament like the rubric, yet as fanctioned by *Convocation* are the law of ecclefiaftics *fubfidiary* to the rubrics of the Book of Common Prayer) cannot, and efpecially fince the final revifion which gave us the prefent Book of 1662, govern, control, or limit the rubric, which is *ftatutable*, while the Canons (of 1603) are not. The reafon for the apparent difcrepancy of the Canons (of 1603) and the rubric will be found in the time the Canons were promulgated. It then feemed almoft hopelefs to enforce the ftatutable ornaments of the rubric, fo the Bifhops acquiefced in the loweft poffible amount of "ornaments," ritual and ceremonial under the preffure of Puritan neceffity. The old canons and the rubrics were almoft ignored—fo the Canons of 1603 were promulgated, to compafs bare decency and order. We obey the *fpirit* of the Canons of 1603 in exact proportion as we adhere to the *letter* of the rubric. And here it may be noted in regard to the phrafe "veftment *or* cope" in the firft book of Edward VI. that the chafuble was always called "*the* veftment," and it has been thought that the allowance of the cope refers to the cafe of a *Miffa ficca*.[1]

† Thefe Inventories are acceffible in Mr. Chambers' Strictures, Legal and Hiftorical; Mr.

[1] This ought only to apply to Good Friday (*if*, not having the mafs of the prefanctified, we are right in not celebrating on that day); as a fufficient number of the faithful ought always to be encouraged to ftay at all times, whether they actually communicate or not, which will not be difcovered till afterwards, fo as to make a quorum in the fenfe of the rubric—even if they go out after the Prayer of Oblation or the Exhortation, it will be too late for the Prieft to ftop. Abfent fick perfons who communicate fpiritually ought alfo to be counted in. Thus there can be no great difficulty in offering the Holy Sacrifice daily according to the mind of the Church: "Note alfo, that the Collect, Epiftle, and Gofpel appointed for the Sunday *fhall ferve all the week after*, where it is not in this Book otherwife ordered." Book of Common Prayer. The only prohibitory rubric is the third at the end of the Communion Service. But no Prieft in a parifh which had *above* "twenty perfons of difcretion," &c. would be legally precluded from acting on his own judgment, and celebrating if he communicated one perfon only, or even if one perfon only fpiritually communicated. It fhould be borne in mind that in parifhes where there is a fmaller number of "perfons of difcretion," &c. than the number mentioned in the rubric, the "twenty perfons" might ufually be made up either by perfons accidentally ftaying in the parifh, or by thofe who might come from a diftance, fo that fave where the Prieft acted rigidly upon the rubric requiring perfons to give notice the night before, he would have no opportunity of knowing who were going to communicate at leaft till after the Prayer for the Church Militant, and therefore if the convenient number were prefent at the beginning of that Prayer, he muft make the Oblation, and having done that, muft, as already ftated, *confecrate*.

ornaments, viz. crucifixes, crosses, altar candlesticks, altar cloths, lecterns, altar-frames, corporals, Eucharistic and other vestments, (on this point, however, viz. the vestments being *statutable*, there was never any question), and divers other ornaments and utensils, being in actual use in and after Edward's second year. A complete inventory of these "ornaments of the church and of the ministers" is given in the Appendix to this Manual. It should be remembered that ornaments in use in the specified year are *lawful* ornaments; but even if they cannot be found among the statutable ornaments of the second year, as, e.g. the white bands, black scarf, organs, hassocks, and the like, and these are certainly *not* found among the ornaments of the second year, they are equally *lawful* ornaments if not at variance with them, or with the Service Book. The first book of Edward VI. is the structure with which these ornaments must be in harmony. And, as has been already shown, since the Eucharistic vestments are given *nominatim* in that Book, the altar-lights secured by Injunctions of 1547, and the altar-cross (or crucifix, if it be preferred), proved to be lawful by the Carlton Ride inventories; all is given that is required for Catholic ritual, even were the old canon law not of *statutable* authority—and there is no doubt it is. The Eucharistic vestments, the altar lights, and the altar cross of *statutable* authority, even without the old canon law, which is statutable also.

It is now time to consider how far Ritual and Ceremonial not specified *nominatim* in the Rubrics of the Prayer Book are affected by the Act of Uniformity, by the 2nd article of Canon XXXVI. to which subscription at Ordination is required, and by Canon XIV. equally binding upon spiritual persons. How far Ritual and Ceremonial not expressly named in the Book of Common Prayer are consistent with the Act of Uniformity, the 2nd article of Canon XXXVI. and Canon XIV. of 1603.

The statute of 1 Eliz. c. 1, which enforces the Act of 2 and 3 of Edward VI. c. 1, orders, "That all ministers shall be bound to say and use the Matins, Evensong, Administration of each of the Sacraments, and all other common and open prayer in such order and form as is mentioned in the said Book so authorized by Parliament, and *none other or otherwise*." And the statute 14 Charles II. enacts, "That the former good laws and statutes of this realm which have been formerly made, and are still in force for the uniformity of Prayer and Administration of the Sacraments, shall stand in full force and strength to all intents and purposes whatever, for the establishing

---

Perry's Lawful Church Ornaments; the Ecclesiologist, Nos. cxiii. cxiv; and Stephen's edition of the Book of Common Prayer, vol. i. fol. 352-61. A selection from Mr. Chambers' Collection is given in the Appendix.

and confirming the said Book . . . hereinafter mentioned, to be joined and annexed to this Act."

The 2nd Article of Canon XXXVI. orders, "That he (the person to be ordained) will use the form in the said Book prescribed, in Public Prayer and Administration of the Sacraments, *and none other*."

Canon XIV. provides, "That all ministers shall likewise observe the orders, rites, and ceremonies prescribed in the Book of Common Prayer, as well in reading the Holy Scriptures and saying of Prayers, as in administration of the Sacraments, *without either diminishing in regard of preaching, or in any other* respect, or adding anything in the matter or form thereof."

In regard to the Act of Uniformity, it should be borne in mind that Elizabeth's Act of Uniformity was followed by Injunctions explanatory of the very Rubrics of the Book which the statute enforced. The Act is aimed against the practice of the Puritans who endeavoured to avoid everything the Book *enjoined*, but which they disliked, and failing this to get rid of the Book altogether. Hence the need to insist on the complete use of the Service Book. The Act which restored the furniture to the altar and the vestment to the Priest could never mean to forbid the details of Catholic Ritual and Ceremonial and to limit every gesture of reverence: it would not specifically enjoin them, for who would expect an Act of Parliament to be a complete manual of directions for the performance of Divine Service? it was rather meant to exclude *interpolated* prayers; matters of Ritual and Ceremonial were not, strictly speaking, within its scope. The explanatory Injunctions of Elizabeth sufficiently prove that her Act of Uniformity does not regard the Rubrics of the Prayer Book as a perfect directory for Divine Worship; and the unavoidable, but most important corollary is, that those Rubrics cannot be argued from *negatively*; they cannot be interpreted as forbidding what they do not enjoin.

The terms of Canon XXXVI. are precisely the same, and when it is considered "That these Canons, being a hundred and forty-one, were collected by Bishop Bancroft out of the Articles, Injunctions, and Synodical Acts passed and published in the reigns of Edward VI. and Queen Elizabeth," (Collier's Ecc. Hist. vol. ii. p. 687,) the *animus* of them, and of the Article in question, must be self-evident: it was against the depravers of the Liturgy, not against the faithful and learned Priests who scrupulously carried out its Rubrics. In the words of Blomfield, Bishop of London:—
"No[*] one who reads the history of those times with attention can doubt

---

[*] *Apud* Robertson's "How to Conform to the Liturgy," p. 8.

that the object of the legiflature who impofed upon the Clergy a fubfcription to the above declaration, was the fubftitution of the Book of Common Prayer for the Miffal of the Roman Catholics, or the Directory of the Puritans."

Canon XIV. cautions the Puritan preacher not to diminifh from the Service Book by preaching doctrine inconfiftent therewith, and not to add anything in refpect of form or matter: thus admitting the Liturgy to be the confervator of doctrine, and Ritual and Ceremonial to be the fafeguards of Sacraments and teachers of dogma. For "matter" and "form" are well-known theological terms having a technical meaning,* and point mainly to the prefervation and right adminiftration of the Sacraments—which certainly were in danger at the time of the promulgation of thefe canons. Thefe terms were probably alfo intended to check fuch irregularities as the omiffion of the crofs in Baptifm, the making the father anfwer queftions with the godfathers and godmothers, the omiffion of the Abfolution, *Venite*, *Te Deum*, Leffons, &c. a Sermon being fubftituted, the mutilation of the Communion Service and omiffion of the Prayer of Confecration†—irregularities which not only affect the "order" of Divine Service, but in the cafe of the Sacrament of the Altar, entirely vitiate it, and that not by changing, but by omitting the "form" of words. The Rites and Ceremonies of the canon mean exactly the fame things as they do in the title of the Prayer Book: "The Book of Common Prayer, and Adminiftration of the Sacraments, and other Rites and Ceremonies of the Church." It is clear that Rites and Ceremonies are here ufed in diftinction to Sacraments—meaning the Occafional Offices, and not what we term "Ritual and Ceremonial." Had it been fo, the title would have run fomething after this manner:—"The Book of Common Prayer and Adminif-

---

* " With what *matter* was this child baptized ?
" With what words (= *form*) was this child baptized ?"—Miniftration of Private Baptifm of Children in houfes. Book of Common Prayer.
Here "matter" and "form" (*words*) are technically ufed. It fhould be remarked that till 1603 the paffage ftood—"With what thing, or what matter they did baptize the child ?" It is noteworthy that the men who revifed the Book of 1559, and put forth the canons of 1603, eliminated as unneceffary the word "thing" and ufed "matter" in its purely theological and technical meaning. The revifion of the Prayer Book and collection of the canons were going on at the fame time—the word is ufed in the fame fenfe in the Canons of 1603 and the Book of 1604.

† See "Lawful Church Ornaments," pp. 292, 293, 329, for hiftorical proof that fuch depravation of the Prayer Book was not unfrequent at the period of the compilation of the canons of 1603.

tration of the Sacraments *with the ceremonies and rites thereof.*" However, Ritual and Ceremonial, (viz. such ancient uses of the Church of England as are consistent with the revised Service Book, and needful for the right and due administration thereof), are included in the canon under the words, Rites and Ceremonies, and indeed the former must, of necessity, be more or less elaborately employed in carrying out the latter.

* And if it be argued, for instance, that the Bishop's or Priest's conse-
The argument crating of the oil for the anointing of a sick person is a *fresh*
for anointing of *rite or office, that* cannot be argued as a prohibition of such
the sick. action to the Episcopate or Priesthood; for the consecration of churches is a parallel instance as far as any modern law goes; yet the Bishops continue a practice which would be illegal on the principle that silence is prohibition; and moreover, they use an office which can make no claim to authority such as the Prayer Book possesses. *Custom* is indeed a sort of ecclesiastical common law and sanctions this; but as *desuetude* does not repeal a law, so it would appear that any diocesan Bishop is *free* to act upon the ancient Canons and Provincial Constitutions. In regard to the "mixed chalice," i. e. with wine and water, a custom enjoined and used by Bishop Andrewes; practised in Prince Charles' chapel at Madrid; ordered by Laud;† authoritatively recommended by Cosin; pronounced lawful by Palmer in his Origines Liturgicæ; used by authority in the Church in Scotland; and by many learned and holy Priests down to the present day; is little likely to be a violation of the Act of Uniformity or of the canons of 1603.

It now only remains to thank those who have aided in the compilation of this Manual.

And first, the thanks of the editor are due to his friend, the Reverend Frederick George Lee, S.C.L., F.S.A., his fellow-labourer and joint-compiler, who, himself engaged on a like work, kindly and most liberally handed over to the editor the whole of his carefully-collected and valuable notes, containing many important authorities not generally known; the whole of which notes have been incorporated into the volume.

---

* See "Lawful Church Ornaments," pp. 484, 485.
† "And the Presbyter shall then offer up and place the bread and *wine prepared* for the Sacrament upon the LORD's Table, that it may be ready for that Service." Rubric before the Church Militant Prayer in Archbishop Laud's Prayer Book (1637).
"Prepared" is the technical epithet always applied to the chalice which contains the element of wine mingled with a small proportion of water, thus *prepared* to be consecrated by the Priest.

Preface.

To ensure correctness nearly every proof-sheet has been revised, amongst others, by the following eminent ritualists:—The Rev. Thomas Chamberlain, M.A., Student of Christ Church, and Vicar of S. Thomas the Martyr, Oxford; the Rev. Philip Freeman, M.A., Vicar of Thorverton, Devon; the Rev. F. G. Lee, F.S.A.; and the Rev. J. M. Neale, M.A., Warden of Sackville College, East Grinstead. Thanks are likewise due to John D. Chambers, Esq., M.A., for permission to reprint his valuable letter on the legal effect of the "Judgment" of the Privy Council in the case of the churches of SS. Paul and Barnabas, Diocese of London, in the Appendix; and to the Rev. T. W. Perry, who has kindly allowed a liberal use in the way of extracts of his work on Lawful Church Ornaments.

The Commentary on the Daily Service is a *resumé* from the *first* volume of "The Principles of Divine Service." The permission to make such extensive use of this erudite and noble work is here gratefully acknowledged by the editor; he would also express his gratitude for the elaborate corrections and important additions which the *Directorium* received from its author. But it must be distinctly understood that Mr. Freeman is not to be identified either as a ritualist or a theologian with every direction in this Manual. Nor is the editor committed to every statement in his book.

The admirable paper in the Appendix on the Music of "The English Church" has been contributed by the Rev. Thomas Helmore, M.A., to whose kindness and courtesy the editor owes much.

The valuable paper on Floral Decorations was furnished for the Appendix by the Rev. John Oakley, M.A. [now Curate of S. James's, Piccadilly.]

The editor must also express his obligations to the Rev. John Jebb, M.A., Rector of Peterstow, for valuable information, and for permission (for which thanks are also due to Mr. Parker, his publisher) to incorporate some extracts from his work on "The Choral Service of the Church" into the text. These passages occur in Parr. 133, 136.

Great use has been made of that well-known, correct, and most useful publication, "The Churchman's Diary." Indeed it has formed the basis of the *Directorium*, and the permission to make this use of it adds another obligation to many which are due to its editor.

And here it is proper to add an expression of thanks to J. W. Hallam, Esq., for the unwearied pains which he took in illustrating this Manual; it is needless for the editor to commend either the beauty or the ecclesiastical correctness of the drawings.

The illustration of the Priest vested for "Holy Communion" is from a brass in the possession of the Rev. F. G. Lee, who is most anxious to restore it to the church, from which it has been severed, if such can be discovered.

The portion of the present English Rite, which the frontispiece is intended to illustrate, is the ascent of the Priest and Sacred Ministers to the midst of the Altar, before the celebrant takes up his position at the north-side of the Altar, and the Epistoler and Gospeller go to their respective steps, immediately before the singing of the Introit.*

The editor, on behalf of the compilers, of all and any who have aided in putting together these pages, and of himself, commends this Manual to the care of Almighty God, trusting He will deign to bless it to His glory, and to the edification of His Church.

✠ DEO GRATIAS.

Orwell Rectory,
Monday in Easter Week, A.S. 1858.

P. S.—Since the compilation of the *Directorium Anglicanum*, the Judgment of the Privy Council in the matter of the Churches of S. Paul and S. Barnabas has been delivered (on March 21st, 1857,)—a decision for which we must all be grateful, not only as setting at rest a *vexata quæstio*, but as securing to those who love "the beauty of holiness" the unmolested use of Lawful Church Ornaments,—though far be it from the advocates of Ritual and Ceremonial according to the use of the Church of England, to force the *maximum* of *statutable* ornaments upon those who are contented to abide by the *minimum*, or to advise the revival of all the minutiæ of ritual detail which were practised in mediæval times. It would not have been right, however, to have omitted them in such a treatise as the present. And it is a source of great satisfaction to the editor to find that he has only one unimportant matter to alter in consequence of that Judgment, viz. that "the fair white linen cloth" put upon the altar at the Communion-time must not be edged with lace, or adorned with embroidery,† as it is directed to be at p. 25.‡ The Judgment, however, does not prohibit lace, embroidery, and colour on the "linen cloth" used for covering what remains of the Blessed Sacrament after the communion of Priest and people.

J. P.

---

* The Frontispiece of the Second Edition represents the Elevation of the Chalice.

† Embroidery is that particular kind of work which entirely covers the surface of the original material. Every kind of work is not embroidery.

‡ Second Edition, p. 28.

Preface to the Second Edition.

XACTLY feven years ago the Directorium Anglicanum was firft publifhed. It had occupied the editor and fome of his affiftant compilers many years in its preparation, and its publication was looked forward to with much intereft. The original lift of fubfcribers is an evidence of this; while the rapid fale of a confiderable edition, in the fhort fpace of fix months from its firft iffue, was no uncertain indication of that renewed intereft in the fubject of ritual which was being taken in the Church of England, and which is in fo many quarters now both extending itfelf and bearing abundant fruit.

When this Manual was firft put forth, that doctrinal progrefs, thanks be to God! which is the wonder of many amongft ourfelves,—creating deep intereft in other portions of the Chriftian Family,—had been practically made and fealed; and this while queftions of external improvement had fcarcely been thought of. For the battle concerning the ufe of the Surplice in the Pulpit and the Prayer for the Church Militant (as it is commonly called) was of no great fervice in the Catholic Revival, except as indicating a readinefs on the part of a fection of the clergy to do what the exprefs law of the Church commanded when that law was made clear and indifputable to them. For any practical purpofes the battle might as well never have been fought. Preaching in the furplice was a queftion of extremely fmall moment; while a return to the Communion-table to read the Prayer for the Church, &c. was only an undefirable completion of that peculiar Reformation-rite, which in the great majority of Anglican Churches, for the laft three centuries, has tended to give the faithful an empty piece of the verieft formalifm in lieu of that Euchariftic Sacrifice, which is their precious heritage and greateft privilege. When, too, the rubric immediately preceding the commencement of Morning Prayer exprefsly ordered the ufe of the ancient Euchariftic and Catholic veftments, it muft be owned

xxviii   **Preface to the Second Edition.**

that the excitement occasioned by the attempt to win back the surplice for the pulpit was hardly commensurate with the gain; especially when,—with perhaps the single instance of the Vicar of Morwenstow in the diocese of Exeter,—the ancient vestments were nowhere assumed,* and the Rubric referred to was deliberately ignored.

Now, however, the work of reform and restoration in questions of external worship is going on with remarkable success. Enquiry generates further enquiry, and the result of enquiry has been to enlist a large number of learned and earnest men in the good work, so that even in the most neglected dioceses and parishes of England some approximation to greater decency—some outward and visible improvement is taking place. The outcries which from time to time have been heard against changes for the better were loud and piteous. For a while they inconvenienced some of our spiritual rulers, and terrified, for example, the respected Archdeacons of the diocese of Oxford. But neither the anonymous fabrications of Mr. Charles P. Golightly, nor the bitter malignity of the *Record* against theological colleges which were not Puritanical, could stay the progress of Catholic Reform. On our side we felt confident that nothing would be lost and everything gained by enquiry, and so it has turned out. Now the rationale of the science is better understood.† Since the publication of

---

* The writer is informed, on high and unquestionable authority, that the Cope was constantly worn in the diocese of Lichfield within the last 35 years, and this, too, on one occasion in the presence, and with the full approbation of, the late pious and devoted Dr. Henry Ryder, Bishop of that See.

† "'Tractarian' Ritual is reasonable because of its use in teaching the poor and uninstructed. Even if it were not disastrously true that the majority of preachers are far too ill-instructed themselves to have much probability of teaching others successfully, yet a great proportion of the poor is not accustomed to follow the thread of an argument or discourse for ten minutes together, not to say for thirty or forty, and even if it were, two-thirds of the language employed in most sermons is hopelessly unintelligible to the hearers. How can we most easily get a half-savage street-Arab or country clown to understand that there is a Mighty Being Whom he should adore, that there is a brighter and better world than this for which he should strive? Is it by putting him into a dark corner of a large, bare, and shabby room, to hear a gentleman read something carelessly out of one or two books for half-an-hour, and then roar something else excitedly for double that time? Will that get the unlettered peasant or artisan down on his knees in awe and prayer? On the other hand, will not the sight of a building far more beautiful and stately than any other he knows, will not the sound of sweet singing, and the example of numerous worshippers bending and prostrating themselves, speak directly to his eyes and ears and thus make their way into his slow mind? More than a thousand years ago the Emperor Charles the Great conquered the Saxons, and imprisoned their chief. One heathen Saxon, thirsting for revenge, followed the Emperor to his capital, and sought him out for the purpose of murder. On inquiry at the palace he was directed to the Cathedral,

Preface to the Second Edition. xxix

the DIRECTORIUM ANGLICANUM, nearly twenty books or tractates have been issued on the subject of the practical adoption of external religious observances; and these, of course, have very considerably helped on the good work. In addition to which, however, actual, visible, and palpable improvements have taken place in the manner of conducting Divine Service in so many places that continued progress is certain. Church-of-England people only need to see what may be made of our altered and circumscribed services by a careful performance of them in the spirit of ancient times to thank GOD for having preserved so much for us, in days of violent change or shifting belief,—in the times of Thomas Cranmer and Oliver Cromwell,—and to take courage and action for the future. "There is no question," wrote the late Mr. A. Welby Pugin, "that in the abstract the *Book of Common Prayer* is exceedingly Catholic, and that the rites of the Church of England, when solemnly administered, are close approximations to the ancient service; and all theologians will admit that the old priests who used the present Communion Service, with intention, consecrated most truly, and, consequently, that Mass was celebrated under the new form in hundreds of parochial and other churches long after the

---

and arriving there he found the terrible warrior, poorly clad, prostrate before the Altar, while the solemn rite of the Holy Eucharist was being celebrated. The thought which flashed across the heathen's mind was 'How great must that GOD be to Whom so great a king abases himself thus! It is by His might that my gods have been overcome.' And the intending murderer sought baptism, and became a Christian noble at the Court of the monarch he had meant to kill. If the Emperor had been sitting in a pew listening to a fluent gentleman in black, his life would have been forfeit, and the course of all European history have been changed.

"Once more, it is a constant complaint amongst clergymen that the young men are inaccessible to religious influences. Wherever 'Tractarian' ritual is in the ascendant, young men throng the choir and frequent the services. Is it not wise to bring them to divine worship instead of driving them away? Not long ago, Canon Clayton, a Puritan champion, preached a sermon at Cambridge against Ritual, in which, like Balaam of old, he blessed what he meant to curse. He said that 'Tractarians' made the 'Sunday Service palatable and even interesting to unconverted and unscriptural minds.' No doubt he avoids that pitfall himself, but a little more familiarity with his Bible might have taught him different language. There we are told in the Gospels that the publicans and sinners loved Christ's teaching better than the Pharisees did, there we learn from S. Paul that when worship is properly performed, 'and there come in one that believeth not or one unlearned, he is convinced of all, he is judged of all, ... and so falling down on his face he will worship GOD, and report that GOD is in you of a truth.' (1 Cor. xiv. 24, 25.) And because of these three merits, because it trains the body for the service of Heaven, because it accustoms the soul to gratitude towards GOD, and because it attracts and teaches the ignorant and careless, 'Tractarian' ritual is reasonable."—Rev. Dr. Littledale's *Catholic Ritual in the Church of England*, pp. 8, 9. London: Palmer, 1865.

accession of Elizabeth."* Truly our heritage is the Catholic Faith, whole and undivided, and with it those Catholic practices, which follow as a matter of course. To use plain words, certain Protestant traitors who eat the bread of the Church of England while they deny or refuse to proclaim her doctrine, and seldom carry out the explicit directions of her Service Book, made an attempt in the case of SS. Paul's and Barnabas', London, to obtain the sanction of the law for their sins of omission and commission. Large sums of money were spent both in attack and defence. Both sides were in earnest. But the formal and final decision was so completely in favour of Catholics that as yet no further attack has been made. True, an Irish peer, the Marquis of Westmeath, has complained in his place in the House of Lords of the satisfactory progress which is being made in the Church of England, but he has been answered by the Bishop of London in the following speech which—while advocating a change in the law— most conclusively admits that the restored practices complained of are perfectly legal, and can only be "put down" by an important and radical alteration of the law:—

"The Bishop of London was much obliged to the noble marquis for bringing these matters before the house. The matter was a very serious one, and he spoke the sentiments of all his right rev. brethren when he said they regarded it as very serious. The questions touched upon by the noble marquis were so intimately connected with fresh legislation that he did not know what would be the best remedy for these evils. He had had occasion more than once to refer to the highest legal authorities as to how these difficult matters were to be dealt with; and he confessed that the result was no more than this—that there was a rubric at present in existence which made it extremely difficult to act in these cases. The rubric he alluded to was that which said that the ornaments of the church and the furniture thereof were to remain the same as they were in the second year of the reign of King Edward the Sixth. That rubric he hoped and believed was capable of such an interpretation as he had always been in the habit of putting on it; but at the same time the existence of such a rubric introduced great uncertainty in the law. If there was the slightest hope that their lordships and the other house of parliament would take into consideration the alteration of this and other rubrics, he could say for himself and his right rev. brethren that they would support an alteration. There was another way in which the law might be altered, and he would pledge himself to vote for it. There was a phrase in the rubrics equally objectionable. It said that when the clergyman had any doubt as to the interpretation of these rubrics reference should be made to the Bishop of the diocese, and, if his decision was not satisfactory, to the Archbishop of the province, whose decision should be final. At first sight it would appear that that was a solution of the difficulty; but in many cases when he had attempted to apply this solution he had been met by this answer, and one which he believed could not be got over. The rubric said, ' If the clergyman had any doubt;' but these gentlemen always rejoined that they had no doubt, and did not want to refer to the Bishop or Archbishop or any one else (a laugh.) The law in this respect was obviously in a most unsatisfactory state (hear). It was said that these evils could

---

* Earnest address on the Establishment of the Hierarchy, p. 10. London: Dolman, 1851.

Preface to the Second Edition.

not be put down until a new court was established; but it was not a new court that was required, but a revision of the law (cheers). Bishops had a twofold authority. They had the authority which their advice naturally carried with it; and he was glad to say that by far the great majority of the clergy throughout the kingdom were always ready to accommodate themselves to the advice of their bishop in such matters; but, of course, if they did not there was nothing to fall back upon but the legal authority of the bishops. That legal authority was decided by the written law, and when the written law was in this unsatisfactory state (hear, hear) it became very difficult for the bishop to do more than to protest and to use his personal interest to stop abuses. There were two other parties who might do much to discourage these things. The first was the patrons of livings, who ought to take great care as to the principles of the gentlemen whom they presented for institution. There were also the parishioners, who had some power in the matter. Once a year they were called together for the election of churchwardens, and churchwardens had considerable legal powers as to the arrangement of such matters. In the churches to which the noble marquis had alluded what had taken place might be supposed to be the will of the parishioners, as expressed by their election of churchwardens. He trusted that in the district churches—for it was principally in them that these practices were carried on—the parishioners would see that a solemn duty devolved on them in respect to the choice of churchwardens. His opinion on these subjects was expressed at considerable length in his primary charge; and the sentiments of his right rev. brethren were also well known. The most rev. prelate (the Archbishop of Canterbury) had occasion, some years ago, when presiding over another diocese, to investigate some objectionable practices at a church at Leeds; and his grace's sentiments were then expressed quite as clearly as his had been. It would be the greatest mistake to suppose the bishops were not quite aware of the great evils which the noble marquis had pointed out; and if in any way he could discourage and discountenance such practices he should always be ready to do his duty. The distressing part of the matter was, that many of the gentlemen who made themselves conspicuous in this way were men of deep convictions, and who were in many cases sacrificing their health in their efforts amongst the destitute poor in this large diocese (cheers)."—*Standard*, June 17th, 1865.

This, then, is the present position of the Ritual revival. Of the strict legality of those restored forms and methods of worship—e. g. the use of Plain Song by a special choir, vested in cassock and surplice, in their proper place, the chancel; the use of incense, and lights, at celebration; crosses, both on the altar and on the rood-screen, flowers, banners, processions, ancient hymns, the Eucharistic and ancient vestments, the sign of the cross, bowing towards the altar, reverences at the *Gloria Patri*, &c. &c.—there can be no manner of doubt; and if all those who allow their legality and value acted as the respected Incumbent of S. Mary Magdalene's, Munster Square, acts, still greater progress would be made. Apropos of the attack by Lord Westmeath, Mr. Stuart writes as follows in the *Guardian* of August 2, 1865. He is replying to some faint-hearted anonymous scribe:—

"SIR,—I do not see that I have at all misrepresented 'Sacerdos,' or I would very readily acknowledge it.

"I must protest against the miserable, trembling, cowardly attitude which he recommends the clergy to assume towards their Bishops.

Preface to the Second Edition.

"He says—'I am further anxious that clergy whose views are the same as my own should not unduly provoke the Bishop to renew and enforce this appeal to Parliament.'

"Why not? Our own appeal is to the heart and conscience of the nation at large, and to what else can the Bishop of London himself appeal? These public attempts to put down Catholic faith and worship in the Church of England do a deal of good. They force upon an ignorant and prejudiced people some little knowledge of the truth of Catholic principles, and this is just the very thing we most want. The Gorham trial taught England the doctrine of Baptismal Regeneration; Dr. Pusey's suspension and the Denison, Cheyne, and Brechin trials, taught the doctrine of the Real Presence and the Eucharistic Sacrifice; the Poole persecution taught the doctrine of Confession; and the St. Barnabas' and St. George's-in-the-East Riots taught the nature and lawfulness of Catholic worship: and just so, depend upon it, any future 'raid' upon the Church will be overruled to the same good ends, if only we ourselves act sincerely and conscientiously in what we do.

"If the Bishop of London is inclined to 'run-a-muck' at Catholic faith and Catholic worship, by all means let him do so. He has as good a right to his opinion as we have to ours. If he wishes to Puritanize the Church, as I believe he does, let him take all lawful means towards his object; and if we wish to Catholicize the Church, as we avowedly do, let us take all lawful means towards our object too; and 'God defend the right!'

"Who is this awful despot, this terrible Turk, this Pope *in posse*, who is ready to cut off all our heads in five minutes if we 'provoke' him? He is a constitutional officer of the Church, and himself subject to its laws as much as any one else.

"The ministry of the Church of England would be unendurable to men and Christians on the terms which 'Sacerdos' seems to suggest.

"EDWARD STUART.

"*Munster Square, Regent's Park.*"

Under these circumstances, united action alone can preserve to us and to our children that which, by GOD's gracious mercy, has been handed down to the present time. If we are to remain a portion of the One Universal Church, and not to be degraded to the position of a mere sect, we must be prepared not only to theorize but to act. And those who are agreed in principle must be careful to act in unison. Though much has been done, much remains to be accomplished. With increased knowledge, and new stores of information, Prudence and Discretion must be present to guide the parish priest both as to the manner and time of particular reforms and restorations.

As regards the position of the priest at the altar, during the celebration of the Holy Eucharist—one important point for consideration—the Editor of this Second Edition of the DIRECTORIUM ANGLICANUM, strongly recommends that most able and exhaustive treatise, *The North-side of the Altar*,* by his friend, Dr. Littledale, to the attention of all readers of this book. Though the reform on this point has been very considerable, as yet it is by

---

* *The North-Side of the Altar: a Liturgical Essay*, by Richard F. Littledale, M.A., LL.D. Third Edition. London: G. J. Palmer, 1865.

no means general, which it ought to be. If the object of the change be carefully and intelligibly set forth beforehand, both publicly and privately, this reform could be at once readily effected.

The abolition of the use of black stoles, except for the Good Friday Services and for the funerals of adults, is a point which ought certainly to be aimed at. They have no doubt been introduced within the last forty years, and their symbolism is neither pleasing, flattering, nor edifying. Within the memory of many, only D.D.'s wore a wide black silk scarf during Divine Service in our cathedral and collegiate churches. Other clergy wore simply cassock, surplice, and hood. In so doing they followed the ancient tradition.

In addition to this practice which especially needs reform, the various rules and directions, taken from ancient sources, set forth in the DIRECTORIUM ANGLICANUM, should be carefully considered, with a view to the discovery of what is practically lacking, and of amending that which requires improvement. The following are leading practices which need to be generally restored:—(1.) The use of the Eucharistic vestments; (2.) The use of, at least, two lights at the celebration of the Holy Eucharist; (3.) The use of wafer bread in lieu of the ordinary bread commonly provided; (4.) The celebration of the Sacrament of the Eucharist at such a time on every Sunday and festival of obligation that the faithful generally may be able to be present at it; (5.) The use of incense.

It now becomes the duty of the Editor of this Second Edition to set forth what has been done on his part. The original compiler of the DIRECTORIUM having made over the book to him, with full permission to amend and make alterations where either were required, he has devoted a considerable time to a very agreeable labour. Independently of having received several valuable suggestions from the Editor of the First Edition, nearly fifty communications from various clergy and others had to be carefully considered. Every statement, consequently, has been tested by recognized authorities; and all references have been carefully and thoroughly collated. The great principle on which the book was formerly compiled, viz. that what was not specifically, legally, and actually abolished in the sixteenth century is still in force, has always been regarded in its revision. Nor has it been forgotten that the Church of England of the nineteenth century is substantially one with the Church of England of the ninth century; and consequently—in the face of modern Latin customs—national peculiarities have been consistently and properly respected. Where the language of the First Edition appeared at all obscure or vague, alterations have been made;

and references backwards and forwards, as far as poſſible, avoided, either by judicious additions or by a few eliminations. Several Occaſional Offices have been added; here and there a new arrangement, on a ſmall ſcale, has been made, and the "Cautels of the Maſs"—ſo valuable as indicating the mind of our beloved Church in times gone by—have been tranſlated and printed at length. The "Gloſſary" has been added to, and ſeveral notes interſperſed throughout.

The Editor deſires, in the firſt place, to expreſs his warm acknowledgments to the Original Editor and Compiler, for much valued help, without which—as the Firſt Edition is rare and cannot be eaſily obtained—he would have had to tranſcribe the whole of the volume.

For the ſelection of Edmund Sedding, Eſq., architect, as the illuſtrator of this volume, the writer is indebted to the diſcrimination and good judgment of the ſame kind friend. Mr. Sedding's able drawings, ſo full of Catholic feeling and a correct taſte for the beſt form of Chriſtian art, tell their own ſtory. They will be appreciated wherever this book finds its way.

He is indebted to John D. Chambers, Eſq., Recorder of Saliſbury—to whom his thanks are publicly tendered—for permiſſion to reprint the form for "Bleſſing a New Houſe," which in its preſent ſhape was uſed in the Benediction of 16, Prince's Gardens, Hyde Park. His obligations are due, likewiſe, to the Rev. H. A. Walker, M.A. of Oriel College, for a tranſlation from the Sarum Rite of another ſervice printed in this Edition.

And, finally, with a general acknowledgment of his ſincere thanks to many who have rendered him valuable aſſiſtance by the loan of books, by advice, counſel, and ſuggeſtions, to Mr. Boſworth, the accompliſhed publiſher, for the production of it in ſo handſome a form, and to Meſſrs. Whittingham and Wilkins for the taſte exerciſed in the printing—he commends this Manual to the Bleſſing of Almighty GOD, and to the attention and charitable conſideration of his brethren, the Clergy of the Anglican Communion; with an earneſt hope and conſtant prayer that it may in no degree hinder, but,—by reminding members of the Church of England of their ancient ſtandard,—may rather tend to promote, that Viſible Re-union amongſt the ſeparated portions of the Chriſtian Family, which, in GOD's good time and way, will be completely accompliſhed.

F. G. L.

19, Coleſhill Street, Eaton Square, London, S.W.
Auguſt 3, 1865.

List of Books and Editions

EITHER REFERRED TO OR USED IN THE COMPILATION OF THIS TREATISE.

LCUINUS, Op. fol. Lut. Par. 1617.
Altar, The, or Meditations in verſe on the Great Chriſtian Sacrifice. London: 1847.
Ambroſius, S. Op. 5 vols. fol. Bas. 1567.
Andrewes', Bp. Works. Lib. Ang. Cath. Theol.
Andrewes Epiſc. Preces Privatæ Quotidianæ. Londini: 1848.
Anſelmus, S. Op. fol. Lut. Par. 1675.
Auguſtinus, S. Op. fol. Bas. 1569.

Bailey's Ritual Ang. Cath. London: 1847.
Baldeſchi's Ceremonial according to the Roman Rite (Dale's tranſlation) 8vo. London: 1853.
Bangor Miſſal (apud Maſkell).
Balſamon, Theod. Commentarius in Canones Apoſtol. et Conc. fol. Paris: 1620.
Baſilius, S. Op. ap. Frob. fol. Bas. 1532.
Bayford's edition of the Judgment of the Right Hon. Stephen Luſhington, D.C.L. delivered in the Conſiſtory Court of the Biſhop of London, in the caſes of Weſterton *v.* Liddell (clerk), and Horne and others: and Beal *v.* Liddell (clerk), and Park and Evans, on December 5, 1855. London: 1856.
Beauty of Holineſs, The, By Rev. F. G. Lee. London: 1860.
Bede's Hiſtory. Ed. Stephenſon. London: 1841.

Bethell, Bp. Doctrine of Regeneration in Baptiſm. London: 1845.
Bennett's Principles of Book of Common Prayer. London: 1845.
Bennett's The Euchariſt: its Hiſtory, Doctrine, and Practice. London: 1846.
Bingham's Works. 2 vols. fol. London: 1726.
Biſſe's Beauty of Holineſs in Common Prayer. (Pocock's edition). Cambridge: 1846.
Blackburn's The Stone Altar in connexion with the Euchariſt, in the time of Pope Sergius the Firſt, &c. Cambridge: 1845.
Blunt's Duties of the Pariſh Prieſt. London: 1856.
Blunt's Sketch of the Reformation in England. London: 1850.
Bona, D. Joannes Card. Op. 4 vols. fol. Antverpiæ: 1677.
Bona de divina Pſalmodia. 4to. Antverpiæ: 1677.
Booke of the Common Prayer and Adminiſtracion of the Sacraments, &c. London: 1549.
Boke of Common Prayer and Adminiſtracion of the Sacraments, &c. London: 1552.
Book of Common Prayer; containing the Office for the healing of thoſe diſeaſed with the King's evil, entituled "At the healing." London: 1709.
Book of Common Prayer and Adminiſtration of the Sacraments, and other Rites and Ceremonies of the Church, according to the Uſe of the Church of Ireland. Dub-

lin: Printed by and for George Griefon, in Effex Street. 1736.

Books of Common Prayer:—

Book of Common Prayer and Adminiftration of the Sacraments and other Rites and Ceremonies of the Church, according to the Ufe of the Church of England. London: (Mafters' Edition, reprinted from the Edition of 1662, according to the Sealed Copy in the Tower,) 1848.

The Firft Book of Edward VI. 1549.—The Second Book of Edward VI. 1552.—The Firft Book of Queen Elizabeth, 1559.—King James's Book, as fettled at Hampton Court, 1604.—The Scotch Book of Charles I. (Abp. Laud's), 1637.—King Charles the Second's Book, as fettled at the Savoy Conference, 1662.—Victoria Book, collated with the fealed Book in the Tower of London, and other copies of the fame. 7 vols. fol. (Pickering's edition.) London: 1844.

Book of Common Prayer. Copy of Alterations prepared by Royal Commiffioners in 1689. Ordered by Houfe of Commons to be printed, June 2, 1854.

Book of Common Prayer, according to the Ufe of the Church of Scotland (with the imprimatur of Patrick, Lord Bifhop of S. Andrew's, Dunkeld and Dunblane). Edinburgh: 1849.

Book of Common Prayer, adapted for General Ufe in other Proteftant Churches. (Bunfen.) London: 1852.

Borromæi, S. Caroli, Inftructionum Fabricæ Ecclefiafticæ. Paris: 1855.

Boutell's Monumental Braffes of England. London: 1849.

Boutell's Chriftian Monuments. London: 1854.

Brechin's, Bp. of, Primary Charge. London: 1858.

Brett's Coll. of Liturgies. 8vo. 1845.

Breviarium Monafticum, O.S.B. 4to. Venetiis: 1596.

Breviarium Romanum. Dublinii: 1808.

Brev. Sarifbur. (Seager's edit.) Fafc. P. et S. London: 1843-55.

Burn's, Richard, Ecclefiaftical Law, 9th edit. (Edited by Robert Phillimore.) 4 vols. 8vo. London: 1842.

Cæremoniale Epifcoporum. fol. Paris: 1633.

Calendar of Anglican Church (Illuftrated). Oxford: 1851.

Camdenus, Gul. Annales rerum Angl. et Hib. Regn. Elizabeth. Lond. 1615.

Cardwell's Two Books of Common Prayer of Edward VI. compared, &c. Oxford: 1841.

Cardwell's Hiftory of Conferences. Oxford: 1841.

Cardwell's Documentary Annals. 2 vols. Oxford: 1844.

Cardwell's Synodalia. 2 vols. Oxford: 1842.

Caffianus. Op. fol. Atrebati: 1628.

Catalani, Jos. Cæremoniale Epifcoporum. 2 vols. fol. Romæ: 1744.

Chambers' Tranflation of Sarum Pfalter. London: 1852.

Chambers' An Order of Houfehold Devotion. Pfalter and Manual. London: 1854.

Chambers' Lauda Syon. London: 1857.

Chambers' Companion to Confeffion and Holy Communion, tranflated and arranged from the Ancient Englifh Offices of Sarum Ufe. London: 1853.

Chambers' Strictures, Legal and Hiftorical, on the Judgment of the Confiftory Court of London, in December, 1855, in the Cafe of Wefterton v. Liddell. London: 1856.

Chamberlain's The Chancel; an Appeal for its Proper Ufe. London: 1856.

Chamberlain. In what fenfe may the Holy Eucharift be called the LORD's Supper. A Letter to the Lord Bifhop of S. Andrew's. London: 1855.

Chriftian Remembrancer. A Quarterly Review. London: Mozleys.

Church Schemes. Ecclefiological Soc. London.

Church Hiftorians of England. London: 1853-58.

Churchman's Diary. London: 1858.

Churchwardens: a Few Words to. Parts I. and II. (Suited to town and manufacturing diftricts.) Ecclefiological Society. London: 1844, 1851.

List of Books and Editions.

Churchwardens: A Few Words to. Suited to country parishes. Part I. London: 1846.
Church Worship. (Churchman's Library.) London: 1854.
Chrysostomus, S. fol. Etonæ: 1612.
Clay's Book of Common Prayer, illustrated. London: 1841.
Clemens, S. Alexand. Op. fol. Paris: 1572.
Clemens, S. Rom. Epis. 8vo. Paris: 1568.
Codex Canonum Ecc. Universal. Paris: 1661.
Collier's Ecc. History. fol. London: 1708-14.
Comber's Works. 2 vols. fol. Oxford: 1701, 2.
Conciliorum Omnium Gen. et Prov. Collect. Reg. 31 vols. fol. Paris: 1644.
Conciliorum Collectio. Paris: 1672.
Constitutions and Canons Ecclesiastical, of 1603, (Corrie's edit. of The Homilies). Cambridge: 1850.
Cope and Stretton's Visitatio Infirmorum. London: 1848.
Cosin's Works (vol. v.), Lib. Ang. Cath. Theology. Oxford: 1855.
Corpus Juris Civilis Romani. 2 vols. fol. Antverpiæ: 1726.
Crosthwaite's Communio Fidelium. Oxford: 1841.
Cyprianus, S. Op. fol. Bas. 1525.
Cyrillus, S. Alexand. Op. fol. Paris: 1638.
Cyrillus, S. Hierosolym. Op. fol. Paris: 1720.

Day-hours of Church of England. London: 1858.
Damascenus, S. Joannes. Op. 2 vols. fol. Paris: 1712.
Daniel's Thesaurus Hymnologicus. 4 vols. 8vo. Halis. 1841-55.
Dionysius Areopagita, S. (Pseudo) Op. ed. Corderius. Venet. 1755.
Directory, A, for the Publicque Worship of God in the Three Kingdomes. 4to. London: 1644.
Dodson, Sir John, his Judgment delivered in the Arches' Court of Canterbury, on Saturday, Dec. 20, 1856, in the Appeal, Liddell v. Westerton. Law Report. Times Newspaper, Dec. 22, 1856.

Donne's Works. London: 1839.
Dugdale's Monasticon. fol. London: 1655.
Durandus, Gul. Rationale Divinorum Officiorum. 4to. Lugduni: 1510.
Durandus on Symbolism (Neale and Webb's translation). Leeds: 1843.
Durantus, Jo. Ste. de Ritibus Ecclesiæ. fol. Romæ: 1591.
Dyce's Book of Common Prayer, with Plain Tune. 2 vols. 4to. London: 1843.

Ecclesiastic and Theologian. London.
Ecclesiological, late Cambridge Camden Society's Transactions.
Ecclesiologist. London.
Epistolæ Gildæ. Ed. Stephenson. London: 1838.
Eucharist, on the Celebration of the Holy (reprinted from the "Theologian and Ecclesiastic." August, 1849.) London: 1849.
Eusebius Pamphilus (Cæsar. Episc.) Hist. Ecc. fol. Bas. 1549.
Exeter, Bishop of, Letter to the Rt. Hon. Dr. Lushington, on his Judgment in the cause of Westerton v. Liddell (Clerk). London: 1856.
Exeter Pontifical. Ed. Barnes. 8vo. Exeter: 1847.

Freeman's Principles of Divine Service. 2 vols. 8vo. Oxford: 1855-57.
French's Tippets of the Canons Ecclesiastical. 8vo. London: 1850.
Forms of Bidding Prayer (H. O. Coxe). Oxford: 1840.
Fuller's Church History of Britain. fol. 1665.
Fust's, Sir H. J., Judgment in the Court of Arches in the case of Faulkner v. Litchfield. London: 1845.

Gavanti Thesaurus Sacrorum Rituum. 2 vols. 4to. Venetiis: 1792.
Gibson's Codex Juris Ecclesiastici Anglicani. 2 vols. fol. London: 1713.
Goar, Jac. Euchologion. fol. Paris: 1647.
Goar, Horolog.
Gregorie's Works. 4to. London: 1695.
Gregorius Nazianzenus, S. Op. ed. Ben. fol. Paris: 1778.

Gregorius Nyſſenus, S. Op. fol. Paris: 1638.
Gregorius M., S., Op. ed. Ben. fol. Paris: 1705.
Grindal's, Abp., Remains. Parker Soc. Cambridge: 1843.
Guide to the Euchariſt (Churchman's Library). London: 1858.

Hallam's Monumental Memorials. London: 1854-58.
Hardwick's Hiſtory of the Chriſtian Church (Middle Ages). Cambridge: 1853.
Hardwick's Hiſtory of the Chriſtian Church during the Reformation. Cambridge: 1856.
Harington's Conſecration of Churches. 8vo. London: 1844.
Harriſon's Hiſtorical Inquiry into the true Interpretation of the Rubrics, &c. London: 1845.
Helmore's Manual of Plain Song. London: 1851.
Herbert's Prieſt to the Temple. London: 1849.
Hereford Miſſal (apud Maſkell).
Heylyn's Hiſtory of the Reformation. 4to. London: 1674.
Hieronymus, S. Op. fol. Lond. 1620.
Hierurgia Anglicana. London: 1848.
Hiſtory of Chriſtian Altars. Eccleſiological Soc. London: 1847.
Hittorpius de Divinis Catholicæ Ecc. Officiis. fol. Coloniæ: 1568.
Holy Oblation, the. London: 1848.
Homilies, the, (ed. by Corrie for Syndics of Univerſity Preſs.) Cambridge: 1850.
Hook's Church Dictionary. London: 1854.
Hooker's Works. 2 vols. 8vo. Oxford: 1850.
Horæ B. V. M. ad uſum Ecc. Sariſb. 4to. 1527.
Horæ B. V. M. ad legitimum Sariſburienſis Eccleſiæ Ritum. 4to. Paris: 1535.
Humphry's Hiſtorical and Explanatory Treatiſe on the Book of Common Prayer. Cambridge: 1853.
Hymnale ſec. uſum inſig. ac præclar. Ecc. Sariſb. Littlemore: 1850.

Hymnarium Sariſburienſe cum rubricis et notis muſicis. Pars Prima. Londini: 1851.
Hymnal Noted. London: 1851-1858.

Illuſtrations of Manners and Expenſes of Ancient Times in England. 4to. 1797.
Ignatius, S. (Martyr), Epiſtolæ. fol. Baſ. 1569.
Imitatio Chriſti. Geræ et Lipſiæ. 1847.
Inſtrumenta Eccleſiaſtica. 2 vols. 4to. London: 1847, 56.
Iſidorus, S. Hiſpalenſis. Op. 2 vols. fol. Matriti: 1778.

Jebb's Choral Service of the United Church of England and Ireland. 8vo. London: 1843.
Johnſon. The Unbloody Sacrifice (Lib. Ang. Cath. Theol.) Oxford: 1847.
Johnſon's Collection of Canons, &c. of Church of England. 2 vols. 8vo. London: 1720.
Johnſon's Clergyman's Vade Mecum, containing Codes of the Primitive and Univerſal Church. 2 vols. London: 1731.
Juſtinus Martyr, S. Op. ed. Ben. fol. Paris: 1742.
Juſtorum Semita. 2 vols. Edinburgh: 1843.

Keble on Euchariſtical Adoration. Oxford: 1857.
Keeling's Liturgiæ Britannicæ. London: 1851.
Kennet's Parochial Regiſter. fol. 1728.
Ken, Bp., Life of, by a Layman. 2 vols. London: 1854.

Laud's, Abp., Trial. London: 1705.
Laud's Summarie of Devotions. Oxford: 1667.
Lectures to Ladies. 8vo. Cambridge: 1855.
L'Eſtrange's Alliance of Divine Offices. London: 1659.
Liber Feſtivalis. 1483.
Lightfoot's Temple. 4to. London: 1650.
Lightfoot's Works. 13 vols. London: 1825.
Lingard's Anglo-Saxon Church. London: 1844.
Littledale's North Side of the Altar. 8vo. London: 1865.

List of Books and Editions. xxxix

Littledale's Mixed Chalice. 8vo. London: 1864.
Liturgies, Ancient, of Gallican Church. (Neale and Forbes' Ed.) Burntisland (Pitsligo Press). 1855.
Liturgy of S. James. (Neale's Ed.) London: 1858.
Liturgy of S. Mark. (Neale's Ed.) London: 1858.
Liturgies of Edward VI. Parker Soc. Cambridge: 1844.
Liturgies and Occasional Forms of Prayer set forth in the Reign of Queen Elizabeth. Parker Soc. Cambridge: 1847.
Lives of English Saints. 14 vols, London: 1844-48.
Loss and Gain. London: 1848.
Lyndewode, Prov. Ang. Edit. Prima.

Mabillon (Joannes), De Liturgia Gallicana. 4to. Lut. Par. 1685.
Manuale ad usum percelebris ecclesiæ Sarisburiensis. 4to. Londini: 1554.
Martene De Antiquis Ecc. Ritibus. 4 vols. Rotomagi: 1700.
Maskell's Ancient Liturgy of the Church of England. First Ed. London: 1844.
Ditto. Second Ed. 8vo. London: 1846.
Maskell's Monumenta Ritualia Ecclesiæ Anglicanæ. 3 vols. 8vo. London: 1846, 47.
Maskell's Doctrine of Absolution. 8vo. London: 1849.
Maskell's Holy Baptism. 8vo. London: 1848.
Maskell's History of the Martin Marprelate Controversy. London: 1845.
Mede's (John) Works. fol. 1677.
Merbecke. Book of Common Prayer, Noted. (Pickering's Ed.) London: 1844.
Merbecke. (Rimbault's Ed.) London: 1845.
Millard's Historical Notices of the Office of Choristers. London: 1848.
Miscellaneous Sermons, edited by Rev. F. G. Lee. London: 1860.
Missale ad usum Sarisbur. 4to. Paris: 1516.
Missale ad usum Sarisburiensis. fol. Paris: 1526.
Missale Romanum. fol. Antverpiæ: 1677.

Missale Romanum. Mechliniæ: 1846.
Monro's Parochial Work. Oxford: 1851.
Montague's, Bp., Articles of Inquiry. Cambridge: 1841.
Neale's History of the Holy Eastern Church, 4 vols. and Appendix. London: 1847-50.
Neale's Tetralogia Liturgica. Londini: 1849.
Neale's Life and Times of Bishop Torry. London: 1856.
Newland's Confirmation and First Communion. London: 1853.

Oakley's Order and Ceremonial of the most Holy and Adorable Sacrifice of the Mass explained. London: 1848.
Oblations, on the Term in the Communion Service and its importance as to the time of placing the elements on the LORD's Table. London: 1856.
Office for the Holy Communion according to the Use of the Church of Scotland. 4to. Edinburgh: 1853.
Optatus, S. (Milevitanus). Op. fol. Paris: 1631.
Ordo Recitandi Officii Divini. London: 1858.
Original Letters relative to English Reformation. Parker Soc. 2 vols. Cambridge: 1846, 47.
Origines. Op. 2 vols. fol. Paris: 1619.

Palmer's Antiquities of the English Ritual. 2 vols. 8vo. Oxford: 1839.
Parish Clerks and Sextons, a Few Words to. Ecclesiological Soc. London: 1846.
Patrick's, Bp., Christian Sacrifice. London: 1672.
Perceval's Apology for the Doctrine of the Apostolical Succession. London: 1841.
Perceval's Original Services for the State Holidays, with documents, &c. London: 1838.
Perry's Lawful Church Ornaments. London: 1857.
Pinnock's Clerical Papers. Cambridge: 1852-58.
Planché's History of British Costume. London: 1841.

Plain Directions for the Simple Celebration of the Holy Communion. London: 1858.
Plummer's Observations on the Book of Common Prayer. London: 1847.
Pontificale Romanum. fol. Parisiis: 1664.
Pontificale Sarisbur. (apud Maskell.)
Popular Tracts, Illustrating the Prayer Book of the Church of England. IV. Nos. London.
Portiforium, seu Breviarium Sarisbur. 4to. Parisiis: 1556.
Position of Priest at the Altar. (Reprinted from the "Ecclesiastic," May, 1858.) London: 1858.
Prayer Book: and how to use it. (Churchman's Library.) London: 1854.
Presence of Non-Communicants at the Celebration of the Holy Eucharist, how far a Catholic Practice. (Tracts on Catholic Unity. No. 7. By Members of the Church of England.) London.
Private Prayers, put forth by authority during the Reign of Queen Elizabeth. Parker Soc. Cambridge: 1851.
Privy Council, The Judgment of the Committee of, in regard to the Churches of SS. Paul and Barnabas, in the Appeal, Liddell v. Westerton, delivered March 21, 1857. (Printed from the authorized Official Document, published in *The Union*.) London: 1857.
Processionale Sarisbur. 4to. London: 1555.
Procter's History of the Book of Common Prayer. Cambridge: 1855.
Prudentius. Op. fol. Paris: 1589.
Pugin's Glossary of Ecclesiastical Ornament and Costume. 4to. London: 1846.
Pugin's Present State of Eccles. Architecture in England. London: 1843.
Purchas' Book of Common Prayer Unabridged; a Letter to Rev. James Hildyard, B.D. London, 1856.
Pusey's Councils of the Church. Oxford: 1857.
Pusey's Doctrine of the Real Presence. Oxford: 1855.
Pusey's Presence of Christ in Holy Eucharist. Oxford: 1853.

Pusey's The Real Presence of the Body and Blood of our Lord Jesus Christ, the Doctrine of the English Church. Oxford: 1857.
Pusey's Letter to the Bishop of London. Oxford: 1851.
Renaudotii Eus. Collectio Liturgiarum Orientalium. 2 vols. 4to. Paris: 1716.
Right of all the Baptized to be present at the Celebration of the Holy Eucharist. London: 1854.
Rituale Angl. Bangor. MSS.
Rituale Romanum. 4to. Parisiis: 1665.
Robertson's How shall we conform to the Liturgy of the Church of England. 8vo. London: 1844.
Rock's Church of our Fathers. 3 vols. 8vo. London: 1849.
Rock's Hierurgia. London: 1851.
Russell's Obedience to the Church in things ritual. London: 1847.

Sacramentarium Ecclesiæ Catholicæ. Part I. London: 1857.
Sacristan's Manual. London: 1854.
Saravia. On the Holy Eucharist. (Ed. by Archdeacon Denison.) London: 1855.
Sarum Psalter. (Cambridge Univerfity Library.)
Smith's Devout Chorister. London: 1854.
Sparrow's Rationale. London: 1657.
Sparrow's Rationale. Oxford: 1843.
Sparrow's Collection of Articles, Injunctions, Canons, &c. of Church of England. London: 1671.
Spelman's History and Fate of Sacrilege. London: 1853.
Spirit of the Church. London: 1857.
Statement of Particulars connected with the Restoration of the Round Church, by the Chairman of the Restoration Committee. Cambridge: 1845.
Stephens' Edition of Book of Common Prayer. (Ecc. Hist. Soc.) 3 vols. London: 1849, 50, 54.
Strype's Works. 26 vols. 8vo. Oxford: 1821-28.

List of Books and Editions.

Taylor's, Bp. Jeremy, Works. (Eden's Edit.) 10 vols. London: 1847-54.

Thorndike's Doctrine of the Holy Eucharist. (Edit. by Chambers.) London: 1855.

Tracts for the Times. 6 vols. London: 1834-41.

Trower's Review of the Judgment of the Right Hon. Sir John Dodson, Knt., D.C.L. delivered in the Arches' Court of Canterbury, on December 20th, 1856, in the Case of Liddell v. Westerton, considered with especial reference to the Legality of Crosses as Church Ornaments. London: 1857.

Union Review, The. A Magazine of Catholic Literature and Art. London: 1863-1865.

Wall's History of Infant Baptism. (Cotton's Edit.) 4 vols. 8vo. Oxford: 1836.

Wettenhall's, Bp., Gifts and Offices. Dublin: 1679.

Wheatly's Rational Illustration of Book of Common Prayer. London: 1729.

Why Non-Communicants should remain during the " Missa Fidelium." London: 1857.

Wilberforce, Archdeacon. Doctrine of Holy Eucharist. London: 1853.

Wilkins' Concilia. 4 vols. fol. London: 1737.

Wilson's, Bp., Short and Plain Instruction for the better understanding of the LORD's Supper. (Cleaver's Edit.) London: 1851.

Wren's Injunctions, (apud Cardwell's Doc. Ann.)

Wright's Directorium Scoticanum et Anglicanum. (Not published.) London: 1855.

York Missal, (apud Maskell.)

Zurich Letters. Parker Soc. 2 vols. Cambridge: 1842-45.

Contents.

	PAGE
THE Celebration of the Holy Eucharist	1
The Vestments	13
The Order of Administration	26
Cautels and Directions (Cautelæ Missæ)	83
The Calendar	97
Matins and Evensong	109
The Creed of S. Athanasius	147
The Litany	148
Prayers and Thanksgivings upon several occasions	150
The Collects, Epistles, and Gospels	151
The Sacrament of Holy Baptism	152
The Ministration of Private Baptism of Children in houses	155
The Ministration of Baptism to such as are of riper years	157
The Order for Confirmation	160
The Order for Holy Matrimony	161
The Order for the Visitation of the Sick	164
The Communion of the Sick	165
The Order for the Burial of the Dead	168
The Churching of Women	171
A Commination or Denouncing of God's Anger against Sinners	173
The Ordinal	174
APPENDIX	187
Cautels (the Bread and Wine)	189
Of the Veiling of the Cross, &c. at Passiontide	191
Of the Folded Chasuble	191
Of the Preparation of the Altar and its Ornaments, for Holy Communion	192
The Sign of the Cross	193
Directions for the Celebrant	193
The Parts of the Altar	194
Additional Notes for Deacon and Sub-deacon	196
Solemn Service in the Absence of a Sub-deacon	199
Directions for Acolytes or Lay Assistants	200
Directions for Servers	201
Directions as to Chalices and Patens	204
Solemn Eucharistic Service in Presence of a Bishop assisting pontifically	205
Form of Consecration of Churches, &c	206
Office for the Restoration of a Church	218
Office for Expiation and Illustration of a Church	220

Contents.

	PAGE
Service for Bleſſing and Laying the Foundation-Stone of S. Mary's, Aberdeen	222
Service for the Solemn Bleſſing and Opening of S. Mary's, Aberdeen	228
Office for the Benediction of a Dwelling-houſe	240
Various Benedictions	245
Old Veſtments to be burnt	248
Reconſecration and Reconciling of Churches	248
The Oil of Chriſm, the Oil of the Sick, and Holy Oil	248
The Sacrament of Abſolution	249
Form for the Admiſſion of a Choriſter	250
Floral Decorations	252
Altars and Doſſels of Village Churches	258
Flowers on the Altar	258
Flower Vaſes	258
Feaſts of Obligation	259
Feaſts of Devotion	259
Rules for a Sacriſty or Veſtry	260
Cleanſing of Church Furniture	260
Proceſſions	262
The Maſter of the Ceremonies	263
Proceſſional Banners	264
The Verger and Churchwardens' Staves	264
The Proceſſional Croſs or Crucifix	265
Form of Bidding of Prayer	265
Palm Sunday and its Office	266
Ornaments of the Church, &c	270
Extracts from the Carlton Ride Inventories	276
Judgment of the Privy Council in the Caſe of the Knightſbridge Churches	279
Comment thereon by the Recorder of Saliſbury	280
On the Muſic of the Engliſh Church	284
Gloſſary	288
Index	297

List of Illustrations.

1. FRONTISPIECE. THE HOLY EUCHARIST. The elevation of the Chalice. The Deacon kneels to the right of the Priest, holding up the edge of the Chasuble. The Sub-deacon kneels behind. At the extreme right is the Thurifer, while two Acolytes hold elevation-tapers. The general plan, as well as the details of this, are from illuminated MSS.
2. BISHOP. The Chasuble here is of an ancient form. Priest in Cope, &c. Priest in Surplice and Hood. (The Hood is of the ancient shape).
3. PRIEST, in Chasuble. The Chasuble here is of a modern form. Acolyte (in Cassock, Alb, Scarlet Cincture, and Scarlet Zucchetto). Deacon, with Book of the Gospels.
4. PLAN showing the arrangement of a Chancel.
5. A BIRD'S-EYE VIEW OF A CHANCEL.
6. DESIGN FOR CROZIER AND PASTORAL STAFF.
7. MITRE, RING, GLOVES, PALLIUM, RATIONAL, AND SANDALS.
8. THE CHASUBLE, STOLE, AND MANIPLE. (N.B. There is a slight error in the description of the Stole in this plate. The ordinary Stole should be 8 feet 3 in.; the Eucharistic Stole should invariably be 9 feet in length).
9. THE COPE, MORSE, AMYSS, ZUCCHETTO, AND BIRRETTA.
10. THE OBLATION OF THE ELEMENTS,—Arrangement of an Altar.
11. ELEVATION OF AN ALTAR VESTED. (Different designs have been purposely given where an Altar is represented).
12. CREDENCE PREPARED FOR HIGH CELEBRATION.
13. DIAGRAM, showing the distinction between the north side and the north end of the Altar. Diagrams relating to the position of the Ministers at High Celebration.
14. CHALICE AND PATEN. (N.B. It is, perhaps, better for enabling the Sacred Particles to be removed that the plate of the Paten be not engraved, but be quite plain).
15. ALTAR LINEN.

The Directorium Anglicanum.

The Celebration of the Holy Eucharist.*

"Vidi civitatem sanctam Jerusalem novam descendentem de cœlo, paratam sicut sponsam ornatam viro suo."

HE celebration of the Holy Eucharist is the principal act of Christian Worship, inasmuch as it calls directly into action the office of our great High Priest, not only to present our prayers to the Father, but to plead anew the merits of His Own adorable Sacrifice. It should therefore have all possible dignity imparted to it by a carefully-observed Ritual. It is well

---

* "Commonly called the Mass."¹—First Prayer Book of Edward VI.

¹ It bore this name even in the 3rd of Elizabeth, 1561 :—" Paid for 4lb. of candles on Christmas-day morning, for the Mass, 12ᵈ."—Illustrations of Manners and Expenses of Ancient Times in England, 142, 4to. 1797.

The word "Missa," or Mass, has no connection whatever with the doctrine of transubstantiation. All the world know it has several meanings. First, the words of dismission at the end, " Ite Missa est." Secondly, the word was applied to any *offering* or sacrifice *sent up* to God. Thirdly, it was frequently applied to any festival. It is a trite remark by many of the English Divines, that nowhere was the doctrine of transubstantiation necessarily inculcated in the unreformed service. It remains, therefore, in substance, what it was before; viz. *The celebration of the Eucharist.*

The term Eucharistia was preserved much more in the English than in the Roman Use. E. g. " Post introitum vero Missæ unus ceroferariorum panum, vinum et aquam quæ ad *Eucharistiæ* ministrationem disponuntur, deferat."—Sarif. Rubr. See Maskell's Ancient Liturgy, Ed. 1846, p. 32.

" Moneantur laici, quod reverenter se habeant in consecratione *Eucharistiæ*, et flectant genua; maxime in tempore illo, quando, post elevationem *Eucharistiæ*, hostia sacra dimittitur."—Concilium Dunelmense, 1220. Ibid. p. 94, note 26.

See also ibid. p. 108, no'e 52. The Gallican Church also used the term *Eucharistia* frequently.—See Mabillon, De Liturgia Gallicana, p. 52.

Mass : this title for the Holy Eucharist is still preserved in the English names, Christmas, Michaelmas, Lammas, Candlemass, Roodmass, Martinmas, Childermass, &c. With regard to the frequency of celebrations the English Church orders it on all Sundays and Festivals, and contemplates it daily by directing that " the Collect, Epistle, and Gospel for the Sunday shall serve *all the week* after, where it is not in this Book otherwise ordered." In S. Cyprian's time it was certainly daily :

" Episcopatus nostri honor grandis et gloria est pacem dedisse martyribus, ut sacerdotes, qui sacrificia Dei quotidie celebramus, Hostias Deo et victimas præparemus."—Epist. liv. ad Cornelium.

B

The Celebration of the Holy Eucharist.

when the Liturgy* can be used by itself;† and it should not be begun without the intention of going through the whole.‡ As there is one Altar, so can there be but one Priest, (acting in that capacity,) whose place is to stand at first *at*, i. e. in front of, the Altar at the north side, and after the Gospel *in medio altaris*, (see Par. 21), facing the east. He is never to leave the footpace except when communicating the faithful. Clergy acting as Gospeller§ and Epistoler, whether Priests or Deacons, should stand below the footpace, facing eastward. The parts which should be said by them

---

* "The traces of the form of worship used by the Christian converts, which we find in the New Testament, refer to the Eucharist, as being emphatically the Christian Service. Hence naturally arose the ecclesiastical use of the word *Liturgy*,[1] to designate the form employed by the Church in celebrating that Office."—Procter. History of the Book of Common Prayer, p. 281.

† "It has always been held that the Holy Communion should not be celebrated unless the Office of one of the Hours had been previously recited; whether of Tierce, Sext, or the Ninth Hour."—Maskell. (See Anc. Lit. pp. 153, 154, 155, for the English positive Rule).

‡ "In too many churches, Sunday after Sunday, in lieu of that oblation which GOD desires to receive, and which our Blessed Saviour Himself especially directed His Apostles and their successors, the Christian Bishops and Priests of all ages, to make, is only offered a mutilated and unmeaning worship, entirely novel and utterly pointless,—consisting of that part of the present Eucharistic Office which takes in the Nicene Creed, or the prayer for the Church Militant. The officiating Priest—while, perhaps, the choir is singing an introit—goes deliberately and solemnly to the Altar, which he knows to be wholly unprepared for the celebration of the Sacrament, there being no sacred vessels nor oblations, and there reads a fragment of the Liturgy, known popularly, but incorrectly, as the "Communion Service." Now it may be safely asserted that three Sundays out of four, in a large majority of our churches, this gross and corrupt following of the Apostles is still continually perpetrated."—"The Vain Oblation," p. 249. Miscellaneous Sermons, edited by Rev. F. G. Lee. London: Masters, 1860.

§ The Gospeller or Deacon, even though he be in Priest's Orders, should wear his stole (under his dalmatic) as a Deacon, (see p. 13, sect. 4), being about to fulfil a diaconal function, for " it pertaineth to the office of a Deacon . . . . to assist the Priest in Divine Service, and especially when he ministereth the Holy Communion." (The Ordering of Deacons). The Epistoler or Subdeacon, if the ancient Sarum and present Roman Rule be followed, should wear no stole at all.

Both Gospeller and Epistoler wear the maniple. In the old English Ordinals this vestment is given to the Subdeacon as his especial badge. See Pont. Sarisbur. apud Maskell. Mon. Rit. iii. 182, and Pont. Exon. apud Barnes, p. 84.

The Canon (XXIV. of 1603), allows of two assistants—Deacon and Subdeacon in old times, now simply Gospeller and Epistoler. Ancient custom assigns to the former a place

[1] "In classical Greek, λειτουργία denotes any public service, religious or secular. In the LXX translation it is used for the ministry of the Levites (e.g. 1 Chron. xxvi. 30, εἰς πᾶσαν λ. Κυρίου); in the New Testament, for the *ministry of prophets and teachers* (Acts xiii. .2); and in ecclesiastical writers, for any sacred function, and in an especial and strict sense for the Eucharistic Office. Thus we speak of the *Liturgies* of S. James, S. Mark, S. Chrysostom, &c. for the service used in celebrating (the Sacrament of) the LORD's Supper, in the churches of Antioch, Alexandria, Constantinople, &c." Λειτουργία is also used for the whole action of sacrifice in the account of Simon, son of Ozias, in Ecclesiasticus, ch. l. ver. 14, 19.

The Altar. 3

are the Gospel and Epistle, the Exhortations, and the Confession.[*]
Where there is only one assistant, he should read the Epistle and Gospel on
the proper sides. When the Priest (being without Epistoler or Gospeller)
reads them, he should do so from the Service Book, placed on the book-
rest, which, in the first instance, should be put on the Epistle side, and then
on the Gospel side, by the lay-server.

For this Service there is required,
1. An ALTAR.[†]

---

on the south side (*ad latus Epistolæ*) on the step next to the Altar platform, to the latter
a place on his own step behind the Gospeller, a little towards the right. Both stand facing
the east. For the position of the Sacred Ministers, when *directly assisting* the Priest, see *infra*
Parr. 16, note [*]; 20, note [†]; 72, notes [*], [†], [‡]; and Appendix, p. 169, ii.
If at Church Festivals, &c. or on occasions where many are present who purpose communicating, an additional cleric to the Gospeller and Epistoler be required to help the Priest in
the distribution of the Sacrament, he should stand on the lower step of the sanctuary behind
the Celebrant.

[*] The greater part of the Rubrics of the Book of Common Prayer only contemplates one
Priest[1]—assistants very rarely. Whether the maximum or minimum of ritual be observed,
ancient Catholic rules and traditions should of course be followed.

[†] The table on which the Eucharistic Sacrifice is offered has been called an Altar " from
the beginning." The Prophet Malachi[2] speaking in prophecy of the Eucharistic Sacrifice
terms " the Table of the LORD," in reference to IT an " Altar." S. Paul tells the Hebrews[3]
that " We have an Altar, whereof they have no right to eat which serve the tabernacle."
It is to be observed that the same Apostle calls the Christian, Jewish, and Gentile Altars,
tables; thus defining an Altar to be a Table whereon a Sacrifice was offered.[4] And so,
Bishop Andrewes:[5] " The holy Eucharist being considered as a sacrifice, it is fitly called
an Altar, which again is fitly called a Table, the Eucharist being considered as a Sacrament."
In the first century we find S. Ignatius[6] assert that " In every church there is one Altar."
In the second century S. Justin Martyr[7] alludes to the passage in which the Prophet Malachi
calls the Table of the LORD an Altar. And Origen[8] and S. Cyprian perpetually refer to the
Altar of the Christian Church. In the fourth century we have a cloud of witnesses. The
historian Eusebius,[9] S. Optatus Milevitanus,[10] S. Ambrose,[11] S. Jerome,[12] S. John Chrysostom,[13]

[1] No stress can be laid upon the word " Priest" in
the Rubrics, when defining the duties of his assistants.
See for instance the Versicles a.ter the Creed at
Matins and Evensong.
[2] Malachi i. 7, 12.   [3] Heb. xiii. 10.
[4] 1 Cor. x. 18—21, and ix. 13.
[5] Answer to Cardinal Perron, Minor Works, edit.
1854. p. 20.
[6] "Ἐν θυσιαστήριον πάσῃ τῇ ἐκκλησίᾳ.—S. Ig. in
Epis. ad Phil.
[7] Διὰ τοῦ ὀνόματος τούτου θυσίας ἅς παρέδωκεν
'Ιησοῦς ὁ Χριστὸς γίνεσθαι, τουτέστιν ἐπὶ τῇ εὐ-
χαριστίᾳ τοῦ ἄρτου καὶ τοῦ ποτηρίου, τὰς ἐν παντὶ
τόπῳ τῆς γῆς γινομένας ὑπὸ τῶν Χριστιανῶν,
προλαβὼν ὁ Θεὸς μαρτυρεῖ εὐαρέστους ὑπάρχειν
αὐτῷ.—Justinus M. Dial. cum Tryph.
[8] Orig. Hom. iii.   S. Cyp. Epit. passim.
[9] Hist. Ecc. lib. x. c. 4. 'Ἐφ' ἅπασί τε τὸ τῶν
ἁγίων ἅγιον θυσιαστήριον, ἐν μέσῳ θείς.
[10] Lib. vi. contra Parmen.   " Quid est altare, nisi
sedes et Corporis et Sanguinis Christi?'
[11] " Ille super altare, qui pro omnibus passus est."
[12] Hieron. lib contra Vigilan.   " Christi altaria."
[13] S. Chrys. Hom. xx. in 2 Cor. ix. τοῦτο θυσιαστήριον μὲν γάρ θαυμαστὸν διὰ τὴν ἐπιθεμενὴν ἐν
αὐτῷ θυσίαν.

The Celebration of the Holy Eucharist.

The length of the altar will vary according to the size of the church or chancel, but it should never be less than six feet.* In large churches it may be even ten or twelve feet. The width about two feet six inches. It should be three feet six inches high, and raised as much as possible above the level of the nave. In all cases the slab or *mensa* of the Altar should be *of one stone*† without fracture or blemish; and the thickness of the slab

---

and S. Augustine,[1] and to these may be added Prudentius, who flourished in Spain in the fourth century, and Sidonius Apollinaris in France during the fifth century.

* The dimensions of the altar of the church of Perranzabuloe, near Truro, were five feet three inches, by two feet three inches, and its height four feet. When taken down, the headless remains of S. Piran, the patron saint, were discovered immediately beneath it, the feet of the buried saint pointing as usual to the east; it was, in fact, both Altar and Tomb: and hence the remarkable peculiarity of its position, lying lengthwise east and west. About sixteen miles from S. Piran's a similar ancient church has been more recently discovered, at Gwithian, so named from an Irish saint there martyred. Here also the Altar was of stone, but placed in the usual position, standing north and south, against the middle of the east wall.

The original high Altar remaining in 1844, in S. Mary's, Forthampton, Gloucestershire, is five feet three and a half inches long, and two feet ten inches high; its breadth is two feet three inches, and the thickness of the *mensa* five and a half inches.

In the first part of the Ecclesiological (late Cambridge Camden) Society's Transactions, will be found a paper on Chantry Altars, by Mr. Bloxam, in which eight of these Altars, still remaining, are described. Five of these were solid masses of masonry, surmounted by a slab of stone, varying from three feet three inches to six or seven feet in length, and from one foot four inches to three feet in breadth; the height rather more than three feet; and *the thickness of the slab six inches.*

† "Let[2] no Altars be consecrated by unction with chrism, unless they be of stone."[3]—The Excerptions of Archbishop Ecgbriht, A.D. 750. (Johnson's Collection).

[1] Civ. Dei. l. viii. cap. ult.—"Quis audivit aliquando Fidelium stantem sacerdotem ad altare etiam super sanctum corpus martyris ad Dei honorem cultumque constructum, dicere in precibus; Offero tibi sacrificium Petre vel Paule."

[2] "The C.C.C.C. MS. justly makes this a distinct Canon; with this title *Canon Epaonensis*, and it is the sense of No. XXVI. Canon of Epone, in the year 517."

[3] In continental Churches it is usual for a small piece of stone to be let into the middle of the *mensa* to consecrate upon.

This inserted Altar-stone was called "ara," (see Gavantus, P. I., Tit 20), in contradistinction to altare, i.e. the slab and whole structure of the Altar. The same name is also applied to a consecrated Altar-stone of jasper or marble, set in gold or silver, laid upon an unconsecrated Altar of stone or wood. "Domina Petronilla de Benstede dedit sumto Albano unum super-Altare rotundum de lapide jaspidis, subtus et in circuitu argento inclusum, super quod, ut fertur, sanctus Augustinus Anglorum apostolus celebravit."—Monasticon Ang. t. ii. p. 221. The jasper in Christian symbolism indicates Faith, "*jaspis fidei*," porphyry or any red marble was used in default of the symbolical jasper. It was formerly the custom in cathedrals to place this Altar-stone upon the ordinary consecrated stone *mensa*, either *causa reverentiæ* to the blessed Eucharist, *causa honoris* to the great festivals, or *causa dignitatis* of the celebrating bishop.

This "*ara*" was also styled the "*super-Altar*," the term now technically used for the ledge of the Altar, whereon stand the cross and candlesticks.

The "*ara*" was sometimes made of oak wood, covered with plates of precious metal, and sometimes *laminæ* of ivory.

"*Ara*" is also the correct word for the portable Altar (*tabula itineraria*) for "The Communion of the Sick."

Messrs. Neale and Webb in their translation of the First Book of Durandus' "Rationale Divinorum Officiorum," p. 41, have the following note: "The true ecclesiastical distinction between *altare* and *ara* is, that the former means the Altar of the true GOD, and is therefore alone used in the Vulgate answering to the Greek θυσιαστήριον, as opposed to *ara* (βωμος) an Altar with an image above it. See Mede, folio 386."

about six inches. The *mensa*, the part of the Altar on which the Eucharist is consecrated, being either of stone or marble, is supported on a wooden frame which consists of either four sides, or of four or six low pillars of wood.

It is well, perhaps, that the Altar should not be imbedded, or fixed to the wall, though many of the ancient Church of England altars undoubtedly were so fixed. In many places it will be found extremely convenient to have a passage around it. Behind it should be a Dossal Cloth,* Reredos, Painting, or Triptych, in front of which stands the Cross. (See Altar-Cross). There should be no Niches unless filled with statues, nor Tables of Commandments.† The Altar is raised on a platform, which forms a footpace extending from three to four feet from the east wall, and in length not reaching more than six or eight inches beyond the ends of the Altar. The ascent to this should be by at least two steps, each of the same height with the platform, and about fifteen inches in

---

" Of Altars, that they be of stone."—(Lanfranc) Canons of the Council of Winchester, A. D. 1070. (Johnson's Collection).

Elizabeth's Injunctions *permitted* wooden Altars, and the Canon of 1571 (never in force), speaks of a table " ex asseribus composite junctam." These " asseres" however might be of any material, iron, stone, zinc, as well as of wood. But these, and such like Injunctions, Canons, and Articles, it is a notorious legal fact, have not a shred of authority belonging to them. The only document which can claim any weight is the 82nd Canon of 1603—4, now in force, though subject to the act of Uniformity. This Canon simply speaks of the Table as " decent and convenient" but makes no mention of the *material*, and even if it did, it would be of no force, as the Canon would be overruled in this particular, as it is in the matter of the Altar being moveable. For the Rubric inserted at the last review directs *the communicants, not* the Table, to be *conveniently* placed for the receiving, implying plainly that the Altar was not to be moved for their convenience. The Altar is therefore *a fixture*, " *not moveable*," but " *to be removed* only by authority," as the font, pulpit, or other fixture.

The Book of Common Prayer, made by the Act of Uniformity part of the statute law of the land, orders such ornaments to be retained and be in use as were in this Church of England by the authority of parliament in the second year of King Edward the Sixth. Therefore whatever was the law of the Western Church in this matter before the Reformation is the law of the English Church now. The Canons of Archbishop Ecgbriht, of the Council of Winchester, are the statutes in which it is embodied. The more we multiply cases of stone Altars pulled down and sold in the later years of Edward VI. and Elizabeth, the more abundantly shall we prove that they were the ordinary and legitimate " ornaments of the Church " in the period to which our Rubric refers us.

* There should be no Cross embroidered on the Dossal where the Altar-cross is in use. Where no Altar-cross has been provided—a metal Cross of rather large size securely affixed to the Dossal is to be preferred to an embroidered one.

† The proper place for the Tables of Commandments, if put up at all, is at the east of the *Nave*.

breadth. From the lowest step to the *septum* or sanctuary rail, there should be at least twelve feet in collegiate churches, and, if possible, never less than six.

The slab of the Altar should be covered with cere-cloth,* which in its turn is covered by the superfrontal, which hangs down about ten inches below: whilst the frontal, or antependium, which with the superfrontal makes up the covering or vestment of the Altar, hangs down in front. The frontal and superfrontal should each have a fringe. The *ends* of the Altar need not be covered, save by the "fair white linen cloth," (see *infra*). They were, however, often vested in ancient times, as, indeed, they usually are at the present day. As the Altars of the English Church are not now affixed to the eastern wall, the back of the Altar may be vested. The extract below † from the *Monasticon Anglicanum* shows—from the phrase "frontlets of the same," in an inventory of Altar Vestments—that the Cloths were intended to hang over the back of the Altar. The superfrontal and the cere-cloth should fit closely.

Along the back of the *mensa* extends a ledge from six to twelve inches in height, and from five to seven inches in breadth, according to the size of the Altar; it is sometimes called the "super-Altar," the "Altar gradine," or "retable:" upon it are placed two Lights, and between these a cross of metal, with the addition of flower vases on Sundays and festivals.

On the top of the superfrontal are placed the three linen cloths,‡ the

---

* A waxed cloth extended over a consecrated Altar-stone to protect it from damp, dirt or irreverence. It should be made of strong linen, and close at the corners; a quantity of virgin wax should then be melted in an iron vessel, and applied to the cloth while held a short distance from the fire.

† "Imprimis, a costly cloth of gold, for the high Altar, for principal feasts, having in the midst images of the Trinity, of our Lady, four Evangelists, four angels about the Trinity, with patriarchs, prophets, apostles, virgins, with many other images, *having a frontlet of cloth of gold*, with scriptures, and a linen cloth enfixed to the same; *ex dono Ducis Lancastriæ*. Item, a purpur cloth, with an image of the Crucifix, Mary and John, and many images of gold, *with a divers frontlet of the same suit*, with two Altar Cloths, one of diaper. Item, a cloth of gold, partly red and partly white .... *with a frontlet of the same suit*, having in the midst the Trinity .... Item, a cloth of white, with treyfoils of gold .... *having a frontal of the same.*"

"*Item*, a cloth for the hie Awtᵣ of blew baudekin, with the picture of our LORD, Mary and John, and *a front of the same*. Item, an one Awter Cloth of white fustyan, with red roses, with a Crucifixe, Mary and John, broydered, and *front of the same*, and two curtains."—In the Inventory of S. Paul's in capella carnariæ. Jacob's Hist. of Faversham.

‡ The cere-cloth, superfrontal, and the three linen cloths should always remain upon the

two under ones not to exceed the length of the *menfa*, but the uppermoft fhould hang down at each end, nearly to the platform, and fhould hang down in front not above two inches below the flab. This " fair white linen cloth,"* as well as the two under ones, fhould have five croffes worked upon it, correfponding to the five croffes on the Altar-ftone, in the centre and four angles, with borders of various patterns. All the Altar linen as well as all the veftments of the priefts fhould be marked with a crofs.

Many of the old Englifh Altars were provided with curtains.

A curtain may hang at each end of the Altar. Thefe hangings are either fufpended by rods projecting from the walls or reredos, or elfe they reft on detached pillars generally of brafs, erected by the ends of the Altar.

The only niches that are defirable are thofe of which the Reredos or Altar-fcreen not unfrequently confifts. The reredos is very often formed of three funk panels filled with fculpture; thefe fhould be of marble or alabafter, with a feries of fmall figures in relief, painted and gilt, ufually reprefenting the principal events in the life of our Bleffed LORD.

2. The CREDENCE† is a fmall fide-table for the reception of the elements previous to their oblation, and is provided to enable the celebrant at the

---

Altar. It is ufual, during the Daily Office, and at all times when the Liturgy is not being celebrated, to cover the " fair white linen cloth," as a protection againft duft, &c. with a ftrip of green filk, hemmed and marked with five croffes. This covering fhould exactly fit the *menfa*.

* See Gavanti Thefaurus Sacrorum Rituum. Pars I. Tit. xx. Ed. Venetiis, 1792. Where it will be feen that in the weft it is permitted to ufe *two* linen cloths, fo that the under one be large enough to fold *twice* over the *menfa*. " Duplicatam unam concedit Rubrica, ut fint tres: non ergo duæ, tuta confcientia fufficiunt."

It was anciently the cuftom of the Englifh Church to fpread a purple pall[1] upon the menfa, and over this the three linen cloths. The cere-cloth now performs the function of the purple pall,[2] but the beautiful fymbolifm of its colour, which typifies blood, as well as kingly power, is ftill retained in the fuperfrontal, which always may be, and generally is, crimfon or red.

† See Ecclefiologift, Vol. vii. pp. 178—218, and Vol. viii. pp. 9, 92—147, for elaborate papers on the Credence.

[1] In S. Æthelwold's Benedictional there is an Altar covered with a purple pall.

Bifhop Leofric gave to Exeter Cathedral, ' v. paellene weofod fceatas,' five purple palls.—Cod. Dip. Ang. Sax. t. iv. p. 275.

[2] Queen Ælgive gave to Ely Cathedral, amongft other ornaments, a purple pall, " Defuper biffus fanguineo fulgore in longitudinem altaris ad cornua ejus attingens ufque ad terram cum aurifrifo, altitudinem habens, fpectaculum decoris magni pretii adminiftrat."—Thomæ Elien. Hift. Elien in Anglia Sacra. tom. I. p. 607. See alfo, Epiftola Gildæ. Ed. Stevenfon, p. 51, " Sub fancti abbatis amphibalo, latera regiorum tenerrima puerorum, inter ipfa ut dixi, facrofancta altaria nefando enfe haftaque pro dentibus laceravit (Damnoniæ tyrannicus catulus Conftantinus), ita ut facrificii cœleftis fedem purpurea ac fi coagulati cruoris pallia attingerent."

Holy Euchariſt to place the Bread and Wine reverently upon the Altar as required by the Engliſh Rubric. The Credence is ſometimes ſupported on a ſhaft or bracket, or formed at the bottom of a niche, or conſiſts of a ſhelf over the Piſcina.

Where no conſtructional ſtone Credence exiſts, it is cuſtomary to uſe a ſmall moveable table for receiving the elements before they are conſecrated, or in fact any expedient may be adopted ſo as to prevent the elements being placed on the Altar until the Oblation takes place. The judgment in the caſe of SS. Paul's and Barnabas', Knightſbridge, pronounced the Credence-table to be a neceſſary "Legal Ornament" in the Church of England.

3. The PISCINA is a ſtone baſon with an orifice and drain to carry away the water which has been uſed at the Waſhing of the Prieſt's hands in accordance with Pſalm xxvi. 6, and for rinſing the chalice *after the Purifications*, and is one of the appurtenances of an Altar which in ancient times was never diſpenſed with. It is generally conſtructed at the bottom of a ſmall niche on the Epiſtle ſide of the chancel, eaſtward of the ſedilia, and theſe frequently conſtitute a portion of the ſame deſign.

Where there is no Piſcina, a baſon of metal is the uſual ſubſtitute.

4. The AUMBRYE, or Locker, is a ſmall cupboard for the preſervation of the Sacred Veſſels, and is generally conſtructed in the north or eaſt wall[*] of the chancel near the Altar: the door is uſually elaborately carved in oak, or ornamented with floriated iron-work, and is always furniſhed with a lock.

5. The SEDILIA, three ſeats for the Prieſt, Goſpeller, and Epiſtoler, during the Celebration, conſiſt of arched receſſes conſtructed in the maſonry of the ſouth wall of the chancel within the ſanctuary, and are frequently ſurmounted by rich canopies delicately groined. They are either level, or graduated, following the ſteps of the Altar, the higheſt ſeat being neareſt the eaſt end. The Sedilia may be furniſhed with embroidered cuſhions. They ſhould be only occupied during the Sermon.

---

[*] What look like Aumbryes in the eaſt walls are almoſt invariably ancient Tabernacles for the reſervation of the Bleſſed Sacrament. Many ſuch exiſt in Scotland. Vide Gentleman's Magazine, Jan. 1862.

The Furniture of the Altar.

Where Sedilia do not exist, a bench, or stall, or stools, should be placed in a similar position against the south side wall of the Sanctuary.

It is perhaps needless to add that no chairs should under any circumstances be placed at the north and south ends of the Altar, whether facing the congregation or otherwise, except on the north side (facing the south, a little below the platform) for a Bishop when present.

The proper place for the *Bishop's Throne* is below the Sanctuary, at the extremity of the stalls, nearest to the *septum*, on the south side, and is moveable, except in cathedrals.

THE FURNITURE OF THE ALTAR.

THE CHALICE, in which there are four parts. The foot, the stem, the knop, and the bowl.

The foot should extend considerably beyond the bowl, to prevent the possibility of its being upset. On one division of the foot it is usual to engrave the LORD'S Passion: this should be always turned towards the celebrant. The stem unites the foot to the bowl, and on it is fixed the knop for the convenience of holding the chalice. The knop is variously enriched with enamel, jewels, tracery and tabernacle-work, whilst the stem is frequently engraved or enamelled.

The height of the stem is generally about four inches, and seldom exceeds six. The bowl should vary from three to six inches in dimension, and of a proportionable depth; it should have a plain rim of about an inch, below that it may be enriched with engravings, inscriptions, and chasings.

The Chalice should never have *turn-over* lips, which are extremely liable to cause accident in communicating the faithful.

Chalices are made of silver either whole, or parcel gilt, occasionally of pure gold and jewelled.

The PATEN is made to fit the top of the Chalice. Legends and jewels are admissible on the outer rim only. If the whole surface of a silver paten cannot be gilt, it is usual to gild the middle.

The CRUETS, or FLAGONS should be either of glass or of hammered metal.

THE BURSE. See infra p. 32, note.

The OFFERTORY BASIN, is a vessel of pewter, latten, or precious metal.

It ſhould not be large, as when removed from the credence to receive the velvet purſes, and placed upon the Altar by the Prieſt, it would occupy too much ſpace.

The ALTAR-CROSS* is a metal croſs with a foot to it. Uſually it is between two and three feet high. It is often jewelled, and not unfrequently has upon it an engraved repreſentation in *alto relievo* of our LORD's Paſſion. The foot of the Croſs ſhould be on a level with the bowls of the Candleſticks.

Two† Altar Lights. Theſe lights ſymbolize that CHRIST is the very true Light of the world; HE is ſo, becauſe HE is the GOD-MAN, and poſſeſſes *two* natures in His own Perſon. And the lights are *two* on the Altar, becauſe they ſymbolize the ſame union of Divinity and Humanity in the Bleſſed Sacrament.

Altar CANDLESTICKS‡ are made in gold, ſilver, or ſilver parcel gilt, copper gilt, latten, braſs, cryſtal or wood.

---

* " He (Paulinus) alſo brought with him many rich veſſels of king Aeduini, among which were *a large gold croſs*, and a golden chalice, dedicated to the uſe of the Altar, which are ſtill preſerved and ſhown in the church of Canterbury."—V. Bede, Hiſt. Ecc. lib. II. c. xx. § 148. A. D. 633. Stevenſon's ed.

" The Altar in the Queen's (Elizabeth) chapel was furniſhed with rich plate: two fair gilt candleſticks, with tapers in them, and a maſſy ſilver crucifix in the midſt thereof."—Heylyn, Hiſt. Ref. p. 124, fol. 1661.

To prove that in the order to deſtroy images, croſſes could not have been included, the following facts may be of importance. That in almoſt all ancient illuminations (all that the compilers have ever ſeen) of Altars, a croſs and not a crucifix is diſplayed; moreover, the preſent Roman rule is obeyed, if a croſs—a ſimple croſs—is placed on the ſuper-Altar. Thus, a croſs can ſcarcely come under the category of " images," and was conſequently retained. The croſs has been ruled to be legal by the judgment in the Knightſbridge Churches' caſe: only it muſt not be affixed to the Altar.

† The Syriac, probably the oldeſt form of the Eaſtern Rite, has *two candles* to this day:

" *Et cum* (*Sacerdos*) *accendit cereum, ad latus dextrum dicit:* In lumine tuo videmus lumen.

"*Ad latus finiſtrum dicit:* Pius et ſanctus, qui habitat in habitaculis lucis."—Renaudot, tom. ii., Lit. Or. Coll. p. 12.

‡ The two Altar candles ought never to be lighted except at the celebration of the Holy Euchariſt.[1]

" In the earlieſt times, the fourth Canon of the Apoſtles, ſo praiſed by Beveridge, mentions ' *lamps* at the holy Offering.' Beda ſpeaks in one of his homilies[2] of the ' walls of the Church being carefully adorned, and many lights being lit ' at the Divine ſervice. A *pharus*, or can-

---

[1] If light is required in the Sanctuary at late Service, it ſhould be provided by Standard Candleſticks placed on the ground. Candles in Coronas and Branch Candleſticks placed upon the retable may and ſhould be lighted about the Altar. The Sarum Rule, as well as the preſent Latin Rule, enjoins lights at the Altar during Evenſong or Veſpers.

[2] Lingard's Anglo-Saxon Church, p. 291.

The Furniture of the Altar.

There are five parts in an Altar candlestick. 1. The foot. 2. The stem. 3. The knop, which for convenience of lifting is put in the middle. 4. The bowl to receive the droppings of wax. 5. The pricket terminating

delabrum, hung over the Altar of the Cathedral Church at York, in the beginning of the eighth century, which Altar was decked with silver and gems.[1] King Edgar's Canons enact, 'Let a light be always burning in the Church, when a mass is sung.' The poem of the monk Ethelwolf on the abbots of Lindisfarne, speaks of the numerous candelabra in the church glittering like stars.[2] By the Constitutions of Giles de Bridport, Bishop of Salisbury,[3] anno 1236, the parson was to provide the candelabra, but the parishioners the 'wax candles in the chancel, and also sufficient *light* throughout the whole year, at Matins, Vespers, and the Mass, and blest bread, with candles, in every Church in the Christian world.' By a provincial constitution of Archbishop Reynolds, which embodied the then existing custom, A.D. 1322: 'Let two candles, or one at the least, be lighted at the time of high mass.'[4] And Lyndewode, commenting on this Constitution, adds, 'Note, that the candles to be burned at the celebration of the mass, must be of wax rather than *any other material. For the candles so burning signifieth* CHRIST *Himself, Who is the brightness of the eternal light*.' In which he repeats the ancient observation of Isidore of Seville (in the seventh century):[5] 'Under the type of this corporeal light, that light is shown forth of which we read in the Gospel, He was the true light which lighteneth every man.' As we have already proved *in extenso*, this, and all other Canons, where not expressly avoided by some subsequent Parliamentary authority, or *contrariant or repugnant* to the then laws, statutes, and *customs of the realm*, or to the King's prerogative, 'are now still to be used and executed as before,' by the 23 Henry VIII, c. 19. That this Canon was in universal force throughout England up to Henry VIII.'s death, we know by the illuminations in the MSS. Service-books and the prints in the Missals, Breviaries, Antiphonaries, and other printed books published up to the last year of his reign, which invariably represent the Altar with two lighted candles upon it, and no more; so also by the Inventories of church goods before and hereafter referred to.

"Beside this, the first Injunctions of King Edward, of May, 1547, the authority of which I have discussed already, repeat nearly *totidem verbis* Archbishop Reynolds' Canon, and the reason of it: 'No torches or candles, tapers, or images of wax were to be set before any image or picture, but only two lights upon the high Altar *before the Sacrament, which, for the signification that* CHRIST *is the very true Light of the world, they shall suffer to remain still.*'[6] This last Injunction was enforced by Archbishop Cranmer in his Visitation Articles

---

[1] Poema de Archiepis. Ebor., Gale, ii.
[2] Act. SS. Ben. vi. 331.
[3] Wilkins' Conc. i. 714.
[4] See Johnson's Can. ii. 338.
[5] Orig. vii. 12.
[6] It seems clear this cannot be referred to the light before the pyx, because that was never more than one, and that only in Churches possessing considerable means. (Constit. of W. de Cantilupe, Wilk. I. 557. Cardinal Pole's Constit. 1555). Cromwell's Injunctions, 1536, forbid all but one light before the sacrament of the Altar, meaning the pyx, or tabernacle; the Proclamation of Henry VIII, in 1538, and the Injunction of 1539 (Wilkins, iii. 842—847,) authorize candles on Easter-day before Corpus Christi, showing they were not there before. The reason given in Reynolds' Constitutions, which refer to the celebration of the Mass by name, and in Edward's Injunctions, is precisely the same; both must refer, then, to the same thing. In the Private Prayers of that date, some of which are given in the Sarum Missal, to be used at the time of communion, the celebration is frequently called the Sacrament; and Cranmer, in his Injunctions of the second year, refers the lights to the Altar, not to the pyx. And the doubtful Injunctions of 1549-50 speak of the candles on the LORD's Board. The authority of Cosin must be considered as decisive, who speaks of them as two lights on the Communion Table; and, finally, the continued practice of the English Church.

The Celebration of the Holy Eucharist.

the ftem on which the taper is fixed. Frequently, and more conveniently in fome inftances, a focket is ufed.

It is convenient alfo when the Service Book does not contain the Action on one page, to have a Card containing the Canon or Prayer of Confecration in a large type, though there is no mediæval authority for this practice.

It is a fymbolical and Catholic cuftom to ufe incenfe during Divine Service. This cuftom continued all through the reigns of Elizabeth, James I, and indeed we find its occafional ufe down to the time of George III. (See *Hierurgia Anglicana*).*

By the exprefs command of GOD incenfe was very frequent in the fervice of the Jewifh Temple. (Exod. xxx. 1, 3, 9; xl. 5; Levit. xvi. 12, 13; S. Luke i. 10, 11).

It will be remembered that frankincenfe was prefented to the new-born JESUS. (S. Matt. ii. 11).

S. John particularly mentions (Rev. viii. 3, 4) how "another angel came and ftood at the altar, having a golden cenfer; and there was given unto him much incenfe, and that he fhould offer it with the prayers of all faints upon the golden altar which was before the throne. And the fmoke of the incenfe, which came up with the prayers of the faints, afcended up

---

of the fecond year, one of whofe inquiries was this: 'Whether they fuffer any torches, candles, tapers, or any other lights to be in your Churches, but only two lights *upon the high Altar.*' And in his Communion Book, in force till Whit-Sunday in the third year, the Prieft was ordered to go through the fervice 'without *varying any other* rite or ceremony in the mafs,' of which we know the two lights formed one. This Canon, therefore, and ufage, was in force up to the end of that fecond year, and beyond, and was not either '*contrariant or repugnant*' to the ftatutes or cuftoms of the realm, or to the King's prerogative, but in harmony therewith."—Chambers' Legal Argument.

* Where it will be feen that incenfe was alfo ufed at the Coronation of George III.[1]

[1] *Incenfe in Churches.* S. Mary the Virgin, Cambridge:
"1562 For frankincenfe to perfume the church, 1d. For do. 2d.
1573 Item, for perfumes and frankincenfe for the church, 8d."

All Hallows, Steyning, London:
"1563 In the time of ficknefs, item, for juniper for the church, 2d.
1625 The time of GOD's vifitation, item, paid for 10 lbs. of frankincenfe, at 3d. per lb. 2s. 6d."

Jefus Chapel, Cambridge:
"1588 Juniper to air the chapel on S. Mark's Day."
—Tranfac. of the Cambridge Camden Society, P. iii. p. 271.

Incenfe in churches recommended by the "Divine" Herbert:
Circa 1631. "The country parfon takes order ... fecondly, that the church be fwept and kept clean without duft or cobwebs, and at great feftivals ftrewed and ftuck with boughs, and *perfumed with incenfe.*"— Prieft to the Temple, ch. xlii. The Parfon's Church.

Form ufed by Abp. Sancroft for the Confecration of a Cenfer:
1685. So likewife when a *cenfer* is prefented and received, they fay: While the king fitteth at his table, my fpikenard fendeth forth the fmell thereof. (Cant. i. 12). Let my prayer be fet before Thee as incenfe; and let the lifting up of my hands be as the evening facrifice. (Pfalm cxli. 2.)—The Form of Dedication and Confecration of a Church or Chapel.

before God out of the angel's hand." It is confidered that S. John adapted his wondrous language to the ceremonial of the Liturgy then followed by the Chriftians in celebrating the Euchariftic Sacrifice, at the period the Evangelift committed to writing his myfterious revelation.*

The primitive Chriftians adopted the ufe of incenfe at the Celebration of the Liturgy from the Jewifh Service. In the fecond of the Apoftolical Canons we find it ordered thus: "let it not be allowed to prefent any thing on the Altar, but oil for the lamps, and incenfe for the time of the Holy Oblation." The Liturgy of S. James commences with burning of incenfe.† (Vide the fpecial Section on this fubject).

---

* Incenfe is fymbolical of the prayers of the faithful, which are fo often defcribed in Holy Scripture to be an odour of fweetnefs before heaven. "The four and twenty elders fell down before the Lamb, having every one of them harps and golden vials full of odours, which are the prayers of faints."—Rev. v. 8.

† See "Εὐχὴ τοῦ θυμιάματος τῆς εἰσόδου τῆς ἐνάρξεως."—Neale's Tetralogia Liturgica, p. 5.

The Vestments.

"Myrrha et gutta et cassia a vestimentis tuis, a domibus eburneis: ex quibus delectaverunt te filiæ regum in honore tuo.
"Astitit regina a dextris tuis in vestitu deaurato: circumdata varietate." Ps. xlv. 9, 10.

HE ordinary dress of all connected with the Church down to Choristers is (1) the Cassock and (2) Square or College Cap.

The Eucharistic Vestments are (3) the Amice (*Amictum*); (4) the Alb; (5) the Girdle; (6) the Stole; (7) the Maniple; (8) the Chasuble.

Besides these there are the special vestments for the assistant Ministers of the Altar, viz. (9) the Dalmatic for the Gospeller; (10) the Tunic for the Epistoler.

These are also worn together with (11) the Mitre, (12) Gloves, (13) Sandals, (14) Pastoral Staff, and (15) Ring, by Bishops; and with the (16) Crozier, and (17) Pall, by Archbishops.

1. To the Daily Office—(18) the Surplice, and the Academical Hood, or (19) the Tippet (in the case of non-graduates); and Birretta. (20) The Amys (*Almutium*) may be worn instead of the Hood or the Tippet. Choristers and Acolytes wear over their cassocks a cotta or surplice. (18.)

2. In Processions, and therefore, strictly speaking, at funerals, (21) the Cope should be worn over the Surplice, and always (22) the Birretta.

---

1. The Cassock,[1] or Priest's Coat, is single breasted, and fastened from the throat to the feet by numerous buttons, extending the whole length. At the back the Cassock is very full, from the loins downwards, and sometimes trails a considerable length on the ground. It has

[1] A Cassock of black cloth or serge, either single or double breasted, is very suitable for clerics when engaged in ordinary parochial work.

The Vestments.

a narrow upright collar, and close sleeves. It is bound round the waist with a band a yard and a-half long and three inches broad, called a Cincture.

The recent English Cassock is sometimes folded over in front, and kept close by the Cincture.

The material of a Cassock may be of either silk, stuff, or cloth.

2. The ACADEMICAL SQUARE, or TRENCHER CAP, may be used (either worn or carried in the hand) together with the hood and surplice—*never* with the Alb and Vestment, nor with the surplice and cope, or amyss, with which vestment the Priest's cap, or "Birretta," is always used.

The Trencher Cap is a regular part of the clerical dress. At the Universities it was not formerly worn by laymen, who used the *round cap*, such as the Doctors of Law and Medicine wear on state occasions there. The *Hat*, worn by clergymen with their gowns (by a very modern innovation at Cambridge) is forbidden by Archbishop Parker (App. to *Life*, Book ii. No. 28), and *Caps* are directed to be worn, except in journeys, by the Clergy.[1]

3. The ALB[2] is a vestment of white linen reaching to the feet; the sleeves are tight, in order that the hands of the Priest may be at liberty when celebrating the Eucharist. It should not be plaited into folds, but should fall straight and with a very moderate looseness. It has usually a worked red border and is secured round the waist by a girdle. The apparels should either go round the bottom edge and wrists, which is the most ancient style, or they may consist of quadrangular pieces, varying from twenty inches by nine, to nine inches by six for the bottom, both before and behind, and from six inches by four to three inches for the wrists.

These apparels were not sanctioned by the First Book of Edward VI, but are ordered by our present Rubric, which requires the *whole* of such "ornaments" of the Church and of the Ministers, as were in use in the second year of Edward VI. by authority of parliament.

As the alb, like the *properly*-made surplice, is never open in front, the aperture being only large enough to admit the head, the Priest puts it completely over his head, passes through his right arm and then his left. He then binds it with the girdle round his *loins*, and adjusts it all round, so that it be a finger's breadth from the ground.

4. The STOLE is spoken of under the name of *Orarium*, as early as the Council of Laodicea.[3] It was properly made originally of white linen, afterwards it was made of silk or stuff, and enriched with embroidery and even jewels. The ends are *slightly* widened to admit of an embroidered cross, and terminate in a *fringe*. There should also be a cross in the middle.

The Eucharistic stole is three yards in length and three inches in width, it is worn crossed upon the breast of the celebrating Priest at the Holy Sacrifice, the ends appearing below the Vestment, at other Sacraments it is worn pendant. An Archbishop or Bishop wears the stole pendant at celebration.

The Deacon's stole is worn over the left shoulder and tied under the right arm.

---

[1] It was an ancient custom to wear in choir the Priest's Cap, or "Birretta," over the skull-cap; hence it was usual, for the convenience of taking off the two caps together at those parts of the service, where out of reverence to the Holy Name or otherwise, the head was bared for a short while, to sew the skull and square cap together; so that out of this grew the celebrated "pileus quadratus;" which time has handed down to us, though somewhat altered, in the present Trencher or College Cap of our English Universities.

[2] At the enthronization of Bishop Walton of Chester, A. s. 1661, "All the members of the Cathedral habited in their albs received a blessing from his lordship." Kennett's Register, Vol. I. b. 537, fol. 1728.

[3] "Itaque Diaconus Orarium defert in sinistro humero."

"Subdiaconi vero, ac cæteri inferiores ministri Orariis sive Stolis uti omnino prohibentur." Synod. Laodicena, A. s. 360. Canon xxii. xxiii.

"The *Orarium* was a sort of *scarf*, Du Pin calls it a *stole*, which the Bishop and Priest might have on each shoulder, the Deacon on the left only, the Minister or Sub-Deacon on neither." Johnson's Vade-mecum, Vol. II. p. 111.

When the Cotta or Short Surplice is worn, the stole should never extend beyond its hem. Consequently this short stole is usually two yards and six inches long.

When the long ministerial surplice is worn, which is the old Anglo-Saxon type, a stole of the Saxon type should be worn, viz. one reaching to the hem of the surplice, a stole of this character will be nine feet long and about two inches and a half wide. A surplice of this character is regarded by some as far more graceful than the equally correct short surplice.

The stole—like the maniple—will be of the same colour and material as the vestment of the day.

The stole when crossed on the breast of the Priesthood for the Eucharistic Sacrifice is kept in position by the girdle of the Alb.

[With regard to the Stole, it is at present generally worn by the parochial clergy at matins and evensong, seldom in the college chapels of the two Universities during the recitation of the divine services. This diversity of *use* arises from the fearful neglect of the Holy Eucharist in many parish churches, and the consequent undue exaltation of the Daily Service. Whilst the more frequent celebrations in the college chapels led to the traditional custom of wearing only the surplice and hood at matins and evensong, reserving the stole for the Eucharist. In some cathedrals the stole is worn in choir in singing the Daily Service, in others it is not so worn.

It certainly is not the present usage of the West to wear the stole during the recitation of the divine Office,[2] but it should be remembered that our Daily Service, by one side of its descent, comes from the *East*,[3] and that we may therefore look to Eastern precedents and suggestions. The East is, perhaps, a safer guide on this subject than the West.

Of the identity of the *Epitrachelion*[4] of the holy Eastern Church, with the *stole* of the Western, there can be no doubt; and there is every appearance of this vestment being understood in the East, as the proper badge of the ἱερεύς, as such. It is accordingly worn in all ministrations and prayers, even in those recited preparatory to the public office at home, much more is it indispensable in the recitation of "The Hours."[5] To this must be added, that when the Hours by being said separately from the Liturgy,[6] acquire the dignity of an independent office, not only is the *epitrachelion* = "stole" worn, but also the *phænolion* = "chasuble," or "principal vestment." So high does the East raise the *vestiary* position of the "Hours."

In the West there are also traces of the Eastern idea of the stole, viz. that it is the very badge of the Priest's ministry. (See XXVIIIth Canon of Council of Mayence, § 13, under

---

[1] *Vide* Preface to the Second Edition.

[2] The old Sarum term is *Service*, the Roman *Office*, for the "Hours." The common phrase "Divine Service," (see Rubric after *The Absolution*, and immediately before the *Lord's Prayer* at Matins), is a direct tradition from the old English Use, in contradistinction to the Roman term "Office."

[3] See "The Principles of Divine Service," by the Rev. Philip Freeman, M.A.

[4] "We now come to the *Epitrachelion* which is one form of the Latin *Stole* .... instead of being thrown round the neck and hanging down on each side, as is the case in the Latin Church, the head is put through a hole in the upper extremity, and it simply hangs down in front. It looks, however, nearly the same as a stole, because it has a seam all down the middle .... *it is worn by the Priest in every sacred function.*"—Neale's History of the Holy Eastern Church, (Gen. Iut.) p. 308.

[5] *Ibid.* p. 313.

[6] The eucharistic vestments of the Holy Eastern Church are, for the Priest, the *stoicharion*, which answers to the alb, but is often made of the richest silk or velvet. The *epimanikia*, which in some degree answers to the maniple, but they do not resemble it in shape, and are worn on *both* hands instead of on the left only. They hang down, like a kind of *cuff*, in two peaked flaps, and are fastened under the wrist with a silken cord run along the border, by which they are drawn in and adjusted to the arm. The *epitrachelion*, a form of the stole, a broad strip of brocade or rich silk, with a hole at one extremity for the head to go through, it hangs down simply in front, and is bound upon the *stoicharion* by the *zone*. The *phænolion* is in all respects precisely the Western chasuble. Instead of the *epitrachelion* deacons carry the *orarion*. It is worn over the left shoulder.

The Vestments.

Pope Leo III.) where the stole is ordered to be worn as a badge of sacerdotal dignity[1]. (See Bona, Rer. Lit. i. 24, 6; and Durandus, Rat. Div. Off. L. iii. fol. 25, *de stola*).

Again, we have traces of *vestiary* dignity, beyond the mere surplice, being accorded to the "Hours," and moreover to matins and vespers in the West. "Formerly," says Palmer, (Vol. ii. 314), "the cope was used by the clergy in processions, and on solemn occasions in morning and evening prayers." And so it is still at "solemn vespers," when the officiant is vested "in cotta and cope."[2] He does not, however, wear the stole, according to the decrees of the Sacred Congregation of Rites, September 7, 1816, and September 11, 1847. Now of "the *original* identity of the cope and *casula*, there appears," says Palmer, (Vol. ii. 312), "from the writings of Isidore Hispalensis," (see Gav. Thes. p. 122), and Durandus (lib. iii. cap. 9), "to be no doubt." And thus we have in East and West a recognition of a decidedly priestly vestment at matins and vespers, viz. in the East *phænolion* (chasuble) and *epitrachelion* (stole); in the West *cope* (chasuble). It should, however, be borne in mind, that though the cope and chasuble were *originally* identical, the Western Church has from time immemorial used the chasuble as the eucharistic, the cope as the choral and processional vestment.

There then arises, though it is not absolutely necessary, the consideration, that our matins and evensong are something more than the Hours, or at least than the mediæval idea of them. They are said with much solemnity on Sundays and Festivals more especially;—a reason for a liberal interpretation in this matter of vestments. East and West say, give to this office, at any rate on high days (*East* says always), something more distinctively priestly than the mere surplice. May we not then go back to the probably primitive conception of the stole, as the priestly[3] officiating vestment, bearing in mind the fact of its having been traditionally retained in the English Church at Matins and Evensong? It would fall below the tradition of even the modern West, as expressed by the cope (though without the stole), at high vespers, i. e. on Sundays and Festivals, to wear the *mere* surplice on all occasions, high and low. The West originally no less than the East had doubtless some priestly vestment for the "Hours;" but when the Daily Service became depressed it was analogous and natural that it should lose its stole and cope on ordinary occasions.

To these considerations it may be added, that though there does not appear to be any exact authority for wearing the stole during the Daily Service, this arises from there *not* having been formerly any service of *grand obligation* like our Matins and Evensong. The stole, however, *must* be worn at baptisms, and as these may occur in the daily office "upon Sundays and other holy-days," another reason arises for its use on solemn Vespers and Matins of festivals, apart from honour due to feasts of obligation, &c. It is, therefore, well to wear the stole always, crossed at the celebration of the holy Eucharist, pendent at other sacraments, solemn Vespers, and simple Matins and Evensong.]

The Editor of this second edition is bound to admit that he can find no satisfactory authority for the use of the stole, either at Matins or Evensong. There is nothing of a distinctive sacerdotal nature in either of our daily offices—nothing in fact, which, as a matter of principle, a layman might not say, and notwithstanding the authorities adduced in the paragraphs above standing in brackets (pp. 16, 17) he maintains that the customs so recently current at Cathedral and Collegiate Churches (in perfect harmony and accordance with the directions and practice of the Western Church—of which the Church of England is a portion) is that which it would be wise and well to follow still.—(ED. 2nd ED.)

---

[1] It is true Bona raises the question whether the cassock or any long vestment may not be meant, but there is no certain example of this use. *Orarium* certainly means *Stole* in the canon of Braga.

[2] See Ceremonial according to the Roman Rite, translated from the Italian of Joseph Baldeschi, by J. D. Hilarius Dale. Part II. c. iv. p. 63.

[3] The real origin of the stole is probably that combined with the *phænolion* or chasuble; it represents, and is derived from the "curious ephod" of the high priest.

5. The CHASUBLE, or CHESABLE (*Casula*), commonly called by way of excellency the *Vestment*, is the upper or last vestment put on by the celebrant. Its primitive form was perfectly round, with an aperture in the centre for the head, as we find it figured in the Benedictional of S. Æthelwold. In England its shape continued nearly circular, for six centuries after the mission of S. Augustine; even when a change was made, the only alteration seems to have been that the opposite parts of the circumference were made to come to a point. This form of the Vestment was in use for many ages, and is that which is frequently figured on memorial brasses; but from the middle of the fourteenth century to the present time, the Chasuble[1] as worn by the Priesthood of the Church of England has generally been made in the shape of a *vesica piscis*, and the ornaments with which it has been decorated during that period, are far more elaborate, and consequently richer and more beautiful.

The Orphreys (bands of gold or rich embroidery) of the Vestment consist of a border, a broad stripe in front, and a Latin Cross on the back, extending throughout the whole length and breadth. The *oldest* orphrey however was in the form of a *Pallium*, and came down in a Y shape from the shoulders back and front.

The Chasuble is six feet from point to point, and three feet three inches in its greatest width.

This vestment should be large and *pliant*, as it will then accommodate itself to the positions of the body, and will afford the most beautiful combination of folds. Plain velvet, satin, or silk, *with a thin lining*, are the best materials for ordinary use, as it will then fold up without injury, and not tear and fret the antependia when it comes in contact with them.

The embroidery of the Orphreys tells with surprising effect and richness; but when cloth of gold or figured silks are used, the pattern should be small, as the plain surfaces between the Orphreys are necessarily small, and a large pattern cut up has a confused and disjointed appearance. Powdering is better than diapering for a Vestment, the reverse for a Cope.[2]

The Vestment like the antependium will be of the colour of the Day.

Where there are not funds for more than one Vestment, (a complete set) a Chasuble of fine white silk with gold Orphreys is recommended.

---

[1] "The forms and ceremonies of their worship resemble those of the Greek Church from which they are derived. Their vestments are the same, or nearly so: and here I will remark that the sacred vestures of the Christian Church are the same, with very insignificant modifications, among every denomination of Christians in the world, that they have always been the same, and never were otherwise in any country, from the remotest times where we have any written accounts of them, or any mosaics, sculptures, or pictures to explain their forms. They are no more a Popish invention or have anything more to do with the Roman Church than any other usage which is common to all denominations of Christians. They are and always have been of general and universal—that is of catholic —use; they have never been used for many centuries for ornament or dress by the laity, having been considered as set apart to be used only by the Priests in the Church during the celebration of the worship of Almighty GOD. These ancient vestures have been worn by the Bishops, Priests, and Deacons of that in common with the hierarchy of every other Church. In England they have fallen into disuse by neglect; King Charles I. presented some vestments to the Cathedral of Durham long after the Reformation, and they continued in use there almost in the memory of man,"—Curzon's Armenia, p. 223.

"The Altars in Swedish Churches are richly adorned and furnished with candlesticks and crosses; the vestments of the Priests are also handsome and varied: their usage in these details differs little from the Church of Rome."—Two Summer Cruises in the Baltic, by the Rev. R. E. Hughes, M.A., Fellow of Magdalen College, Cambridge, p. 344.

"In the meanwhile the Priest, kneeling on the Altar-steps was invested by the Candidatus and Kyrke Sanger (precentor) with the mäffe hacke, a crimson velvet Chasuble, embroidered in front with a gold glory surrounding the Holy Name, and behind with a gold floriated cross."—Rev. Henry Newland's Forest Scenes in Norway and Sweden, p. 181.

[2] The "$\phi\alpha\iota\lambda o\nu\eta\varsigma$," or cloak, mentioned by S. Paul in his Second Epistle to S. Timothy, iv. 13, is considered to be no other than the Vestment which the Apostle used when he celebrated the Holy Eucharist.

A white molefkin Chafuble¹ with Orphreys of fcarlet cloth fhaped in the form of a Pallium in front and behind ◊ is well adapted for a village Church, where the ancient colours fometimes cannot be ufed on account of the poverty of the parifh. A Veftment of this kind is of good quality, as all things fhould be in the Houfe of God, of handfome appearance, and of not greater coft than a furplice of fine linen.

When the molefkin Chafuble is wafhed, the Orphreys muft be taken off—they are fewn on like the apparels of an Alb.²

6. The AMICE (*Amictum*) is an oblong fquare of fine white linen, and is put on upon the caffock or prieft's canonical drefs. It is embroidered or *apparelled*, as it is technically termed, upon one edge. In vefting, it is placed for a moment like a veil, upon the crown of the head, as an emblem of falvation, (Eph. vi. 17: *Take the helmet of falvation*), and then fpread upon the fhoulders, and fecured by means of two ftrings, one at each end, which are tied crofs-wife over the breaft. The apparel, which has a crofs in the middle, and is fewed upon it, is from two to three inches wide and extends from ear to ear, forming a kind of embroidered collar, which fhould be arranged fo as to leave the neck free and uncovered.³

The apparel of the Amice cannot be too rich in its ornamentation.

7. GIRDLE (*Cingulum*) is a cord of white cotton or filk taffelled at the end, with which the alb is girded, and adjufted to a convenient length. It is about three yards long.

The girdle is fometimes red.

8. The MANIPLE (*Manipulum*) is three feet four inches long and three inches wide, it is of the fame colour and make as the ftole and fringed at the ends. Embroidered croffes are added to the extremities, which are *very flightly* widened to admit of them.

The Maniple⁴ was originally made of the fineft linen to wipe the chalice at the Offertory or Firft oblation. In very early ages it began to be enriched with embroidery. It is attached by a loop to a button on the left fleeve of the alb, and varies in colour and character with the veftment.

9. The DALMATIC (*Dalmaticum*)—the Gofpeller's Diaconal Veftment at the Sacrament of the Altar—is a loofe robe with large fleeves, partly open at the fides. From the fhoulders behind and before alfo, according to ancient cuftom, are fufpended filk or gold cords with taffels,⁵ which reach within a foot from the hem of the veftment. The Dalmatic fhould extend to the apparel of the alb, and the fleeves fhould be fufficiently fhort not to cover the wrift apparels. The fide openings fhould extend nearly to the hip. There is of courfe no opening in front, but only an aperture for the head as in the cafe of the Alb and Veftment. The Dalmatic has an apparelled collar, and apparels before and behind, in the midft of the open part of the veftment. It has alfo two ftraight Orphreys paffing over the fhoulder and extending to the

---

¹ "Item, one Awter Cloth of *white fuftyan* with red rofes, with a crucifixe, &c."—Jacob's Hift. of Faverfham.

² Some Chafubles have a hood attached to them—but the *Hooded Chafuble* is never ufed as the Principal Veftment, and confequently may be claffed amongft Proceffional rather than Euchariftic veftments. It is called *cafula proceffuria*, or a Proceffional Chafuble. It feems never to have come into general ufe, and is not fo well adapted for ordinary fervices, ceremonials, and proceffions as the Cope.

³ No fhirt-collars, no gloves, nor rings fhould be worn, the hair fhould be fhort, and the face fhaven.

⁴ "Manipuli ufus non ab Aaron, fed ab antiquis patribus Chriftianis initium duxit." Martyr. Bedæ.

⁵ Formerly the fides of the Dalmatic were made to open over the fhoulders to the extent of a few inches, in order to afford a free paffage for the head in putting on the veftment. Thefe flits had an unfeemly appearance when the Dalmatic was adjufted; and therefore filk or gold cords paffing through thefe apertures were contrived to loop or lace them together, and to the end of thefe cords taffels were added as well for weight as for ornament. It was foon found as needlefs to open the Dalmatic on the fhoulder as it would be the Alb or Veftment—but the cord and taffel are ftill attached to the fhoulder as a decoration, and diaconal mark.

The Dalmatic denotes the Kingly Power of CHRIST—and is therefore moft fuitable for the Gofpeller.

"Ufum Dalmaticarum à Silveftro inftitutum fuiffe prodiderunt."—Alcuinus lib. de divinis officiis, cap. x.

The Celebration of the Holy Eucharist.

front and back hem, it has also an Orphrey across the breast and back. It will be seen that this vestment is the same before as behind. The Stole is worn beneath the Dalmatic, and is just visible through the right lateral aperture. The Maniple is affixed to a button upon the left wrist apparel of the Alb. The Dalmatic is of the same colour and material as the Principal Vestment.

10. The TUNIC—the Epistoler's Diaconal[1] Vestment at the Sacrament of the Altar—is of the same shape as the Dalmatic, and follows the same law in regard to shape and colour as the Dalmatic.

Where the colours were not used in regard to the Tunicles (i. e. Dalmatic and Tunic) it was customary to have the Tunic of blue silk.[2]

The Tunic which the Bishop wears beneath his Dalmatic differs only in *length* from that worn by the Epistoler—it should reach midway between the knee and ankle. The Dalmatic as worn by a Bishop is shorter than that worn by the Gospeller, it should extend not more than three inches and a half beyond the knee.

Whatever may have been the colour of the Chasuble the *Episcopal* Tunic and Dalmatic were anciently of a bright purple or sky-blue. At the present time they usually follow the colour of the Vestment. The ancient use seems preferable.

11. The MITRE. There are three sorts of Mitres.

The *Plain Mitre* (*simplex*) made of white linen, the only ornamentation being gold or crimson lining or fringe to the *infulæ* or hanging lappets. This Mitre is used for processions, such as on Rogation Days; for laying the first stone of a Church, School, or College, and by assistant Bishops at Holy Communion.

The gold Embroidered Mitre (*aurifrigiata*) has no gems nor plates of gold or silver upon it, but for its ornament a few small pearls, and is made out of white silk wrought with gold, or of simple cloth of gold. The Orphreyed Mitre is used at Celebrations of Holy Eucharist and at Confirmation.

The Precious Mitre (*pretiosa*) is adorned with gems and precious stones, and often made out of sheets of gold and silver. It was anciently worn on high and solemn festivals, and at synods held in a Cathedral Church.

12. The GLOVES[3] (*Chirothecæ*). The Episcopal Gloves should be made of silk, and richly embroidered.

13. The Sandal is in shape like a high half-boot. It is about six inches high and has no heel, properly so called. Sandals are usually of costly materials, embroidered with various devices, and sometimes enriched with precious stones. They are put on immediately after the Buskins, which are made of precious stuff, or cloth of gold. The length of them is usually about eighteen inches.[4]

14. The PASTORAL STAFF[5] in form somewhat resembles a shepherd's crook, an apt emblem

---

[1] The Epistoler of our canon (XXIV. of 1603) is in the place of the sub-deacon.

[2] "Hyacinthus, quoniam aeris et cœli speciem imitatur, eorundem mentes electorum, omni spe ac desiderio cœlestia quærentes significat. Cujus nobis coloris sacramentum commendans Apostolus, ait: Si consurrexistis cum Christo, quæ sursum sunt quærite, etc."—Beda, de Tabern. Lib. ii. cap. ii.

See also Durand. de *tunica*, Lib. iii. fol. xxvii. Ed. 1653.

The Dalmatic and Tunic are frequently expressed by the simple word "Tunacles," as in the first Prayer Book of Edward VI.

Where there are not funds for a complete set of Tunicles of the canonical colours, it is well to provide two of plain white silk with gold orphreys.

[3] Those which were actually used by the venerable Wykeham are of red silk, embroidered with the Holy Name in gold, and are still preserved at New College, Oxford.

[4] Bishop Waneflete's Episcopal Buskin and Sandals are still preserved at Oxford in the College of S. Mary Magdalen.

[5] "And whensoever the Bishop shall celebrate the Holy Communion in the Church, or execute any other public ministration: he shall have upon him, beside his

of the paſtoral office of a Biſhop over his flock. The upper end is curved, the lower end pointed to ſhow the authority of the Church over the obedient and diſobedient, according to the Latin line,

"Curva trahit mites, pars pungit acuta rebelles."

It is ſometimes bound with a *vexillum* or banner of the Croſs—ſometimes with a *ſudarium*, which is moſt correct, its true uſe being to roll round the ſtaff, not only to hinder the gilding of the burniſhed ſtaff from being tarniſhed, but to preſerve the Epiſcopal Glove.

The Paſtoral Staff is carried by the Biſhop in the left hand, for this obvious reaſon—viz. to keep his right hand free to beſtow, whilſt uplifting it, his bleſſing, as at Holy Communion and other Adminiſtrations of the Church, or as he walks to and from the Altar in proceſſions.

In proceſſions the Crook is carried *forwards*, in bleſſing it is held laterally but ſtill *outwards*. The crook turned outwards[1] denotes juriſdiction over a dioceſe.

Several fine and ancient examples are in exiſtence. An excellent deſign alſo is given in the "Inſtrumenta Eccleſiaſtica." One of ſingular elegance was deſigned by G. E. Street, Eſq., F.S.A., and executed by Mr. Skidmore, for preſentation to the late lamented Biſhop of Graham's Town. An equally clever deſign for a ſtaff for the Biſhop of Central Africa was made by R. Jewell Withers, Eſq. Many of the Engliſh Biſhops now bear their paſtoral ſtaves.

15. The EPISCOPAL RING[2] is generally[3] made of pure gold, large and maſſy, with a jewel, uſually a ſapphire, but not unfrequently a deep broad emerald, or a ruby, ſet in the midſt; it is often enriched with *ſacred* devices and inſcriptions. The ring ſhould be worn on the annular or laſt finger but one of the *right* hand.

16. The CROZIER, or ARCHIEPISCOPAL CROSS, is a Croſs borne on a ſtaff—the lower end pointed as in the Paſtoral Staff. The Crozier is ſeldom of a metal leſs coſtly than ſilver, and is ſometimes wrought of gold and ſparkles with jewels. The Archiepiſcopal Croſs is never carried by the Archbiſhop, but by one of his chaplains choſen to act as Croſs-bearer or "croyſer." The crozier ought according to Catholic cuſtom to have a figure of our LORD hanging nailed to the rood *on each of its two ſides*. A double crucifix of this kind is conſidered to be peculiar to an archiepiſcopal, as diſtinguiſhed from a proceſſional croſs. Thus one figure of CHRIST crucified looks towards the Archbiſhop as he follows it, whilſt another meets the eyes of thoſe in front: if the crozier have only one crucifix it muſt be turned to face the Archbiſhop. The croſs is always floriated.

17. The PALL (*Pallium*). The correct form of this enſign of juriſdiction may be ſeen on the Arms of the See of Canterbury. The Archiepiſcopal Pall is a circle of plain white lambs' wool with a pendent before and behind, reaching down to the feet. The Pall is marked with

rochette, a ſurplice or albe, and a cope or veſtment, and alſo a paſtoral ſtaff in his hand, or elſe borne or holden by his chaplain."—Rubric in firſt Book of Edward VI.

[1] In ancient times *Mitred Abbats* carried the paſtoral ſtaff with the crook turned *inwards* and in the *right* hand, to denote rule over the members only of their own houſes. But this cuſtom was by no means univerſal.

[2] The Ring not only ſymbolizes the temporal dignity of the Biſhop, but is a ſymbol of the Faith with which CHRIST has eſpouſed His Church. The father gave a ring to his prodigal ſon when he returned to him. From this paſſage in the Goſpel the uſe of the Ring is ſuppoſed to have been adopted in the Church. The Ring worn by the Biſhop ſignifies the faithfulneſs, with which he ſhould love the Church confided to his care as himſelf, and preſent her ſober and chaſte to her heavenly Spouſe. 2 Cor. xi. 2: "I have eſpouſed you to one huſband, that I may preſent you as a chaſte virgin to CHRIST." The Biſhop therefore being in the place of CHRIST, wears the Ring of the Bridegroom.—V. Durandus, Lib. iii. fol. xxix. Ed. 1683.

[3] The epiſcopal Ring of Abp. Lee, of York, (now in the poſſeſſion of the Rev. F. G. Lee, D.C.L.,) is of *ſilver gilt*, with the ſacred name engraved upon it, and contains an amethyſt of large ſize.

four purple croffes¹—two on the round part, viz. one at each point whence the pendents iffue, and one on each end of thefe pendents which terminate in a fringe. The Pall is *double* in a portion of the round part—this double part is let fall on the Archbifhop's *left* arm. Befides the *four* purple croffes the Pall is ornamented with *three* golden pins.² Thefe pins, which formerly faftened the Pallium to the Veftment, now pierce neither pall nor chafuble, but by means of little eyes or loops of filk are faftened to the pall as follows—one on the left arm on that part of the pallium which is *double*; the fecond of thefe pins is ftuck in front, at the part whence the pendent ftarts from the circle; the third behind in a like pofition. The fecond and third pin is fixed upon the crofs.

In addition to the above "Ornaments of the Minifter" is the now obfolete "RATIONAL." This was an oblong fquare, and lefs often an oval, of beaten gold, or filver gilt ftudded with precious ftones. It had given to it the name of the ancient Jewifh Rational, Aaronic breaftplate. The Rational was affixed to the breaft of the Bifhop upon the Chafuble by three filvergilt pearl-headed pins, and was only worn at the Celebration of the Holy Euchariſt. It feems not to have been ufed by Englifh Bifhops fince the fourteenth century. This ornament occurs on the Chafuble of the Bifhop Gyffard in Worcefter Cathedral; alfo on the effigy of another Bifhop in the Ladye Chapel of the fame, fuppofed to be either S. Wulftan or Bifhop William de Blois. It may be feen alfo on a figure of Laurence S. Martin, Bifhop of Rochefter, (who died A.D. 1274), in Rochefter Cathedral.

18. The SURPLICE (*Superpellicium*) is a loofe flowing garment of linen, with expanding fleeves, worn by ecclefiaftics of all ranks.

The old Englifh Surplice reaches well nigh to the feet, it is very full, and has large broad fleeves widening as they outftretch themfelves all down the arms to the hands, from which they hang drooping in maffes of beautiful folds. With a round hole at the top, large enough to let the head go through with eafe, it has no kind of opening in front, not even a fhort flit above the breaft,³ thus needing neither tie nor button to faften it at the neck. Immediately it is thrown on the fhoulders, it fits itfelf in becoming drapery about the wearer's perfon, fo that this garment is one of the moft graceful of thofe employed in the facred miniftry.

A long minifterial furplice of this character is admirably adapted for the more folemn fervices, fuch as that of Matrimony; it is alfo fuitable to be worn by Priefts with the choral cope.

The Short Surplice (*cotta*) reaches to the knees—the fleeves of the cotta fhould not extend beyond the hem of the garment.

The Cotta is admirably fitted for Matins and Evenfong.

It is alfo fuitable for lay-clerks.

Surplices fhould *never open in front*.⁴ Nothing can be more unfeemly, efpecially when no

---

¹ The way for putting on the Pall is to make the two pendents droop, one before, the other behind, directly upon the orphrey of the Chafuble, and the circular part to go round the perfon in fuch a manner that it may fit, not about the neck, but over the arms. In the Roman Church it is at prefent hung upon the fhoulders.

The Pall given by the Pope to the Roman Bifhops is now marked with fix black croffes, four on the round part, two on the pendents, which do not reach below the waift.

² Thefe golden pins originally faftened the Pall to the Veftment. In ecclefiaftical coftume every detail muft have a purpofe, to be really beautiful; and the moment anything is added fimply for ornament, or is made extravagantly large, it is offenfive.

³ This, however, does not feem to have been invariably the cafe, for in a picture of the Purification, of the latter half of the fifteenth century, two ecclefiaftics wear full furplices reaching almoft to the feet, and not faftened at the neck, but having an opening in front, which reaches far down the breaft, and difplays a crimfon caffock.

⁴ "This coat (viz. the High Prieft's coat of the Ephod) he put not on after the ordinary fafhion of putting on coats, which were open before; *but this he put on like a furplice, over his head*; and this hole was edged about with an edging of the fame ftuff woven in,

cassock is worn,—an impropriety of too frequent occurrence,—than to see the opening surplice reveal the details of modern full dress. The aperture of the surplice sleeve readily permits the arm to be withdrawn so that the hand can reach the cassock pocket. With the alb the handkerchief can be carried in the girdle.

The "winged" surplices—that is, surplices with the sleeves slit open, and hanging uselessly from the back of the shoulders, are barbarous mutilations of the ample and majestic sleeves and flowing drapery of the ancient surplice. These surplices are much used in France, and the folds are crimped and plaited into narrow divisions—they are both inconvenient, and, as might be conjectured, perfectly unmediæval.

19. The ACADEMICAL HOOD, or COWL, when used as an ecclesiastical vestment should not be worn as at the Universities, viz. hanging by a ribbon, and reaching nearly to the ground behind—a custom of questionable taste, as it has entirely altered the character and uses of that garment. At the time the canon was promulgated, the hood was worn over the shoulders like an Amyss or cape, upon this cape the cowl or hood (which gave its name to the whole vestment) was affixed behind at the back of the neck; this cowl terminated in a purse-like strip called its tippet or liripipe.[1] The tippet of the cowl ought not to reach below the cape. This vestment should be either buttoned down in front, or brought to meet in front, by being stitched together down the breast, so that in putting it on the wearer has to pass his head through it.

20. The TIPPET is a cape of black *stuff*, which clergy who are not graduates are permitted to wear over their surplices when officiating, in lieu of the academical hood: "it shall be lawful for such ministers as are not graduates to wear upon their surplices instead of hoods some decent tippet of black, so it be not silk."—Canon LVIII. of 1603.

" — Likewise all deans, masters of colleges, archdeacons, and prebendaries, in cathedral and collegiate churches, (being priests or deacons,) doctors in divinity, law, or physic, bachelors in divinity, masters of arts, and bachelors of law, having any ecclesiastical living, shall usually wear gowns .... with hoods or tippets of silk or sarcenet, and square caps, and that all other ministers admitted or to be admitted into that function shall also usually wear the like apparel as is aforesaid, except tippets only."—Canon LXXIV. of 1603.

The spirit of the *Canons* is, that non-graduates are permitted to substitute the tippet for the academical hood during divine service only; that all clerics, being graduates, are to wear the hood agreeable to their degrees, not only over their *surplice* but over their usual habit, the *gown*; whilst dignitaries, and beneficed clergy, if not of a lower degree than M.A. or S.C.L. may substitute a *tippet of silk* for the hood, to be worn over their ordinary apparel in public, viz. the *gown*.

The proctors in the University of Cambridge wear the tippet in place of the hood. But this tippet at the present day is no other habit than a Cambridge M.A. hood *laid flat*.

---

that the hole should not be rent."—A Handful of Gleanings out of the Book of Exodus, by John Lightfoot, D.D. London, 4to. 1643.

It would seem from this extract that in the reign of Charles I. the surplice open in front was unknown.

[1] It is well known in the case of the furred Amyss, that at the beginning it was outwardly of black cloth, and inside lined with fur, and that afterwards the fur was worn outside.

The tippet or liripipe is easily recognized in the hoods worn by graduates of Cambridge and Dublin; though less noticeable it is also seen in the Oxford B.D. Hood, and it is also not a little curious that while these hoods have entirely departed from their original shapes in the parts intended to cover the head and shoulders, so that they now serve no other purpose than that of a mere badge, the tippets should have remained comparatively unaltered. In regard to tippets as worn by the *laity* they were in mediæval times of considerable length. Peers of the time of Henry VII. might wear tippets a yard and a half long. The gentry were required to wear them a yard long and an inch broad. Attendants, huntsmen, and abigails wore them a minimum length of a few inches. Inferior persons were ordered to have " no manner of tippets bound upon them."

The anomalous "ribbons" are looped up, and the *liripipe* and *folded cape* form two stole-like appendages, which are crossed upon the breast and held in position by a hook and eye, whilst the cowl and upper part of the folded cape serve as a capacious tippet. Under this "tippet" is worn what is called by University robe-makers "*the Ruff*,"[1] which is not unlike an amice of black silk without a neck apparel.

There is no doubt that the Cambridge M.A. hood *as worn quasi* "tippet," gives the correct shape of the habit permitted to non-graduates by the Canons.

21. The AMYSS or CHOIR TIPPET (*Almutium*) is a large fur cape, which entirely overspreads the shoulders and breast, reaching down as far as the elbows, its "tippets," i.e. two strips of fur in front, fall, stole-like, below the knees, retaining the whole way down the same breadth, about three inches. This vestment had originally a large roomy hood hanging down from all around the neck. The hood portion was early disused, and in its stead a square cap was worn. The Amyss used to be worn over the surplice by Canons and Rectors, according to ancient custom, in choir during the recitation of the Divine Offices, instead of the academical hood.[2]

22. The COPE (*Cappa pluvialis*) is in shape an exact semi-circle with a border (Orphrey) on the straight side, frequently very rich with figures of saints, and sometimes the whole vestment is covered with diaper-work. The length of the straight side of a cope opened out should be ten feet. It is fastened across the chest by a clasp called a Morse. A hood which might be used was in ancient times attached to the back of it; but at the present time this, with the border or orphrey, is only retained that the embroiderer may enrich the dress with tabernacle niches of saints or devices, heraldic and symbolical.

The Cope used in penitential processions is of coarser material and plainer ornamentation than the choral Cope. The Cope is also worn in the Dry Service,[3] which should never be used except on Good Friday—when its colour is black.

It[4] was an ancient custom in the English Church for Priests to wear choral Copes at solemn Vespers. They were worn also by *all* the assistant Clergy in choir on great feasts. And at High Mass according to the Salisbury Use the assistants and rulers of the choir were required to be vested in copes.

---

[1] This ruff is simply a breadth of silk of about two yards long; it is tied upon the left shoulder, and has a cord under the right arm, forming an armhole. It is *gathered* round the neck.

[2] The Amyss as worn by Canons and Rectors is made for the former of white ermine, for the latter (usually) of the skin of the gray squirrel—this is the celebrated Gray Amyss—"the *Amice* gray," as Milton incorrectly spells it; the tails of the ermine are sewn round the edge. It is proper when the Bishop is a "Lord Spiritual" to wear a SPOTTED Amyss.

The "tippets" or points of the Amyss, especially when worn with the Cope, much resemble a Stole, which however if the Western rule regarding vestments be followed in reference to the saying or singing of Matins and Evensong, or in processions, is not worn on such occasions. It is correct in saying office to wear only Cassock, Surplice, and Hood, the hood being by Canon 25 (vide also the last rubric in the first Prayer Book of Edward VI.) in the place of the Amyss for ordinary clerics. When these last wear the Amyss, it should be black—the fur brown. The "tippets" of the Amyss can always be distinguished from the Stole by their rounded terminations, and by small plummets of lead appended to weigh them down.

[3] The Dry Service is unfortunately sometimes used on Sundays and Holidays, but an early Communion supersedes this objectionable practice at all times.

[4] Independent of the rubric at the beginning of the Book of Common Prayer, which states that "such ornaments of the Church, and of the Ministers thereof . . . shall be retained, and be in use;" the XXIVth Canon A.D. 1603, enjoins that at the Administration of the Holy Communion "the principal Minister," i.e. the celebrant, "shall use a decent Cope, being assisted with the gospeller and epistoler:" this Canon however has no power to substitute the Cope for the Vestment (chasuble) when actual celebration takes place.

At a coronation the Archbishop who performs the act is vested in a Cope. *Vide*, "The Form and Order of Her Majesty's Coronation," and as may be seen in Hayter's well-known picture. The Sub-Dean of Westminster wears one also, and Copes of cloth of gold are likewise worn by the Canons of Westminster. Copes are also worn by the Bishops who sing the Liturgy.

The colour of the cope is guided by the same unvarying law which determines the colour of other vestments.

The copes used at the present time in the University of Cambridge are of fine scarlet cloth, with a hood that may be worn. Both cope and hood are lined with ermine.

23. The Priest's Cap, is either a skull cap of black silk or velvet or a Birretta.

This is worn with the Chasuble, Cope, or Amyss, when *the academical* square cap would be out of place, (see Illustration). The Birretta is in shape like the lower half of a pyramid inverted; and in the centre of the crown is placed a tassel, the lower edge is often bordered with a band of velvet. It is worn with a point in front.

The Birretta, which should always be used at funerals, should be invariably raised from the head, by the right hand, at the Sacred Name, the singing of the *Glorias*, or the Invocation before, and the Ascription after, a Sermon.

The Order of Administration.

"The Order of the Administration of the Lord's Supper, or, Holy Communion."*

Colours.†

IF there are more sets of vestments than one, the following order should be observed in the use of them :—

---

* An ellipse¹ for " The Order of the Administration of *the Sacrament* of the Lord's Supper, or Holy Communion."
" In the Catechism the ellipse is expressly supplied in the question which inquires, 'How many Sacraments hath Christ ordained in His Church?' to which the answer is, 'Two only, as generally necessary to salvation, viz. Baptism, and the Supper of the Lord.' In the other case the ellipse is also (though not quite so plainly) supplied in the Prayer Book itself. The Office indeed is called, ' The Order of the Administration of the Lord's Supper, or, Holy Communion,' without any immediate mention of the word Sacrament. But if we look to the Title of the Prayer Book, we find it to be inscribed, ' The Book of Common Prayer, and Administration of the Sacraments, and other Rites and Ceremonies of the Church,' and from thence I conceive we should supply the word ' Sacrament' both to this office and that of Holy Baptism.
"' The general title and contents of the Book therefore, for the Sacramentary,' (like the Ordinal, the Psalter, &c.) as a distinct Book, would stand thus:
' The Administration of the Sacraments :
 1. The Administration of the Lord's Supper (i.e. the one Sacrament, or Holy Communion).
 2. The Ministration of Baptism, (i.e. the other Sacrament).' "—A Letter to the Lord Bishop of S. Andrew's, by the Rev. T. Chamberlain. (Masters).
† The Sarum use of the colours was different, as will be seen from the subjoined translation of the general rubric on that matter contained in the Sarum Missal, usually found preceding the Ordinary of the Mass. " . . . . in the Paschal season,² of whatsoever the mass be said, (except in the Invention of the Holy Cross,) the ministers of the Altar shall use white vestments at the mass; so be it likewise on the Feast of the Annunciation of the Blessed Mary, and in the Conception of the same, and in both Feasts of S. Michael, and in the Feast of S. John the Apostle, in the Nativity of our Lord, and in the octave, and throughout the octave of the Assumption, and of the Nativity of the Blessed Mary, and in the Commemoration of the same throughout the whole year, and throughout the octave, and in the octave of the Dedication of

---

¹ The term "*Lord's Supper*" was first introduced into the Book of Common Prayer, (Edward VI.'s First Book,) to signify the consecration as distinct from the communion. "The Lord's Supper and Holy Communion;" the latter having come in the year before, (Sparrow's Collection, "The Order of the Communion, 1547,") to signify the *receptionary* part of the office.
² i.e. from Easter Day to the Octave of Corpus Christi.

*White.**—From the evening of Christmas Eve to the Octave of Epiphany, inclusive, (except on the two feasts of S. Stephen and the Holy Innocents); from the evening of Easter Eve to the Vigil of Pentecost,

the Church. But let them use red vestments[1] in all Sundays throughout the year without the Paschal time when it is the service of the Sunday, and in Ash-Wednesday, and the Cœna Domini, and in each Feast of the Holy Cross, and in every Feast of Martyrs, Apostles, and Evangelists, without Paschal time; but in all Feasts of a Confessor or many Confessors, let them use vestments of a yellow (*crocei*) colour."—Rub. Sarif.

"The Rubrical colours for vestments were directed [by Sarum use] to be as follows:—Red on every Sunday, and every Festival of Martyrs, Apostles, and Evangelists throughout the year, except from Easter to Trinity Sunday, when they were always white. They were also white on the Feasts of the Annunciation, and of S. Mary, S. Michael, and S. John; yellow on Confessors' days; black on Vigils and Ember days. For other days no particular directions were given. . . . . We may presume that the *colours* employed for the Altar followed the same rule; but the Rubric seems not to have been very strictly observed."—J. D. Chambers' Strictures on Dr. Lushington's Judgment, p. 113. London: W. Benning, 1856.

In another rubric, immediately following the mass for S. Felix, occur these directions:—
"But in *vigils* and ember days let the mass of the Fast ever be said; but if a Feast of Nine Lessons fall thereon let the mass of the Feast be said after terce, the mass of the Fast after sext, both at the principal Altar; but so that the deacon and sub-deacon be robed in albs with amices without tunicles or chasubles at that mass, that is of the fast; but the clerks in the choir shall use black copes."—Rub. Sarif.

Black vestments were undoubtedly used in vigils and masses for the dead.

Though no mention is made in the Sarum Rubrics of the colour of the hangings of the Altar, they as a matter of course followed the same law which obtained in the matter of the vestments of the priest, &c. and were consequently always of the colour of the day or season.

Again, no mention is made of any vestments or altar-hangings of blue or green, and yet these frequently occur in the ancient inventories of church furniture; as, for instance, in Dugdale's Monast. viii. 1209, of York Cathedral; *ibid.* 1387, of Lincoln Cathedral; *ibid.* 1362, of S. George's Chapel, Windsor; and in the illuminated MSS. in the British Museum, and elsewhere.

There is no direction as to the colour on Ferial Days. The colour, if not green[2] as at present, might vary according to that of the preceding Sunday; and if so, there was probably an exception during Advent and Lent, when black vestments were most likely used.

* *White*, emblematical of Purity.

Red, colour of Blood, and is proper to all Martyrs' Days; and is an emblem of the fiery tongues in the form of which the HOLY GHOST descended on the Apostles.

Green, the least expressive of colours, or perhaps as the prevailing colour of nature.

Violet, a mourning colour; used on the Feast of Holy Innocents, because the Church deems it no prejudice to mourn for the great wickedness of the crime which cut them off from the earth—especially directed against our Blessed LORD Himself—even whilst celebrating the memory of these earliest and very glorious Martyrs.

[1] This reasonably accounts for the tradition of the Church of England, in the question of altar coverings—a few years ago almost all being of crimson.

[2] The great number of green vestments described as existing, renders it most probable that green was the Sarum ferial colour; there is no other way of accounting for the numerous vestments of that colour.

on Trinity Sunday, on Corpus Christi Day and throughout its Octave; on the feasts of the Purification, Conversion of S. Paul, Annunciation, S. John Baptist, S. Michael, S. Luke,* All Saints, on Maundy Thursday, and at the celebration on Easter Eve, on all Feasts of Our Lady, and of Saints and Virgins not Martyrs, at Confirmations, Harvest Festivals, Marriages, and on the Anniversary Feast of the Dedication of the Church.

Red.—Vigil of Pentecost to the next Saturday, Holy Innocents, (if on a Sunday), and all other Feasts.

Violet.—From Septuagesima Sunday to Easter Eve; from Advent to Christmas Eve; Ember Week in September; the Rogation Days; and on Holy Innocents, unless on Sunday.

Black.—Good Friday and funerals; on public fasts *et de missis de requiem*.

Green.—All other days.

Some ritualists say the Altar should be stripped on Good Friday.

Cloth of gold is said to supply all other colours.

The vestments used at the celebration of the Holy Eucharist should be of the same colour as the Frontal of the Altar. The Superfrontal may always be Red.

1. *Time of Vesting the Altar for a Festival.*

IN time for the Evensong next before, being its first Vespers.

2. *The fair white Linen Cloth.*

"The Table, at the Communion-time having a fair white linen cloth upon it."†

IT is well to have one fair white linen cloth with a border worked in colours for Festivals.

No cushion should be allowed upon the Altar, and only one book (for the Celebrant,) with a small brass desk to support it.‡

---

* Amongst the Latins, Red is the colour for S. Luke's Day. It is said to be doubtful whether he was martyred.

† The fair white linen cloth should cover the top of the Altar, and hang down two feet at the ends thereof, but not over the front, more than an inch or two to show a border of lace or embroidery. It should never cover the Antependium.

‡ The Book of the Gospels and the Book of the Epistles are placed upon the credence.—Masters' Edition of the Book of Common Prayer, according to the *sealed copy* in the Tower, printed in red and black, with the old Elzevir type, is sometimes used for this function; but the Oxford edition rubricated, in octavo, and printed in a plain large type, is perhaps more convenient.

The Order of Administration.

3. *Vestments for Choristers.*

See infra, Appendix.

4. *Assistant Deacons.*

DEACONS assisting in other capacities than the above—when *e. g.* a Bishop celebrates—wear surplice and stole deacon-wise, but no hood*—the hood, a purely choir vestment, never being worn at a Celebration of the Holy Eucharist.

5. *Diaconal Vestments.*

FOR the Vestment of the Deacons, i.e. Epistoler and Gospeller, see infra, Appendix, where they are marked thus (*).

6. *Vestments, Episcopal and Sacerdotal.*

FOR the Vestment of the Celebrant, if a Bishop, see infra, Appendix; if a Priest, infra, Appendix, where the Eucharistic Vestments are marked thus (+).

7. *Prayers for Choristers.*

When vested.

CLEANSE me, O LORD, and keep me undefiled, that I may be numbered among those blessed children, who having washed their robes, and made them white in the blood of the Lamb, stand before Thy throne, and serve Thee day and night in Thy Temple. Amen.

Before Service.

O LORD, open Thou my lips, that my mouth may show forth Thy praise, and purify my heart, that I may worthily magnify Thy glorious Name; through JESUS CHRIST our LORD. Amen.

After Service.

Grant, O LORD, that what I have sung with my mouth, I may believe in my heart; and what I believe in my heart, I may steadfastly fulfil; through JESUS CHRIST our LORD. Amen.

---

* According to the Rubrics of the Roman Church, those religious orders who wear hoods are directed to adjust them before celebration under the ecclesiastical vestments. They are usually enveloped in the amice, but sometimes hang over the back of the chasuble.

8. *Orationes cum Diaconus paramentis induitur.*

Ad Amictum, (infra).

Ad Albam vel Superpellicium, (infra).

Ad Zonam, (infra).

Ad Stolam, (infra).

Ad Dalmaticum:

Da mihi, Domine, sensum et vocem, ut possim cantare laudem Tuam ad hanc missam.

Vel ad Tunicam:

Indue me, Domine, vestimento salutis, et indumento lætitiæ circumda me semper.

Ad Fanonem, (infra).

9. *Orationes cum Sacerdos induitur sacerdotalibus paramentis.*

Cum lavat manus dicat:

DA, Domine, virtutem manibus meis ad abstergendam omnem maculam : ut sine pollutione mentis et corporis valeam Tibi servire.

Ad Amictum imponendum capiti suo:

Spiritus Sanctus superveniet in me, et virtus Altissimi obumbrabit caput meum.

Ad Albam:

Miserere mei, Deus, miserere mei: et munda me a reatibus cunctis, et cum illis qui dealbaverunt stolas suas in sanguine Agni mereamur perfrui gaudiis perpetuis.

Ad Zonam:

Præcinge me, Domine, zona justitiæ, et constringe in me dilectionem Dei et proximi.

Ad Stolam, dum imponitur collo:

Stola justitiæ circumda, Domine, cervicem meum, et ab omni corruptione peccati purifica mentem meam.

Ad Fanonem, dum imponitur brachio sinistro:

Indue me, Pater clementissime, novum hominem, deposito veteri cum actibus suis, qui secundum Deum creatus est in justitia et sanctitate veritatis.

Ad Casulam, cum assumitur:

Domine Qui dixisti, Jugum Meum suave est et onus Meum leve, fac ut istud portare sic valeam quod consequar Tuam gratiam.

The Order of Administration.

10. *Præparatio ad S. Eucharistiam.*

FOR THE CELEBRANT ALONE.

Ante S. Eucharistiam:

EUS Qui de indignis dignos, de peccatoribus justos, de immundis mundos facis: munda cor et corpus meum ab omni contagione et sorde peccati, et fac me dignum altaribus Tuis ministrum, et concede propitius, ut in hoc altari, ad quod indignus accedo, hostias acceptabiles offeram pietati Tuæ pro peccatis et offensionibus meis et innumeris quotidianisque excessibus; et pro omnibus hic circumstantibus, universisque mihi familiaritate et affinitate conjunctis, atque me odio aliquo insectantibus et adversantibus, cunctisque fidelibus Christianis vivis et mortuis: et per Eum sit Tibi meum votum atque sacrificium acceptabile: Qui Se Tibi Deo Patri obtulit in sacrificium, Jesum Christum Filium Tuum Dominum nostrum, Qui Tecum vivit et regnat in Unitate Spiritus Sancti Dominus.

Post S. Eucharistiam:

Gratias Tibi ago Domine sancte, Pater omnipotens, æterne Deus, Qui me peccatorem, indignum famulum Tuum, nullis meis meritis, sed sola dignatione misericordiæ Tuæ satiare dignatus es pretioso Corpore et Sanguine Filii Tui Domini nostri Jesu Christi. Et precor ut hæc sancta communio non sit mihi reatus ad pœnam, sed intercessio salutaris ad veniam. Sit mihi armatura fidei, et scutum bonæ voluntatis. Sit vitiorum meorum evacuatio, concupiscentiæ et libidinis exterminatio: charitatis et patientiæ, humilitatis et obedientiæ augmentatio: contra insidias inimicorum omnium, tam visibilium quam invisibilium, firma defensio: motuum meorum, tam carnalium quam spiritualium perfecta quietatio: in Te uno ac vero Deo firma adhæsio, atque finis mei felix consummatio. Et precor Te, ut ad illud ineffabile convivium me peccatorem perducere digneris: ubi Tu cum Filio Tuo et Spiritu Sancto sanctis Tuis es Lux vera, Satietas plena, Gaudium sempiternum, Jucunditas consummata et Felicitas perfecta. Per Christum.

11. *The Chalice and Paten.**

HE Chalice, over which is folded the Purificator—having placed upon it the Paten, upon this the Pall,† and over this a Veil of silk of the colour of the season, the burse or corporal case, also of the colour of the season, containing a white linen corporal,

---

* At the oblation of elements, viz. before the Prayer for the whole state of CHRIST's Church, the Chalice should be placed in the centre of the Altar, behind the Paten. This was the Sarum custom, and is *now* the present Roman use; though before the fifteenth century the celebrant was ordered by the Roman rubrics to place it on the left of the Host, to catch, as it were, the Blood which flowed from the spear-wound in our Blessed LORD's right side.

The most ancient known custom—that of the Syriac Liturgy of S. James—is to place the elements side by side at the oblation, one behind the other, for consecration, thus effecting a cruciform arrangement by the successive positions.—See Renaudot's Lit. Or. vol. ii.

† The Pall or Chalice-cover is a small piece of cardboard, about six inches square, covered

being laid on the top of all—is placed upon the Altar at the beginning up to the oblation of the Elements, unlefs at High Service, when it is placed on the Credence, and not put on the Altar until the Offertory. After the Offertory is completed the Chalice is covered with the Pall, the Paten with the corner of the corporal.*

12. *The Credence.*

THE Credence—about three feet by two feet in fize—fhould be placed at the fouth end of the Altar. If the Aumbrye is ufed as a Credence—which is certainly undefirable—it will ufually be found on the north: but the Epiftle fide is by far the moft convenient for either a permanent or moveable Credence. It fhould be covered with a green embroidered cover fringed, over which fhould be placed a white linen cloth. Upon it fhould be arranged before Service begins, the Holy Veffels, viz. the Chalice and Paten; the Cruets or Flagons, for wine and water; a metal Plate or Canifter for the wafers or breads, which fhould lie upon fair white linen, and be covered with a napkin to preferve them from duft or other defilement; and a fair linen maniple, for the *lotio*

---

with linen on both fides. Once every fix months the linen fhould be removed, carefully burnt in the facrifty, and the afhes thrown down the pifcina. Formerly, when the Corporal was much larger than at prefent, its ends ufed to cover *both* the holy veffels. The Pall is therefore fuppofed to be a part of the Corporal, and perhaps reprefents a Corporal folded. It is better and moft convenient that it be not fringed with lace, nor anything which hangs over.

The Burfe is ufually nine inches fquare, the Corporal about eighteen inches.

The Chalice-veil of filk, about one foot eight inches, with embroidered crofs.

* A like direction is found in the Coronation Service. "And firft the QUEEN (kneeling) offers BREAD and WINE for the Communion, which . . . . are by the Archbifhop received from the QUEEN, and reverently placed upon the Altar, and *decently covered with a fair linen cloth*."—The Coronation of her Majefty Queen Victoria.

Immediately follows the *Secreta* of the Coronation: "Blefs, O LORD, we befeech Thee, thefe Thy gifts." It is to be obferved that in the Form and Order of Coronation the oblation of the unconfecrated elements precedes the oblation (offertory) of the "purfe of gold," the Queen's *fecond oblation.*

When the Eucharift is celebrated as a diftinct fervice, the proper place for bringing in the elements and placing them upon the Credence is co-ordinately with the proceffion and Introit. The Sarum (and old French) ufe *allowed* it till the firft Collect, (fee Mafkell's Ancient Liturgy of the Church of England, p. 34), but ftrictly fpeaking it fhould accompany the Introit, and in the *Syriac* it was quite at the beginning.

When Matins, Litany, and the celebration of the Holy Eucharift follow in fucceffion, the proper place for bringing in the elements and placing them on the Credence is after the Litany, before the proceffion and Introit. They may be placed on the Credence *before* Matins if

manuum, and the Mundatory or Purificator, for the wiping of the chalice after the purifications. It is convenient to have a perforated Spoon on the Credence.

The Offertory bason and alms-bags should also be placed on the Credence, also a ewer and a metal or glass bason (where there is no Piscina) for the Priest to wash his hands after the Offertory. Also there should be thereon the Book of the Gospels, and the Book of the Epistles.

13. *Hour of Celebration.*

HE Holy Communion may be celebrated at any hour, from break of day till twelve o'clock: there should be no Celebration commenced after that hour. The Holy Sacrament should invariably be received fasting, according to the practice of the Universal Church. Bishop Sparrow* reckons nine A. M. as the ancient canonical hour for Celebration. At any rate, putting aside Catholic usage, as a marriage by act of Parliament must be celebrated before noon, and it is declared by the rubric that it is "convenient that the married persons receive the Communion at their marriage," it would seem to be implied that the Communion must be celebrated in the forenoon. See also *Ecclesiologist*, Vol. XIII. pp. 53—56, in condemnation of the afternoon Celebration.

14. *The Communion, or Houselling Cloth,*†

AY be spread over the Septum or Rails, where there are any, or else placed in readiness to be used during the Communion of the People. Abroad it is the custom in some places for the servers or acolytes to hold it at either end.

---

if there be no sacristy to deposit the elements during the time the Morning Service is being recited.

At plain service the elements are placed upon the Credence by the clerk who serves; at solemn service by either the Deacon or Sub-deacon, or by the assistant priest.

* Sparrow's Rationale, p. 251. Ed. London, 1661.

† Mentioned in Coronation Service :—

"Whilst the King receives, the Bishop (Bishops, George II. &c.) appointed for that Service, shall hold a towel of white silk, or fine linen, before him."—Order of Coron. of Geo. IV.

The Houselling cloth has not since been used in the Coronation Service.

It is still spread in some churches in the diocese of Winchester; at S. Mary's, Oxford; at S. Mary's, Prestbury, near Cheltenham, and at All Saints, Leamington. It is placed over the rails before the communicants.

15. *The Altar Lights.**

HESE should be lighted immediately before the Communion Service by the Clerk in cassock, or in cassock and surplice. He should make a reverence before ascending to light them, and commence on the Epistle side.

---

* Testimony of S. Jerome:—
"Per totas orientis ecclesias quando Evangelium legendum est, accenduntur Luminaria, jam sole rutilante, non utique ad fugandas tenebras, sed ad signum lætitiæ demonstrandum, ... ut sub typo luminis corporalis, illa lux ostendatur de qua in Psalterio legimus—Lucerna pedibus meis verbum Tuum, Domine, et lumen semitis meis."—Hier. Epist. adversus Vigilant.

"They reduced candles formerly sans number in churches to two upon the High Altar, before the Sacrament; these being termed 'lights' shows they were not *lumina cæca* but burning."—Fuller's Church History, p. 374, fol. 1655.

Speaking of the Queen's Chapel, Heylyn writes: "The Altar furnished with rich plate, two fair gilt candlesticks with tapers in them, and a massy crucifix of silver in the midst thereof."—Hist. of Reform. p. 124, fol. 1660.

In the 42nd Canon of those enacted under King Edgar, (Thorpe's Ancient Laws and Institutes of England, Vol. II. p. 252—3,) we find, "Let there be always burning Lights in church when Mass is singing." Ditto 14th Canon of Elfric, pp. 348—9 of the same volume.

"Lights were received in the primitive church to signify to the people that GOD the Father of Lights was otherwise present in that place than in any other. . . . . We must not be hasty in condemning particular ceremonies, for in so doing in this ceremony of Lights, we may condemn the Primitive Church that did use them, and we condemn a great and noble part of the Reformed Church, which doth use them unto this day."—Dr. Donne's Sermons, p. 80, fol. 1640.

"Semper in ecclesia Lumen ardeat dum missa decantetur."—King Edgar's Canons, (A.D. 968). The above is from Lambard's Latin version.

"Who perceiveth not that by this right way the tapers came into the Church mysteriously placed with the Gospel upon the Altar, as an emblem of the True Light?"—Gregory's Works, 1st Edition, p. 108. London, 1671.

"Ut sub typo luminis corporalis illa Lux ostendatur de qua in evangelio legitur—'Erat Lux vera Quæ illuminat omnem hominem.'"—S. Isidore of Seville (Orig. vii. 12).

Lights are placed on the Altars of the several Oxford College Chapels and Parish Churches mentioned below: Merton, Magdalen, Worcester, University, Jesus, Pembroke, Queen's, Exeter, Lincoln, All Souls, Balliol, S. Edmund Hall, S. Mary Hall, Corpus Christi, Oriel, Trinity, S. John's, Brasenose, New College. Also at S. Peter-in-the-East, S. Paul, S. Michael, S. Thomas the Martyr, SS. Philip and James, S. George, S. Fridefwide, S. Giles, S. Mary. At Cambridge: Trinity, St. John's, Caius,[1] King's, S. Peter's, Jesus,[2] Magdalen, Emanuel.[3] And in the following cathedral and parish churches: Westminster Abbey; Ely Cathedral

---

[1] They were removed when the chapel was lighted with gas, having been, it is presumed, most improperly used to light the sanctuary at evensong.

[2] Date 1777.

[3] The gift of Archbishop Sancroft.

It should be observed that these two Eucharistic lights should never be used as mere candles for lighting the Sanctuary. Other brackets for candles or the Coronæ and standard lights are sufficient for that purpose. The two lights are symbols and *in honorem Sacramenti*, and must be *cæca lumina*, save when Celebration is intended. The Judgment in the Knightsbridge Case decided their strict legality.

When Matins, Litany, and Communion, or Matins and Communion, are celebrated together, the lights should not be lighted till just before the Communion Office begins. Other lights may be lit at the Gospel, at the Offertory, or immediately before the Consecration or Canon. Two lights are the minimum according to the plain existing law of the Church of England.

(when there is a celebration of the Holy Eucharist); Christ Church Cathedral; Lincoln Cathedral; Bristol Cathedral (post-Reformation); Salisbury Cathedral (at early Communion); Shrewsbury parish Church; Exeter Cathedral; Lichfield; Manchester Cathedral; Bruton, Somerset; West Tennant, Somerset; Theale, Berks; Thoverton, Devon; S. Paul's, Brighton; Marlborough S. Mary, Wilts (from time immemorial); Beaumaris, Anglesea; All-Hallows, Barking, City of London; Clifton Hampden, Oxfordshire; Cuddington, Bucks; Walpole S. Peter, Norfolk; Chapel of S. Edmond (ibid.); Skipton, Christ Church, Yorkshire; Kilndown, Kent; Benefield, Northants; Eastnor, Hereford; Cuddesdon, Oxford; Worminghall, Bucks; S. James' Chapel Royal; S. Gregory's Canterbury, Kent; S. Margaret's, Canterbury, Kent; S. Paul's, Knightsbridge; S. Barnabas, Pimlico; S. Alban's, Holborn; Ilam, Stafford, (the candlesticks are put on the Altar on days when Holy Communion is administered; an ancient practice. The present incumbent, who has held the living fifty years, found the custom and retained it); New Shoreham, Sussex; Old Shoreham, Sussex; Withyam, Sussex; Crowborough, Sussex; Rotherfield, Sussex; S. Paul's in the city of Exeter; Littlemore, Oxford; S. Saviour's, Leeds, York; S. Paul's, Shadwell, York; Hackness, York (ancient); S. Martin, Liverpool; Sheen, Stafford; S. Augustine's College Chapel, Canterbury, Kent; Lavington, Sussex; Graffham, Sussex; S. Alban's, Manchester; Stoke South, Sussex; Holy Trinity, Coventry, Warwickshire; Butleigh, Somerset; Balstonborough, Somerset; Wasperton, Warwick; S. Paul, Birmingham; Holy Trinity, Bordesley; Shevioke, Cornwall; Stoke, near Coventry; Low, near Coventry, date 1730; Empshott, Hants; S. Columba, Edinburgh; S. John's, Aberdeen; S. Mary's, Aberdeen; S. Drostane's, Deer; S. Margaret's, Forgue; Arley Chapel, Cheshire; Sackville College Chapel, East Grinstead, Sussex; Christ Church, Hoxton; S. Ethelburga, City of London; S. Bartholomew's, Cripplegate; S. Mary Magdalen, Chiswick; S. Andrew, Wells-Street, London; Christ Church, Clapham; Crawley, Sussex; Parish Church, Leeds; S. Mary, Brompton, (until *stolen* two or three years ago); Cowley, Oxford; Sandford, Oxfordshire; S. Mary-le-Strand, London; Wantage, Berks; Sunningwell, Berks; S. Mary, Stone, Kent; Malling Abbey Chapel; S. James, Enfield, Middlesex; Leigh, Essex; S. John Baptist, Harlow, Essex; S. Hugh, Harlow, Essex; S. Ninian's Cathedral, Perth.[1]

[1] More than two thousand churches in England have lights upon the Altars.

16. *The Procession and Introit.*

THE Choir proceed from the Sacrifty, two and two, holding their caps* with both hands before the breaſt, and preceded by the verge-bearer, take their places in the chancel, laterally, firſt inclining before the Altar, two and two. Theſe are followed by the Celebrant and the miniſters of the Altar, (preceded by the ſerving-clerks in caſſock and ſurplice,) in the following order:

1. Epiſtoler
2. Goſpeller } with bodies erect, and eyes turned to the ground.
3. Celebrant

The Goſpeller and Epiſtoler *walk together*, the Celebrant *alone*.

On arriving at the foot of the Altar-ſteps, the clerks take their places north and ſouth, facing eaſt on the lower ſtep in front of the Altar, and the Celebrant and Miniſtrants ſtand humbly before the ſteps of the Altar, *until the commencement of the Introit*, when the Celebrant advances to the Altar, and the Goſpeller and Epiſtoler alſo take their places.†

---

* On no account muſt the Prieſt place his Birretta upon the holy Altar, (he ſhould give it to the lay clerk who ſerves, if at plain ſervice; and to the ſub-deacon or Epiſtoler at ſolemn ſervice; who will place it on the credence, or in the Prieſt's ſeat of the ſedilia, and return it to him after the Liturgy is over), nor his handkerchief, which may be carried in the girdle of his alb under his veſtment. In fact, nothing ſhould be placed upon the Altar but what immediately relates to the Euchariſt; even the "ornaments," viz. the Croſs and Altar-lights, and Flower Vaſes are placed upon the *altar ledge*.

† It is an *old* and proper practice for the *Goſpeller to go to the right hand of the Celebrant*, while the *Epiſtoler aſcends to his left*. After the Introit is ſung the Prieſt goes to the book on the north ſide or Goſpel corner, and the ancient cuſtom is for the Goſpeller to go to his ſtep next to the altar platform on the ſouth ſide, and the Epiſtoler on his own ſtep on the north ſide; of courſe all facing the eaſt.

The poſition of the hands and feet.—The hands of all the miniſters ſhould be joined before the breaſt, with the fingers extended. The chief exceptions are in Collects and ſimilar prayers, the intonations of the Creed, the Prefaces, and the Conſecration Prayer to the words "Body and Blood," and of the Gloria in excelſis; in theſe caſes the celebrant (only) holds his hands open and extended, the palms facing each other. The feet are put cloſe together. In ſitting the ſame rule is obſerved, the legs ſhould not be croſſed, and the hands ſhould be placed in the lap.

17. *The Pater Noster* and Collect for Purity.*

" And the Priest† standing at the north side of the Table shall say the Lord's Prayer, with the Collect following, the people kneeling."

HE Celebrant, continuing to stand on the north side with his face to the east, recites the Lord's Prayer in monotone or otherwise, the Ministrants *standing* in their places. The Pater Noster and Amen here are said by the celebrant alone.

18. *The Commandments and Kyrie Eleisons.*‡

" Then shall the Priest, turning to the people, rehearse distinctly all the TEN COMMANDMENTS ; and the people still kneeling shall, after every Commandment, ask God mercy for their transgression thereof, for the time past, and grace to keep the same for the time to come, as followeth."

HESE are said by the Celebrant, still standing at the north side of the Altar, but with his face towards the Faithful.

The Service Book should be laid open on the palm of the left hand, and held steadily with the right. The Rubric of the Scotch Rite of 1636 (v. Laud's Prayer Book) desires that mercy shall be asked " for the transgression of every duty therein ; either according to the letter, or to the mystical importance of the said commandment."

---

* The Celebrant says the " Pater Noster," *alone*. The rubric in the Morning Prayer has nothing whatever to do with the question, for the Communion Office is governed by Special Directions. The Sarum custom was for the Priest to say the *Pater* and the Oratio, *Deus cui omne cor patet*, as a preparation as it were for the Holy Sacrifice.

The Lord's Prayer was doubtless in the early part of the Gregorian Office in all churches, but the Roman removed it to the sacristy in the *Præparatio ad Missam*. It is also at the beginning of, or early in, the Syriac, the Nestorian, and the Mozarabic Rites, and was probably universal.

† Though the Lord's Prayer and Collect for Purity are removed from the sacristy to the Altar, they are still a *Præparatio ad Missam*. Hence the " Amen " at the end of the Pater Noster is not printed in italic type, as it is said by the Priest ; but in the Collect the Priest seems to extend the *Præparatio* to the Faithful who make it their own, by the answer " Amen." It will be observed that the Amen of the Collect is printed in the usual italic type.

‡ The *Kyrie Eleisons* occupy their old place, as in the Sarum Rite. As to *the Commandments*, they form invariable capitula taken from Exodus xx., and are prefixed to each Kyrie. In the Sarum Use, at certain seasons (v. Maskell, Anc. Lit. Appendix), addresses to the three Persons of the Holy Trinity are similarly inserted. It is also worthy of record, that on the eve of Pentecost the Sarum Rite began with the Lord's Prayer, after which lessons were read

The Celebration of the Holy Eucharist

19. *Collects for the Church and Queen.*

"Then shall follow one of these two Collects for the Queen, the Priest standing as before, and saying."

STANDING as before," viz. in the position the Priest was in before rehearsing the Commandments—at the north* side of the Altar, with the face eastwards.

The Second Collect is to be preferred. It is the ancient and famous " Deus in cujus manu corda sunt regum," found in the Gregorian Sacramentary, and ordered to be used *daily* in some parts of the *Sarum dominions*, e. g. in Scotland (v. Maskell's Anc. Lit. p. 28, note), and doubtless elsewhere. It is of course in one of the " missæ pro rege " in the Sarum Missal. The first Collect on the contrary *seems* to be a new one, though very likely there was an original. Its containing a Prayer for the whole Church as well as for the King, though a recommendation, does not warrant a preference over the Second Collect.

20. *The Collect for the day—The Epistle†—The Gospel—The Creed.*

"Then shall be said the Collect of the Day. And immediately after the Collect the Priest

---

from the law of Moses *without titles*, each lesson being followed by a response and collect.—Miss. Sarif. fol. cii. London, 1526. [It must be admitted that the introduction of the Ten Commandments was a singular and grievous innovation, for which no ancient precedent whatever can be found.—ED. 2nd ED.]

A portion of the Decalogue was read on the *Feria* iv. *post Oculi*, followed by the response : " *Miserere mei, Domine, quoniam infirmus sum, sana me, Domine.*"—Ibid. fol. xlvi. London, 1526.

* *The north side* (as distinguished from *the north end*, the Altar being a parallelogram) is the technical phrase for *the north part of the west side*, called also the Gospel or left corner. It occurs in the Syriac Liturgy of S. James :—" *Venitque* (i. e. *sacerdos*) *a latere septentrionali ad australe.*"—Renaudotii Lit. Or. Coll., tom. ii. p. 24. Vide Dr. Littledale's pamphlet *The North Side of the Altar*, 2nd Edition. London : Palmer, 1865.

The corresponding rubric in the Nonjurors' Office explains their north side to mean the north end ; and thereby shows by implication that the then practice of the Church of England *did not*.

† According to the Use of Sarum the Epistle was read at a lectern or desk in the midst of the Choir ; " Subdiaconus per medium chori ad legendam EPISTOLAM in pulpitum accedat."—Miss. Sarif. The Hereford Use was, " Deinde legatur EPISTOLA super lectrinum a subdiacono ad gradum chori."—Miss. Herf.

It is also according to Catholic usage to read both Epistle and Gospel from the jube or roodloft, if the chancel is deep, so that the Faithful cannot hear.

According to the Roman Rite the Epistle is read towards the Altar on the south side.

shall read the Epistle,* saying, *The Epistle* [or, *The portion of Scripture appointed for the Epistle*] *is written in the* —— *Chapter of* —— *beginning at the* —— *Verse.* And the Epistle ended, he shall say, *Here endeth the Epistle.* Then shall he read the Gospel (the people all standing up) saying, *The holy Gospel is written in the* —— *Chapter of* —— *beginning at the* —— *Verse.* And the Gospel ended,† shall be sung or said the Creed following, the people still standing, as before."

---

* At Solemn Service, the Epistle and Gospel should be read by an Epistoler and Gospeller. The usage of the Universal Church is for these Ministers to stand during the greater part of the Communion Service as well as the Priest. The exceptions in the Church of England are at the Confession and Absolution, the Prayer of Access, the Consecration, the receiving of the Sacrament, and the Benediction.

The Gospeller's Office is to assist the Priest; the Epistoler to assist the Gospeller: or rather the Gospeller is to assist at the Holy Eucharist, directly and principally; the Epistoler to assist in it indirectly and subordinately. When there are none to assist who are deacons, it is customary for Priests to act as Gospeller and Epistoler at Solemn Service, i.e. to discharge for the time being, the office not of their actual, but of their inferior and implied order,—accordingly they wear the habits and badges not of the order to which they have attained, but of that through which they have passed, and which they are fulfilling. According to an injunction of Abp. Grindal, a layman in surplice and cassock might read the Epistle.

When there is only a celebrant, a chorister or clerk, habited simply in cassock and surplice down to the knee, or Cotta, should always serve the Priest.

When the Gospel and Epistle are read *in pulpito vel a lectrino*, one pulpit or lectern may serve. It is better, however, to have two—one on either (the proper) side.

It would seem, from a comparison of the Sarum Rubrics, that on Sundays and principal Feasts this was the use. But on Ferial days they were read from their respective steps of the choir. They were, as a rule, either *both* read from the pulpit, from the rood-loft, or from the choir. "Quandocumque enim legitur epistola in pulpito, ibidem legatur et evangelium."— Rub. Sarif.

But whenever the Gospel was read, the Gospeller's[1] face was of old turned to the north, "et semper legatur Evangelium versus aquilonem."—Rub. Sarif.

When the Gospel and Epistle are read from the rood-loft, the former is read from the north and the latter from the south side.

In all other cases the Epistle is read on a lower step than that from which the Gospel is, and from the south side, and the Gospel from the north.

According to Mr. Maskell, the Gospel was *originally* read on the north side, the Deacon turning to the *south*, where the men sat, who were addressed as the chief objects of the Church's teaching in her public offices, and from them the women were to learn at home, as S. Paul admonishes. It would seem from the will of Maud, Lady Mauley, dated 1438, that the Gospel and Epistle were both read from the south side, when not read in the pulpit, but, of course, on different steps, the Gospeller probably looking northwards. See "Ancient Liturgy of Church of England," pp. 46, 47, second edition.

† The Gospeller is not directed to say, "Here endeth the holy Gospel," inasmuch as ancient ritualists teach us that the Gospel being everlasting has no end; or because, as some of them hold, that the Gospel finds its proper end in the creed.

[1] The present Roman use is for the *Celebrant* to face respectively the Gospeller and Epistoler at a time when they exercise their special function.

The Celebration of the Holy Eucharist.

OTHER Collects ("Plures collectæ dicendæ," Sarif. Miss.) besides the one for the day, used to be said according to the Sarum Rite; the number varying with the season.* But the rubric orders that the use of Collects shall be *uneven*, probably for the reason that an uneven number is symbolical of the desire of the Church for unity; an exception, however, was made in the week of the Nativity.† But the number was not to exceed seven, because that was the number of petitions in the Lord's Prayer (besides the seven gifts of the Holy Ghost‡); this reason is given in the rubric, and is curious, because there is reason for saying that originally the Roman Rite had *no* Collect, but only the Lord's Prayer in the Collect's place, as the Mass of S. John Lateran still had in the days of Durandus, L. iv. fol. xliv.

The Sarum rule supplemented, when necessary, the even number of Collects by adding that of All Saints. (1 Dom. Adv.) The First Book of Edward VI, clearly reckons the Collect for the King as one, and so makes *two* at Communion, for it says "Then the Collect for the daie" (which no doubt then came *first*, according to the old way) "with one of these two Collectes followying, for the Kyng." ... "The *Collectes* ended," &c. Now *except* on the ground of "imparity"—which may be attained (according to the Sarum Rule of supplementation of Collects when needful) by adding, as the English Rite conveniently permits, another Collect from those appended to the Communion Office with the rubric that they may be said after the Collects either of Morning or Evening Prayer, *Communion*, or Litany, at the discretion of the Minister—the presumption is certainly that the rubrics about additional or "memorial" Collects given in our Prayer Book, were evidently meant to apply to the Holy Communion Office, from the mere fact of their being in our "Missale" so to call it; and on looking back to the Sarum, we certainly do find "memoriæ" of Saints' Days were said "ad missam," e. g. the leading rubric, 1 Dom. Adv. So in e. g. Miss. 2 Vigil. Nativ., memoria de S. Anastasia, after

---

* The number varied greatly. Through Lent there were seven on week-days, only *one* on Sundays. In the Trinity period, three on week-days, three on Sundays—(1) of the day, (2) of the Trinity, (3) of All Saints.

† " Ita tamen quod ad missam impar numerus ipsarum collectarum semper custodiatur nisi in ebdomadâ Nativitatis Domini tantum."—Sarif. Missal.

‡ " Item, in collectis dicendis semper impar numerus observatur. Una propter Unitatem Deitatis. Tres propter Trinitatem Personarum. Quinque propter partitam passionem Christi. Septem, propter septiformem gratiam Spiritus Sancti. Septenarium numerum excedere non licet."—Cautelæ Missæ. Sarif. Missal.

the Collect. Again as to the Collects for Advent Sunday, Christmas Day and Ash-Wednesday, though we have not a traditional rule applying to the first and third of these seasons, we *have* in the case of Christmas Day perfect analogy for the others; for the first, the Collect *De Nativ.* was said "in missa" every day till the Circumcision. Secondly, the Collect for Easter Day was used *at Communion*, after the Collect for the day, on every *week day* in Easter, though not on Sundays (rubric ibid.) Whilst the Trinity Sunday Collect was said after the Collect for the day, on all *Sundays* after Trinity, but not on the week-days. These instances cover the whole ground; and distinctions between Sundays and week-days being now done away, it remains that in seasons when the Collect is to be repeated *at all*, it is to be repeated at the Holy Communion. The only question is whether it should be used at the Daily Service, for which there is no precedent or analogy. Of course *head* Collects are only spoken of, viz. the Collects for Advent Sunday and Ash-Wednesday. For "Memoriæ" of Festivals in the ordinary office there is abundant precedent.

The law of connection of the Mass and the ordinary Service as to Collects was this:—

1. The number of Collects in both must be the same on any given day.

2. Both must begin with the Collect for the day, "de Die."

3. But after that the two sets diverge. The Breviary set always contained the "*de Pace*" and "*de S. Spiritu*" memorials. The Missal set *sometimes* contained the *de Pace* (as in Lent and Trinity periods on weekdays), but this set varied much with the season.

4. Since the *number* of Collects at Mass varied according to a rule, as *supra*, the ordinary Service clearly took its cue from thence; and hence perhaps we obtain a sort of rule for our present practice, viz.—to use the same number of Collects, and in fact the same Collects at both Services; and if the scrupulous ritualist object to there being an *even* number of Collects, at either the Holy Communion, or at the ordinary Service, the proper remedy for the "parity" has been already suggested by the use of the Collects at the end of the Office. However the rule does not very clearly hold, as we have the Collect for the Queen at Holy Communion and not at Matins, unless indeed the Prayer for the Queen *counts* as a Collect, a conclusion which would after all only complicate an already intricate matter.

It would therefore be proper to say the Collects of "commemorated" Feasts at both the Communion and the ordinary Office; but the *head* Collects of Seasons, viz. Advent and Lent, at Holy Communion only;

"imparity" being always attainable by the use of the Collects at the end of the Office for the Holy Communion.

On Saints' Days the Sunday Collect should be omitted, for our Service-Book directs, that "the Collect, Epistle, and Gospel appointed for the Sunday shall serve all the week after, *where it is not in this Book otherwise ordered*."

The Choir, after the announcement of the Gospel, turning eastwards, sings "Glory be to Thee, O LORD." And after the Gospel is sung, "Praise to Thee, O CHRIST."

In announcing the Epistle and Gospel the wording of the directions in the rubric should be strictly followed, thereby avoiding such errors, as "the portion of Scripture appointed for the Epistle" *is taken out of*, &c. The words "portion of," &c. obviously apply to those instances where "the Epistle" is taken from other parts of Scripture than the Epistles.

The Gospel should be given out as "according to" ("secundum") each Evangelist, the Catholic theory being that there is and can be but one Gospel, though expressed "according" to the four writers.

21. *The Creed.*

HE Celebrant now proceeds to the midst of the Altar immediately before the cross, and, extending his hands, intones the first sentence of the Creed.* At the words "Maker of heaven and earth," he joins them. At the words "And was made Man," he will either bow profoundly or genuflect—as will also the Deacon and Subdeacon; at the words "Worshipped and glorified," all three will bow reverently; and at the words "Resurrection of the body," draw the sign of the cross on their breasts.

The Sarum rubric directs everything before the Epistle to be said at the Epistle corner (*in dextro cornu*) of the Altar, the Creed and everything after it in the middle of the Altar. The rubric in our *Ordo* substitutes the north side (Gospel or left corner, *in sinistro cornu*) for the Epistle corner at first, but curiously enough at the Creed gives no direction "to stand as before," as before the Collect for the Queen, evidently intending that it should be sung, with the rest of the Function,—where it is not specially ordered

---

* On bowing at the Name of JESUS, and at the Gloria Patri, see among others two Constitutions in Wilkins, Conc. tom. iii. p. 20. At the words "down from heaven" the Hereford Missal has this rubric, "*et fiet genuflexio dum dicetur*." To "*genuflect*" is to kneel on the right knee; to "*kneel*,"—on both knees.

otherwife, as in the Exhortations (*Pax*, v. infra), Abfolution, Comfortable Words, and *Surfum Corda*—as it was of old, in the middle of the Altar. The ancient Englifh rubric is as follows:—

Ex Miff. Sarifb. Ed. Herbriant. Paris, 1516. *Fol.* cxlix.

"Sciendum eft autem quod quidquid a facerdote dicitur ante Epiftolam in dextro cornu altaris expleatur præter inceptionem '*Gloria in excelfis*,' fimiliter fiat poft perceptionem facramenti. Cetera omnia in medio altaris expleantur nifi forte diaconus defuerit. Tunc enim in finiftro cornu altaris legatur evangelium."

When the Celebrant intones the firft fentence of the Creed, the Deacon or Gofpeller fhould ftand immediately behind the Celebrant, on his own (the Deacon's) ftep, and the Sub-deacon or Epiftoler fhould again ftand behind the Deacon on his own (the Sub-deacon's) ftep. At the words "Maker of heaven and earth," the Deacon fhould proceed to the predella or altar-ftep, immediately to the right of the Celebrant and the Sub-deacon to the predella or altar-ftep immediately to the left of the Celebrant, remaining in that pofition (unlefs for convenience fake they fit down in the fedilia, if the mufic be long and tedious) until its conclufion.

22. *Notices of Holy-days,** *Fafting-days, &c., Banns of Matrimony, &c.*

"Then the Curate fhall declare unto the people what Holy-days, or Fafting-days, are in the week following to be obferved. And then alfo (if occafion be) fhall notice be given of the Communion; and the Banns of Matrimony publifhed; and Briefs, Citations, and Excommunications read. And nothing fhall be proclaimed or publifhed in the Church, during the time of Divine Service, but by the Minifter. Nor by him anything, but what is prefcribed in the Rules of this Book, or enjoined by the Queen, or by the Ordinary of the place."

HE proper way of giving notice of days to be obferved during the week is thus: "Thurfday in this week is the Feaft of S. ——; Wednefday is the Vigil of that Feftival." "Monday and Tuefday in this week, being within the Octave of Eafter, (or Whitfun Day,) have fpecial fervices appointed for them."

---

* The minor Feftivals, or black-letter days, although they have no proper offices, nor are publicly commemorated, ought, neverthelefs, like the others, to be announced on the preceding Sunday, and, as far as may be, obferved according to the direction given in the Canons:—[1]

"*Due Celebration of Sundays and Holy Days*. All manner of perfons within the Church

[1] It is of courfe proper to ufe the colour of the day. See Appendix for Colours to be ufed on thefe Feftivals.

At the same time, the celebration of the Holy Sacrament, during the week and on the following Sunday, should be announced. The Exhortations which come after the Prayer for the Church need only be used when it is wished to give some special "warning" to the people, either of their coming too little or too carelessly, as it may be.

When *notice* of Communion is given, the Priest may use any short form that is convenient.*

When he giveth *warning* the whole exhortation is read, in which case it is read after the sermon, and from the pulpit, as a kind of homily, rather than a notice.

In the "sealed books," after the word Communion, is this clause, "*and the Banns of Matrimony published.*" These words have been omitted in later editions of the Prayer Book,—the Queen's printer, the delegates at Oxford, and the syndics at Cambridge, having not only committed a breach of the Act of Uniformity, but having assumed to themselves the province of Convocation. The Marriage Act, 26 Geo. II. c. 33, on which this unauthorized omission is based by a wrong interpretation thereof, would seem to provide for the publication of Banns of Matrimony after the Second Lesson at Evening Prayer in churches where *there is no morning service*; and after the Second Lesson at Morning Prayer *as well as after the Nicene Creed* when the services are divided; *but when they are combined, not after the Second Lesson,* but after the Creed, as the unmutilated rubric directs. For the words of the Act are not, during Morning Prayer or Matins, but "during the time of morning service," i. e. such divine offices as take place before noon.

Such is the course for those who regard Parliament as having authority to alter or interpolate rubrics.

---

of England shall from henceforth celebrate and keep the Lord's Day, commonly called Sunday, and other Holy Days, according to God's holy will and pleasure, and the orders of the Church of England prescribed in that behalf; that is, in hearing the word of God, read and taught; in private and public prayers, in acknowledging their offences to God, and amendment of the same; in reconciling themselves charitably to their neighbours, where displeasure hath been; in oftentimes receiving the Communion of the Body and Blood of Christ; in visiting of the poor and sick; using all godly and sober conversation."—Canon 13.

The fact that the minor Holy Days are without proper offices does not detract from the obligation of keeping them holy, any more than in the case of Vigils and Rogation Days, which in that respect are equally destitute, and yet the Prayer Book positively declares that they are "to be observed."

* It is customary to use the first paragraph of the first exhortation, down to the word "Christ" inclusive, for this purpose.

It should be remembered, however, that the Act of Uniformity demonstrates that the power of the Crown is limited in the matter of rubrical alterations to the necessary changes occasioned by the birth and death of any of the Royal family. And since that review when the Prayer Book was finally settled by the united authority of Convocation and Parliament, no argument for the independent legislation of the Crown or Parliament on ecclesiastical matters can be drawn from the precedent of antecedent times.

The rubrical direction of the "sealed books," the only authorized standard of our present Prayer Book, must be observed, and such observance is moreover in accordance with the right interpretation of the Marriage Act.

23. *The Sermon or Homily, in Communion Office.**

"Then shall follow the Sermon, or one of the Homilies already set forth, or hereafter to be set forth, by authority."

AFTER the Creed is finished the Celebrant and Ministers—i. e. the Deacon and Sub-deacon—take their seats in the sedilia, each in his own place, and the Preacher ascends the pulpit. [The other assistant clergy, lay-clerks, and acolytes should sit on stools placed for them on the lower step of the sanctuary, on either side facing north and south.] If the Preacher be not one of the Ministrants,

---

* " We would observe that as the bulk of our congregations, in towns as well as in rural districts, is composed of ignorant persons, it is very desirable that preachers should generally avoid ' long trains of naked reasoning,' and that their sermons ' should be comparatively short.' We believe that much of the indifference with which sermons are heard by the lower and uneducated classes arises from the fact that the Clergy, in their studies, so often lose sight of the wants and capacities of these classes, and think and write in a style which, though familiar and intelligible to themselves, is far otherwise to the majority of their hearers. With the teaching of our Lord and the Apostles before them, and knowing the copious use which all popular writers and speakers have made of '*similitudes* and *illustrations*,' it is surprising to us that the Clergy should so neglect them in their sermons. The most habitually callous and reckless will listen when they hear the daily occupations, thoughts, and habits of themselves or of their companions, referred to and described, accurately and intelligibly, and adduced, as they may constantly be, to illustrate and enforce high and holy truths, principles, and practices. There must be something to arrest, and keep alive, the attention of the ignorant, the indifferent, and the worldly, or it is of little use to preach sermons. The mere recitation, or dull reading, of a well written essay, in which the allusions, illustrations, and references are mostly scholastic and conventional, and the words and sentences barely English, is but a feeble instrument for turning men, women, and children, from the errors and temptations which beset them. Monotony of matter, and monotony of manner, we regard as one of the very greatest defects in

he preaches in his caffock, furplice, ftole (*pendent*), and hood; if the Gof-peller or Epiftoler preach, he takes off the dalmatic or the tunicle, lays it on the fedilia, and wears a Prieft's ftole (*croffed*) if he be a Prieft, or a Deacon's (over the left fhoulder and tied on the right fide) if he be a Deacon.

The preacher, when neither Celebrant, Deacon, nor Sub-deacon, fhould wear caffock, cotta, and ftole of the colour of the day.

If the Celebrant preaches he lays his Veftment on the Altar, and wears, of courfe, the alb and croffed ftole, except he be a Bifhop, who wears the ftole *pendent* under the epifcopal tunic and dalmatic, only laying afide the Veftment.

The Preacher fhould precede the Sermon with the words, " In the Name of the FATHER, and of the SON, and of the HOLY GHOST. Amen"—

---

the preaching of the prefent day. And it is ftrange to obferve how entirely men of the moft oppofite ftyles of preaching agree in adopting a monotonous mannerifm in the delivery of their fermons, even of thofe parts in which there is, per force, a palpable variation in the matter. For inftance, thofe who fimply read, or who *intone* their fermons, often deliver the moft folemn and affecting texts, and other quotations, with as little feeling and emphafis as they exhibit in the delivery of the moft formal and technical matter: while, on the other hand, the lachry-mofe, the grandiloquent, and the ranting mannerift, will, refpectively, throw juft as much of their peculiar quality into the mere announcement of the chapter and verfe where a certain text is to be found as they would employ in delivering the moft awful and pathetic paffages of which our language is capable. If every man's experience did not teach him this, it would be incredible that educated and even learned men could be conftantly guilty of fuch a violation of common fenfe, good tafte, and propriety. That it muft neceffarily lead many perfons to fuppofe that the whole manner is *put on*—a piece of mere profeffional conventionalifm—irre-fpective of any feeling or thought about the matter—is very obvious, and muft be as injurious, morally, as it is phyfically—in the ' wear and tear ' of a perpetual mannerifm—to both paftor and people."

" Relaxed throat is ufually caufed, not fo much by exercifing the organ, as by the kind of exercife : that is, not fo much by long or loud fpeaking as by fpeaking in a *feigned* voice. Not one perfon in, I may fay, ten thoufand, in addreffing a body of people, does fo in his natural voice, and this habit is more efpecially obfervable in the pulpit. I believe that relax-ation of the throat refults from violent efforts in thefe affected tones, and that fevere irritation, and often ulceration, is the confequence."—W. C. Macready.

" The evil of fpeaking in a feigned or unnatural voice has already been touched on in the former part of this treatife, and the opinion of Mr. Macready on the point given. It is, un-fortunately, rather difficult to convince perfons that this is the cafe with themfelves, whilft thofe who know them and their natural tone in converfation can eafily detect the difference. This feigned tone is fometimes adopted under an idea of giving increafed folemnity or impref-fivenefs to the reading; but as nothing that is unnatural is really impreffive, it is a great miftake. If the feeling exift, the tone will follow ; if it do not, the remedy is to ftrive after *it* rather than its expreffion."—Dyfphonia Clericorum.

during the saying of which he will make the sign of the cross. "The LORD be with you," is also an ancient form of salutation that has been used before the Sermon; to which the people reply, "And with thy spirit." The first form is much preferable to the use of a prayer in this place.

It should be remembered that the Preacher has no legal right to deliver an introductory prayer in the pulpit before the Sermon; because there has been none provided by the rubric. In the Canons of 1604,* a bidding of prayer is ordered, and which was to terminate with the LORD's Prayer; but no rubric commanding such observance is in the present Prayer Book, 1662. In fact no prayers should be used publicly, but those that are prescribed, lest through ignorance or carelessness anything be uttered before GOD contrary to the Catholic Faith.

The Preacher should never kneel in the pulpit; as to his prayer before preaching he had better say it in his chamber, or in the sacristy, or in his place in the sanctuary, or in his stall in the chancel.

The doxology at the end of the Sermon should be said turning eastwards.

24. *The Offertory.*†

"Then shall the Priest return to the LORD's Table, and begin the Offertory, saying one‡ or more of these sentences following, as he thinketh most convenient in his discretion."

AID by the Celebrant as an antiphon, not as an exhortation, standing before the midst of the Altar with his face eastwards and with hands joined. After the Priest has said an Offertory sentence, the choir will sing it.

---

* The Canon (LV.) probably referred to Lectures apart from the Holy Communion. Then the Bidding Prayer is in place and might precede the Litany.

† The real rationale of the offertory of money occurring in this place is as follows:

The Sacramental elements *are* the oblations, and all other kinds of oblations at this time grew, merely and purely, out of this one.

When the Priest presents the oblations, not only do the Faithful therein provide, according to the ancient idea, a real *material gift*, however small, out of their own substance, to constitute the substance of the Sacrifice; but (2) since so small a gift as is needed for the Christian "mincha" or meat-offering (Malachi i.) cannot really be divided amongst a multitude, *the rest* provide other gifts for several purposes—gifts, we may say, to CHRIST for His Ministers, His temple, His poor members, and the like; and (3) the Faithful here symbolically desire to give up themselves in body, soul, and spirit, "ready to be offered," and uniting consecration and oblation—their "reasonable service" first reaches the Altar herein.

‡ It seems preferable that one Offertory sentence instead of several should be recited by the

The Celebration of the Holy Eucharist.

"Whilft thefe Sentences are in reading, the Deacons, Churchwardens, or other fit perfon appointed for that purpofe, fhall receive the Alms for the Poor, and other devotions of the people in a decent bafin, to be provided by the Parifh for that purpofe, and reverently bring it to the Prieft, who fhall humbly prefent and place it upon the Holy Table."

The alms fhould be collected in bags, and are placed by the Deacons, Churchwardens, Clerks in furplices, or other fit perfons, reverently, on the bafin held by the Epiftoler, who then gives the bafin to the Celebrant to prefent. The alms-bowl is moft conveniently placed on the fouth end of the Altar, and after being prefented fhould be removed to the credence, or elfewhere

The Faithful fhould ftand during the Offertory, until they have made their offering, after which they fhould kneel.

25. *The Oblation of Bread and Wine, commonly called the Firft Oblation.*

" And when there is a Communion, the Prieft fhall then* place upon the Table fo much† Bread and Wine, as he fhall think fufficient."

Prieft. At Solemn Service the choir will immediately fing it as an anthem; during which time the alms will be placed upon the Altar, and the Gofpeller will then bring the bread and wine from the credence to the Prieft. The bread fhould be brought firft, then the wine, and where it is cuftomary the water. This laft fhould be brought by the Epiftoler.

The alms-bowl fhould never be kept on the Altar, but on the credence. See fupra, par. 12.

* If there be no credence nor fide-table, the churchwardens fhould be required to provide one. But doubtlefs this neceffary adjunct to the Altar will be now found in all churches, as it has been fo recently and fo diftinctly *authorized.* See fupra, p. 7, par. 2.

† " So much " *and no more*—the bread and wine not required for confecration being replaced on the credence. The cuftom of offering fruits in kind, as bread, at the Altar, had been long obfolete at the time of our revifion. In the Firft Book of Edward VI. the parifhioners were to " offer euery Sunday, at the tyme of the offertory, the jufte valour and price of the holy lofe," *not the loaf itfelf,* which it was clear the Parfon was to provide himfelf with, in the fhape of wafers,[1] only he was thus to be indemnified *therefore.* Then, as now, he was " to take *fo muche* bread and wine, as fhall fuffice for the perfons," &c. That which was not wanted, might indeed be well confidered to be offered in the *gifts of money* paid for it, but was rather looked upon as part of the facred furniture and equipments, and as fuch needed no dedication at that time to the fervice of God.

Hence it is *quite wrong* to oblate and leave upon the Altar the bread and wine not needed

---

[1] " It is mete that the breade prepared for the Communion, bee made through all thys Realm, after one fort and fafhion : that is to fay, vnleauened, and round , as it was afore, but without all manner of printe, and fome thyng more larger and thicker then it was, fo that it may be deuided in diuers pieces, &c."—Rubric of Edwd. VI.'s Firft Book.

IN prefenting the alms, and offering the oblations (viz. the Sacramental elements provided by the Faithful* for confecration and prefentation, and fignifying their defire to give themfelves to God, and alfo as an oblation to God the Father of His own creatures, Bread and Wine, as an humble acknowledgment that our food and all we have are His gifts, which He, by the operation of God the Holy Ghost, turns into our heavenly and daily bread), the Prieft fhould ftand erect; he fhould never kneel on this occafion; the Prieft himfelf and no other,† fhould place the Sacramental Bread and Wine on the holy Table.

The Celebrant now moves to the Gofpel corner, and the Gofpeller advancing to the middle of the Altar moves the chalice to the Epiftle corner: then removing the burfe from the chalice, he takes out the corporal with his right hand, laying it on the midft of the Altar. He then puts the burfe on the Altar towards the north fide, and fpreads the corporal with both hands. It is not to hang over. He then arranges the book, and ftands on the right‡ of the Celebrant. The Epiftoler having gone to the credence and taken therefrom the metal plate with the wafers or breads, which are folded in a linen cloth — accompanied by the Clerks, the fenior of whom bears the cruet or flagon with the wine, and the other with the water-cruet where it is cuftomary, — goes to the right of the Gofpeller, and places the plate with the bread on the right of the chalice.

---

for the Eucharift, inftead of replacing fuch unoblated elements back again on the credence. All bread and wine deftined for this holy ufe fhould be fet apart with prayer¹ for the purpofe, when it is provided, *of courfe in the facrifty*, before it is placed on the credence.

* "The Bread and Wine for the Communion fhall be provided by the Curate and the Churchwardens, at the charges of the Parifh."—Rubric, Book of Common Prayer.

† This of courfe does not apply to the preparation of the chalice, &c. by the deacon and his affiftants, on the epiftle corner of the Altar.

‡ The right of the Prieft is always the deacon's proper place when miniftering at the Altar, (*ad dextrum cornu altaris*). The deacon never goes to the left corner of the Altar at all, in the Sarum Rite, except at the benediction before the Gofpel,—*in cornu altaris finiftro a facerdote in cornu altaris dextro ftante*,—and in moving the book and folding up the corporal whilft the Prieft is making the ablutions after communion, affifted by the fub-deacon on the right.

¹ The following Prayer (flightly altered) from the "Office of the Prothefis," from the Liturgy of the Holy Eaftern Church, is recommended. "O God, our God, Who didft fend forth the Heavenly Bread, the nourifhment of the whole world, our Lord and God, Jesus Christ, as a Saviour and Redeemer and Benefactor, bleffing and hallowing us; Thyfelf blefs this oblation, and receive it to Thy Altar: remember, of Thy goodnefs and love to men, him who is about to offer it, and thofe for whom it is about to be offered; and keep us without condemnation in the celebration of Thy holy Myfteries. For bleffed and hallowed is Thy glorious Name, Father, Son, and Holy Ghost, now and ever, and to ages of ages. Amen."

He then takes off the veil* from the chalice, folds it in three, and places it near the back of the Altar. He next takes off the pall, and places it to the right of the corporal on the Altar.

The Gospeller then goes to the Epistle corner of the Altar, and, taking the plate in his left hand, with his right removes the paten from the chalice, and places it on the left thereof. He then takes either a wafer or one larger piece of bread and places it on the paten, together with sufficient smaller breads or wafers for the communicants,† and gives the metal plate, with the bread not needed, to one of the Clerks, who replaces it on the credence.

The Epistoler meantime wipes the bowl of the chalice with the purificator, which he lays down on the Epistle side, when the Gospeller taking the chalice with his left hand, and the wine-cruet from the hands of the Epistoler with his right, pours wine into the chalice. The Epistoler then, taking the water-cruet from the Clerk with his right hand, pours in a little water.‡ The Gospeller places the paten on the chalice, which he gives with both hands to the Celebrant, who proceeds to the midst of the Altar, and places the chalice on the middle of the corporal.

The Gospeller and Epistoler go to their respective steps.

---

* When the Celebrant is a Bishop the chalice and paten are without the veil.

† In order that the Priest's own bread, which is to be used for the ostension and fraction, may be distinguished from the other breads.

‡ "Quo dicto (offertorio) ministret ea quæ necessaria sunt sacramento; scilicet panem, vinum et aquam in calicem infundens."—Missale in usum Herford.

"Putting thereto a little pure and clean water."—Rubric after the Offertory in Edward VI's First Prayer Book.

In Bishop Andrewes' Form of Consecration of a Church and Churchyard, there is this rubric: "Cæteris rebus ordine gestis episcopus . . . vino in calicem effuso, et *aqua admixta*, stans ait."

Palmer's Origines Liturgicæ, vol. ii. p. 76, 8vo., 1832.
Collier's Eccl. Hist., vol. ii. p. 726.
Brett on the Liturgy (instances Archbishop Laud), p. 404, edit. 1838.

This practice is symbolical of our LORD's Incarnation; the wine as the more precious Element representing His Divinity, the water as the inferior, His Sacred Humanity. ἄρτος προσφέρεται καὶ οἶνος καὶ ὕδωρ. Justin Martyr, Ap. 2.

This practice is mentioned by S. Cyril of Jerusalem. Cat. Lect. xiii. 21.

According to another view the water symbolizes the people united to CHRIST. The Armenian Church, however, a very ancient one, has never mixed water with the wine.

It is still kept up at Sandford, Oxon, where the ancient cruets remain, and are in use.

"It is certain that the primitive Christians did offer water mingled with wine in the Eucharist. Justin Martyr, Irenæus, Clemens Alexandrinus, and Cyprian do especially mention it; and though we know there were several heretics that used water only in the Sacrament, yet we have not heard of any, in the most primitive times, that used wine alone, either in the Church or without it."—Johnson's Unbloody Sacrifice.

26. *Lotio manuum.**

WHERE this ancient custom obtains, this is the proper place for it; as ritualists hold that the "Washing" originated in the fact that the hands of the Priest were soiled by the offerings, which often included the fruits of the earth. It has now received a mystical signification, the Priest saying *secreto*, while washing his fingers, "I will wash my hands in innocency," &c. This form had better take place, where indeed it *originally* did, at a piscina or basin on the Epistle side of the Altar:† the mode of ablution at the piscina is not by *immersion* of the fingers, but by an assistant pouring water upon the hands of the Celebrant from an ampulla, ewer, or basin; "*Infundat ei aquam in manibus*,"‡ as the old rubric gave direction.

When there is no piscina, the Celebrant had better stand at the Epistle corner of the Altar looking to the south, when the senior Clerk or Acolyte brings in both hands from the credence a napkin folded, and the junior§ the basin in his left hand, and the water-cruet in his right, which he pours over the four fingers and thumb of the Priest, who uses the napkin provided. They then return and place the towel and basin on the credence.

27. *The Commemoration of the Living and the Dead.*

"After which done, the Priest shall say,‖

---

* "Et canat cum suis ministris offertorium. Postea lavet manus."—Missale Ebor.
  This, then, is the best place in our present office for this very proper and highly typical ceremony. Bishop Andrewes directs that it should be done immediately before the Prayer of Consecration. Either of the following antiphons or prayers may be found convenient to be used in secret: " Lavabo inter innocentes manus meas; et circumdabo altare tuum, Domine;" or " Munda me, Domine, ab omni inquinamento mentis et corporis; ut possim mundatus implere opus sanctum Domini." " Ye saw then the Deacon give to the Priest water to wash, and to the Presbyters who stood around God's Altar. . . . . The washing, therefore, of hands (before the Holy Communion) is a symbol."—S. Cyril of Jerusalem, Cat. Lect. xxiii. 2.

† " Eat sacerdos ad dextrum cornu altaris et abluat manus."—Sarif. Mis.

‡ *Liber usuum Cisterciensium.* Martène, Monach. Rit. p. 151.

§ In the Roman Pontifical, on the ordination of a Sub-deacon, a *basin* and towel are delivered to him as symbols of his office, a custom that dates from the fourth council of Carthage, at the end of the fourth century, and no doubt from an earlier period.—Baronius ap. Binium, concil. tom. i. p. 588.

‖ Wheatley, following Bishop Patrick (Christian Sacrifice, p. 77), considers that the term

The Celebration of the Holy Eucharist.

"Let us pray for the whole state of CHRIST's Church militant here in earth."*

HE Celebrant, who is standing at the middle of the Altar, looking eastward, outstretching his hands and joining them again, will pause at the words, "*alms and oblations,*" and having first verbally oblated the alms, he will take the chalice

"oblations" refers exclusively to the elements of bread and wine, offered up for consecration. Johnson maintains that it has a prospective reference to the oblation of our LORD's Body and Blood.

The elements being thus offered on the Altar, the Priest turns him to the people, and says, "Let us pray for the whole state of CHRIST's Church militant here in earth." Then the Priest turns him to the Altar, and says, "Almighty and Everlasting God," &c. (See Rubric in Edward VI's First Prayer Book). "*Stans ad medium altaris clare et distincte dicat;*" as the Sarum Rubric directs.

The ancient English Use was to offer the oblations both together, the paten with the host being placed upon the chalice containing the wine and water. The rule, however, was not universal, as the Rubric in the York Missal directs the oblations of Bread and Wine with water to be made separately, and this is the usage of the modern West: the Roman prayers however are different. The following are the old English Rubrics on the subject:

"Deinde dicat offertorium.

"Quo dicto ministret ea quæ necessaria sacramento: scilicet panem, vinum et aquam in calicem infundens: benedictione aquæ prius a sacerdote petita hoc modo:" ...

"Sacerdos sic dicens:" ...

"Et postea sumat patenam cum hostia et ponat super calicem in manibus suis, dicat devote:" ...

"Qua dicta reponat calicem, et cooperiat eam cum corporalibus: ponatque panem super corporalia decenter, ante calicem vinum et aquam continentem, et osculetur patenam: et reponat eam a dextris super altare sub corporalibus, parum cooperiendo."—Herford. Missale.

"Post offertorium vero porrigat diaconus sacerdoti calicem cum patena et sacrificio: et osculetur manum ejus utraque vice. Ipse vero accipiens ab eo calicem: diligenter ponat in loco suo debito super medium altare: et inclinato parumper elevet calicem utraque manu offerens sacrificium Domino, dicendo hanc orationem," &c. dicta oratione. "Qua dicta reponat calicem, et cooperiat cum corporalibus: ponatque panem super corporalia decenter, ante calicem vinum et aquam continentem, et osculetur patenam et reponat eam a dextris sub corporalibus parum cooperiendo."—Sarif. Missale.

"Postea lavet manus et componat hostiam super corporales pannos et dicat:" ...

"Item, calicem cum vino et aqua et dicat."—Ebor. Missal.

This Prayer should be said very deliberately, short pauses being made in particular places for the purpose of commemorating especial persons, as at the words "all Bishops and Curates," "especially to this congregation," "all them who in this," &c., "that with them we." The Priest should always in addition to the above, privately commemorate the saints whose festivals fall on the day, or about the day, on which he celebrates the holy eucharist. This Prayer must of course always be said by the Celebrant.

* As some ritualists have gone so far as to assert that this prayer is a compromise, *because* the title does not correspond with the contents, and as this apparent anomaly (supported as it is

The Order of Administration. 53

with the paten thereon with both hands, and will offer the sacrifice to GOD, holding the chalice or paten before his breast.

The following form of *Secreta*, (which is quite a model,) from the Hereford Missal, is strongly recommended to be said *secreto* during the

by the history of the successive reviews our Service Book has undergone since the first revision of our offices in the reign of Edward VI.)[1] has been a cause of distress to many both of the clergy and laity, it may be a source of comfort to the Faithful to point out that strictly speaking the title is *not* at variance with the contents of the prayer. The Church militant here in earth is indeed the title and *main* subject of the prayer, but it is not necessarily the *exclusive* subject; the whole Church and those departed in faith and fear are also its objects, if the subsequent words are sufficiently large to comprehend them, which they are. The most ancient *actions*, so to speak, of the Church with reference to the departed, was not prayer, strictly speaking, but remembrance. So in the Syriac—no doubt the oldest existing form—" Memoriam agimus—even of B. V. M. and of All Saints." (Renaudotius, tom. ii. pp. 17, 33, 98, 99). This was all. Now this is just what the English Church does in the prayer for "the Church militant;" she prays for the living, the Church militant—she *prayerfully remembers* the departed (in this particular prayer[2]), and as this is done in a manner that "with them we may be partakers," &c., the title need not specify anything more. There is yet another sanction—the LORD'S Prayer makes exactly this degree of memory of the departed in "Thy kingdom come," and the Church in the *earliest* ages did no more in the Holy Eucharist. With regard to the *title* of the prayer it is notoriously *ancient* as far as "Church," in the English use. For on Good Friday (the only day in the year that she had an intercession with the oblation, though anciently without doubt it was the place for the Roman intercession), the rubric was *Oremus*—" *Et primo pro universali statu ecclesiæ.*"—Sarif. Miss. fol. lxxviii.

And more than this—there is a pre-Reformation prayer with a heading almost word for word the same, and which goes on, not prayerfully to remember, but *to pray for the dead.*

"¶ *A generall and devout prayre for the goode state of oure moder the Churche militant here in erth.*

Omnipotens et misericors Deus, rex cœli et terræ, tuam clementiam suppliciter deposco; ut per interventum et meritum gloriosæ Dei genetricis semper virginis et omnium sanctorum angelorum patriarcharum prophetarum apostolorum martyrum confessorum monachorum, virginum viduarum, et omnium supernorum civium Dominum apostolicum et omnem gradum ecclesiasticum episcopum nostrum reges et principes nostros, famulos et samulas tuas atque locum istum una cum universa ecclesia catholica in omni sanctitate et pace custodias; omnesque cum sanguinitate affinitate familiaritate commissione et elemosynarum largitione nobis junctos et omnes Christianos a vitiis et a peccatis emundes virtutibus illustres, pacem et salutem mentis et corporis nobis tribuas, hostes visibiles et invisibiles a nobis removeas, aeris temperiem indulgeas, fruges terræ concedas, carnalia desideria repellas, infirmis nostris sanitatem restituas, lapsis reparationem navigantibus atque itinerantibus fidelibus iter prosperum et salutis portum,

---

[1] The "memento" of the Faithful departed was left out in the Second Book of Edward VI, and was not restored till the final revision of the English Service Book of 1662.

[2] In the first Post Communion Collect the dead in CHRIST are emphatically prayed for, not merely prayerfully remembered. Blessed be GOD, the English Church still supplicates for those who have gone before, when she prays that "we and ALL HIS WHOLE CHURCH may obtain *remission of our sins*, and *all other benefits of His Passion.*"

paufe at the oblation of the elements. "Sufcipe fancta Trinitas hanc oblationem quam tibi offero in memoriam paffionis Domini noftri Jefu Chrifti, et præfta, ut in confpectu tuo tibi placens afcendat, et meam et omnium fidelium falutem operetur æternam, per Chriftum."

The Celebrant then replaces the chalice in the midft of the Altar, on the middle of the corporal, and takes therefrom the paten with the breads, which he places before the chalice. He covers the paten with that corner of the corporal* neareft to him on his right hand. He then proceeds with the prayer, *junctis manibus*.

It is convenient after the words "*any other adverfity*" for the Celebrant to paufe, and call to mind diftinctly and individually any in fuch eftate, as he is bound by promife, requeft, or duty efpecially to commemorate. At the commemoration of the faithful departed he fhould extend his hands (*disjunctis manibus*) with the palms facing each other, and paufe after the words "*and fear,*" and fhould call to mind diftinctly and by name, any faithful dead whom he defires, or is requefted, efpecially to commemorate. In the paufes for *fecretæ*, and intervals for commemorating the Living and the Departed, the Prieft fhould not be long left he fhould weary the Faithful. Five minutes *is ample for all fuch paufes throughout the entire fervice.*

During the prayer for the whole ftate of CHRIST's Church, the Gofpeller and Epiftoler ftand on their own fteps.

28. *The Exhortation and Invitatory.*

"At the time of the Celebration of the Communion, the communicants being conveniently placed for the receiving of the Holy Sacrament, the Prieft fhall fay this Exhortation."

---

tribulatis gaudium oppreffis elevationem, captivis liberationem falutarem concedas inimicis noftris ac difcordantibus et nobis veram charitatem largiaris, rectoribus noftris pacem tribuas, errantes corrigas, incredulos convertas, ecclefiæ tuæ fanctam fidem augeas, fymoniacam herefim, et omnes herefes et cifmata in ecclefia tua catholica deftruas, et *omnibus fidelibus vivis et defunctis*, in terra viventium vitam eternam pariter et *requiem* concedas. Per Chriftum Dominum noftrum. Amen. Pater nofter. Ave."

"Horæ Beatæ Mariæ Virginis ad ufum ecclefiæ Sarum ex officina Chriftophori Ruremundeñ, 1531. Venundantur in cimiterio Sancti Pauli fub interfignio fancti Auguftini."

This Church militant prayer before the Reformation is extracted from a Sarum book of Hours in the poffeffion of J. D. Chambers, Efq., to whofe kindnefs and courtefy the Editor is indebted for the above verbatim copy.

* The old Englifh (as well as the Roman) cuftom is, to place the bread on the corporal without anything intervening. In the Eaft the bread is retained in the "holy difk"=paten, and fo placed on the cloth.

HILE the first exhortation, "Dearly beloved in the Lord," is being read by the Epistoler, as it may be at solemn Service, it should be read from his own step looking to the west, the Gospeller standing on his own step. The last paragraph is a doxology, and should be said facing eastwards; the exhortation to charity corresponds in idea, though not in position, to the ancient *Pax*; the people reply *Amen*.

"Then shall the Priest say to them that come to receive the Holy Communion."

The last exhortation, "Ye that do truly," should be read by the Celebrant, who, however, sometimes directs the Gospeller or Epistoler to say it.

29. *The Confession.* *

"Then shall this general Confession be made, in the name of all those that are minded to receive the Holy Communion, by one of the Ministers, both he and all the people kneeling humbly upon their knees, and saying."

HE Confession is more usually chaunted in monotone by the Gospeller, who kneels, facing the east. The Celebrant stands in the midst of the Altar, of course also facing the east. At Plain Service the assistant *alone* says the Confession, in the name of those about to communicate.

30. *The Absolution.* †

"Then shall the Priest (or the Bishop being present) stand up,‡ and turning himself to the people, pronounce this Absolution"

THE Celebrant here fronts the people, and standing in the midst of the Altar, pronounces the Absolution, *junctis manibus*, making the sign of the cross with the right hand at the words "Pardon and deliver you," &c.

---

* The confession is said all kneeling except the Celebrant, "capite inclinato, junctis manibus."
† The Priest should always pronounce the absolution and the benediction without the use of the book.
‡ This refers to the case of the Celebrant being without Gospeller or Epistoler or Assistant, when of course he will make the Confession kneeling, *junctis manibus*.

31. *The Comfortable Words.*

AFTER the Absolution the Priest turns to the east to say the "Comfortable Words."

32. *The Surſum Corda, &c.*

AT the *Surſum Corda* the Celebrant, turning towards the people, first outſtretches his hands, then raiſes them, joining them before his breaſt at *gratias agamus.*

33. *The Daily, and the Proper, Preface.**

ERE the Celebrant turns to the Altar. He opens his hands, (the palms facing each other), at "*It is very meet*," he places them on the Altar at *the Preface*, he joins them before his breaſt at the *Sanctus*. All incline moderately. The ſaying or ſinging of the people commences at "Holy, Holy," &c., and not at "Therefore with Angels." During the Sanctus the faithful kneel.

34. *The Prayer of Humble Acceſs.*†

"Then ſhall the Prieſt, kneeling down at the LORD's Table, ſay in the name of all them that ſhall receive the Communion, this Prayer following."

THIS is to be ſaid by the Celebrant kneeling before the midſt of the Altar with his hands upon the corporal. The Deacon and Sub-deacon as well as all the Acolytes or Lay-clerks are to kneel. After the Prayer of Humble Acceſs the Celebrant riſes and

---

* "Ad dicendam vel cantandam præfationem erigat ſe ſacerdos honeſte et ponat manus ſuper altare ex utraque parte calicis et dicat hoc modo . . . . Tunc ſacerdos elevans aliquantulum brachia junctis manibus dicat: *Sanctus*."—Miſſale Hereford.

It is to be deplored that the words "Holy, holy, holy" have not always been printed in our Rite ſeparated from the Preface immediately preceding them, "Therefore with angels." In all the ancient Liturgies the triſagium is ſung by the Faithful. Perhaps the Celebrant's tone and manner might aſſiſt in underſtanding where they ought to be ſilent, and where not.

Our own compoſers ſet merely the *ſanctus* to muſic, leaving the introductory part to be ſung by the Prieſt.

† The Confeſſion, and the Prayer of Humble Acceſs, are the only prayers at which the

The Order of Administration. 57

ſtands before the midſt of the Altar, looking to the eaſt, as indeed he does throughout the whole function, ſave where it is otherwiſe ſpecially ordered.

35. *The Canon.*

THIS is ſo called becauſe it has been laid down as the Rule or Canon which is to be rigidly followed by the Prieſt who offers the Holy Sacrifice.

The Prayer of Conſecration*—containing the Commemoration of the Paſſion, the Invocation, and the Conſecration Proper, i. e. the Words of Inſtitution.

The Celebrant does juſt what CHRIST did, as near as we can imitate His Action. "He takes," when he ſays, "He took," and preſents to GOD the element; he breaks,† when he ſays, "He brake it," and deſigns it to reception by laying his hand upon it, and in a manner imparts it when he ſays, our LORD gave it, ſaying, "Take, eat," &c., and he makes it the Body of CHRIST by the words of conſecration, "HOC EST CORPUS MEUM."

"When the Prieſt, ſtanding before the Table,‡ hath ſo ordered the Bread and Wine, that he

---

Celebrant kneels during the whole function, and only at the latter, when he has an Aſſiſtant, or at ſolemn Service, when there will be Goſpeller and Epiſtoler.

* The prayer of conſecration, which was taken from the Sarum Canon, ſhould be ſaid by the Prieſt as the preſent rubric enjoins, "ſtanding before the table." According to the direction in the Sarum Miſſal the beginning of the Canon is ſaid "manibus junctis et oculis elevatis." "Hear us, O merciful FATHER, &c." ſhould be ſaid *extenſis manibus*.
See alſo Eccleſiologiſt, vol. xii. p. 91, for legal opinion on the poſition of the celebrating Prieſt, viz. before the altar, facing the eaſt.
Vide Laud's Trial, p. 116, fol. ed. London, 1705. Jebb in his *Choral Service*, pp. 508, 9, inſtances Andrewes, Wren, and Coſin, as invariably adopting this poſition. Montague likewiſe practiſed the ſame, as may be ſeen in the charges brought againſt him in the Houſe of Commons.—Reports *in loco*.

† In the Sarum Rite, at "fregit," there is this direction, "Hic tangat hoſtiam;" the "fraction" not taking place till after the Conſecration. The Old Engliſh Church, as does the Roman Church at the preſent day, divided the Sacred Hoſt into three—a practice which all our clergy ought to reſtore and follow; the Eaſtern Church into four, following S. Chryſoſtom; and the ancient Liturgy of S. James into two. The preſent Engliſh Rubric, inſerted at the laſt reviſion, preſcribes a breaking of the Bread during the benediction, thus imitating our LORD's Action more cloſely than any other Liturgy.

‡ This phraſe (ſtanding before the Table) means of courſe before the midſt of the Table. The rubrics of our Book of Common Prayer and Adminiſtration of the Sacraments for the moſt part have reference to an Officient or Celebrant alone (ſuppoſing that aſſiſtant Miniſters would follow the Catholic uſe); now the Celebrant before the prayer of conſecration is

I

may with the more readiness and decency break the Bread before the people, and take the Cup into his hands, he shall say the Prayer of Consecration, as followeth.*

Almighty GOD, our heavenly FATHER, Who of Thy tender mercy didst give Thine only SON JESUS CHRIST to suffer death upon the cross for our redemption; Who made there (by His one Oblation of Himself once offered) a full, perfect, and sufficient Sacrifice, Oblation and satisfaction, for the sins of the whole world, and did institute, and in His holy Gospel command us to continue, a perpetual memory of that His precious death, } COMMEMORATION OF THE PASSION.

kneeling before the midst of the Altar in the prayer of humble access—in accordance with *the place* he has occupied since the Creed—the revisers of the Liturgy having endorsed the old English rule that everything after the Creed should be said in the middle of the Altar (v. supra, p. 42, par. 21). Therefore "standing before the Table" means standing in the midst thereof, in contradistinction to *kneeling* at the middle of the Altar, in which position the previous rubric had left the Celebrant.

This direction was inserted at the last revision, with the rubrics about the paten, fraction, and chalice. There had been no rubrics having special reference to this Action since the First Book of Edward VI. Doubtless it was this absence of minute and reverent rubrical detail which led to the remarkable statement of the Judicial Committee of the Privy Council in the case of the Knightsbridge churches, delivered March 21, 1857, that the Second Book of Edward VI. contained no consecration of the elements. In which case it would follow that the English Church was cut off from CHRIST for more than one hundred years.

Yet this Book of Common Prayer, of which it is asserted, that "*the Prayer for the Consecration of the Elements was omitted,*" (see Judgment of the Committee of the Privy Council in regard to the churches of SS. Paul and Barnabas, p. 28. Painter and Sons' edition, printed verbatim from the authorized official document), was the very Service Book[1] which Pope Pius IV. offered to confirm, on the condition of the return of Queen Elizabeth to the Roman obedience. See "Lawful Church Ornaments," by Rev. T. W. Perry, pp. 172, 173. Masters.

To "break the Bread before the people" means in presence thereof,—not that the Faithful actually see the "fraction" itself, but that the Celebrant may be seen as he inclines in the act of the breaking, and as he elevates the paten, and shows the chalice, as he raises it, above his head. This Action is of course best seen by the Faithful when the Priest stands before the middle of the Altar with his face to the east—an arrangement which secures his undistracted attention during the awful Action. For the Celebrant should never look about him, least of all at so dread a moment.

* Some of the English clergy say the following before the prayer of consecration in secret. "Most merciful God, look graciously upon the gifts now lying before Thee, and send down Thy HOLY SPIRIT upon this Sacrifice, that He may make this bread the Body of Thy CHRIST, and this cup the Blood of Thy CHRIST; and that all who are partakers thereof may obtain remission of their sins, be confirmed in godliness, and be filled with Thy HOLY SPIRIT. Amen." But the English (as the Roman) Church holds, that the words of Institution are sufficient for

---

[1] The main difference between the second book of Edward VI. and the book of Elizabeth consists in the latter restoring to the Church the ancient ornaments which the former had taken from her; the variations in the *text* are very slight, so that the two books, with the important exception alluded to, are in point of fact identical.

The Order of Administration. 59

until His coming again; Hear us, O merciful FATHER, ⎫
we most humbly beseech Thee, and grant that we re- ⎪
ceiving these Thy creatures of bread and wine, according ⎬ THE INVOCATION.*
to Thy SON our SAVIOUR JESUS CHRIST's holy institution, ⎪
in remembrance of His Death and Passion, may be par- ⎭
takers of His most blessed Body and Blood: Who in ⎫
(*a*) *Here the Priest*   the same night that He was betrayed (*a*) ⎪
is to take the Paten   took Bread, and when He had given ⎪
into his hands: thanks, (*b*) He brake it, and gave it to ⎪
(*b*) *And here to*   His disciples, saying, Take, eat, (*c*) THIS ⎪
break the Bread: IS MY BODY,† Which is given for you. ⎪
(*c*) *And here to*   Do this in remembrance of Me. Like- ⎪
lay his hand upon all   wise after Supper He (*d*) took the Cup, ⎬ THE CONSECRATION PROPER.‡
the Bread.   and when He had given thanks, He ⎪
(*d*) *Here he is to*   gave it to them, saying, Drink ye all ⎪
take the Cup into his   of this, for THIS (*e*) IS MY BLOOD OF THE ⎪
hand: NEW TESTAMENT, Which is shed for ⎪
(*e*) *And here to lay*   you and for many for the remission of ⎪
his hand upon every   sins: Do this, as oft as ye shall drink ⎪
vessel (be it Chalice   it, in remembrance of Me. *Amen.*" ⎭
or Flagon) in which
there is any Wine to
be consecrated.

    The Celebrant at the Consecration Prayer inclines humbly, *extensis manibus*. Before the recital of the Words of Institution the Celebrant should remove the pall from the chalice.§   At the words "Body" and "Blood" he should

---

the consecration, as may be gathered from the rubric concerning the consecration of further bread and wine.

  * Though it be true that GOD the FATHER effects the consecration of the elements by the operation of GOD the HOLY GHOST, it is unnecessary to pray *expressly* for the HOLY GHOST to consecrate the elements of Bread and Wine, because GOD knows perfectly all that is necessary for a valid consecration. See Palmer, Orig. Lit. tom. ii. pp. 138-40.

  † It may not be generally known to our readers that the custom, invariably followed in Latin Service Books, of placing the words of Consecration in the Mass in large type characters, was followed in one instance in a Church of England Prayer Book, a copy of which is in the possession of the Rev. F. G. Lee. In the early part of the reign of King Charles the Martyr, a very limited number of copies of the folio Book of Common Prayer, A.D. 1627, printed by Bonham Norton, and John Bill, was issued; though, as Dr. Bandinel of Oxford believed, the edition was immediately suppressed, owing to the opposition of the growing Puritan party. Anyhow, copies are remarkably rare, the only one at the Bodleian, at Oxford, being composed of two imperfect copies. The Prayer of Consecration, which stands on one page (thus avoiding the necessity of turning over of pages) contains no Rubrical directions, but has the words "This is My Body," "This is My Blood of the New Testament," printed in black letter capitals. Both Wheatley and Palmer, as well as Maskell and Proctor, overlook this important and curious fact. [Ed. 2nd Edition.]

  ‡ So our Church, with the whole West, and the Sarum, emphatically, as see *Cautelæ Missæ*, clearly holds,—containing imitation of the Action, and Recital of words of Institution.

  § "*Et tunc discooperiat calicem.*"—Missale Sarif.

  ¹ There was a variety of practice as to elevating the cup, covered or uncovered. It would seem that the use of the English Church was to elevate uncovered. See Maskell, Anc. Lit. p. 96.

make a crofs over the elements. At the words " Who, in the fame night," he fhould reft his elbows on the Altar, bowing down. The paten, and alfo the chalice are held in the left hand; the fign of the crofs being made with the right hand. After the words " This is My Body which is given for you," the " Hoftia" fhould be placed on the paten, and the Celebrant, with his affiftants, fhould reverently genuflect. Then rifing, the Celebrant fhould at once elevate Iᴛ with the firft finger and thumb of both hands, for the worfhip of the Faithful, while he is faying " Do this in remembrance of Me."* After the words " This is My Blood of the New Teftament," he fhould place the chalice on the centre of the corporal and, with his affiftants, genuflect again; after which he fhould in like manner elevate the chalice with both hands, while he is faying " Do this as oft as ye fhall drink of it, in remembrance of Me." After the Confecration, the Celebrant will keep his right finger and thumb joined until after the Ablutions. The Lay-affiftants at the Altar and members of the choir fhould be inftructed to bow profoundly at the Confecration and Elevation. It is quite wrong to turn to the people at the breaking of the bread, lifting up of the paten, and fhowing of the cup.†

It is ufual at the Fraction—"He brake it"—to divide the wafer or bread into *two* particles. The ancient divifion into *three*‡ particles, as was formerly practifed by the Church of England *after* the confecration, and is ftill directed in the modern Roman rubric, had now better take place *immediately* after the Prayer of Confecration, when one of the two particles can be divided. In the firft Fraction there is a typical allufion to the Sacrifice of Cʜʀɪsᴛ on the crofs, in imitation of Hɪs ᴏᴡɴ Aᴄᴛɪᴏɴ at the Laft Supper.

---

* Vide *The Elevation of the Hoft*, by R. F. Littledale, LL.D., reprinted from the *Union Review*. London: G. J. Palmer, 1864.

† The oftenfion or elevation of the chalice, *after* the confecration, which was the ancient Englifh cuftom, was prohibited by a Rubric in Edward VI's Firft Prayer Book, but this rubric has been omitted at all the fubfequent revifions, therefore the prohibition altogether falls to the ground.

The paten and chalice ought to be taken off the Altar reverently with both hands.

If wafer bread is not ufed, the Bread fhould be cut through previoufly to the fervice. The breaking of the Bread in the Prayer of Confecration, of courfe means the Prieft's own Bread. The "facrificium," as the Sarum, and the "hoftia," as the York, Rubric, calls It.

The greateft care fhould be taken to avoid the facrilege of allowing the fmalleft Particle to fall from the paten, or from the ciborium, or pyx, in communicating the Faithful.

‡ It does not feem that the Church of England meant to exclude the ancient Fraction by directing a Fraction *during the Confecration*. See Palmer, v. ii. p. 146.

The Order of Administration. 61

After the consecration the Celebrant will replace the pall on the chalice. The paten, standing in front thereof, will remain uncovered.

No one should sit after consecration, but all should remain kneeling or standing, till after the final consumption of the Holy Sacrament.

After the Consecration Prayer it is most desirable that no person passes before the Blessed Sacrament, without genuflecting, bowing, or some token of reverence.

36. *Preces Secretæ*

AY be said by the Celebrant standing humbly before the midst of the Altar. The following are strongly recommended. (*Ex Missali Sarum*). They should be written out plainly, printed, or illuminated:—

Dicendæ post Consecrationem.

Unde et memores, Domine, nos servi Tui, sed et plebs Tua sancta, ejusdem Christi Filii Tui Domini Dei nostri tam beatæ Passionis, necnon et ab inferis Resurrectionis, sed et in cœlos gloriosæ Ascensionis, offerimus præclaræ Majestati Tuæ de Tuis donis ac datis, Hostiam pu✠ram, Hostiam sanc✠tam, Hostiam imma✠culatam: Panem sanc✠tum vitæ æternæ, et Cali✠cem salutis perpetuæ.

Supra quæ propitio ac sereno vultu respicere digneris; et accepta habere, sicuti accepta habere dignatus es munera pueri Tui justi Abel, et sacrificium Patriarchæ nostri Abrahæ: et quod Tibi obtulit summus sacerdos Tuus Melchisedech, sanctum sacrificium, immaculatam Hostiam.

Supplices Te rogamus Omnipotens Deus: jube hæc perferri per manus sancti Angeli Tui in sublime altare Tuum, in conspectu Divinæ Majestatis Tuæ: ut quotquot ex hac altaris participatione, sacrosanctum Filii Tui Cor✠pus et San✠guinem sumpserimus: omni bene✠dictione cœlesti gratia repleamur. Per eundem Christum Dominum nostrum. Amen.

Memento etiam, Domine animarum famulorum famularumque Tuarum (*N. et N.*) qui nos præcesserunt cum signo fidei, et dormiunt in somno pacis: ipsis Domine, et omnibus in Christo quiescentibus, locum refrigerii, lucis et pacis, ut indulgeas, deprecamur. Per eundem Christum Dominum nostrum. Amen.

Nobis quoque peccatoribus famulis Tuis de multitudine miserationum Tuarum sperantibus, partem aliquam et societatem donare digneris cum Tuis sanctis Apostolis et Martyribus: cum Joanne, Stephano, Matthia, Barnaba, Ignatio, Alexandro, Marcellino, Petro, Felicitate, Perpetua, Agatha, Lucia, Agnete, Cæcilia, Anastatia, et cum omnibus Sanctis Tuis: intra quorum nos consortium non estimator meriti, sed veniæ, quæsumus, largitor admitte. Per Christum Dominum nostrum.

Per quem hæc omnia Domine, semper bona creas, sancti✠ficas, vivi✠ficas, bene✠dicis, et præstas nobis. Per ip✠sum, et cum ip✠so, et in ip✠so est Tibi Deo Patri Omnipo✠tenti, unitate Spiritus ✠ Sancti omnis honor et gloria. Per omnia sæcula sæculorum. Amen.

The above should be said with no pauses nor delays; immediately after the elevation: so that not too much time be taken up, nor the service too considerably lengthened.

37. *The Communion of the Priest.*

"Then shall the Minister first receive the Communion in both kinds himself, and then proceed to deliver the same to the Bishops, Priests, and Deacons, in like manner (if any be present)."

THE Priest,* according to the ancient usage of the Universal Church, communicates himself STANDING. When he is so doing he should not repeat the words aloud;† nor need he use the last clause at all.

Standing in front of the Altar, with his back to the people, he should incline moderately at taking the paten in his left hand, saying *secreto*, " LORD, I am not worthy that Thou shouldest come under my roof, but speak the word only, and my soul shall be healed." Then he communicates himself of the BODY over the paten, with his right hand, making the sign of the cross with the Blessed Sacrament and reverently inclining his head. He should then communicate of the BLOOD, saying *secreto*, " What shall I render unto the LORD for all His benefits that He hath done unto me? I will take the cup of salvation, and call upon the Name of the LORD." He should take the chalice by the knop with both hands, always inclining the head at the Name of JESUS. The Celebrant *alone communicates standing;* he next communicates the Gospeller and Epistoler —if they desire it, are fasting, and have not already offered the Holy Sacrifice at an earlier hour—who kneel on their own steps respectively; after them the Clergy present in surplices and stoles communicate on the sanctuary step; then the choir; and then the Clergy who may be simply in their ordinary dress.

---

* " *Hic*," says the York Missal, just before the Priest communicates, " *inclinet se sacerdos dicens orationes sequentes,*" " *inclinet*" referring merely to bowing the head.

† It is " *dicit*," everywhere in the Uses Roman and English, without any *secreto*. Of course the first person should be used.

38. *The Communion of the People.*

"And after that to the people alſo in order, into their hands, all meekly kneeling. And when he delivereth the Bread to any one, he ſhall ſay."

F there be a large number of communicants the Celebrant may place the Bleſſed Sacrament of the Lord's Body into the ciborium,* as being larger, leſs liable to accident, and more convenient than the paten.

Non-communicants† have an undoubted legal right, and are bound by ancient canons to be preſent during the whole rite, on all Sundays and Holy days of obligation. The Bleſſed Sacrament‡ is given to the people

---

* The ciborium, as uſed in the Weſt, is a veſſel in which the Bleſſed Sacrament is reſerved. It is, in fact, a chalice with a cover, ſurmounted by a croſs. The pyx was originally uſed for this purpoſe: this veſſel is of various ſhapes, from that of a dove to a round box with a conical top, terminated by a croſs. Amongſt Latins, ſmall pyxes for carrying the Bleſſed Sacrament to the ſick are round and flat—ſufficient to contain the *Hoſtia*, and are invariably of precious metal. The pyx was alſo uſed for Altar-Breads: *S. Paul's Cathedral*, "Item, a painted pyx for the Altar-Breads. In the Chapel of S. Rhadegund: Item, 2 wooden pyxes for the Altar-Breads."—Dugdale's Monaſticon.

The ciborium, or elſe a chalice, is alſo uſed in the Weſt in communicating the Faithful.

A Conſtitution of Abp. Peckham, (A.D. 1279), orders the pyx to be lined with linen. Abp. Winchelſea's Conſtitutions, (A.D. 1305), ſpeak of the pyx as one of thoſe articles to be provided at the charge of the pariſh. The pyx is therefore an *authorized* veſſel for uſe in the Church of England.

† In the Firſt Prayer Book of Edward VI, thoſe who did not receive were to depart, not out of the church, but out of the *quire*, except the Miniſters and Clerks engaged in the Euchariſt Service. In the Book of 1552 the Puritan party introduced a ſentence of excluſion, which was withdrawn when the Prayer Book was laſt reviſed by the Church's repreſentatives in 1662, when it again became legal, right and proper for all who were in the Church's communion to take part on all occaſions in the Euchariſtic Sacrifice.

‡ "Approaching therefore come not with thy wriſts extended, or thy fingers open; but make thy left hand as if a throne for thy right, which is on the eve of receiving the King. And having hollowed thy palm receive the Body of Christ ſaying after it Amen. Give heed leſt thou loſe any of It, for what thou loſeſt is a loſs to thee as it were from thine own members. For if any one give thee gold duſt wouldſt thou not with all precaution keep it faſt, being on thy guard againſt loſing any of it and ſuffering loſs? How much more carefully then wilt thou obſerve that not a Crumb falls from thee of What is more precious than gold and precious ſtones.

"Then having taken of the Body of Christ, approach alſo to the Cup of His Blood; not ſtretching forth thy hands, but bending, and ſaying in the way of worſhip and reverence, 'Amen, be thou hallowed by partaking alſo of the Blood of Christ.'"—S. Cyril of Jeruſalem, Cat. Lect. xxiii. 21, 22.

kneeling at the sanctuary step. If there are rails these should be covered with a linen cloth (see supra, p. 33, par. 14, and note); if there are no rails a cloth may be held before the communicants by the Clerks. The Sacrament of the LORD's Body should be taken in the palm of the right hand, which should be carefully raised to the mouth supported by the left. The Gospeller is to follow the Priest with the chalice, which he should always retain in his hand, even when he places it in that of the communicant.

The communicants should be careful to kneel where they are instructed to kneel, and should hold the head and body erect. It is obviously impossible to communicate people who put their faces on the floor, or who kneel off and away from the kneeling-cushions, without the greatest danger to the Blessed Sacrament and the most painful and singular inconvenience to the clergy.

39. *Consecration in one kind.**

" If the consecrated Bread or Wine be all spent before all have communicated; the Priest is to consecrate more according to the Form before prescribed: beginning at [OUR SAVIOUR CHRIST in the same night, &c.] for the blessing of the Bread; and at [Likewise after Supper, &c.] for the blessing of the Cup."

F the first Rubric in the Communion Office
(So many as intend to be partakers of the Holy Communion shall signify their names to the Curate at least some time the day before.)
were attended to, additional consecration would be very infrequent.

The rubric is a perfectly correct and simple transcript of the old Sarum rule in the " Cautelæ Missæ "—that if a priest found there was no wine in the cup, after he had consecrated the bread, he was to begin at " Simili

---

" Let us approach then with a fervent desire, and placing our palms in the fashion of a cross, receive the Body of the Crucified."—Damascen. Orthodox. Fid. Lib. iv. c. 13.

" Whosoever wilfully throws IT away, shall for ever be excluded from communion."—Conc. Tolet. xi.

These catholic usages are endorsed by Bishop Sparrow. See Rationale, p. 272. London, 1657.

* Some ritualists are ignorant that the words of Institution are all that is necessary for valid consecration. This is the old rule. The whole preceding prayers, necessary or not, (which they are not, any more than the prayer to sanctify the water at Baptism,) *count;* and so the Action is ample as well as sufficient. It is, however, discreet to take care always to consecrate enough at first.

The Order of Administration.

modo," the previous part of the Office *reckoning*. So with the bread, if a Priest died, or fainted, in the act of consecrating it, another Priest was to take up the rite at "Qui pridie." What this proves is, that *un-oblated* elements might be consecrated, the previous oblation *counting*. The whole of this old provision is in some measure a justification of ours.

40. *The Post Communion.*

"When all have communicated, the Minister shall return to the LORD's Table."

WHEN all have communicated the Celebrant is to return to the LORD's Table with the ciborium, or the paten, and the Gospeller with the cup.

41. *The Veiling of the Blessed Sacrament.*

"And reverently place upon it what remaineth of the consecrated Elements, covering the same with a fair linen cloth."

HE Ministers having returned to the Altar, the Priest takes the Blessed Sacrament and places It in the chalice, (in the middle of the Altar), on which he puts the paten, covering both with the pall or chalice cover, i.e. with "a fair linen cloth."*

42. *The* LORD's *Prayer*† *and Collects.*

"Then shall the Priest say the LORD's Prayer, the people repeating after him every petition."
"After shall be said as followeth."

HE Celebrant still stands in the midst and fronting the Altar. It is much to be desired that the former of these Collects were put back into the place which it occupied in the First Prayer Book of Edward VI, between the consecration and

---

* A veil of *linen and lace; this chalice-cover is only used for the veiling of the blessed Sacrament after the communion of the people*, and must not be confounded with the chalice-veil of silk, of the colour of the season.

† The LORD's Prayer was anciently said, in the Sarum use, not only towards the end of the canon after the consecration and the 'Oratio pro mortuis,' but after the Rite was over, (see Sarif. Missale. Rubric at the end of the Missa). And this is probably the reason why it is put after the reception in our Canon.

K

administration, where Bishop Overall always insisted on saying it, and as it is in Laud's Prayer Book. But its *original* place, however, was the conclusion of the canon, *before* the words of consecration, " Hanc igitur *oblationem* servitutis nostræ . . . placatus accipias ; . . . quam oblationem tu Deus . . . *rationabilem*, acceptabilemque facere digneris . . ."—*Sarif. Missale. Canon Missæ.* And as then it was a desire for the acceptance of the Sacrifice* before it was offered, so may it very well be used here for Its acceptance after It has been offered.

43. *The Gloria in excelsis*

S then to be intoned by the Celebrant in the midst of the Altar, both himself, the Gospeller, and Epistoler following exactly the directions as to position given in section 21, as regards the creed.

The Celebrant usually intones the words " Glory be to GOD on high," and the choir sings the remainder of the hymn.

44. *The Blessing.*†

" Then the Priest (or Bishop, if he be present) shall let them depart with this Blessing."§

HE Gospeller and Epistoler are then to kneel on their respective steps, whilst the Celebrant facing west, but not turning his back on the Blessed Sacrament, gives the Blessing. Saying the words, " The peace . . . His Son JESUS CHRIST," the Celebrant

---

* In the Eastern Liturgies prayers for grace and acceptance after reception are very common. See S. Mark's, the Coptic, S. Basil, Armenian, &c.

† The right hand is always used in blessing, confirmation, &c. The Bishop, when he uses the pastoral staff, as directed by the Rubric, carries it in his left hand, according to the usage of the Church.

In blessing the old rule was for the Priest to make the sign of the Cross once: the Bishop at the mention of each Name of the Persons in the blessed Trinity.

" Quid est signum Christi, nisi Crux Christi ? Quod signum nisi adhibeatur sive frontibus credentium, sive ipsi aquæ ex quâ regenerantur, sive oleo quo chrismate unguuntur, sive sacrificio quo aluntur, nihil horum rite perficitur."—S. August. Hom. cxviii. in Joan.

‡ This benediction is a peculiar function of the Bishop's Office, if present, because *the less is blessed of the better*, Heb. vii. 7.

§ The Blessing is compounded of (1) the " Pax," and (2) the Blessing. Therefore at any other service the " Pax " being peculiar to the Holy Communion should not be given, but

outſtretches his arms, but when actually giving the Bleſſing, he places his left hand open on his breaſt, and with his right makes the ſign of the croſs over the people.

45. *The Occaſional Collects.*

"Collects to be ſaid after the Offertory, when there is no Communion, every ſuch day one, or more; and the ſame may be ſaid alſo, as often as occaſion ſhall ſerve, after the Collects either of Morning or Evening Prayer, Communion, or Litany, by the diſcretion of the Miniſter."

ONE of theſe collects ſhould be ſaid daily as a Poſt Communion. The firſt is a prayer for ſafety in all worldly changes; the ſecond, for the preſervation of our ſouls and bodies; the third, for a bleſſing on God's Word; the fourth, for direction and ſucceſs in all our undertakings; the fifth, for excuſing the defect of our former prayers; the laſt, for the acceptance of all the reſt of our ſupplications.

46. *Miſſa Sicca.**

"Upon the Sundays and other Holy-days (if there be no Communion) ſhall be ſaid all that is appointed at the Communion, until the end of the general Prayer [*For the whole ſtate*

only the Bleſſing (2). Palmer, however—but with no ſufficient reaſon—Vol. ii. p. 161), conſiders our formulary to be a judicious enlargement of benedictions which were uſed in the Engliſh Church before the year A. D. 600. "Benedictio Dei Patris omnipotentis, et Filii, et Spiritus Sancti, maneat ſemper vobiſcum."—Saxon Office, *ad finem completorii.*
"Benedictio Dei Patris et Filii, et Spiritus Sancti, et pax Domini, ſit ſemper vobiſcum."—Benedictiones in quotidianis diebus, MS. Leofric, Exon. fol. 332. See alſo Proctor, pp. 331, 332.

* The term *Miſſa Sicca* (Dry Service), is generally uſed for the Office, conſiſting of the firſt part of our Communion Service, and ending after the prayer for the Church Militant, followed by one or more of the collects, printed at the end of the Office, and concluding with the bleſſing, and has therefore been retained in the text.
The following is the Rationale of this anomalous Service.
The uſe of *an Office ſelected from the Liturgy* is of very ancient uſe in the Church, and is *univerſal* in the Eaſt, from whence no doubt the Weſt derived it as early as the thirteenth century or earlier. Not only in Egypt on Wedneſdays and Fridays, but throughout the Eaſt, (the *Greek* Eaſt certainly, and the Armenian Church), is there uſed *every day*, when there is not celebration, on Sundays, &c. whether there is or is not, either after Sexts or Nones, (according to the time of the year), a very full Office ſelected from the Liturgy, (Bona, Div. Pſalmod. c. 18, p. 904). "Quibus additur *Typicum,* quod *loco miſſæ* recitare ſolet." This "Typicum," which means, both in Greek and Slavonic (ſee Neale, Hiſt. of H. E. Church,

of CHRIST's *Church militant here in earth*] together with one or more of thefe Collects laft before rehearfed, concluding with the Bleſſing."

"And there ſhall be no celebration of the LORD's Supper, except there be a convenient number to communicate with the Prieſt, according to his diſcretion."

"And if there be not above twenty perſons in the Pariſh of diſcretion to receive the Communion; yet there ſhall be no Communion, except four (or three at the leaſt) communicate with the Prieſt."

"And in Cathedral and Collegiate Churches and Colleges, where there are many Prieſts and Deacons, they ſhall all receive the Communion with the Prieſt every Sunday at the leaſt, except they have a reaſonable cauſe to the contrary."

Gen. Int. p. 941) "the likeneſs or *imitation*," viz. of the Liturgy, conſiſts of the *Sunday Euchariſtic Office* up to a certain point, viz. 1. Pſalms 103—146. 2. The Hymn "Only Begotten SON," correſponding to the Weſtern "*Gloria in Excelſis.*" 3. The Beatitudes with reſponſes, like our Commandments and reſponſes. 4. Epiſtle and Goſpel, (ſee Bona, p. 905). Then, in lieu of the Euchariſtic Preface and Terſanctus, another form of Terſanctus. Then the Nicene Creed in the old place of *Creed and Reception.* Then deprecation and LORD's Prayer, much as in the Liturgy, certain Hymns and the *Pſalm of Thankſgiving* after Communion, (Pſalm 34).

The Armenian has a ſimilar Office at Nones. The Egyptian Church was therefore not peculiar in having on Wedneſdays and Fridays "all the Euchariſtic Service, except what was proper for celebration," (Socrates, l. c. ap. Bingham). Neither is there *in the abſtract* any poſſible objection to a Service ſo ſelected, provided it keeps a remote diſtance from the Liturgy. Ordinary Offices *always* borrow ſomething, e.g. the collect, from the Euchariſtic; it is a queſtion of degree how much they ſhould borrow. The ſo-called Miſſa Sicca of the thirteenth and ſixteenth centuries in the Weſt was ſimply ſuch a diſtant parallel. The Prieſt was veſted in his ſtole and all his ſacerdotal veſtments. The Office *omitted the canon altogether* except the LORD's Prayer, but had the *Præfatio,* which the Eaſt had not, and the *Terſanctus* like the Eaſt. But the *Secreta,* or oblationary prayer was *omitted,* exactly as is ordered in our Book, (ſee rubric to Church Militant prayer, "if there be no alms or *oblations,*" &c.,) as being ſacrificial, Durandus l. iv. c. i. 23. This is very remarkable, and ſhows the exact ritual learning of our Reviſers (of 1662). It is worthy of note that it was our firſt and leaſt deſtructive reviſers (of 1549, not 1552), who ordered the ſaying of the Office, as far as the offertory, if there was no Communion. It is moſt likely that they had the Eaſtern precedent before them, the Egyptian more eſpecially, which from ſo well-known a writer as Socrates they might reaſonably have had. It would ſeem that they intended ſuch uſe of the abridged Office to take place *daily,* if there was no Communion. For the rubric which enjoins it on Wedneſdays and Fridays, as chief Euchariſtic days, ends thus: "and the ſame order ſhall be uſed *all other days* whenſoever the people be cuſtomarily aſſembled to pray in the church, and none be diſpoſed to communicate with the Prieſt." And this is no doubt, or probably, the reaſon why the matins in that Book ends ſo abruptly, viz. becauſe *either* Celebration, or the ſhort Office was to follow. Hence the ſo-called Dry Service is not objectionable in the abſtract, when regarded as *a ſort of ordinary Office,* but only when it is ſubſtituted for, and, as it would ſeem, preferred to the Liturgy. It were to be deſired that the term "abridged Office," or "ſhorter Service," were uſed inſtead of *Miſſa Sicca* or Dry Service. Without doubt the proper name for it would be the "proanaphoral" or the "Service of catechumens."

[Practically this "Dry Office," or whatever people chooſe to call it, has taken the place of actual celebrations—a ſtone being offered inſtead of bread,—though our "Reformers" of the

The Order of Administration. 69

*AILY Eucharist.* However un-primitive and un-Catholic our present custom be, it is plain from the rubric enjoining "that the Collect, Epistle, and Gospel appointed for the Sunday shall serve all the week after, where it is not in this Book otherwise ordered," that celebration on ferial days, i. e. on other days besides Sundays and Festivals, is contemplated by the Church. The Holy Sacrifice ought to be offered if there be four, or three at least, to communicate with the Priest, and this is required that he may "solemnize so high and holy mysteries with all the suffrages and due order appointed for the same."*—(Edward VI's First Book). If the Celebrant sees three people in church, therefore, he should presume that they intend to communicate, and go on to celebrate the Eucharist.

On Good Friday,† when the Dry Service is celebrated, the Priest should wear a cope instead of a vestment (chasuble), and is permitted to use a surplice in the place of the alb. Vide First Prayer Book, Edward VI, *in loco.*

47. *The Bread and Wine.*‡

AFER bread is the order of the Church of England, with a permission to use "the best and purest wheaten bread;" which lax and unprimitive permission most unhappily has led to the ordinary use of the latter.

When wafer bread is used, it is convenient to place on the credence a

---

present day are continually and successfully undoing the mischief. It is impossible, therefore, having this "corrupt following of the Apostles" (of Protestantism) before our eyes, not to see the evil; and seeing the evil clearly in all its baneful bearings, steps should be taken to rectify it. Neither East nor West, at this or any other period, ever sanctioned so profane and empty a ceremony. It is idle to attempt to justify the Anglican Reformers on this important point. ED. 2nd ED.]

* This need not practically ever prevent celebration at least on Sundays and Festivals; for even if people withdrew after the prayer for the Church, if the oblation has been made, as of course it will have been, the service must go on. Much more should absent sick persons, who will of course communicate spiritually, be counted in.

† Good Friday is the only day in the year for which proper Collect, Epistle, and Gospel are appointed, when no celebration takes place. The Priest vested in the *black cope,* not chasuble, would end the Service with the Church Militant prayer, collect, and blessing.

‡ "That a Priest never presume to celebrate Mass, unless he hath all things appertaining to the housel, viz. a pure oblation, pure wine, and pure water. Wo be to him that begins to celebrate unless he have all these; and wo be to him that puts any foul thing thereto, as the

canister* containing wafers. When ordinary loaf bread is used, which is much to be deprecated, a square thereof should be divided into breads, and placed on a metal plate. The Celebrant will generally know how much to consecrate, and should be careful to do so, and also to consecrate with the least.

No one should be permitted to arrange the wafers, or prepare the bread, (viz. to cut the square and divide it into breads) save the Deacon; when there is no Deacon the Priest must do it himself. It is of course prepared in the sacristy.

It would seem to be lawful in the Church of England to use either leavened or unleavened bread.†

The wine should be the pure juice of the grape. Tent wine‡ is the present customary use of the English Church.

Jews did, when they mingled vinegar and gall together, and then invited CHRIST to it by way of reproach to Him."—Canons made in Edgar's reign, A.D. 960.

Our custom of using common baker's bread, adulterated, as it often is, with alum, and potatoes, and bonedust, is as alien to the spirit of our forefathers, as it is in itself un-Catholic, unseemly, and irreverent.

* Amongst the furniture of the Altar of Bishop Andrewes' chapel was a "silver and gilt canister for the wafers, like a wicker basket, and lined with cambric laced."—Hierurgia Anglicana, p. 8.

† Unleavened bread in the Holy Eucharist, remarked by Alcuin A.S. 789, thus:—"Panis qui in Corpus Christi consecratur absque fermento ullius alterius infectionis debet esse mundissimus."—Epist. lxix. ad Lugdunenses.

"Without deciding the much disputed point, whether our Blessed LORD employed leavened or unleavened bread when He instituted the Holy Eucharist, it is suggested, that if we test the merits of the two kinds of bread by their purity, the unleavened will undoubtedly be the best. Its elements are perfectly simple, and can be mixed together before one's own eyes, without the necessity of adding any foreign substance to render the bread such as is desired. 'Apertissimum est,' says S. Anselm, 'quia melius sacrificatur de azymo, quam de fermentato: tum quia valde aptius et prius et diligentius fit; tum quia Dominus hoc fecit.'"—See "On the Celebration of the Holy Eucharist," pp. 6-7, Masters, a work that ought to be studied by every Priest.

‡ Claret wine has always been used, until the present year (1858), in the Royal Chapels, except in the German Chapel, where white wine is still used. Red wine (Malaga) is used on feast days in the Latin Church in some countries.

48. *The Consumption and Purification.*

"And if any of the bread and wine remain unconsecrated, the Curate shall have it to his own use: but if any remain of that which was consecrated, it shall not be carried out of the church, but the Priest and such other of the Communicants as he shall then call unto him, shall, immediately after the Blessing, reverently eat and drink the same."

THE Celebrant genuflecting immediately after the Blessing, and without any private devotions, stands before the midst of the Altar, whilst the Sub-deacon or Epistoler, going to the left hand of the Priest, closes the Book, and the Deacon or Gospeller, going to the right, uncovers the chalice for the consumption of the Blessed Sacrament. This should be taken at once by the Celebrant, who then presents the chalice to the Epistoler, who having received the wine-cruet from the clerk, pours some wine with his right hand into the chalice, when the Celebrant, moving about the chalice with his wrists, in order to take off any particles which may adhere to the inside of it, drinks its contents, if possible by the side where the particles adhere. The Celebrant having again presented the chalice to the Gospeller, resting it on the Altar, the latter pours in some wine, then gives the wine-cruet to the clerk, and the Epistoler taking the water-cruet into his right hand, pours some water into the wine *over the fingers** of the Priest. The Celebrant then drinks off the ablutions.† The Epistoler then having returned the water-cruet to the clerk to place with the wine-cruet on the credence, puts the purificator into the hands of the Celebrant, who wipes the chalice and paten,‡

---

* "Qua dicta eat sacerdos ad dexterum cornu altaris cum calice inter manus, digitis adhuc conjunctis¹ sicut prius : et accedat subdiaconus et effundat in calicem vinum et aquam : et refinceret sacerdos manus suas ne aliquæ reliquiæ corporis vel sanguinis remaneant in digitis vel in calice."—Sarum Missal.

† "Cum vero aliquis sacerdos debet bis celebrare in uno die: tunc ad primam missam non debet percipere ablutionem ullam, sed ponere in sacrario vel in vase mundo usque in finem alterius ; tunc sumatur utraque ablutio."²—Sarif. Missale.

‡ The Bangor and Hereford uses were to lay the chalice *upon its edge* upon the paten that it might drain thereon.—See Dr. Rock's "Church of our Fathers," vol. iii. part ii. p. 167, for an illustration of this rite.

The following are the old English rubrics on the subject :—

¹ i. e. so that the first finger and thumb of each hand might be within the chalice, and thus washed as well as the cup with wine and water poured over them.

² This rule should be carefully observed in case of duplication.

and dries his fingers with it. The Gospeller at the same time folds the corporal, and puts it into the burse, and covering the chalice, on which have been placed the purificator and paten, with the silk veil, of the colour of the season, lays the burse upon it, and putting it on the credence, returns to his place on the right of the Celebrant. They all three stand for a few moments before the Altar, then descend to the floor, and having together bowed to the cross, return to the sacristy in the order in which they came. During the consumption of the Blessed Sacrament it is a pious and edifying custom for the choir to sing *Nunc Dimittis*. One of the acolytes or servers may remain to extinguish the Altar lights, beginning with that on the Gospel side.

This rubric was first inserted in the Book of Common Prayer at the final revision. It is evident from it that the faithful should not leave the church until the solemn ceremony of the consumption is ended. (See Cleaver's edition of Bp. Wilson's "Short and Plain Instruction for the better understanding of the LORD's Supper," p. 139).

49. *Duplication.*

IT is not proper nor canonical for the same Priest to celebrate more than once in the same day, except on Christmas Day, and in cases of necessity, nor of course must the Assistant Ministers receive the Blessed Sacrament more than once in the same day, though present at more than one celebration.

"Bis in die celebrare nullus præsumet, nisi in diebus Nativitatis et Resurrectionis Dominicæ; et tunc in prima missa ablutio digitorum vel

---

" Post perceptionem ablutionum ponat sacerdos *calicem super patenam*: ut si qua remaneat stillet; et postea inclinando se dicat:

" Adoramus crucis signaculum, per quod salutis sumpsimus sacramentum."—Sarum Missale.

" Eat sacerdos in medio altaris, ibidem calicem *super patenam jacentem* dimittens: et se cum magna veneratione respiciendum crucem inclinans, dicat in memoria passionis Domini . . . . Adoremus, &c."—Bangor Missal.

" Tunc ponat *calicem jacentem super patenam*, et inclinet se ad altare, et eat ad sacrarium et lavet manus suas, et in eundo dicat:

" Lavabo inter innocentes manus meas: et circumdabo altare tuum, Domine."—Hereford Missal.

The bowl of the chalice when laid upon the paten should face the west.

calicis a celebrante non fumatur." Wilkins' Concilia, tom. i. p. 531. (This is from a Provincial Constitution of Archbishop Langton).

The 55th of the Excerpts of Archbishop Egbert, a contemporary of Venerable Bede, declares:—"Et sufficit sacerdotem unam missam in una die celebrare, quia Christus semel passus est, et totum mundum redemit." —Wilkins' Concilia, tom. i. p. 104.

50. *Directions for the Use of Incense at High Celebration of the Holy Eucharist.*

A QUARTER of an hour before the celebration the Thurifer should present himself at the sacristy, put on his cassock and *cotta*, and in default of the acolytes assist the Sacred Ministers to vest.

The Priest, Deacon, and Subdeacon being vested, the blessing of the Incense to be used in the procession takes place, immediately before leaving the sacristy. The Celebrant receives the spoon from the Deacon, who says, "Be pleased, reverend father, to give a blessing;" he then takes incense from the *navicula* or incense-boat (held by the Deacon, who receives it from the Thurifer,) and puts it on the burning charcoal in three several portions, each time sprinkling it in the form of a cross. Then in accordance with the Deacon's prayer, he blesses the incense with his right hand, saying, "Be thou blessed by Him in whose honour thou art to be burned." The thurible is held by the Thurifer whilst the incense is put in. The procession then moves into the aisle in the following order:—

1. Thurifer with thurible smoking, preceded by the cross-bearer.
2. Acolytes.*
3. Clergy, two and two in reverse order; the part nearest the celebrant being the place of honour.
4. Procession of celebrant.
    α. Subdeacon and Deacon.
    β. The Celebrant.

N.B.—If a Bishop be present he precedes the celebrant. This supposes him not to act *pontifically*.†

---

* In the West a lighted torch is carried in the outside hand.
† When a Bishop assists pontifically he goes last in the procession, with an attendant Priest on either side.

The Celebrant standing before the midst of the Altar, turns round by his right, and then with his side to the Altar, puts incense into the thurible, the Deacon ministering the spoon and holding the boat as before. The Priest then blesses (*secreto*) the incense with the words already mentioned. He then receives the thurible from the Deacon,* and incenses the midst of the Altar† and the two corners. The Celebrant himself is then incensed by the Deacon.‡ After the Introit the Priest again incenses the Altar.§ The next incensing takes place before the Gospel,∥—the midst of the Altar is alone incensed by the Deacon,—the lectern from which the Gospel is read is *never* incensed.

When the oblations¶ are placed upon the Altar they are incensed by the Celebrant, who is afterwards incensed by the Deacon.** An acolyte then incenses the choir.†† The next and last incensing takes place (in the West) after the consecration. When the consecration and adoration of the sacred Body are over, the Deacon rises and removes the pall from the chalice; and after the consecration and adoration of the Precious Blood he replaces it,—the chief assistant having incensed the Body and Blood of our Lord.

N.B.—When a Bishop assists *pontifically* he blesses the incense.

α. The Thurifer genuflects when he leaves or enters the choir; or leaves or approaches the Altar *after* consecration, and on passing or re-passing from one side to the other. When the Blessed Sacrament is not present, he bows reverently to the Cross.

β. When a thurible does not contain incense which has been blessed, he will hold it in his left hand; but when it does contain incense which has been blessed, *vice versa*. During the more ceremonial parts of the function, such as at the singing of the Gospel, &c. and during pro-

---

* "Accepto thuribulo a Diacono." Rom. Miss.
† "Et ipse sacerdos thurificet medium altaris, et utrumque cornu altaris." Missale Sarisb.
‡ "Deinde ab ipso diacono ipse sacerdos thurificetur." *Ibid.*
§ "Et postea incenset altare." Missale Ebor.
∥ "In fine alleluia, vel sequentiæ, vel tractus, diaconus antequam accedat ad evangelium pronuntiandum thurificet medium altaris tantum. Nunquam enim thurificetur lectrinum ante pronuntiationem evangelii." Missale Sarisburiense.
¶ "Hoc peracto accipiat thuribulum a diacono et thurificet sacrificium: videlicet ultra ter signum crucis faciens, et in circuitu et ex utraque parte calicis et sacrificii: deinde locum inter se et altare. Et dum thurificat dicat: Dirigatur Domine ad te oratio mea, sicut incensum in conspectu tuo." Missale Sarisb. In all the Greek Liturgies, the oblations are here incensed, e. g. Liturgy of S. Chrysostom in the Euchol. Græc. Goar.
** "Postea thurificetur ipse sacerdos ab ipso diacono." *Ibid.*
†† "Deinde acolytus thurificet chorum." See also Maskell *in loco*, p. 62. *Ibid.*

ceſſions, he places the little finger in the ring of the coverlet, and the thumb of the ſame hand in the ring of the chain that holds the large cover; on other occaſions, ſuch as when he proceeds to receive incenſe, &c. he generally holds it at the top of the chain under the coverlet, in ſuch a manner, however, that the large cover will be ſomewhat raiſed.

γ. After each incenſation the Thurifer having removed the charcoal and remains of the incenſe, and hung up the thurible in the veſtry, takes his place in choir.

δ. If the Thurifer has to go to the ſacriſty to renew the fire, he ſhould be attended by two acolytes to render him any aſſiſtance required.

ε. The Thurifer ſhould occaſionally raiſe the cover a little, and gently ſwing the thurible, leſt the fire be extinguiſhed.

ζ. Where gas is laid on in the ſacriſty it will be found convenient and economical to have a jet fitted with frame, upon which may reſt a ſmall iron pan, ſo perforated that the charcoal put into it may eaſily be ignited by the flame of the gas paſſing through it. The pan ſhould have a ſmall handle. This plan is eſpecially uſeful in the ſummer ſeaſon, as, by a gutta-percha tubing the jet may be temporarily placed in the ordinary ſtove or fire-place; and during the winter months when the ordinary fires are burning may be carefully laid by.

η. The thurible with its boat is placed on the credence. Alſo the ſpoon and a ſmall pair of tongs. This latter is carried out to the veſtry, where the prepared charcoal is being heated.

θ. The thurible, *Navicula* (Incenſe boat) ſpoon, and caniſter of Incenſe ſhould be kept together in a cupboard. It is recommended to let the thuribles hang from pegs, and the other articles ſtand upon a ſhelf a little above.

PLAIN SERVICE.*

51. *The Altar Lights.*

THE candles should be lighted by the clerk, acolyte, or server, (in cassock and surplice) immediately before the celebration.

52. *Directions for celebrating Holy Communion when there is only a Celebrant, attended by one or more lay servers or acolytes.*

THE Celebrant should be vested in his cassock. In silence he is to register (i.e. to set the markers in the proper places) the service-book in the Vestry, and to hand it to the server. He then washes his hands, and puts the wafers or the breads on the metal plate. He places the paten on the chalice, with the purificator between, and over these a veil of silk, of the colour of the season, the burse containing the corporal being laid upon the top of all. He next puts on the vestments.

(1.) The Amice. The Priest rests it for a moment like a veil, upon the crown of his head, and then spreading it upon his shoulders, arranges and fastens it.

(2.) The Alb. The Priest puts it completely over his head, passes through his right arm, then his left. He then binds it with the girdle round his *loins*, and adjusts it all round, so that it be a finger's breadth from the ground.

(3.) The Stole. This he *crosses* on the breast and confines with the girdle.

(4.) The Maniple. This he puts on the left arm by means of a loop, which he fixes on a button upon the sleeve of the alb.

---

* This only differs from the sung or solemn Service in this, that the celebrant, (who is always served by at least one assistant or choir boy,) performs the function without the Epistoler or Gospeller, and that all the parts directed to be sung by the Priest are only said; and parts directed to be sung by the choir are said by the server.

(5.) The Chasuble.

The Celebrant may for convenience attach a white handkerchief to his girdle.

For devotions to be used by the Priest whilst vesting, and *Preparatio ad Eucharistiam*, see pp. 30-3.

While the Celebrant is vesting, the acolyte, in his cassock, should place the service-book on the desk upon the north side of the Altar, and arrange the breads, cruets, and all that may be required on the credence.

The Celebrant, preceded by the acolyte, takes the chalice by the knop with his left hand, putting his right on the burse, and proceeds to the Altar, holding the chalice near his breast. On arriving before the Altar, he inclines, places the chalice, &c. on the centre, descends to the floor, and turning to the Altar, says (*secreto*) the Introit; after which he ascends to the Altar,* and going to the Gospel side, begins with the LORD's Prayer and Collect for Purity.

53. *The Collects.*

THE Celebrant "standing as before," viz. in the position he was in before rehearsing the commandments, at the Gospel or north side with his face towards the Altar, (see Par. 19), says the Collects.

54. *The Epistle and Gospel.*

THE Celebrant goes to the south or Epistle corner, bowing to the Cross as he passes, and reads the Epistle, looking towards the East. The book is placed upon the altar-desk, which the acolyte or lay-clerk has removed to the Epistle side. This being ended, the Priest, with hands joined before his breast, goes to the book which the acolyte has removed to the north side. The book is placed obliquely, its back being south-west. The Priest, having signed himself with the cross on forehead, mouth, and breast, reads the Gospel, his hands being joined.

If the Name of JESUS occurs he inclines towards the book.

---

* If the vested chalice and paten and burse thereon be on the credence, and not borne by the Celebrant from the sacristy, he here places the holy vessels on the Altar, in the midst thereof.

55. *The Creed.*

THE Celebrant now proceeds to the middle of the Altar, and extending his hands at the firſt words, but joining them again, ſays the Creed. The acolyte will have placed the ſervice-book to his immediate left.

56. *The Sermon.*

AFTER the Creed, if there be a Sermon, the Celebrant, for convenience' ſake, takes off the chaſuble, which he lays upon the Epiſtle ſide of the Altar,* and proceeds to the pulpit.

57. *The Offertory and the Firſt Oblation, commonly called The Oblation of bread and wine.*

AFTER the Service the Celebrant returns to the Altar, puts on the chaſuble, and ſays the Offertory, during which the alms (if any) are collected.

The Celebrant receives the bags which contain the alms in a baſin or offertory-diſh, and preſents them, ſtanding. The alms-diſh may be placed on the ſouth ſide of the Altar, and ſhould be removed by the acolyte to the credence or elſewhere, after it has been preſented.

The Celebrant then takes from off the veiled chalice the burſe in both hands. Taking out the corporal with his right hand and ſpreading it in the middle of the Altar, he puts the burſe on the Altar towards the north ſide againſt the retable. Then having moved the veiled chalice towards the Epiſtle corner, ſpreads the corporal† with both hands on the centre of the Altar. He then takes off the chalice veil, folds it, and places it near the back of the Altar on the Epiſtle ſide. He removes

---

* The chaſuble is the only ornament of the Prieſt which it is permitted to lay upon the Altar. Caps, gloves, and the like ought never to be tolerated upon the Altar, and if incautiouſly placed there, ought inſtantly to be removed by one of the aſſiſtant Miniſters, Sacriſt, or other officer.

† In the modern Roman rite the corporal is partially ſpread out at the beginning of the function, and the burſe leant againſt the ſuper-altar then, and not at the offertory, as with us.

the pall and places it a little to the right. He then takes the paten from the chalice. The acolyte then brings the wafers or breads to the Celebrant, who places them on the paten.* He then prepares the chalice, the acolyte having brought the cruets—the wine in the right hand and the water in the left—from the credence. He places the chalice on the centre of the corporal, putting on it the pall, and the paten immediately in front of it, covering the same with the right hand corner of the corporal.

58. *Lotio Manuum.*

See p. 51, Par. 26.

59. *The Commemoration of the Living and the Dead.*

See p. 51, Par. 27, and Note.

60. *The Exhortation and Invitatory.*

THE Celebrant joins his hands in pronouncing them, unleſs he holds the book, looking to the weſt.

61. *The Confeſſion.*

THIS is ſaid by the aſſiſtant or acolyte kneeling before † the Altar with joined hands, (ſee p. 55, Par. 29).

62. *The Abſolution.* ‡

THE Celebrant fronts the people, and pronounces the abſolution, (ſee p. 55, Par. 30, and Note).

63. *The Comfortable Words.*

See p. 56, Par. 31.

---

* "Laiyng the breade upon the corporas, or els in the paten, or in ſome other comely thyng, prepared for that purpoſe."—King Edward's Firſt Book.
† "Ad gradum altaris."—Sariſ. Miſ.
‡ "Deinde erectus ſignet ſe in facie dicendo abſolutionem."—Rubric in Bangor Miſ.

64. *The "Surfum Corda," and "Gratias agamus."*

See p. 56, Par. 32.

65. *Preface with Ter-Sanctus.*

See p. 56, Par. 33, and Note.

66. *Prayer of Humble Accefs.*

See p. 56, Par. 34, and Note.

67. *The Canon.**

See p. 57, Par. 35.

68. *The Confecration.*

See pp. 57-61, Par. 35, and Notes.

69. *The Communion of the Prieft.*

See p. 62, Par. 37.

70. *The Communion of the People.*

WHEN the Celebrant has communicated, holding the paten or ciborium in his left hand, he takes a wafer or a bread between the thumb and finger of the right hand, and approaches the communicants, beginning at the Epiftle fide. On repeating the words, "The Body of our Lord Jesus Christ," he makes the fign of the crofs with the Bleffed Sacrament over the paten, and he places the Body in the palm of the hand of the communicant, and after he has placed It in his mouth the Prieft continues: "preferve thy body and foul." The fame order is to be obferved in communicating each feveral communicant of the Blood. The Rubric does not direct the chalice to be given into the hands of the communicants.

---

* In the Sarum Canon at the word "*fregit,*" (where the *Fraction* takes place in our Canon), is the following rubric, "*Hic tangat boftiam dicens* . . ."

The Order of Administration.

71. *Consecration in one kind.*

See p. 64, Par. 39, and Note.

72. *The Veiling of the Blessed Sacrament.**

See p. 65, Par. 41.

73. *The Lord's Prayer and Collects.*

See p. 65, Par. 42.

74. *The Gloria in Excelsis.*†

See p. 66, Par. 43.

75. *The Blessing.*

IN pronouncing the blessing, the Celebrant, turning to the people, extends both his hands from the words, "The peace of God," down to the words "Jesus Christ;" then placing his left hand open on his breast, he raises his right, and when giving the blessing makes the sign of the cross. After the blessing, he rejoins his hands, and turning to the Altar, consumes what remains of the Blessed Sacrament.

76. *Occasional Collects.*

See p. 67, Par. 45.

77. *The Daily Celebration.*

See p. 69, Par. 46, and Note.

---

* The asterisk or cover, in form of a star, placed on the holy Bread in the Office of the Prothesis, in the Eastern Church, was used by Bishop Andrewes, though probably only for the chalice and instead of the customary pall.—See Hierurgia Anglicana, pp. 9-11. And Neale's Hist. of H. E. Church, p. 350, Gen. Int.

† If it be objected that the *Gloria in Excelsis* is used as a thanksgiving (see Par. 43) when it is essentially a hymn, it may be answered that *as a hymn* it is appropriate. For we read in the holy Gospel that after the Sacrament the Lord and His disciples sung an hymn before they went to the Mount of Olives, S. Matt. xxvi. 30; S. Mark xiv. 26. It should be also remembered that after the end of the Roman Liturgy the hymn of "*The Three Children,*" or the *Te Deum* is sung.

78. *The Bread and Wine.**

See p. 69, Par. 47, and Notes.

79. *The Confumption and Ablutions.* See p. 71, Par. 48.

HAVING uncovered the chalice and paten he genuflects, and partakes of what remains on the paten or on the corporal, and then wiping the paten with the purificator, and laying it on the corporal, drinks off the remainder of the facrament of the Blood. He then takes the chalice to the Epiftle corner, (*Ad dexterum cornu altaris*), and having placed it on the Altar, holding it with his left hand he receives from the clerk a little wine (poured with the right hand) from the wine cruet, in the chalice. He takes care that any particles of the bleffed Body and Blood which may have adhered to his fingers, be reverently removed over the cup. After the firft ablution he fays (*fecreto*), "*Quod ore fumpfimus, Domine, pura mente capiamus: et de muneri temporali fiat nobis remedium fempiternum.*"—(Sarif. Miffale). The acolyte then pours wine and water over the Celebrant's fingers into the chalice, the contents of which the Celebrant drinks, faying, (*fecreto*), "*Hæc nos communio, Domine, purget a crimine: et cæleftis remedii faciat effe confortes.*"—(Sarif. Miffale.) After which the chalice fhould be again rinfed with water only, which the Celebrant likewife drinks. Then, taking the purificator, he wipes both chalice, paten, his fingers, and, if need be, his lips with it. He then folds the corporal, takes with the left hand the burfe, and places the corporal in it with his right. He places the paten on the chalice, between which he puts the purificator, over this the filk veil, and upon this the burfe, as at firft (fee Par. 11.) He then takes the chalice in his left hand, and puts his right on the burfe. Defcending with it to the Sanctuary floor, preceded

---

* "That the Communion be celebrated in due form with an oblation of every communicant, and admixing water with the wine; *fmooth wafers* to be ufed for the bread." Rules for the celebration of Divine Service during Prince Charles's refidence in Spain, A. s. 1623, attributed to Bp. Andrewes. See Collier, ii. 726.

". . . *it fhall fuffice that the bread be fuch as is ufual to be eaten; but the beft and pureft Wheat Bread that conveniently may be gotten.*"—Rubric, Book of Common Prayer.

"It is not here commanded that no unleavened or wafer bread be ufed, but it is faid only 'that the other bread fhall fuffice.' So that though there was no neceffity, yet there was a liberty ftill referved of ufing wafer-bread, which was continued in divers churches of the kingdom, and Weftminfter for one, till the 17th of King Charles," (i. e. till 1643.)—Bp. Cofin's Notes on the Book of Common Prayer, Third Series, p. 481.

by the server, he makes an humble adoration. He then returns to the vestry, reciting the *Benedicite*. He takes off his vestments and folds them, or has them folded, and goes back to the church to say his thanksgiving.

The acolyte extinguishes the Altar lights, beginning at the Gospel side.

80. Solemn and Plain Service.

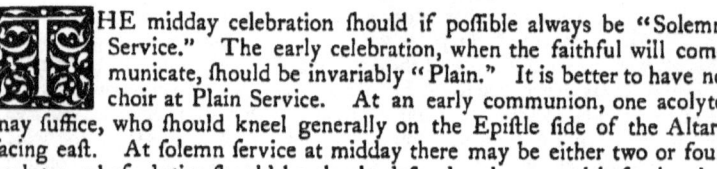HE midday celebration should if possible always be "Solemn Service." The early celebration, when the faithful will communicate, should be invariably "Plain." It is better to have no choir at Plain Service. At an early communion, one acolyte may suffice, who should kneel generally on the Epistle side of the Altar, facing east. At solemn service at midday there may be either two or four acolytes, whose duties should be clearly defined and arranged beforehand.

CAUTELS AND DIRECTIONS.

81. *Cautels of the Mass*—§ *Here follow Directions and Cautels to be observed by the Presbyter wishing to celebrate Divine Service* (Divina*).

I.

HE first Cautel is: that the Priest about to celebrate Mass shall seasonably prepare his conscience by a pure confession, (or) that he shall greatly desire that Sacrament and intend to confess. That he shall know by heart and well the order of performing the function. That his actions be very self-possessed and reverent. Whoever loves GOD loves Him with all his heart, with all his soul, and with all his strength. He is proved not to love GOD, who at the table of the Altar where the King of kings and LORD of all is handled and taken, appears irreligious, irreverent, indevout, unseemly, confused, wandering in his thoughts, or slothful. Therefore let each (Priest) mind that he tarries at an august table. Let him think how it behoves him to be prepared. Let him be cautious and self-possessed. Let him stand erect; not lounging on the Altar. His elbows should touch his sides. When he lifts up his

---

* The celebration of the Eucharist being *the* Divine Service of the Church.

hands, the extremities of his fingers should be just seen above his shoulders. He should suit his understanding to the signs and words, since great things are latent in signs, greater things in words, and still greater things in intention. He should join three* fingers together with which he will make the sign (of the cross); the other two he will lay together in his hand. He will make the sign directly over the chalice, not obliquely; and sufficiently high, lest he upset it. He must not make circles for crosses. When he inclines, he must not do it obliquely, but right before the Altar, and in inclining must bend his whole body.

[*The "Materies."*]

2. The second Cautel is: that he must not think, but know for certain, that he has the appointed matter (*debitas*† *materias*); this is wheaten bread, and wine (mixed) with a modicum of water. Of the wine and water he will be able to be certified after this fashion. Let him test it by his minister‡ who will taste both the wine and the water. But the Priest himself ought not to taste it.§ Let him pour a drop upon his hand, rub it with his finger, and smell it, so that he may be the more certified. He must trust neither the *mark* (*signature* ‖) upon the cruet, nor the colour of it; since both often deceive. He must see that the chalice be not broken. He must look to the wine; if it is corrupted he must in nowise celebrate; if it is sour he must in no wise pass it by. If it is too watery ¶ he must not use it, unless he knows that the wine exceeds the water. And in every case where there is a doubt either in regard to the sourness or the mixture,** or the excessive thickness of the wine, whether it can be used, we counsel the Priest not to use it: because in this Sacrament nothing must be done concerning which there is any doubt, where most explicitly (*certissime*) it is to be said; HOC EST ENIM CORPUS MEUM, *et*,

---

* This is usually the episcopal usage in blessing: a simple Priest ought more properly to bless with the whole hand.

† "Rightly and *duly* administer Thy Holy Sacraments." Prayer of Oblation.—Book of Common Prayer.

‡ Who would not communicate.

§ Because it would break his fast.

‖ Probably alluding to the letters V. and A. with which the wine and water cruets are usually marked, or to some such device.

¶ This evidently refers to the mixed chalice.

** If the Priest (or Sub-deacon at High Mass) had accidentally poured too much water into the wine in preparing the chalice.

Hic est enim calix sanguinis mei. Let him also see that he offer the oblations conveniently and that he pour out the wine discreetly, because this Sacrament ought to be appreciable by the senses, to be seen, touched, and tasted, in order that the sense may be refreshed by the *species*, and the intellect be nourished (*ex re contenta*). Also the water must be poured in the smallest possible quantity, so that it may be absorbed by the wine and receive the savour of the wine. For there is no danger, however small be the modicum of water that is mixed, but there is risk if it be much. Moreover, the water is mixed solely as a symbol, and one drop is as symbolical as a thousand. The Priest should, therefore, take heed not to pour the water with an *impetus*, lest too much should fall into the chalice.

3. The third Cautel is: to read the Canon in a lower tone (*morosius*) than the other parts of the Liturgy. And especially from the place: *Qui pridie quam pateretur accepit.* For then the Priest ought to fetch a breath and concentrate his attention, and to intend to collect his whole self (if he has not been able to do so before) upon each separate word. And whilst he shall say: *Accipite et manducate ex hoc omnes;* he shall fetch a breath and with one inspiration shall say (the words), Hoc est enim Corpus meum: so that any other train of thought shall not intermingle with them. For it seems not reasonable to interrupt a form so short, so important, and so efficacious, whose whole virtue depends on the last word, viz. meum, which is said in the person* of Christ. Wherefore a point ought not to be placed at any word whatsoever. So that by no means should it be said; Hoc est enim, Corpus meum; but should be pronounced altogether at the same time. In like manner the same rule should be observed in the consecration of the Blood. Also in pronouncing the words of consecration over any matter, the Priest should always intend to perform that which Christ instituted, and the Church does.

4. The fourth Cautel is: that if he has to consecrate more hosts (than one) he ought to elevate that one of those which he has determined upon with himself from the beginning of the Mass; and should hold it in regard to the others so that he may direct his sight and intention to all at the same time. And in signing (with the sign of the cross) and in saying: Hoc est enim Corpus meum: he should think upon all which he points at. We counsel also that the Presbyter should know the Canon by heart, in order that he may say it more devotionally; yet he should

---

* Cf. 2 Cor. ii. 10.

always have the Service Book that it may be referred to to help his memory.

5. The fifth Cautel is: that whilst he communicates he should never take the chalice at one draught,* lest by reason of the *impetus* (of the wine against his *fauces*) he should unadvisedly cough, but twice or thrice he should take It warily, that no impediment occur. But if he must take more Hosts than one, as when the Host is renewed, let him first take that which he has used as the Priest's Host (*confecit*) and (also) the Blood; after them the others which remain. He should take his own (Host) before the others, because of his own he believes and has knowledge,† (that the matter is without defect), of the others he indeed believes, but has not certain knowledge. After that the Ablutions, and not before.

6. The sixth Cautel is: that he burdens himself with names of few‡ in the Canon; not always, but when he wishes it he may make mention of them, when he wishes he may omit them, because the Canon is made prolix by a multitude of names, and hence thought is distracted. Yet it is honourable that father, mother, brother and sister should there be named; and specially those in whose behalf the Mass is celebrated. Not, however, that the expression thereof should be vocal, but mental.

7. The seventh Cautel is: that before Mass the Priest do not wash his mouth or teeth, but only his lips from without with his mouth closed as he has need, lest perchance he should intermingle the taste of water with his saliva. After Mass also he should beware of expectorations as much as possible, until he shall have eaten and drunken, lest by chance anything shall have remained between his teeth or in his *fauces*, which by expectorating he might eject. But though a Mass be most devoutly celebrated when an opportunity for contemplation is afforded, yet a measure is to be kept therein, that a man be not notable either for prolixity or haste; for haste is a sign of carelessness; prolixity is an occasion of distraction. The middle course will be safest. But each Mass is to be said by each Priest

---

* This, of course, is inapplicable to us—the privilege of communion in both kinds being invariably restored to all who communicate.

† The Priest, through the *medium* of his minister, would have tested the Priest's own breads by eating one or two of the wafers made at the same batch—besides the hosts intended for the Priest were probably made under his own eye, if not actually with his own hands, as the Cautels evidently imply. See "On the Celebration of the Holy Eucharist," pp. 5—7, a paper reprinted from the *Ecclesiastic*.

‡ The names of those his piety may prompt him to commemorate whether living or dead. All long pauses and prolixity of every kind should be carefully eschewed.

with difpofition, as if it were the firft he was to fay, and never was to be repeated, for fo great a gift ought always to be new. Therefore let the Prieft have diligence in performing It; reverence in handling It; and devotion in taking It. So will the Sacrament be worthily treated in thought and action; the office will be performed rightly, and dangers and fcandals avoided. Alfo in faying the collects the Prieft fhould obferve always to fay an unequal number. One collect on account of the Unity of the Godhead. Three on account of the Trinity of Perfons. Five on account of the five-fold Paffion of CHRIST. Seven on account of the feven-fold grace of the HOLY GHOST. It is not lawful to exceed the number feven. Alfo; when a collect is directed folely to the FATHER, at the clofe fhall be faid: "*through our* LORD JESUS CHRIST." But if it is directed to the FATHER and mention is made of the SON in the fame collect, at the clofe fhall be faid: "*through the fame our* LORD JESUS CHRIST." But if the collect is directed folely to the SON, at the clofe fhall be faid: "*Who with the* FATHER *and the* HOLY GHOST, &c." And if mention be made of the HOLY SPIRIT in any collect, at the clofe fhall be faid: "*of the fame* HOLY SPIRIT, GOD *for ever and ever.* Amen."

82. ¶ *Here begin Cautels to be obferved, as to what is to be done in regard to defect, or accident, which may poffibly arife in the Mafs, and efpecially in regard to the confecration of the Eucharift.*

Firft what is to be done if a Prieft faints.

IF a Prieft faints or dies before the Canon, it is not neceffary for another Prieft to complete* the mafs. If, however, another Prieft is willing to celebrate, he ought to recommence the Mafs from the beginning, and go through the whole rightly.
But if he faints in the Canon,† fome actions having been already performed, yet before the tranfubftantiation and confecration of the Sacrament, then another Prieft ought to recommence from the place where he left off and to fupply juft fo much as is omitted.

---

* Before the Prayer for the Church Militant in our Service Book when the oblations are made.
† In our Service Book—from the Prayer for the Church Militant inclufive to the Prayer of Confecration exclufive.

But if a Prieſt faints in the act of confecration,* ſome words being already ſaid in part, but not altogether completed, according to Innocent, another Prieſt ought to begin from the place, *qui pridie*.

But if a Prieſt faints when the Body is confecrated, but not the Blood, another Prieſt may complete the confecration of the Blood, beginning from the place, *ſimili modo*. If after the confecration of the Body, the Prieſt perceive there is no wine in the chalice, the Hoſt ought to be directly replaced upon the corporal, and when the chalice is rightly prepared, he will begin from the place, *ſimili modo*.

If before the confecration of the Blood he perceive there is no water in the chalice,† he ought forthwith to put ſome in, and go on with the function.

But if after the confecration of the Blood he perceive that water is wanting in the chalice, he ought neverthelefs to proceed; he ought not to mix water with the Blood, becauſe in part would follow the corrupting of the Sacrament: but the Prieſt ought to grieve and to be puniſhed.

If after the confecration of the Blood he perceive that no wine, but only water, has been put into the chalice, if indeed he perceive this before communicating of the Body, he ought to put out the water,‡ and to put in wine with water, and to refume the confecration of the Blood from the place, *ſimili modo*.

If he perceive this after taking of the Body, he ought to take another hoſt *de novo*, again to be confecrated with the Blood, according to the doctors in the ſacred page;§ but he ought to refume the words of confecration from the place, *qui pridie*. But in the end he ought again to take the Hoſt laſt confecrated, and it muſt not hinder him if he has before taken the water and even the Blood.‖ Innocent, however, faith, that if the Prieſt fear ſcandal from prolixity, thoſe words ſhall ſuffice by which the Blood is confecrated, ſc. *Simili modo, &c.* and ſo to take the Blood.

But the queſtion ariſes, if after having communicated of the Body, he

---

* In our rite—either during the confecration *proper*, viz. *the words of confecration*, or during the firſt part of the Prayer of Confecration.

† i. e. *recollect* that the chalice had not been prepared; he could not tell the abſence of a few drops of water by his viſion.

‡ By giving it to the Deacon, who hands it to the Sub-deacon to empty into the piſcina at ſolemn Service; or by emptying it himſelf at low Service.

§ The decrees of Councils and written opinions of doctors and canoniſts.

‖ It is not clear how he could have taken the *Blood* in the caſe contemplated, without he communicated himſelf of the chalice before taking the ſecond Hoſt.

shall have the water already in his mouth, and shall then for the first time perceive that it is water—whether he ought to swallow it or to eject it. Refer *in summa Hostiensis in titulo de celebr. missa.* It is, however, safer to swallow than to eject it; and for this reason, that no particle of the Body may be ejected with the water.

Also: if the Priest after the consecration call to mind that he is not fasting, or has committed some sin, or is excommunicated, he ought, nevertheless, to proceed, with the determination to make satisfaction and to seek absolution.

But if he call to mind any of the aforesaid, before consecration, it is safer to leave off a begun Mass and to seek absolution, unless a grave scandal should thence arise.

Also: if a fly or spider or any such thing should fall into the chalice before consecration, or even if he shall apprehend that poison hath been put in, the wine which is in the chalice ought to be poured out, and the chalice ought to be washed, and other wine with water put therein to be consecrated. But if any of these (contingencies) befall after the consecration, the fly or spider or such-like thing should be warily taken,* oftentimes diligently washed between the fingers, and should then be burnt,† and the ablution, together with the burnt ashes, must be put in the piscina. But the poison ought, by no means, to be taken, but such Blood, with which poison has been mingled, should be reserved in a comely vessel, together with the relics. And that the Sacrament do not remain imperfect, the Priest ought to prepare rightly a chalice *de novo,* and resume the consecration from the place, *simili modo.* And note that according to the doctors, nothing abominable ought to be taken by reason of this Sacrament.

Also: if the Priest does not recollect that he has said some of those things which he ought to have said, he should not be troubled in his mind; for he who says many (prayers) does not always remember which he has said. If even he knows for certain that he has left out some, if they be such as are not necessary to the validity of the Sacrament, such as the *secretæ,* or some words of the Canon, let him go on, and not begin anything over again. If, however, he is convinced of the probability of his

---

* Scil. with a perforated spoon—there should always be one on the credence.

† The Sub-deacon should be sent for a *covered* chalice, he will pour a little water in, and also over the Priest's fingers. The Priest will leave the fly or such-like thing and spoon with the ablutions in the chalice; the Sub-deacon will cover the chalice, and place it on the credence. After service the insect must be burnt and the ashes and ablutions thrown down the piscina.

having omitted fomething which is neceffary to the Sacrament, as the form of words by which it is confecrated, he ought to fay again all the words of confecration over the matter (*materiam*—the technical theological term for the elements), becaufe there has been no confecration. It does not, however, fignify if the conjunction *enim* has been omitted, or other words which go before or follow after the form, (viz. the words of confecration), for they are not of the fubftance of the Sacrament itfelf.

But if the Prieft doubt whether or no he hath left out fome word pertaining to the fubftance of the form, by no means ought he to ufe any conditional form; but without rafh affertion he ought to refume the whole form (of confecration proper) over each matter (viz. the elements of bread and wine), with this intention: that if confecration hath taken place, by no means doth he wifh to confecrate; but if confecration hath not taken place, he wifhes to confecrate the Body and Blood.

Alfo: if during the time of confecration, any diftraction fhould occur from his actual* intention and devotion, neverthelefs he muft ftill proceed with the confecration; whilft habitual intention remains in him; for the great High Prieft, CHRIST, will fupply the defect of His Prieft.

But if in too much diftraction, his habitual intention be withdrawn as well as his actual intention, it feems he ought to refume the words of confecration with actual intention, with this provifo, that he is unwilling to confecrate, if confecration has taken place.

Alfo: if the confecrated Hoft on account of cold, or any other caufe, flips from the Prieft's (hands) into the chalice, whether before or after the dividing of It; he ought not to take It out of the Blood, nor to reiterate anything by reafon of this, or to change aught concerning the celebration of the Sacrament; but he muft proceed in making the fign of the crofs and in other matters, as if he held It in his hands.

If the Eucharift hath fallen to the ground, the place where It lay muft be fcraped, and fire kindled thereon, and the afhes referved befide the altar.†

¶ Alfo: if by negligence any of the Blood be fpilled, upon a table‡ fixed to the floor, the Prieft muft take up the drop with his tongue, and the place of the table muft be fcraped, and the fhavings burnt with fire,

---

* "Habitual intention" is the frame of mind which has a general and pervading intention to do what CHRIST did, and fo fulfil the mind of the Church—"actual intention" is the *confcioufnefs* of "habitual intention" directed to a particular action or thing.

† In a fimilar cafe we fhould put the afhes down the pifcina.

‡ Either the credence, or any fixed table, ledge, or ftand.

and the ashes reserved with the relics beside the altar, and he to whom this has befallen must do penance forty days.

But if the chalice have dropped upon the altar, the drop must be sucked up, and the Priest must do penance for three days.

But if the drop have penetrated through the linen cloth to the second linen cloth, he must do penance for four days. If to the third, nine days. If the drop of Blood have penetrated to the fourth cloth, he must do penance for twenty days, and the Priest, or the Deacon, must wash the linen coverings* which the drop has touched three times, over a chalice, and the ablution is to be reserved with the relics.

Also: if any one by any accident of the throat vomit up the Eucharist, the vomit ought to be burned, and the ashes ought to be reserved near the altar. And if it shall be a cleric, monk, presbyter, or deacon, he must do penance for forty days, a bishop seventy days, a laic thirty.

But if he vomits from infirmity, he must do penance for five days.

But who does not keep the Sacrament well,† so that a mouse or other animal devoured It, he must do penance forty days.

But whoever hath lost It, or if part thereof hath fallen and cannot be found, he must do penance thirty days. That Priest is worthy of the same penance by whose negligence the consecrated Hosts have become corrupted. But during the aforesaid days the penitent ought to fast, and to abstain from communion and celebration. However when the circumstances of the fault and person have been weighed, the aforesaid penance can be diminished or increased according to the judgment of a discreet confessor. But this is to be observed, that wherever the *species*‡ of the Sacrament are found in their integrity, they are severally to be consumed: but if this cannot be done without risk, they are still to be reserved for relics.

Also: if a Host, or part of a Host be discovered under the pall§ or under the corporal, and there is a doubt whether or no it is consecrated, (the Priest) ought reverently to consume it after the taking of the Blood, as you will find more fully set down *in titulo de celebratione missarum.*

Also: in respect to the matter of the Blood see that it be not home-

---

* The *parts* of the linen coverings which the Sacrament has touched are to be washed over a chalice three times with fresh water each time, the ablutions to be poured down the piscina.

† Viz. the reserved Sacrament.

‡ The "form" or outward part of the Sacrament.

§ This probably does not refer to the fourth linen cloth, which was dyed purple and called the pall (see "Church of our Fathers," vol. i. p. 266), but is most likely used in a general sense—meaning any of the altar-cloths, or chalice-veils, &c.

made, or wine so weak, that by no means it hath the nature (*species*) of wine. It muſt not be water red from being ſtrained through a cloth which has been ſteeped in red wine. It muſt not be vinegar, or wine at all corrupted; nor muſt it be claret* (*claretum*), or wine made of mulberries or pomegranates† (*malogranates*); becauſe they retain not the nature (*species*) of wine.

He who performs the function with wine that is on the way to corruption, or having a tendency to corruption, ſins very grievouſly (ſhould he uſe ſuch wine) ſince it retains not the nature (*species*) of wine.

Alſo: care muſt be taken, that only a modicum of water be put (into the wine), becauſe if ſo much is put in as to take away the *species* of wine, it muſt not be uſed.

Alſo: if anything be wanting here, it muſt be looked for *in ſumma et lectura Hoſtien. in titul. de celebr. miſſarum.*

ADDITIONAL NOTES AND DIRECTIONS.

83. *Manner of Turning and Poſition of Hands.*

WHEN the Celebrant turns towards the people he turns from the left to the right.

When the hands are "joined," the palms face each other, and the tips of the fingers touch, the right thumb is placed over the left in the form of a croſs.

When the hands are "elevated," they are raiſed apart, equal to the height of the ſhoulders, palm oppoſite to palm.

---

* " Wine mixed with honey and ſpices, and afterwards ſtrained till it is *clear*. It was otherwiſe called *Piment;* as appears from the title of the following receipt, in the Medulla Cirugiæ Rolandi. MS. Bod. 761. fol. 86: '*Claretum bonum, ſive pigmentum*—Accipe *nucem moſchatam, cariofilos, gingebas, macis, cinnamonum, galangum;* quæ omnia in pulverem reducta diſtempera *cum bono vino cum tertia parte mellis:* poſt *cola per facculum*, et da ad bibendum. Et nota, quod illud idem poteſt fieri de *cereviſia.*' And ſo in R. 5957. *Clarré* is the tranſlation of *Piment.* Orig. 11450."—Gloſſary to Tyrwhitt's Chaucer, London, Moxon, 1843.

† Or a wine made from apples—perhaps cider.

84. *Normal Position of Priest, Deacon, and Sub-deacon.*

HE normal attitude of Celebrant, Deacon, and Sub-deacon, (viz. Gospeller and Epistoler*) is standing. During the collects, the Deacon stands immediately behind † the Celebrant, and the Sub-deacon behind him again. They should occupy the same position at the intonation of the Creed and *Gloria*, and during the Preface; passing, the Deacon to the right, and the Sub-deacon to the left of the Celebrant, at the Sanctus, and when the choir begin the Creed and *Gloria*. The Confession (see Par. 29) should never be sung by the choir nor joined in by the people. It should be said by the Deacon *alone*, "in the name" of the communicants, the Priest remaining standing facing the east. At the Canon,‡ the Celebrant of course stands, the Deacon and Sub-deacon kneel after first consecration, 'until after the second. At the Post-communion the Priest, Deacon and Sub-deacon should again stand one behind the other.

85. *The Vestments of the First Book of Edward VI.*

" Upon the day, and at the time appointed for the ministration of the Holy Communion, the Priest that shall execute the holy ministry shall put upon him the vestment appointed for that ministration, that is to say: a white alb, plain, with a vestment or cope. And where there be many Priests or Deacons, there so many shall be ready to help the Priest in the ministration as shall be requisite; and shall have upon them likewise the vestures appointed for their ministry, that is to say, albs with tunicles.

" Upon Wednesdays and Fridays the English Litany shall be said or sung in all places, after such form as is appointed by the King's Majesty's injunctions; or as is or shall be otherwise appointed by his highness. And though there be none to communicate with the Priest, yet these days (after the Litany ended) the Priest shall put upon him a plain alb or surplice with a cope, and say all things at the Altar (appointed to be said at the celebration of the LORD's Supper,) until after the offertory. And then shall add one or two of the Collects aforewritten, as occasion shall serve, by his discretion. And then turning him to the people shall let them depart with the accustomed blessing.

---

* Perhaps the phrase "Epistoler and Gospeller" has caused more ritual anomalies than any other, by leading persons ignorant of Catholic tradition to limit the functions of clergy discharging those offices to reading the Epistle and Gospel. Whereas it is the Gospeller's function to assist the Priest, and the Epistoler's function to assist the Gospeller.

† It is better for the Deacon to stand a *little* towards the right of the Priest, and the Sub-deacon a little towards the right of the Deacon, an arrangement which obtains frequently in the modern West. The Collect in the Roman Liturgy is said at the Epistle side of the Altar, and the position of Deacon and Sub-deacon is consequently different.

‡ If the Celebrant kneels after the consecration of each Species, as it is ordered in the Roman rite, the Deacon kneels and rises with him; the sub-deacon should kneel after the first, and *remain kneeling* until after the second consecration.

"And whenfoever the Bifhop fhall celebrate the Holy Communion in the church, or execute any other public miniftration, he fhall have upon him, befides his rochette, a furplice or alb, and a cope or veftment, and alfo his paftoral ftaff in his hand, or elfe borne or holden by his chaplain."—Rubric in "The Supper of the Lord, and Holy Communion; commonly called, The Mafs."

ROM a comparifon of the above rubric it would appear, that whenever the Holy Communion was celebrated, the Prieft* who celebrated was to wear an alb with a veftment (i.e. a chafuble), and his affiftants albs with tunicles; but that when no celebration took place, i.e. on Good Friday only, (if we would follow Catholic ufage both in Eaft and Weft,) the Prieft was at liberty to wear a furplice, and that inftead of the veftment he was then to wear a cope.

The Firft Book of Common Prayer, which did not come into ufe till the third year of Edward VI, ought not to have any authority with us as to limiting the Ornaments of the fecond year of Edward. And it would in reality, if it defined the Ornaments of the Celebrant, make but one unimportant difference, viz. that the alb fhould be white and "plain," that is, not without apparels, but of white colour and not enriched with embroidery; the "apparels" are not of courfe part of the alb, but fupplemental ornaments removable at pleafure, whilft amice, ftole, and maniple would be included under the term "veftment," which included thefe appendages of the Prieft's ornaments as well as the chafuble.

86. *Arrangement of Veftments for Solemn Service by a Bifhop in his own Dioceſe.*

N the centre of the Altar, (if the Bifhop do not veft in the facrifty), the epifcopal veftments fhould be placed in the following order: chafuble, dalmatic, tunic, cope (extended), ftole,† girdle, alb, amice, and the gloves on a filver falver; the whole will be covered with the gremial veil. At the Gofpel corner will be placed the coftly mitre,‡ and at the Epiftle corner the plain one, each on its ftand.

---

* As we have the funčtion (though not the order) of fub-deacon difcharged by the Epiftoler, it is defirable to ufe the more ancient defignation.

† The Bifhop's maniple is ufually enclofed in the fervice book in the place of the Gofpel for the day.

‡ The Ribbons are to hang over the antependium. When the Deacon carries the mitre to the Bifhop, he will be careful to let the ribbons fall towards *himfelf*.

The Order of Administration. 95

An antependium, of more than ordinary costliness, should be used.

When the Eucharistic is not preceded by the ordinary Office, the cope will not be required.

A stand for the pastoral staff should be ready, if needed.

87. *The Gremial.*

THE gremial* is a silken apron placed upon the Bishop's lap whenever he sits down in the intervals of the celebration of Holy Communion. An assistant Deacon attends to the placing and replacing the gremial on the lap of the Bishop as required; it is also used for covering the episcopal vestments when placed upon the Altar. See Par. 86.

88. *The Rochet.*

" And whensoever the Bishop shall celebrate the Holy Communion in the Church, or execute any other public ministration, he shall have upon him, besides his Rochette, a surplice or alb, and a cope or vestment, and also his pastoral staff in his hand, or else borne or holden by his chaplain."—Rubric in First Book of Ed. VI.

THE rochet† is a fine linen vestment reaching a little beyond the knees, and with tight sleeves. It is worn under the alb or surplice. It is, in fact, a diminution of the alb.

The costly mitre is used till the Creed, after which the plain mitre is used; after the Offertory the costly mitre is re-assumed, and is used for the rest of the service.

The mitre is removed at the Collects, the Gospel, and during the Credo, and is not resumed till the Absolution, after which it is again taken off, and not used till the final benediction.[1] It is then removed, and at the end of the purifications and ablutions, the Bishop receives it again, and after bowing to the Altar proceeds to the faldstool to take off the sacred vestments.

* The gremial should be three feet long and two feet broad, and should have a border embroidered with gold or silver.

† The rochet is also worn under the chimere.[2] There is however no authority either for its great length or large lawn sleeves.

---

[1] The mitre is not worn during the *Gloria in excelsis Deo*, as in the Roman Rite, in which at the latter part of the *Gloria* the Bishop sits and assumes the mitre which he had laid aside at its beginning. The position of the Angelic Hymn in the English Liturgy gives it another phase, so to speak, to that which it shows in the Rite of S. Peter, and hence the different use.

[2] The chimere is properly a kind of cope with apertures for the arms to pass through. A scarlet one is used in Convocation, and when the sovereign attends Parliament; on ordinary occasions a black satin one is used.

89. *Arrangement of Vestments where there is no Sacristy.*

HE Celebrant, when not a Bishop, vests of course in the sacristy. A Priest may not receive his vestments from the Altar; where there is no sacristy that he may use, he should receive them from a table in the sanctuary.

90. *Altar Lights and other Candles.*

HE candles should be always of pure white wax, those of sperm, composition, or other substance, not being permitted. Oil lamps may be used in extreme scarcity.
Candles of *unbleached* wax should be used *de missis de requiem*, and at Evensong on Wednesday in Holy Week, and during all the services of Maundy Thursday and Good Friday.

91. *The Washing of Corporals.**

AS the corporal is the linen cloth on which has been laid the LORD's Body, the Church orders the washing of it with a minute and pious care.†

---

* The corporal may not be touched after use by laics without especial permission, nor must it ever be washed after use in domestic vessels, until it has been first washed by a clerk in Holy Orders, when it may be touched by laics again. Those corporals which have been employed at the Altar should be left in the burses, and not be taken out and put away in drawers.

† The following was the practice of the mediæval English Church. A favourable time of year should be chosen for this purpose, either the pure air of spring or after the middle of September, when the flies are less troublesome than in summer. Special vessels should be kept for this reverent custom. After Evensong the corporals should be immersed, in the church, in cold water, twice, and rubbed in the hands; and both waters should be poured into the *piscina* over which the chalice is washed: fresh water should then be poured upon them the third time, in which they are to remain all night; and in the morning that water also should be poured into the same *piscina*. They may then be carried from the church, and regularly washed (see the Consuetudines of Udalricus). According to a gloss of Lyndewolde on a Constitution of Archbishop Walter, the use of starch in corporals is forbidden, *at least once*. But the prohibition is merely an interpretation of the Decretum, "Non in serico panno, sed *puro linteo* sacrificium consecretur altaris."

The Calendar.

92. *A Table of all the Feasts that are to be observed in the Church of England throughout the Year.*

All Sundays in the Year.

The Days of the Feasts of
- The Circumcision of our LORD JESUS CHRIST.
- The Epiphany.
- The Conversion of S. *Paul*.
- The Purification of the Blessed Virgin.
- S. *Matthias* the Apostle.
- The Annunciation of the Blessed Virgin.
- S. *Mark* the Evangelist.
- S. *Philip* and S. *Jacob* the Apostles.
- The Ascension of our LORD JESUS CHRIST.
- S. *Barnabas*.
- The Nativity of S. *John Baptist*.

The Days of the Feasts of
- S. *Peter* the Apostle.
- S. *James* the Apostle.
- S. *Bartholomew* the Apostle.
- S. *Matthew* the Apostle.
- S. *Michael* and all Angels.
- S. *Luke* the Evangelist.
- S. *Simon* and S. *Jude* the Apostles.
- All Saints.
- S. *Andrew* the Apostle.
- S. *Thomas* the Apostle.
- The NATIVITY of our LORD
- S. *Stephen* the Martyr.
- S. *John* the Evangelist.
- The Holy Innocents.

Monday and *Tuesday* in *Easter Week*.
Monday and *Tuesday* in *Whitsun Week*.

93.

TO the above Table of all the Feasts that are to be observed in the Church of England through the year, must be added the solemnity of the Feast of Dedication of every parish Church, and of the saint to whom such church is dedicated.

The Feast* of Dedication was originally celebrated on the very day of dedication as it annually occurred, and was afterwards transferred to some other day, especially Sunday. By an Act of Convocation passed in the reign of Henry VIII, A.D. 1536,—never legalized however—the Feast of the Dedication of every church is ordered to be kept on one and the self-same day, viz. the first Sunday in October; and the Church holyday,—

---

* The Sunday within the Octave should be always observed with as great devotion as the feast itself.

that is, the feſtival of the Saint to whom the church is dedicated,—is wholly laid aſide.

In regard to the church holyday, it is obvious that when the church is dedicated to GOD in honour of a ſaint in the Engliſh Calendar whoſe Feſtival is on the " Table of *all* the Feaſts that are to be obſerved through the year," the feaſt ſhould be kept on the feſtival of ſuch ſaint.

Tradition, cuſtom, and the tacit ſanction of eccleſiaſtical authorities allow the commemoration of other Holy and Saints' days than thoſe in the calendar of our preſent Prayer Book. The various dioceſan calendars, the official almanacks of the Stationers' Company, the Churchman's Diary, the Oxford and Cambridge Calendars, the Calendar of the Engliſh Church, the Calendar of the Prayer Book of the Scottiſh Church, the Union Review Almanack, and others contain, amongſt others, the following Commemorations :—S. David, S. Antony, S. Polycarp, S. John Chryſoſtom, S. Dorothea, S. Scholaſtica, S. Colman, S. Mildred, Shrove Tueſday, S. Gabriel, S. Patrick, S. Cuthbert, S. Serf, S. Anſelm, S. Athanaſius, S. Gregory Nazianzum, S. Pancras, S. Columba, S. Baſil, S. Cyriacus, S. Palladius, Tranſlation of S. Thomas of Canterbury, Invention of S. Stephen, Aſſumption B. V. M., S. Bernard, S. Louis, S. Aidan, S. Ninian, S. Adamnân, SS. Coſmas and Damian, S. Wilfrid, S. Frideſwide, All Souls', S. Winifred, S. Margaret, S. Edmund of Canterbury, Preſentation B. V. M., S. Ode, S. Eligius, S. Oſmund, S. Droſtane and S. Thomas of Canterbury.

The feaſt of Corpus Chriſti—kept on the Thurſday after Trinity Sunday—a feſtival obſerved throughout the entire Weſtern Church, as it was formerly in England, is being reſtored very generally amongſt us. Being in honour of our Bleſſed Saviour Himſelf, and in remembrance of His undying love to mankind, all who duly reverence and obey Him will ſee the great propriety and fitneſs of its obſervance. The church and altar ſhould be decorated as for a feaſt of the firſt claſs. White is the colour for the veſtments of the clergy and altar. Proceſſions ſhould be made and ſpecial hymns ſung, e. g. the *Pange Lingua*, *Lauda Sion*, &c. and Sermons delivered in honour of the Preſence of our LORD in the Bleſſed Sacrament.

The Calendar. 99

94. *The Minor Festivals of the Church; commonly called "The Black Letter Saints' Days."* *

S. Lucian, Pr. and M.
S. Hilary, Bp. and Conf.
S. Prisca, Rom. V. and M.
S. Fabian, Bp. of Rome and M.
S. Agnes, Rom. V. and M.
S. Vincent, Span. Deac. and M.
S. Blasius, an Armenian Bp. and M.
S. Agatha, a Sicilian V. and M.
S. Valentine, Bp. and M.
S. David, Abp. of Menevia or S. David's.
S. Cedde, or Chad, Bp. of Litchfield.
S. Perpetua, Mauritan. M.
S. Gregory, M., Bp. of Rome and C.
S. Edward, King of the West Saxons.
S. Benedict, Abbot.
S. Richard, Bishop of Chichester.
S. Ambrose, Bishop of Milan.
S. Alphege, Abp. of Canterbury.
S. George, M.
Invention of the Holy Cross.
S. John, ante Port. Lat.
S. Dunstan, Abp. of Canterbury.
S. Augustine, first Abp. of Canterbury.
Ven. Bede, Pr.
S. Nicomede, Rom. Pr. and M.
S. Boniface, Bp. of Mentz and M.
S. Alban, M.
Translation of King Edward.
Visitation of B. V. M.
Translation of S. Martin, B. and C.
S. Swithun, Bp. Winchester, Transf.
S. Margaret, V. and M. at Antioch.
S. Mary Magdalen.
S. Anne, Mother of B. V. M.

Lammas Day.
Transfiguration of our LORD.
Holy Name of JESUS.
S. Lawrence, Archdeacon of Rome and M.
S. Augustin, Bp. of Hippo, C. D.
Beheading of S. John Baptist.
S. Giles, Abbot and Conf.
S. Enurchus, Bp. of Orleans.
Nativity of B. V. M.
Holy Cross Day.
S. Lambert, Bp. and M.
S. Cyprian, Abp. of Carth. and M.
S. Jerome, Pr., Conf. and Doct.
S. Remigius, Bp. of Rheims.
S. Faith, V. and M.
S. Denys, Areopagite, Bp. and M.
Translation of King Edward the Confessor.
S. Etheldreda, V. and Queen.
S. Crispin, M.
S. Leonard, Conf.
S. Martin, Bp. and Conf.
S. Britius, Bp.
S. Machutus, Bp.
S. Hugh, Bp. of Lincoln.
S. Edmund, King and Martyr.
S. Cecilia, V. and M.
S. Clement, first Bp. of Rome and M.
S. Catharine, V.
S. Nicolas, Bp. of Myra in Lycia.
Conception of B. V. M.
S. Lucy, V. and M.
O Sapientia.†
S. Silvester, Bp. of Rome.

---

* "Sixty-six in number: 16 are of Eastern origin, 17 are British, 15 French, 2 African, 1 Spanish, 16 Italian or Sicilian. Of these 31 commemorate persons or events before the first General Council in 325; 19 belong to the interval between the 1st and 6th Council in 680; 7 between that date and the schism between East and West in the 9th century, and 10 belong to the period subsequent to that Division. Those of S. George, Lammas Day, S. Lawrence, and S. Clement were restored to the Calendar in Queen Elizabeth's reign."—Note in Churchman's Diary.

† This is not a festival, but a note to remind the faithful that certain antiphons begin to be used.

THESE festal commemorations are "to be observed," and the minister should declare unto the people the days on which they are to be observed. See p. 43, Par. 22, note (*). As in the case of Vigils* and Rogation Days the black letter feast days have no proper services provided for them, yet when it is remembered that the Second Book of Homilies contains one "for the days of Rogation Week," it is well to give a short discourse upon the teaching of the minor holy-days of the Church, in order that the faithful may learn the due obligation thereof. Special Hymns may be used. The altar should be properly vested, and processions made on these minor festivals.

95. *A Table of the Vigils, Fasts, and Days of Abstinence, to be observed in the Year.*

| The Eves or Vigils before | The Nativity of our LORD.
The Purification of the Blessed Virgin *Mary*.
The Annunciation of the Blessed Virgin.
Easter Day.
Ascension Day.
Pentecost.
Saint Matthias. | The Eves or Vigils before | *Saint John* Baptist.
Saint Peter.
Saint James.
Saint Bartholomew.
Saint Matthew.
Saint Simon and *Saint Jude*.
Saint Andrew.
Saint Thomas.
All Saints. |

NOTE, that if any of these Feast-days fall upon a *Monday*, then the Vigil or Fast-day shall be kept upon the *Saturday*, and not upon the *Sunday* next before it.

96.

LUKE has no Vigil probably because the Church is doubtful whether he suffered martyrdom. The eve remains.

97.

THE Feast of S. Michael and All Angels has no Vigil, because the *fasted* eve is symbolical of a state of trial through which saints pass before entering heaven, and therefore it is inapplicable to the eve of a Festival in honour of angels.†

---

* It is not perhaps strictly correct to say that vigils have no "offices" appointed for them—the collect used by anticipation is such as far as it goes. And yet when a feast falls on a Monday, the vigil is kept on the Saturday, whilst the office (= collect) is not used then, but on the Evensong of the Sunday.

† This is not equally true of the East as of the West, as a *twelve days' fast* before S. Michael and All Angels was observed in at least one portion of it.

98. *Unfasted Eves.*

HE Feasts which fall generally between Christmas and the festival of the Purification of the Blessed Virgin Mary have no vigils, simply eves, because the Church does not deem it right to multiply fast days at such a joyful season. The Feasts which fall during this period are SS. Stephen, John the Evangelist, the Holy Innocents, the Circumcision of our LORD JESUS CHRIST, the Epiphany, and the Conversion of S. Paul.

99. *Unfasted Eves.*

HE Feasts which generally fall between Easter and Whitsuntide have no vigils, simply eves, for the like reason. The feasts are those of SS. Mark the Evangelist, Philip and James the Apostles, and Barnabas the Apostle.

As exceptions to the above must be noted the Festival of the Ascension of our LORD JESUS CHRIST and Whitsun-day itself, which have Vigils. The Rogation days, the third of which falls on the Vigil of the Ascension, together with Fridays, are the only abstinence days at the above period.

100. *The Concurrence and Occurrence of Holydays.*

FESTIVALS are said to "concur" when one feast is succeeded by another feast, so that the second Evensong of the former "concurs" (viz. takes place at the same Evening Prayer) with the first Evensong of the latter. The "occurrence" of festivals is when they "occur" on the same day, in which case the inferior feast is "translated" to some unoccupied day,—for which unhappily there is no provision in our present Prayer Book,—or at least is "commemorated" by its collect.

101. *Eves or Vigils.**

"NOTE, that the Collect appointed for every Sunday, or for any Holyday that hath a Vigil or Eve, shall be said at the Evening Service next before."

OT that a vigil or eve is implied to be one and the selfsame thing, but that the collect for fast days which have of course neither vigil nor eve must not be said at Evening Service next before.

It should be remembered that fast days have *no* eves, and that festivals *have* always eves; the collect for a festival is *always* said at the evening service next before.

The day before a festival, if fasted, is called its vigil; if unfasted, its eve. If a festival which has a vigil falls on Monday, Saturday is the vigil; Sunday the eve. The Church never fasts on the LORD's Day. An eve is not a fast. It is to be noted in the above case that the collect for the festival will not be said at all on the vigil, but on the eve at the Evening Service next before. That is, not at Evensong on Saturday, but at Evensong on Sunday.

102. *Vigils, Eves, and Evensongs, use of Collects thereon.*

HE collect for a saint's day, and that alone, save in certain exceptional cases, (for which see *infra*), is to be said on its eve at first Evensong, or on its vigil, except the feast fall on a Monday, in which case Saturday is the vigil and Sunday the eve.

---

* The distinction between vigils and eves will be manifest from a consideration of the rubric for S. Stephen's Day. "Then shall follow the collect of the Nativity which shall be said continually until New Year's Eve." Thus though the Circumcision has no vigil, its eve is recognized by the Book of Common Prayer in accordance with Catholic usage, and its collect, and that alone, is to be said on that eve. Again, Christmas Day has a vigil, but if it falls on a Monday, the rubric upon vigils commands the vigil to be kept on the Saturday preceding. In which case, if vigil and eve be the same thing, the Collect for the Fourth Sunday in Advent must be said at the Evening Service on Saturday without the First, thus violating the rubric which orders "this collect is to be repeated every day with the other collects in Advent until Christmas Eve." If however we take Christmas Eve to be the first evensong of the Nativity, that is, the Evening Service next before, the matter is quite plain, the order of collects varies as follows:

Vigil of Christmas.—At Evensong, Saturday Service coll. (1) 4th Sund. in Advent, (2) Advent.

Eve of Christmas.—At Evensong, Sunday Service, collect for Christmas.

Thus if the Feaſt of the Nativity fall on a Monday, Saturday in compliance with the rubric, or note to the Table of Vigils, will be the vigil or faſt day—the Church never faſting on the LORD's Day—and Sunday the eve. The collect of the Nativity will therefore not be ſaid at all on the vigil, but that of the fourth Sunday in Advent and firſt at Evenſong. On the Evenſong of Sunday, being the firſt Evenſong of the Nativity, that is, the Evening Service next before, the collect of the Nativity is alone ſaid, the Sunday is not to be commemorated.

103. *General Rule for uſing Collects of Firſt Evenſong.*

THE collect for the feſtival, and that alone, is to be ſaid at the Evening Service next before, whether it be that of a vigil or eve.*

104. *Concurrence of Firſt and Second Evenſongs of Feſtivals.*

WHEN the ſecond Evenſong of a feſtival concurs with the firſt Evenſong of a commencing feſtival, the proper uſe of collects on ſuch Evenſong will be (1) collect for the office of the morrow, (2) collect for the day.

Thus, the collect of firſt Evenſong takes precedence on concurrence of firſt and ſecond Evenſongs of the feſtivals.

The Feaſts of SS. Stephen, John, and Holy Innocents have *no* firſt Evenſongs. Hence the collects ſhould be ſaid thus:—at ſecond Evenſong of Chriſtmas, (1) Chriſtmas Day, (2) S. Stephen, as *memorial*. Of courſe at Matins of S. Stephen, (1) S. Stephen, (2) Chriſtmas. The ſame order of collects obtains at Holy Communion. At Evenſong on the 26th of December, (1) S. Stephen, (2) Nativity, (3) S. John, as *memorial*. At Matins of 27th, (1) S. John, (2) Nativity. At Evenſong of 27th, (1) S. John, (2) Nativity, (3) Holy Innocents, as *memorial*. At Matins, Holy Communion, and Evenſong of 28th, (1) Holy Innocents, (2) Nativity.

* All holydays have eves or vigils, except faſts, in which caſe the collect is not to be ſaid at Evening Service next before.

105. *Occurrence of Eves.*

WHEN a faint's day falls for inftance on a Sunday, the collects of both feftivals muft be ufed upon the Evening Service next before. The faint's day collect firft, becaufe the faint's day takes precedence of the Sunday, and that of the Sunday after it as a *commemoration.*

106. *Cafes in which the Sunday Collect is added as a memorial to that of the Saints' Day, though it be otherwife ordered.*

IN "the Order how the reft of Holy Scripture is appointed to be read," occurs the following note:
"The Collect, Epiftle, and Gofpel, appointed for the Sunday fhall ferve all the week after, where it is not in this book otherwife ordered."

When a faint's day falls on any day except Sunday, *it is otherwife ordered;* and therefore the Sunday collect ought not to be repeated after the collect for the faint's day, either on the feftival or the Evenfong of its eve or vigil.

Two firft collects are never faid, one after the other, except on the Occurrence of Holy Days, or on the Concurrence of fecond and firft Evenfongs, or that of a faint's day and Sunday, when the latter is faid on the eve and feftival in *commemoration* only, not as forming part of fervice of the day, and alfo during the Octaves of Chriftmas, Eafter, and Pentecoft.

107. *Occurrence of Holydays, Memorial Collect.*

WHEN a feaft day falls upon a Sunday it was ordered in the fervice of Sarum, our legitimate guide in cafes not treated of in our prefent rubric, that the Sunday fervice fhould give way to the proper fervice ordained for the feftival, except fome peculiar Sunday only, and then the one or the other was transferred to fome day of the week following. Our Prayer Book, though filent upon the

The Calendar.

tranflation* of feftivals, evidently allows it, as of courfe the compilers intended its filence to be traditionally explained, as in the antiphonal recitation of the Pfalms and fo many other matters. But where tranflation does not obtain, and a Holyday is not transferred to fome unoccupied day, we muft by the light of the Ufe of Sarum, and the univerfal practice of the entire Weftern Church, act on an analogous principle. Our beft plan will be, according to the cuftom of the moft approved ritualifts, when two Holydays (this term includes Sundays, feafts and fafts) fall together, to obferve the fuperior Holyday, *commemorating* the inferior by the ufe of its collect.

108. *Sundays which take precedence of Saints' days.*

> The Firft Sunday in Advent.
> Fourth Sunday in Advent.
> Firft Sunday in Lent.
> Sixth Sunday in Lent.   Palm Sunday.
> Eafter Day.
> Low Sunday.
> Feaft of Pentecoft.
> Trinity Sunday.

In all other cafes the feftival fhould have precedence of the Sunday.

109. *Holydays which take precedence of other Holydays.*

> Chriftmas Day.
> Circumcifion.
> Epiphany.
> The Annunciation of our Lady.
> Afh Wednefday.
> All the days of Holy Week.
> Monday in Eafter Week.
> Tuefday in Eafter Week.
> Monday in Whitfun Week.
> Tuefday in Whitfun Week.
> Afcenfion Day.
> [Corpus Chrifti Day.]

---

* It would be very defirable if Convocation would authorize the annual publication of an *Ordo recitandi* for the tranflation of feftivals and other ritual matter.

110. *The Services of Holydays not to be mingled.*

T has been shown that when two Holy-days "occur" the only notice commonly taken of the inferior in the English Church is by the use of its collect as a memorial after that of the day; the translation of festivals not being general amongst us. And this *memorial* is to be used at Matins and Evensong, as well as in the Communion Office. The head Collects of Seasons, viz. Advent and Lent, are only used as "memorials" in the Eucharistic, *not* in the ordinary Office.*

111. *The Lessons.*

S to the Lessons, it is perfectly against all correctness and precision of ritual to use the Lessons belonging to one service, and the Epistle and Gospel belonging to another. The Lessons must always belong to the same Holyday as the Collect, Epistle, and Gospel, except on *Ferial*, that is, on ordinary week-days.

112. *Exceptions to the above Rule for the Lessons.*

HE Feast of SS. Philip and James has a *second* as well as first Lesson *at Matins*. If this festival falls on the higher one of Low Sunday, the second Morning Lesson must of necessity (there being no second Lesson for Morning Prayer in the Calendar on May 1st, though there is a second Lesson for the Ferial Evensong), be that of SS. Philip and James; but no further notice must be taken of the festival save by its memorial collect.

---

* Though this is undoubtedly the Sarum Use, yet—as many may be averse to throw away the head collects from the Daily Service, and with them the note of the season, the only one we have left, (since, unhappily, for once that the Eucharistic Service is used, the ordinary Service is used ten or a dozen times)—as a matter of edification the *retention* of the head collects in the ordinary office is strongly advised (since the rubric[1] certainly admits of it, and probably intended it), in those cases where there is not daily celebration, as where this is the case, the omission of the head collect would in some sort depenitentialise Lent and strip Advent of Advent feeling.

[1] See rubric after the collect for Ash Wednesday. The collect for the day (*de die*) is properly so called in ordering it for Matins and Evensong as well as for the Daily Eucharist.

113. *Octaves and Proper Prefaces.*

HE festivals whose Octaves are observed in the English Church by the use of Proper Prefaces for seven days after, are Christmas, Easter, Ascension and Whitsunday. The Preface for Whitsunday is ordered to be used only six days after that festival, because the seventh, viz. the Octave of Whitsunday, would be Trinity Sunday which has a Preface of its own. The two first days of the Octaves of Easter and Whitsuntide are Holydays of obligation.

It is proper during the Octave to say the service of the feast of which the Octave is kept, that is, except on such days as have their own Liturgy, viz. the three Martyr days, which occur during the Octave of the Nativity, and the Mondays and Tuesdays in those of Easter and Whitsuntide. The LORD's Day within the Octave is excepted, as it has its special Eucharistic and Dominical office. This will include the Easter Day anthems, which should be sung at Matins throughout the Octave of Easter.

114. *Days of Fasting, or Abstinence.*

I. The Forty Days of Lent.
II. The Ember Days at the Four Seasons, being the *Wednesday, Friday,* and *Saturday* after
  1. The First *Sunday* in Lent.
  2. The Feast of *Pentecost.*
  3. *September* 14.
  4. *December* 13.
III. The Three *Rogation Days,* being the *Monday, Tuesday,* and *Wednesday* before *Holy Thursday,* or the *Ascension* of our LORD.
IV. All the *Fridays* in the Year, except CHRISTMAS DAY.

AST Days, for which no special service is appointed, may be marked by the use of the collect "O GOD, Whose Nature and Property." Consequently, although the Collect for Ash Wednesday is said in the Communion Office on all the Sundays in Lent, thus giving them a *penitential character*, yet as they are still feast days, the collect "O GOD, Whose Nature, &c." need not be used. By analogy this collect will be used on vigils and not on eves.

The Prayer for those who are to be admitted into Holy Orders is to be said every day in Ember Week, and not only on the three fasting days. The rubric of the Book of Common Prayer, 1637, prepared for the

Church of Scotland by Archbiſhop Laud, is explicit on this point. "A Prayer to be ſaid in the Ember Weeks, for thoſe which are then to be admitted into Holy Orders: and is to be read every day of the week, beginning on the Sunday before the Day of Ordination."—Keeling, p. 52—58.

Some ritualiſts argue that the Ember prayer ſhould only be ſaid on the Ember days. Their argument is baſed on the circumſtance of the 31ſt Canon 160¾ calling the three faſt days which precede the Ordination Sunday, *jejunia quatuor temporum*, commonly called Ember Weeks. The word "weeks" applying to the three faſting days as a technicality, though they do not make up a whole week. The preſent rubric, however, is quite ſufficient, even without the light of the Scotch Prayer Book of Laud, to warrant the uſe of the Ember collect every day in Ember week from Sunday to Saturday incluſive. The firſt prayer might be uſed on the Sunday till Friday incluſive, the ſecond on the final Saturday: the collect "O GOD, Whoſe Nature and Property," &c. will be uſed on the Wedneſday, Friday, and Saturday.

It is incorrect to uſe the Prayer on the ſucceeding Sunday alſo. The ancient uſual day for Ordination in the Engliſh Church was Saturday.

Rogation Days* may be obſerved by the uſe of the collect "O GOD, Whoſe Nature," &c. and by reading part of the ſermon for Rogation week, to be found in the ſecond book of Homilies. Of courſe the Prieſt is at liberty to preach a ſermon of his own inſtead.

During the perambulation the 104th Pſalm, *Benedic, anima mea*, ſhould be ſung. Banners for the perambulation alluded to in Winchelſea's Conſtitution, are expreſsly named "vexilla pro rogationibus."†

It is convenient for the pariſh Prieſt to inculcate this and ſuch ſentences, as "Curſed be he which tranſlateth the bounds and doles of his neighbour," and to ſay certain prayers and collects.

Fridays may be marked by the collect "O GOD, Whoſe Nature," &c. except when Chriſtmas Day falls on a Friday, in which caſe the abſtinence being aboliſhed, it will not be ſaid.

---

* Permiſſion ſhould be gained from the Diioceſan to uſe the Litany.

† Enforced by Parliamentary authority, viz. by 25 Henry VIII, c. 19. This is "the authority of Parliament in the ſecond year of King Edward VI," as ſet forth in the rubric, regulating the ornaments of the church and of the miniſters thereof at all times of their miniſtration, which occurs before the Order for Morning Prayer daily throughout the Year. (See Gibſon's Codex, vol. i., p. 225).

The Order for Morning and Evening Prayer;

OR, MATINS AND EVENSONG.*

115.

"The Morning† and Evening Prayer shall be used in the accustomed place of the Church, Chapel, or Chancel; ‡ except it shall be otherwise determined by the Ordinary of the place. And the Chancels shall remain as they have done in times past."

"And here it is to be noted that, such Ornaments of the Church and of the Ministers thereof at all times of their ministration, shall be retained and be in

---

* The old *Matins and Lauds* are now called *Matins*; *Vespers and Compline* Evensong. So remarked Cranmer writing to Henry VIII.

The ancient rule for the East and West is, that the Holy Eucharist should never be celebrated unless Matins and Lauds, at least, had preceded.[1] "The Litany shall be said *afore High Mass* in the midst of the choir;" and rubric at end of Communion Office, First Book of Edwd. VI., "After *the Litany ended* the Priest shall . . . say all things at the Altar," &c.[2]

† *Hour of Matins.* Matins and Lauds (the Matins or Morning Prayer of the English Church) may be said or sung at any time from 12 A.M. to 12 at noon.

‡ Trullan canons (69th). "That no layman come within the Holy Chancel except the Emperor, when he comes to make his offering, according to tradition."

"We come now to speak of the Chancel Arch and the Rood Screen, two of the most important features in a church. These, as separating the Choir from the Nave, denote literally the separation of the Clergy from the Laity, but symbolically the division between the Militant and Triumphant Churches, that is to say, the Death of the Faithful. The first great symbol which sets this forth is the Triumphal Cross, the image of Him Who by His Death hath overcome Death, and has gone before His people through the valley of its shadow. The images of Saints and Martyrs appear in the lower panelling, as examples of faith and patience to us. The colours of the Rood Screen itself represent their Passion and Victory; the crimson sets forth the one, the gold the other. The curious tracery of network typifies the obscure manner in which heavenly things are set forth, while we look at them from the Church Militant."—Introductory Essay to Neale and Webb's Durandus, p. cii.

For post-Reformation authorities see "Chancel and Roodscreens" in contents of "Hierurgia Anglicana."

[1] For authorities see Freeman's "Principles of Divine Service," vol. ii. p. 116.
[2] The idea is that the praise of the Ordinary Office is a contribution to that of the Eucharistic.

ufe as were in this Church of England by the authority of Parliament, in the fecond year of the reign of King Edward VI."

HE direction that "chancels fhall remain as in times paft," implies that they fhall be feparated from the nave by a Rood-fcreen,* and that the clergy, together with all who are about to affift in the fervice, i. e. the choir, fhould have their places there, and no one elfe.

"The Ornaments of the Church and of the Minifters thereof" are fully defcribed under the heads: "The Celebration of the Holy Euchariſt," and "The Order of Adminiftration." A complete lift of furniture of the Altar, and of the facred veftments is given in the Appendix.

116.

THE Daily Office is ordered to be "fung *or* faid;" i. e. either recited mufically on a fingle note, or with the ufe of certain fimple inflections, which conftitute "Plain Song."

Public worfhip confifts of praife and prayer. The firft part of the fervice is introductory. The office of praife begins with the *Gloria Patri*, and includes the Pfalms (furnifhing topics of praife as well as Divine inftruction); Leffons, Canticles (a defcant of praife on the Leffons and on the whole economy of redemption). The remainder comprifes the Creed (which declares the object of the act of *prayer*, and has alfo an avowed relation to the firft part of the office and is, as it were, a link between the praife of the office and its interceffory function), and the office of prayer; the portion after the third collect being devoted to interceffory prayer.

---

* The Rood Screen fhould be always furmounted by a Crofs. This architectural ornament, fo diftinctively authorized by the judgment of the Privy Council, in the cafe of the Knightfbridge Churches, will of courfe everywhere be reftored.

Croffes exift in the following churches:—Ely Cathedral; SS. Peter and Paul, Worminghall, Bucks.; S. Leonard, Sunningwell, Berks.; S. Barnabas, Pimlico; S. Mark, Penfnett, Staffordfhire; S. Saviour, Leeds; Sackville College, Eaft Grinfted; S. John Baptift, Eaftnor; S. Peter, Puddleftone; S. Ethelburga, London; S. Thomas the Martyr, Oxford; S. Mary, Littlemore; S. Alban, Manchefter; Chrift Church, Clapham; S. Mary Magdalene, London; S. Mary Magdalene, Paddington; S. Andrew, Wells Street, London. This lift has no pretenfion to be a complete one.

The Order for Morning and Evening Prayer.

In the Prayers, Pſalms, and Creeds, with which the people are familiar, it is better not to make the termination *ed* a ſeparate ſyllable. In reading Holy Scripture it may be ſounded ſeparately.

117. *Veſtments for the Daily Service, or Divine Office, &c.*

*Preparatio ad Chorum.**

N *entering Church.*—" This is none other but the Houſe of God: this is the Gate of Heaven."

On *entering the Veſtry kneel down and ſay,*—O Lord, I am come now into Thine Houſe, and am about to { offer before Thee the prayers and praiſes (*Clergy*) aſſiſt in the ſervice (*Choir*) } of Thy Holy Church. Do Thou, in all things, I beſeech Thee, direct and rule my heart and lips, ſo that I may praiſe Thee with the ſpirit and with the underſtanding alſo, and finally be found worthy to ſing Thy praiſes in the choirs of heaven. Amen.

On *putting on the Surplice.*—Have mercy upon me, O Lord, and cleanſe me from all ſtains of ſin, that, with thoſe who have made their robes white in the Blood of the Lamb, I may have grace to attain to everlaſting happineſs. Amen.

Ad Caputium.—Indue me Domine lorica fidei et galea ſalutis et gladio Spiritus Sancti. Amen.

In *paſſing to the Choir.*—Who ſhall aſcend into the hill of the Lord, or who ſhall riſe up in His holy place? Even he that hath clean hands, and a pure heart, that hath not lift up his mind unto vanity, nor ſworn to deceive his neighbour. He ſhall receive the bleſſing from the Lord, and righteouſneſs from the God of his ſalvation.

In *Choir.*—O God, before Whoſe Preſence the very Angels veil their faces, help me to adore Thee preſent in this Sanctuary with reverence and godly fear. May the words of my mouth and the meditation of my heart, be acceptable in Thy ſight, O Lord, my ſtrength and my Redeemer. Amen.

For *Holy Baptiſm and the other Sacraments.* *Ad Stolam.*—Stola juſtitiæ circumda Domine cervices meas, et ab omni contagione peccati purifica mentem meam. Amen.

As applying to ſeveral departments of Services.

Unite our prayers and praiſes to thoſe of Thy Church throughout the world. Amen.
Give unto us the preparations of heart which are from the Lord;—an open mouth to ſhow forth Thy praiſe;—a wiſe and underſtanding heart to receive the knowledge of Thy truth,

---

* This " Preparatio" may be written out, printed or illuminated intelligibly on cardboard, then framed and hung up in the choir veſtry.

and to praise Thee for all the glorious things which Thou haft done ;—a fpirit of fupplication to feek thofe things of which we have need. Through our LORD JESUS CHRIST.

Aperi Domine os meum ad benedicendum Nomen Tuum, munda quoque cor meum ab omnibus vanis, perverfis, atque alienis cogitationibus, intellectum illumina, affectum inflamma, ut dignè attentè ac devotè hoc officium recitare valeam, et exaudiri merear ante confpectum divinæ Majeftatis Tuæ. Per Chriftum Dominum noftrum. Amen.

Chorifters.—Caffock, cotta, (i. e. fhort furplice), fquare cap.

Deacons.—Caffock, furplice, or cotta, filk hood " agreeable to their degrees," or decent tippet of black, fo it be not filk, for thofe not graduates, and biretta.

Priefts.—Caffock, furplice, or cotta, filk hood " agreeable to their degrees," or decent tippet of black, fo it be not filk, if not graduates, and biretta. Note: the caffock fhould reach to the feet.

118.

THE Rector or Vicar may wear, *caufa honoris*, the grey almys over a furplice.*

119. *Mode of proceeding to Choir.*

THE (1) chorifters, (2) Deacons, (3) Priefts preceding the (4) Rector or Vicar iffue from the facrifty with heads uncovered, and advance towards the choir in fuch a manner that the right fhoulder of the one may nearly touch the left of the other; and thus each two maintaining an equal diftance from the other, proceed with meafured ftep, holding their caps with both hands before the breaft. Having arrived in the choir, they bow towards the Altar,† and thofe who

---

* That the *grey almys* (fee Sparrow's Collection, 227) was ufed fince the Reformation is proved by its being forbidden to be worn by a fet of canons put forth in 1571. Thefe canons, never having been fubmitted to the Lower Houfe of Convocation, and never having received the Royal fanction, nor been ratified by Parliament, are of not the flighteft authority. They are confidered to have been fubfcribed and approved by Grindal, Archbifhop of York. Strype's Parker, ii. 57—62.

† Canon VII. of the Synod of 1640. This canon may ferve as a recommendation of this moft reverent practice, though it is not binding as a legal authority, having been paffed in a fynod of Convocation, which had been improperly convened. See alfo Bifhop Jeremy Taylor's " Treatife on Reverence to the Altar."

form each pair, face one another, and retire to their places at opposite sides of the choir, where they remain standing,* till they take their seats laterally north and south, the choristers in the subsellæ, or on the floor of the chancel.†

120.

HE Rector or Vicar goes to the Decani stall, the most western on the south side, either with his back to the roodscreen fronting the east,‡ or else facing the north,—his position depending, in some measure, on the arrangements of the stalls. The Curate,

---

* See Cærem. Epif. Liber I. cap. 18.

† It is the custom in some choirs for the Officiant and choristers to kneel on taking their places, and at the same time to cover up their faces in the sleeves of their surplices. This latter unseemly usage should never be permitted. It is not necessary to kneel on entering the choir, bowing to the Altar is enough; but if kneeling is practised when the choir first take their places, the head should simply be bowed over the joined hands.

‡ *Worshipping towards the East.* Clemens Alex. Strom. I. 7. p. 724. (Wheatley). From the 27th chapter, concerning the HOLY GHOST, to Amphilochius.

He speaks of the written doctrine and unwritten traditions of the Apostles, and says that both have the same efficacy as to religion. The unwritten traditions, which he mentions, are the signing our hope in CHRIST with the cross, turning towards the East, to denote that we are in quest of Eden from whence our first parents were ejected, (as he afterwards explains it). Canons of S. Basil (92nd), now owned only by the Eastern Church. See also Neale and Webb's Durandus, Appendix B.

"The very position of our Blessed SAVIOUR on the Cross as represented in the Great Rood and in stained glass is not without a meaning. In modern paintings the arms are high above the head, the whole weight of the body seeming to rest upon them. And this, besides its literal truth, gives occasion to that miserable display of anatomical knowledge, in which such pictures so much abound. The Catholic representation pictures the Arms as extended horizontally: thereby signifying how the SAVIOUR, when extended on the Cross, embraced the whole world. Thus, as it ever ought to be, is physical sacrificed to moral truth."—Introductory Essay to Neale and Webb's Durandus, p. lxxxv—vi.

"The Priest being in the quire shall begin with a loud voice the LORD's Prayer, called the *Paternoster.*" First rubric in the "Order for Matins daily through the year," in King Edward's First Prayer Book.

See Cardw. Con. p. 314, 351, which will show that the mind of the English Church is not to read prayers westward fronting the people.

Till after the Restoration, there was no instance, it is believed, of the desk for prayers facing westward. Jebb's Choral Service, p. 329.

See also Robertson's "How to Conform," p. 623. A very cautious and moderate writer. It appears that in Elizabeth's time, though the reading-desk might be put up in the body of the church, it never fronted the west; it may have done so between 1552—1553. See rubric of 1552. See Robertson for first introduction, 66. Procter, 180.

For full post-Reformation *examples*, besides those given by Mr. Robertson, the reader is re-

or any other prieſt preſent, ſhould occupy the correſponding Cantoris ſtall.

N. B. In all proceſſions what will be the right hand *in going into the choir* is the place of honour; in returning, the place of honour is the left. In chanting, the firſt verſe is ſung full; the Cantoris ſide takes the ſecond, the Decani ſide the third, and ſo on.

121.

T is quite irregular for any clerics to occupy the ſedilia in the Sanctuary during Matins and Evenſong, or to ſit in eaſy chairs at the north and ſouth ends of the Altar. Note: the legs are not to be croſſed in choir.

122.

THE ORDER FOR MORNING PRAYER,
DAILY THROUGHOUT THE YEAR.

"At the beginning* of Morning Prayer the Miniſter ſhall read with a loud voice ſome one or more of theſe Sentences of the Scriptures that follow. And then he ſhall ſay that which is written after the ſaid Sentences."

HE old rubrics direct the making the ſign of the croſs before beginning any Office,† a practice which it would be well to reſtore.

The Sentences are to be regarded as antiphons, and not as ferred to that book of great authority "Hierurgia Anglicana," pp. 32—40; 73, 109; 260, 261; 363, &c.

* A brief prelude of praiſe in the form of a ſhort hymn,[1] followed immediately by the Sentence, would certainly be in accordance with the pureſt conception of Divine Service. The authority of the injunction of Queen Elizabeth can be pleaded for this ſlight variation from the rigour of the Rubric:—"That there be a modeſt and diſtinct ſong ſo uſed in all parts of the Common Prayers in the Church, that the ſame may be as plainly underſtanded, as if it were mere reading without ſinging; and yet nevertheleſs for the comforting of ſuch as delight in muſick, it may be permitted, that in the beginning, or in the end of Common-Prayers, either at Morning or Evening, there may be ſung an hymn, or ſuch like ſong, to the praiſe of Almighty God, in the beſt ſort of melody and muſick that may be conveniently deviſed, having reſpect that the ſentence of the hymn may be underſtanded and perceived."—Injunctions by Q. Elizabeth, 1559. Sparrow's Collection, ed. 1671, p. 79. This is, in fact, a common cuſtom at many Churches on great feſtivals, and is uſually ſung in proceſſion.

† The ſign of the Croſs is made by lifting the right hand to the forehead and afterwards a

[1] The hymn ſhould be commenced by the choir without any preface, ſuch as "Let us ſing, &c." either by clergy or acolytes.

"exhortations." Confequently, they fhould be mufically recited, alfo not towards the people.*

The following arrangement has been fuggefted :—
    Advent: "Repent ye," "Enter not," "O LORD, correct me."
    Lent and Fridays: "The facrifices," "Rend your heart."
    Sundays and Feftivals: "To the LORD our GOD."
    Vigils and Wednefdays: "I acknowledge."
    Evens: "Hide Thy face."
    Ferial days: "When the wicked man," "I will arife," or "If we fay."

123. *Arrangement of Sentences on Occurrence of Fridays and Feftivals.*

HEN a feftival falls on a Friday, it is well to ufe the feftal antiphon. The feaft of the Nativity being the only feftival which fuperfedes the Friday Abftinence-day, when Chriftmas Day falls on a Friday, of courfe no penitential antiphon fhould be ufed.

---

line to the bottom of the breaft, and then another line croffing the former from the left fhoulder to the right. Whilft performing this action it is proper to invocate (*fecreto*) the Three Perfons of the Ever Bleffed Trinity in token of our faith therein. The Crofs is made with the whole hand. In the act of bleffing anything the Crofs is made over it in the air, and in benediction of the faithful it is made towards the congregation. In the Weft, *at the Gofpel*, a diftinct Crofs is traced with the edge of the thumb on the brow, lips, and bofom. In the Eaft, the Crofs is made with three fingers, that is, the thumb and two fingers, in honour of the TRINITY.[1] The fign ufed to be made at the end of the Gofpel, the Creeds, the LORD's Prayer, the *Gloria in excelfis*, the *Sanctus*, the *Agnus Dei*, the *Benedictus, Magnificat, Nunc Dimittis*, the end of the Liturgy, when the Prieft gives the Benediction, and whenever mention is made of the CROSS OF THE CRUCIFIED.

* When celebration of Holy Euchariſt is about to follow the Ordinary Office the fame arrangement of fentences will obtain. Wednefdays and Fridays were cuftomary days of celebration in the African and Eaftern ufe, in addition to Sundays, efpecially in Lent. A feparate Epiftle and Gofpel was provided, in the Englifh ufes, in Epiphany for Wednefdays and Fridays, and in the Trinity period for Wednefday only.

[1] The Jacobites and Eutychians ufe only one finger.

124. *Position of Hands.*

HE hands should be joined before the breast, with fingers extended, and the right thumb placed over the left in the form of a cross, when kneeling. In sitting the same rule is observed, and the hands should be placed upon the lap. In standing the hands should still be joined before the breast.

125. *The Exhortation.*

"And then he shall say that which is written after the said Sentences."

To be said, turning to the congregation.

126. *The General Confession.*

"A general Confession to be said of the whole Congregation after the Minister, all kneeling."

FTER the Minister," not *with** the Minister. Each clause of the Confession is marked by a capital letter commencing it, a rule which should be carefully observed, as pervading similar places in the Prayer Book, and ought to be repeated in each interval, when the Minister has paused after the manner of the Litany.

127. *The Amen.*

T will be observed that the word "Amen" is printed at the end of the General Confession; but that the first rubric, directing it to be said by the people at the end of all the prayers, occurs after the Absolution: also that the word is printed in a different type at the end of the prayers. In these the Officiant says the prayer or the collect, and there stops, while the people answer their "Amen." In other parts as the General Confession, LORD's Prayer, Creeds, "Gloria Patri," which are repeated by the Officiant and people, there is no such difference, the Minister goes on, and says "Amen" himself, thus directing the people to do the same. The *Gloria* should always be sung or said by both sides of the choir.

---

* The parts which are said *with* the Minister are, the LORD's Prayer and the Apostles' Creed. Those which are said *after* the Minister are the General Confession, and by analogy the prayer, "Turn Thou us, good LORD," in the Commination.

128. *The Absolution.*

"The Absolution, or Remission of sins, to be pronounced by the Priest alone,* standing; the people still kneeling."

THE Absolution should be pronounced "junctis manibus" according to mediæval custom.†

129.

"The people shall answer here, and at the end of all other prayers, Amen."

Vide supra, Par. 127.

130. *The LORD's Prayer.*

"Then the Minister shall kneel, and say the LORD's Prayer with an audible voice; the people also kneeling, and repeating it with him, both here, and wheresoever else it is used in Divine Service."

AUDIBLE voice, "clara vox." "If," says Archbishop Laud, "in some principal part of the service there be a caveat given that the presbyter shall speak with a loud voice and distinctly, it implies that he be very careful in that place that his voice be audible and distinct." The LORD's Prayer was in the ancient office for Matins repeated in a low voice throughout. The Church of England in order to secure distinctness of recitation, as is seemly in the enunciation of the

---

* The old form was said interchangeably, with the exception of the last clause, by Priest and people. Vide Maskell, Anc. Lit. p. 6, 1st edit. P. 12, 13, 2nd edit.
If a Deacon be performing the introductory portion of the service when a Priest also is present, and in his place in the choir, the Priest should stand and pronounce the Absolution, the Deacon kneeling with bowed head and joined hands in his stall, as he is acting as assistant to the Priest, and ready to proceed to lead the people in the next petitions. But when no Priest is present, the Deacon should continue kneeling and proceed to the LORD's Prayer. There is no written authority for the insertion of the prayer, "O GOD, Whose nature and property," or "O LORD, we beseech Thee, mercifully hear our prayers," from the Commination Service, in the place of the Absolution.

"The Priest alone" probably means not in contradistinction to a Deacon, but to the people, in reference to the old custom. In a translation of our Prayer Book, by Elias Petley, dedicated to Archbishop Laud, the Absolution is ordered to be said ὑπὸ τοῦ διακόνου μόνου.

† For bowing the head at the Name of the LORD JESUS, see Canon XVIII., 160¾. Some have held that the head need not be bowed in kneeling, and consequently that the people need not bow the head when in that position, but it is certainly more seemly to do so.

118   The Order for Morning and Evening Prayer.

LORD's own words, orders it to be repeated here with the Minister, and not after him.

The LORD's Prayer concludes the introductory part of Matins. The doxology at the close of it was not added till the last review, it is used here only in the office of Matins. It serves to impart to this Divine summary of all our worship, as the general thanksgiving does to the office itself, the dominant and pervading aspect of praise.

["*Wheresoever else it is used in Divine Service,*"—with this exception, the opening of the Communion Office. The rubric in the Communion Office orders the Priest "standing at the north side of the Table to say the LORD's Prayer with the collect following, the *people kneeling;*" not, observe, saying it with him. In the post-Communion Service it is ordered that the LORD's Prayer shall be repeated every petition after the Priest by the people, and it is unreasonable to suppose that at the last revision there was any intention to make a rubric at Matins abolish in an underhand manner a Catholic rubric in the Liturgy. Indeed the character and predilections of the revisers render such an hypothesis improbable. We should also remember that wherever the LORD's Prayer occurs, save in the commencement of the Holy Communion, the direction for the people to say it with the Minister is usually repeated, although the rubrics are in different terms. "Wherever else it is used in Divine Service," must mean wherever else, except there be a rubric to the contrary; that one rubric to the contrary being in the opening of the Communion Office].

131. *The Versicles.*

"Then likewise he shall say,"

HESE two* pairs of Versicles should be used as the link between our penitential preface or introduction, and the act of worship itself. When we remember that the first pair is from Psalm li. and the second from Psalm lxx, their humbling and penitential character will be manifest. A low pitch is generally assigned to them in musical recitation.

---

* When formerly sung, all turned themselves to the Altar.

The Order for Morning and Evening Prayer. 119

132. *The Praise of the Office.—The Gloria, Versicle and Response.*

"Here all standing up, the Priest shall say,"

WITH the "Gloria" the praise of the Office begins, and here all, clergy, choir, and people, not only stand, but according to the Sarum Use, still retained as a Catholic tradition in many places, they who in choir are ranged laterally, turn to the Altar, the head moderately inclined.*

V. "Praise ye the Lord." R. "The Lord's Name be praised." This Versicle, and its answer, represent for us both the "Allelulia" and "Invitatory." Indeed, the exhortation "Praise ye the Lord," (the old Alleluia) answers the purpose of the regular Invitatory, and was probably intended to do so, when † in the First Book of Edward VI. the *Venite* was ordered to be sung "without any Invitatory," i. e. without any of that exact type which had been customary. Consequently the Versicle and Response forms the Alleluia and Invitatory to the *Venite*, the prelude of the psalmody and worship of the day.

Praise ye the Lord (or Alleluia), is to be said by the Priest, turned to the people.‡

133. *The Venite.*

"Then shall be said, or sung this Psalm following: except on *Easter Day*,§ upon which another Anthem is appointed: and on the Nineteenth day of every Month it is not to be read here, but in the ordinary course of the Psalms.

"*Venite, exultemus Domino.* Psalm xcv."

WHATEVER ‖ loss we may sustain from the general unvarying character of our Invitatory Psalm, this tends to put a singular degree of honour upon the one day in the year on which we lay it aside, the great and supreme festival of Easter, the queen

---

* "Quotiesque dicitur Gloria Patri et Filio et Spiritui Sancto, ad eadem verba Deo humiliter se inclinent."—Canon of English Church, Wilkins, iii. 20. According to the Roman Use, the head is inclined, but they do not turn to the Altar.

† "Praise ye the Lord. (*And from Easter to Trinity Sunday*). Hallelujah!"—Edward VI's First Book of Common Prayer.

The response was added at the last revision, but was first inserted in the Prayer Book for Scotland (1637).

‡ In certain parts of the Western Church the organ does not sound throughout Lent or Advent, except on the Sundays *Gaudemus* and *Lætare*.

§ The Easter Day Anthem should be used at Matins during the entire Octave of Easter.

‖ It may be conjectured, though we have no positive evidence of the fact, that the temple

of feasts. It is not that at other times we fail to acknowledge CHRIST as the Great King, One with the FATHER and the HOLY SPIRIT; but that the one piece of heavenly tidings which we recognize as making Christian praise itself more Christian still, and so claiming to supersede our ordinary Invitatory, is that "CHRIST is risen from the dead, and become the first-fruits of them that slept." The omission of the *Venite* when it occurs in the ordinary course of the Psalms, which has been sometimes animadverted upon as a novelty, was customary throughout the West.*

In some parish churches the *Venite* is often chanted whilst the Psalms are not even said in monotone, but colloquially. It is not necessary to enlarge upon the inconsistency of this practice, which after having given the appropriate musical expression to the invitation to praise, denies it to the act of praise itself. Where partial chanting is used, it would be much more consistent to confine it to the Canticles after the Lessons, though even this is undesirable.

The first seven verses of the *Venite* being of a joyful character, the rest more penitential, it is well suited to precede the Psalms of the day, whether joyful or otherwise.

At the *Venite* the organ usually sounds for the first time. Before it commences, the first half of the first verse is intoned by the Officiant or by the Precentor. The faithful should turn to the east and bow at the *Gloria Patri*.† According to the Sarum rite, (our legitimate guide,) this was always done.

The *Venite* should be recited on the Decani and Cantoris sides, antiphonally.

---

service commenced daily with the 95th Psalm itself, or with some part of it. The Synagogue Service on the Sabbath so commences at this day.—Freeman, Principle of Divine Service, whose interesting note see p. 402.

* " In Brev. Rom. the Psalm was still treated invitatory-wise, but in Sar. not so."—Freeman's note.

† In one widely prevailing variety of the Western Rite, special provision was made for a penitential act in connection with the *Venite*. For it was ordered by the Rubric that at the words, "O come, let us worship, and fall down: and *weep* (*sic*, after the Vulg. and LXX.) before the LORD our Maker," all were "to fall down" accordingly.¹

¹ S. Benedic. ad Vig. The injunction was doubtless borrowed from the Greek Rite which enjoins three reverences (μετανοίας, v. Goar, in loc.) to be made at the words of the Invitatory, "O come, let us worship, and fall down before," &c. Horolog. in loc. Freeman.

134. *The Pfalms.—Eagle Lectern.** *Gloria.*

"Then fhall follow the Pfalms in order as they are appointed. And at the end of every Pfalm throughout the Year, and likewife at the end of *Benedicite, Benedictus, Magnificat,* and *Nunc Dimittis,* fhall be repeated,

Glory be to the FATHER, and to the SON: and to the HOLY GHOST;

Anfwer. As it was in the beginning, is now, and ever fhall be: world without end. Amen."

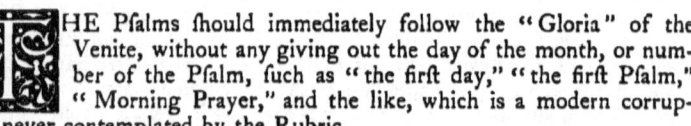HE Pfalms fhould immediately follow the "Gloria" of the Venite, without any giving out the day of the month, or number of the Pfalm, fuch as "the firft day," "the firft Pfalm," "Morning Prayer," and the like, which is a modern corruption never contemplated by the Rubric.

The choir ftand laterally except at the Gloria, the Rector or Vicar fronting the Altar from his Decani ftall.

The Pfalms are chanted antiphonally by thofe who occupy the oppofite fides of the church, the choir leading. They fhould not be faid alternately by Minifter and choir, but antiphonally, viz. by Decani and Cantoris fides refpectively.†

To read the Pfalms colloquially inftead of chanting them, or at leaft faying them in monotone, is incorrect and unedifying. It would be as proper to chant the fermon, or to intone the notices of holydays, banns of marriage, and excommunications. S. Bafil points out as one ufe of the alternate method of finging, in chanting the Pfalms, viz. that they are *alfo* great media of knowledge as well as of praife, though this laft is doubtlefs their firft function.‡ The "Gloria" fhould be faid full, i.e. fhould be fung or faid by both fides of the choir.

In fome parifh churches the "Gloria Patri" is chanted whilft the Pfalms are faid. In this there is nothing abftractedly wrong; fince the "Gloria Patri" is a feparate hymn. Still, as the repetition of the doxology§ after

---

* This is now ufually ufed for reading the Leffons from, and is fometimes placed without the roodfcreen. In mediæval times it ftood in the midft of the choir, fronting the Altar, and the antiphonary was placed on it, and the Precentor who gave out the antiphon took his ftand there. It would be well to reftore the ancient cuftom whenever practicable.

† Where there is *no* choir the Pfalms may be faid by Prieft and people alternately.

‡ διχῇ διανεμηθέντες ἀντιψάλλουσιν ἀλλήλοις.—Ep. 3, ad Neocæs. See Freeman, p. 331, and Jebb, 277, 278.

§ The repetition of the Doxology at the end of every Pfalm was ordered in 1549. Firft Book of Edward VI.

Benedict in his rule fpeaks of the "Gloria Patri" being ufed at the beginning of the offices.

each Pſalm ſignifies our belief that the ſame GOD was worſhipped by the Jewiſh church as by us, and many of the Pſalms (and probably the 95th) were uſed in the Temple worſhip, only the myſtery of the HOLY TRINITY is more clearly revealed to us; and we by this addition turn the Jewiſh Pſalms to Chriſtian hymns: it ſeems improper to diſſociate the Pſalms by ſo different a manner of performance from that hymn which ſo markedly ſtamps them with the character of Chriſtian ſongs. The prophecies of David being now converted into the praiſes of the Church, we ought to aid the Church, not hinder her, in the aſſimilation ſhe deſigned. Beſides this conſideration to *ſay* the Pſalms, and to chant the " Gloria Patri " violates the general rule that the ſervice ſhould be either monotoned, or chanted, throughout.

The chants called Gregorian, there is good reaſon for believing, have David for their author no leſs than the Pſalms, and are the identical melodies to which the Pſalter was ſung from the very firſt in the ſervice of the ſanctuary.

The proper Pſalms for Evenſong on Chriſtmas Day, Eaſter Day, Aſcenſion Day, and Whitſun Day, ſhould be ſaid at the firſt Evenſong of thoſe Feſtivals,—that is, at the Evening Service on their Vigils, as well as at the (Second) Evenſong of the Feaſts themſelves.

135. *The Voluntary* after the Pſalms.*

HE ſanction of old cuſtom is all that can be urged in favour of the voluntary, for it is apt very frequently to add needleſsly to the length of the ſervice, and to become tedious. In large churches where the leſſons are read from the lectern in the centre of the choir, or without the Roodſcreen, at ſome diſtance from the Reader, it might be well to play merely a few bars upon the organ whilſt the Reader is going from his ſtall to the lectern.

The Voluntary, which ſhould be very brief, may plead, however, ſome analogy in that muſical prolongation of the laſt note of the Alleluia of the

---

It has been conjectured that it began to be uſed here ſome time before the age of Benedict as a termination to ſome introductory Pſalms, which were then repeated entirely.—See Palmer, vol. i. p. 220. But ſee Freeman, vol. i. p. 329.

" In hac provincia (Gallia) in clauſula pſalmi, omnes adſtantes concinunt cum clamore GLORIA PATRI et FILIO et SPIRITUI SANCTO."—Caſſianus, lib. ii. c. viii.

* See Neale's letter to Daniel. Vol. v. pp. 3—4 of Daniel's *Theſaurus Hymnologicus.*

Gradual, to which the Sequences were afterwards adapted. Thus viewed, it should be a quiet harmony, winding on out of the last note of " Amen" following the " Glory be to the Father." Its significance would thus be like that of the Sequences,—the echo and prolongation, in the heavenly courts, of the Praise.

136. *The Lessons.*

"Then shall be read distinctly with an audible voice the First Lesson, taken out of the Old Testament, as is appointed in the Kalendar, (except there be proper Lessons assigned for that day :) He, that readeth, so standing, and turning himself, as he may best be heard of all such as are present. And after that, shall be said, or sung in *English*, the Hymn called *Te Deum Laudamus*, daily throughout the Year."

HESE are to be read from a lectern in the midst of the choir, or immediately outside the chancel-screen, the reader fronting the west. They are, however, sometimes read from the Reader's stall in the choir. By the words " He that readeth," an intimation is given that the reader of the lessons is not necessarily assigned to the Officiant at Matins or Evensong. The Reader* in Deacon's orders, to whose office it pertaineth to assist the Priest in Divine Service, reads the first lesson; a Priest, *causa honoris*, might read the second.

" Read distinctly with an audible voice :" this evidently refers to reading according to musical notation with the " clara vox," that is, the lessons are to be read in a chanting tone. In former rubrics the lessons were ordered to be sung in a plain tune, when of course ordinary reading in the speaking tones of the voice was at once put out of the question.† At the last revision the rubric was altered to its present form. The rubric is worded so as to *permit* ordinary reading in the lessons taking the words in their usual conventional meaning, whilst *technically* the *animus* of the rubric is perfectly unaltered.

In cathedrals the lessons are the portions of the service most indistinctly heard, indeed as far as being " understanded of the people," they might as well be read out of the Vulgate. Though doubtless whether read in

---

* A Layman, by custom, may read the Lessons, as the ordinary practice at our ancient universities sufficiently indicates.

† " And (to the end the people may better hear) in such places where they do sing, there shall the lessons be sung in a plain tune after the manner of distinct reading : and likewise the Epistle and Gospel." Rubric of 1549, 1552, 1559, 1604, and Scotch Prayer Book of Laud, 1637. See Keeling, pp. 12, 13, for comparison of Rubrics.

Latin; or, so indistinctly read as to be inaudible, in English, they are to be honoured, and given thanks for, as the Words of GOD, as the founding of the Divine Voice in the ears of men. In cathedrals and large churches it is expedient therefore to read the lessons in a plain tune, or, at least on a high sustained pitch, to the end the faithful may better hear, according to the mind of the English Church.

In parish churches of ordinary size, it may suffice to read the lessons in the speaking tones of the voice, dropping alike the monotone and the chant.

In regard to "the plain tune after the manner of distinct reading," it should be remembered that in ancient times the musical tone (as in the modern Opera recitative, and as in the recitation* of Roman Tragedy), was used not only in the prayers but in all lessons of the Church. The "distinct" reading means the inflexions by which the tone was varied, which were fixed by stated rules: the interrogations, exclamations, pauses, &c. being marked by corresponding rises and falls. For these inflexions, very exact rules are laid down in the ancient treatises on Church Music. So that those who justify a monotonous mode of reading the lessons by the alleged inflexibility of the ancient tone, are altogether mistaken. If they chant, the inflexions of the chant, the end of which is due expression, ought to be used.

When the lessons are read in the speaking tones of the voice, by analogy the due varieties of ordinary speech ought to be used. Those who are capable of managing their voice (and this ought to be a matter of study to all†) ought, even in ordinary reading, so to pitch it, as to lay the prevailing

---

* "At Paris I once saw Mars, with Talma, in a tragedy, where the whole of her part was *plaintive supplication*; and I remarked to my companion at the close, that during the entire representation her voice, said to be the sweetest pronunciation ever known, had never changed from *one note.*" Note to a letter by Ven. Archdeacon Thorp, addressed to the editor of the "Guardian," which appeared in that paper Sept. 19, 1855.

† "Clergymen's sore throat is due entirely to a neglect of observation of the mechanism of speaking; a mechanism which is obvious to any one whose attention is once directed to the matter. Look at a public singer, who wishes to exert the voice to the utmost, at a Greek or Roman statue of an orator, at Raphael's S. Paul preaching at Athens, at most of our really powerful speakers and preachers, and what is the attitude? The lungs are expanded to the full, the windpipe is held straight, the shoulders thrown back, and the arms swung loose; the muscles of the whole trunk have full easy play. Every one of them can be brought to bear in throwing out the voice, because they have nothing else to do; the cartilages of the ribs are stretched so that their elasticity is also made useful, and saves the muscles considerably. Not a single part is overworked, because all act at once, and assist one another. But make a man with clergyman's sore throat read, and you see the origin of his ailment in a moment. The windpipe is bent at an angle, so as to make it difficult to speak at all; the shoulders are brought

stress upon one of its strongest tones; not straining it upon a high key, after the manner of inexperienced readers, but dwelling upon that tone

forward, so that the poor costal cartilages have no chance of exhibiting the beautiful elasticity they are endowed with, and the lungs emptied, so that the relaxed muscles and the diaphragm have to act at an enormous disadvantage, and to strain themselves in order to squeeze out the creaking falsetto which results. Naturally enough all the delicate muscles of the throat are overworked, and affect, secondarily, the mucous membrane that clothes them. There was a quack fellow who made quite a fortune by curing clergymen who had lost their voices. He used to make them promise or swear secrecy concerning his method of treatment, and so it was not generally known that the whole art consisted in teaching them to speak with the chest dilated, and thus to get rid not only of sore throat, but of stammering, and a variety of other impediments arising from feeble muscle. The cure, or rather the prevention, is so simple, and occurs so naturally to every person who has studied ever so superficially the mechanism of speaking, that the ailment ought never to be heard of among educated persons." Dr. Chambers. *Lectures to Ladies on Practical Subjects*. Cambridge: Macmillan.—p. 145.

"Another of your grievances is the feebleness of delivery of the officiating Minister; he has not health or strength to get through his duties on the morning of the LORD's Day in an efficient manner. Of course not. How should he? He shuts up his church from Sunday to Sunday, and instead of saying or singing the service, reads it in a feigned, unnatural voice, and very soon has a 'clergyman's throat,' from the unwonted exertion, and his own wretched reading. One of these Priests, with the usual mysterious malady in his bronchial apparatus, consulted the late Bishop of Lincoln upon the matter, whereupon his Lordship advised as a remedy the saying of Matins and Evensong daily. I know very well what a daily service is, there is no blessing like it, whether for pastor or for flock; and, moreover, the voice rarely gets out of order, and the Priest never feels fatigued by the length of the Sunday Service."— "*The Book of Common Prayer unabridged.*" A Letter to the Rev. Jas. Hildyard, B. D., by the Rev. J. Purchas, M. A., p. 23. London: Masters.

"It is sometimes alleged as an objection to this mode of saying the service (viz. intoning or monotoning it) in the church, that it is one which probably very few clergymen would be found able to use, from want of voice or musical ear. So far, however, as the present writer's experience goes, he must confess that he has found it a much rarer occurrence to meet with a person who can say the prayers reverently, *without* more or less intoning them, than it is to find clergymen who are able to intone them properly. Surely there must be very few indeed, who are unable to sustain one note in their prayers, if it be only one of easy compass to them; and this is, after all, as much as is really necessary for the purpose of intoning. The less it has of the character of a musical performance and the more simple and natural it is, the better." —The Churchman's Library, *Church Worship*, p. 27. London: Masters.

"If the Sunday services are so heavy a drag, if they occasion such wear and tear to the lungs, what must daily prayers be? But, by the same rule, a man who is compelled to take violent exercise once a week, would do well to take none at all on the intermediate days. What is the reason that consumption is so fearfully prevalent among the English clergy, while among their French brethren, certainly not physically stronger, it is almost unknown? Doubtless, in some measure, the most injurious effect of reading instead of intoning, but certainly also because the one set of men tax their lungs to their utmost once a week, the other call theirs pretty equally into play every day. So in like manner, English lawyers, who do not intone, and who speak as much as, or more than, clergymen, are comparatively free from phthisis.

which is moſt natural to them, whether it be baſs or tenor, ſo that the voice may come from the cheſt, and not from the throat, and may admit of that elaſtic ſound, which makes even a low voice audible throughout the largeſt building. A judicious mixture of muſical tones ought to be obſerved, and the converſational quarter tones as little dwelt upon as poſſible. The contrary practice is too general, and the reading of the leſſons, even by thoſe who can chant admirably, is often degraded to the indiſtinct and hurried cadences of the moſt ordinary converſation. The tone ought to be ſlightly elevated above that of common ſpeech, ſo as to partake ſomewhat of the character of a chant, juſt in that degree which a judicious reader of ſolemn poetry ordinarily aſſumes. But to lay down any preciſe rules on this matter is impoſſible, ſo much depends on taſte, judgment, and devotional reverence. Where there is affectation, or a love of diſplay, on the one hand, or irreverence on the other, the caſe is hopeleſs.

It may be obſerved that a good reader will preſerve ſome of the archaiſms of pronunciation which the beſt precedents have made cuſtomary; ſuch as, the making a diſtinct ſyllable of the termination of the paſt tenſe or participle "ed," as err-ed, inſtead of err'd and the like. In a paper of the Spectator, the affectation of ſome young readers, who even then curtailed theſe ſyllables, is remarked upon. In ſolemn poetry, and in the ſpeech of the common people in many parts of England, this more ancient and harmonious mode of pronunciation is kept up; and the dignity of Holy Scripture, and its matchleſs rhythm demand it. It may alſo be obſerved that the word "wind" ought in leſſons of Scripture to be pronounced as in poetry "wind." How the anomalous and inharmonious pronunciation of this word now naturalized in England crept in, it is difficult to ſay. The ancient method is ſtill retained in common ſpeech in Ireland, which, in this particular, as in many others, both of proſody and grammar, has been preſerved from the degrading barbariſms of Engliſh colloquial idioms.

It has been argued that the leſſons ſhould be read colloquially, as read to the people, to diſtinguiſh them from the monotoned or chanted prayers addreſſed to GOD. We may anſwer that as the Praiſe of the office under

---

The reaſon is, that when they exerciſe their voice, the ſtrain is continuous and equable; and when they reſt, the reſt is complete. We believe, and we are ſure we ſhould be borne out by the teſtimony of phyſicians, that daily prayers would be found a preventive of that which they are commonly thought to induce. And we are told by the editors of the 'Guide,' that, in their very numerous inquiries, they found only one inſtance, where daily ſervice, having been commenced, was given up on the ſcore of ill-health."—*Chriſtian Remembrancer*, quoted in Monro's "Parochial Work," 2nd edit. pp. 75, 76.

the form of Scripture meditation is still going on, it is seemly to say the lessons in recitative as a loftier mode than that of the ordinary speaking tone. Doubtless this is so, but generally the *size* of the church will determine the mode of reading the lessons as a practical matter.

It is only necessary to refer to the rubric to see the impropriety of the frequent usage, of announcing the lessons in these terms: "The first or second lesson appointed for this morning (or evening) service is such a chapter of such a book." Or having announced the lesson according to the rubrical formula, to add with imbecile iteration, "such a chapter or verse of such a chapter." The consideration that every one present must know whether the lesson be the first or the second, and whether the service is morning or evening, shows the absurdity of the practice, and the "vain repetition" alluded to, besides being unrubrical, makes the announcement needlessly long.

Equally wrong in announcing the first lesson, if not canonical, is the introduction of the word "Apocryphal;" an innovation not authorized by the Church.

Other irregularities are frequent: such as saying, "Here beginneth such *a chapter at such a verse*," instead of "Here beginneth *such a verse of such a chapter;*" or of mentioning the verse at which the lesson terminates, (in cases where the whole chapter is not read), for which there is no authority whatever.

Where it is directed that a chapter shall be read to a certain verse, it means that verse exclusive; but where it is to begin at a certain verse, it means that verse inclusive.

N. B. Lay persons who have been solemnly and formally admitted to serve in a church choir, or recognized candidates for holy Orders, may, by the analogy of the ancient minor orders, read the Lessons. When the Lessons are read by a layman he should be vested simply in cassock and *cotta*, or in cassock and surplice, with silk hood agreeable to his degree if he be a graduate, or a tippet if he be a literate.

"NOTE, That before every Lesson the Minister shall say, *Here beginneth such a Chapter, or Verse of such a Chapter, of such a Book:* And after every Lesson, *Here endeth the First, or the Second Lesson.*"

In many places "*Thus* endeth" is said instead of "Here endeth." It may be said these are trifles. So they are in themselves. But since the Church makes certain orders, it is an act of obedience to observe them, especially since it is not some "great thing" which is required of us. Befides which, the tranfgreffion of thefe orders implies either an ignorance or inattention to the rubric with which every clergyman ought to be familiar; and which if difregarded in fmaller matters, is fure to be violated in thofe of greater moment.

The Reader in going to the lectern fhould bow towards the Altar. He might alfo, if he be a layman, make a reverence to the Prieft officiating both before and after. He fhould not ftand at the Lectern while the Canticle is being fung after the Firft Leffon, unlefs he turn round and face the Altar, but fhould reverently retire to his ftall, firft bowing towards the Altar. What does he bow to? Nothing.

According to ancient ufage, the faithful fit at the Leffons in the Daily Service, and at the Epiftle in the Liturgy.

137. *The Canticles.*

"And after that fhall be faid or fung, in *Englifh*, the Hymn called *Te Deum Laudamus*, daily* throughout the Year."

HE Leffons and Canticles fhould, in accordance with the ancient ideas and modes of fervice which they reprefent, be confidered primarily as carrying on jointly the work of praife begun at the "Gloria," and going forward in the pfalms without abatement. For the Leffons fupply frefh matter for the Praife of the Office by continually advancing our knowledge of GOD, and of His work on behalf of man; whilft the Canticles defcant on thefe great fubjects, and render due acknowledgment for them in a ftorm of rapturous praife after Scripture meditation.

The option given in the rubrics as to the felection of the Canticles, muft be regulated by Catholic ufage, in the manner following:

TE DEUM AND BENEDICITE.—The hymn Te Deum† is to be fung at Matins on all Sundays and Feftivals (except the Feaft of the Holy In-

---

* In the Sarum Office the *Te Deum* was ufed as an *addition* to the Feftal Service, not forming, as in ours, an integral or *variable* portion of it. If *Te Deum* was *not* faid, nothing elfe was recited in its ftead. The Ancient Offices of the Englifh Church gave this Hymn the title of the "Pfalm *Te Deum*," or the "Song of Ambrofe or Auguftine" indifferently.

† It is cuftomary in many places to bow the head at the "Holy, holy, holy," in the *Te Deum;* the Prieft and choir fhould always do the fame.

This "Creed fet hymn-wife," grows out of the angelic hymn found twice in Holy Scrip-

nocents, when it does not fall on a Sunday), and on Ferial days from Easter to Advent,* and from Christmas to Septuagesima.

It should not be said, according to Sarum Use, in Vigils, nor on Ember Days. Nor should it be said from the Sunday in Septuagesima, inclusive, to Easter Day.

"Or this Canticle.

Benedicite, omnia Opera."

According to the Sarum Use, *Benedicite* would be used *every day* in Lent, including Sundays† and other Holy days.

It is proper also to use it on Septuagesima, (which besides being the first note of the approaching Lent has for its Proper Lesson at Matins Gen. i.), Sexagesima and Quinquagesima.

Benedicite‡ should also be used every day in Advent, Sundays and Saints' days inclusive, according to the mind of our present Prayer Book.

---

ture (Isa. vi. 2, Rev. iv. 8,) with certain variations. The head is therefore bowed at the opening words (Holy, holy, holy) of the hymn in token of the exalted estimation in which the Church holds it, and of our exceeding reverence.

"It appears that this hymn was always sung." Mirroure, lxiii.

"'This angels' song is taken out of the prophet Isay, that see in spiritual vision, our Lord God, set on a high seat, and cherubim and seraphim singing loud either to other, Holy, holy, holy, Lord God of Sabaoth; and therefore, according to the angels ye sing choir to choir, one 'Sanctus' on one side, another on the other side, and so forth on to the other side; and for by cause angels praise God with great reverence, therefore ye incline when ye sing this song.'" Ibid. Sarum Psalter, Chambers' Translation, p. 53. Masters, London, 1852.

* The *Te Deum* is in the Western Church used only on Sundays and holydays, except those in Lent and Advent, Vigils and Ember Days. On these days the *Benedicite* supplies its place, except on the Ember days in Pentecost, when the *Te Deum* is used. The organ is silent in Lent and Advent, unless on the two Sundays Gaudemus and Lætare.

"*Non dicatur Te Deum Laudamus per totum Adventum.*" (Whatever be the service, Chambers' Psalter, p. 53.) Brev. Sarisbur.

"After the first lesson shall follow *Te Deum Laudamus*, in English, daily throughout the year, except in Lent, *all the which time*, in the place of *Te Deum* shall be used *Benedicite Omnia opera Domini Domino*, in English, as followeth," Rubric in Edward VI's First Book, 1549.

See also Keeling for variations, pp. 14, 15.

This rubric would seem to imply that *Benedicite* was to be sung on the Sundays and festivals, as well as on the ferial days in Lent.

† "*Sequens Hymnus (Te Deum) a Septuagesimâ usque ad Pascha non dicetur nisi in Festis.*" Brev. Rom.—no authority however for us.

‡ "There can be nothing more fitting for us, as we have said, than having heard the lessons and the goodness of God therein preached to us, to break out into a song of praise and thanks-

"Then shall he read in like manner the Second Lesson, taken out of the New Testament. And after that, the Hymn following; except when that shall happen to be read in the Chapter for the Day, or for the Gospel on *S. John Baptist's* Day.

Benedictus. S. Luke i. 68."

"Or this Psalm.

Jubilate Deo. Psalm c."

BENEDICTUS AND JUBILATE.*—The Benedictus, if the rigour of the rubric is preserved, is sung at Matins every day, except when it shall happen to be read in the Lesson for the Day, or in the Gospel for the Feast of S. John Baptist, on which occasion, and on no other, shall be used the

giving, and the Church hath appointed to be used (either of them) after each lesson, *but not so indifferently but that the former practice of exemplary Churches and Reason, may guide us in the choice;* for the *Te Deum, Benedictus, Magnificat,* and *Nunc Dimittis* being the most expressive jubilations and rejoicings for the redemption of the world may be said more often than the rest, especially on Sundays or other festivals of our LORD, *excepting in Lent and Advent,* which very times of humiliation and meditation on CHRIST as in expectation, or His sufferings, are not so fully enlarged with these songs of highest festivity (the custom being for the same reason in many churches in Lent to hide and conceal all the glory of their altars, covering them with black, to comply with the season) and therefore in these times may be rather used the following Psalms than the foregoing Canticles as at other times also, when the contents of the lesson shall give occasion, as when it speaks of the enlargement of the Church by bringing in the Gentiles into the Fold of it, for divers passages in these three Psalms import that sense.

"As for the Canticle *Benedicite,* (O all ye works of the LORD,) it may be used not only in the aforesaid times of humiliation, *but when either the lessons are out of Daniel, or set before us the wonderful handiworks of* GOD *in any of the creatures, or the use He makes of them either ordinary or miraculous for the good of the Church.* Then it will be very seasonable to return this song, (O *all ye works of the* LORD, bless ye the LORD: praise Him, and magnify Him for ever;) that is, ye are great occasion of blessing the LORD, who therefore be blessed, praised and magnified for ever."—Anthony Sparrow, one of the coadjutors at the revision of the Book of Common Prayer, 1661, sometime Bishop of Norwich.

This Canticle is called the Song of the Three Children in the Sarum Psalter, and was sung on the LORD's Day at Lauds, and concludes with these two verses which our Prayer Book omits, and puts the *Gloria* instead thereof:[1] "Bless we the FATHER, and the SON, with the HOLY GHOST: praise Him and highly exalt Him for ever.

"Blessed be Thou, O LORD, in the firmament of heaven: worthy to be praised, and glorious, and highly exalted for ever." See Chambers' Translation of the Sarum Psalter, p. 60.

* *Jubilate.* Not in the first Book of Edward VI, except in ordinary course of Psalms. The second Psalm at Lauds on Sundays in the Sarum Breviary.

In some Prayer Books the colon in the second verse is printed after the words "we ourselves:" it should be according to the Sealed Books after the words, "He is GOD:"

The *Jubilate,* called in the Hebrew a Song of Praise, is said by the Jews to have been sung at the Eucharistical sacrifices as the Priest was entering into the temple.

[1] Ye incline at this verse as ye do at Gloria Patri.—Mirroure, lxvii.

Jubilate. The above occasional and very restricted use of the *Jubilate* is a provision of the Church for avoiding the repetition of the same portion of Scripture in sequence.

Benedictus is the distinctive feature of Matins, as *Magnificat* is of Evensong.

Here the office of Praise ends.

138. *The Prime Function—Intercessory Prayer.*

The Apostles' Creed.

"Then shall be sung or said the Apostles' Creed by the Minister and the people, standing; except only such days as the Creed of *S. Athanasius* is appointed to be read."

HE recitation of the Creed is a Prime feature, personal and practical, and stands in avowed relation to the preceding part of the Office. It has ever succeeded hearing, whether of Psalms or other Scriptures, or both, no less than it has preceded or been associated with prayer. It is this that renders the transition to the Prayers from the Praise of the Office, viz. the Psalms, Lessons, and Canticles,—to the Prime tone from that of Matins and Lauds,—though sensible, by no means abrupt. We pass, by a delicately shaded gradation, out of the stage of service in which the objective is dominant, to that in which the subjective claims the larger part, though it can never rightly be the supreme consideration. This function is well performed by the Creed; while it rounds up, fills in, and completes the cycle of Christian doctrine, brought to view by the Lessons, it at the same time turns towards us its subjective and practical side, as the faith of living men, and admonishes that "praying is the end of preaching," and prayer in this world the condition and the instrument of the fruition of GOD.

The Creed* is said aloud, with the Minister still standing, *junctis manibus*, to express the firmness and openness with which we avow in the sight of

---

* The Apostles' Creed was formerly said under the breath; the Athanasian Creed aloud. When the two Creeds changed places in King Edward's Book, 1549, the manner and partly the occasion of using them underwent a change.

After the *Benedictus* in King Edward's First Book, is this rubric:

"*Then shall be said daily through the year, the prayers following, as well at Evensong, as at Matins, all devoutly kneeling.*"

The Order for Morning and Evening Prayer.

God and man, that it is the creed of our Baptifm, and in obedience to the XVIIIth Canon of 160¾.

In faying the Creed the choir and fuch of the clerics as are arranged laterally turn to the eaft* and therefore to the Altar.

> Lord, have mercy upon us.
> Christ, have mercy upon us.
> Lord, have mercy upon us.
> *Then the Minifter fhall fay the Creed and the* Lord's *Prayer, in Englifh, with a loud voice,"* &c.—King Edward VI's Firft Prayer Book.

See Keeling in loc. 22, 23 for fubfequent variations.

* In this work, I have suppofed all the congregation " worfhipping towards the eaft;" but where the internal arrangements of the church do not unhappily admit of this, the Faithful will doubtlefs turn to the eaft according to immemorial ufage. The cuftom is very ancient, and doubtlefs originated in the practice of the Jews, who always turned their faces in the direction of Jerufalem when they prayed. For the Jews before the captivity thus prayed towards the mercy-feat where God vouchfafed to dwell. The primitive Chriftians in like manner, and by an acceptable analogy, turned towards that part of their churches, which contained the Chriftian Holy of Holies. For Chriftian churches are generally placed with the Altar-end to the eaft, and ought always to be fo, as to the place where the Dayfpring from on high vifited us. But this is unfortunately not univerfal; and it is remarkable that in churches which are placed north and fouth, the cuftom of turning to the Altar during the Creed has immemorially prevailed. We turn to the Altar to exprefs more ftrongly our faith in Christ, Whofe death is there fpecially commemorated, and whence His moft bleffed Body and Blood are difpensed to the faithful.

The cuftom of bowing the head at the Name of Jesus has continued to be ufed during the recital of the Creeds, even where—contrary to Catholic ufage and the canons of the Church of England—it has been omitted elfewhere in Divine Service. This can only be accounted for by remembering that the cuftom was early introduced among the ceremonies of baptifm, in which it was ufual to renounce the devil with the face to the weft, and then to turn to the eaft to make the covenant with Christ, the eaft, or region of the rifing fun, being the fource of light. Hence the turning towards the eaft became affociated with the recitation of the Creed.

διὸ καὶ ὁ Θεὸς αὐτὸν ὑπερύψωσε, καὶ ἐχαρίσατο αὐτῷ ὄνομα τὸ ὑπὲρ πᾶν ὄνομα· "Ἵνα ἐν τῷ ὀνόματι Ἰησοῦ πᾶν γόνυ κάμψῃ ἐπουρανίων καὶ ἐπιγείων καὶ καταχθονίων, Καὶ πᾶσα γλῶσσα ἐξομολογήσηται ὅτι Κύριος Ἰησοῦς Χριστὸς εἰς δόξαν Θεοῦ πατρός.—Φιλ. ii. 9, 10, 11.

Canon XVIII. of 160¾.—When in time of Divine Service the Lord Jesus fhall be mentioned, due and lowly reverence fhall be done by all perfons prefent, as it hath been accuftomed, teftifying by thefe outward ceremonies and geftures their inward humility, Chriftian refolution, and due acknowledgment that the Lord Jesus Christ, the true and eternal Son of God, is the only Saviour of the world, in Whom alone all the fervices, graces, and promifes of God to mankind for this life, and the life to come, are fully and wholly comprifed.

Eliz. Injunc. 1559. Sparrow, 81.

It hath been the cuftom of Chriftian men . . . . at the Name of Jesus to bow.—Hooker, Eccl. Pol. xxx. 3, p. 531. ob. 1600.

That due reverence be vifibly done by all perfons prefent when the bleffed Name of the Lord Jesus is mentioned. Bifhop Wren's Injunctions, Card. Doc. An. II. 203.

The Order for Morning and Evening Prayer.

The rubric gives a permiſſion to ſing the Apoſtles' Creed. Now there is no record of this Creed being ſo performed in the Church of England. The Apoſtles' Creed is ſimply recited on one note, and the only inflection is the cadence on *Amen*, adopted in ſome choirs, but not found in the moſt ancient Service Books. The hymn is not conſtructed for chanting, not being divided into verſes; it is however divided into three paragraphs, as the Nicene Creed: the firſt relating to the FATHER, the ſecond to the SON, the third to the HOLY GHOST and to thoſe particulars of the Chriſtian Faith which have reference to the diſpenſation of the Spirit.

At the Name of JESUS in the Creed, the univerſal cuſtom of the Church has been to bow the head. This, however, is more than a cuſtom: it is a poſitive injunction of the Canons of the Church of England, extending however to every occaſion on which that Name of our Bleſſed LORD is repeated, which deſignates His human nature; the preſcribed act of adoration thus marking the indiſſoluble union of that Nature with the Divine. The ſame act is not preſcribed when the deſignation of His Office, CHRIST, is employed.

139. *The " Dominus Vobiſcum"—" Oremus," and Leſſer Litany.*

" And after that, theſe Prayers following, all devoutly kneeling, the Miniſter firſt pronouncing with a loud voice,"

FIRST pronouncing," i. e. *before* kneeling during the " Leſſer Litany."

It will be ſeen that the " Leſſer Litany" ſtood *before* the Creed in our firſt reviſion. But as it was of old uſed as a notice of tranſition to ſome department of ſervice, it is appropriate here, as a ſort of introit, as we paſs from the Praiſe to the Prayer of the Offices.

The ſalutation between Prieſt and people is entirely in the ſpirit, and to the purpoſe, of the old interchange of Confiteor and Miſereatur. It is ſtill to us what that formula was deſigned to be, a touching recognition of the equal need, under difference of poſition, of clergy and laity. Theſe forms, ſaith an ancient council, (Bracarenſe, A. D. 563,) all the Eaſt retains as handed down by the Apoſtles.

The Officiant turns to the faithful, and pronounces, firſt extending and then joining his hands, the Dominus Vobifcum and the Oremus. The clerks and choir refume their lateral pofition.

The "Leffer Litany" ufhering in the LORD's Prayer, Preces, and Collects, is to the *Prayer* what the "Gloria" is to the *Praife* of the whole Office; a prayer fetting the tone and fixing the object of all the reft by being addreffed to the Holy Trinity. It was triple, as with us, at its firft occurrence in the old Eaftern Offices; in our own it was threefold before the LORD's Prayer at Lauds, though ninefold at Prime.

After the Oremus all devoutly kneel, as the Prayer of the Office begins.

When the Service is faid, the choir only repeats the middle verficle; when it is chanted, the three verficles are fung by Officiant and choir.

140. *The Pater Nofter.*

"Then the Minifter, Clerks, and people, fhall fay the LORD's Prayer with a loud voice."

THE LORD's Prayer as ufed in the introductory part of the Office, acted as a fummary of all our worfhip, efpecially of the Office in hand; fo in this place it acts as a fummary, though under a different afpect. In the introductory part the doxology imparts to it that Euchariftic afpect which the "General Thankfgiving" does to the Office itfelf: in this part of the Service, from its pofition and the abfence of the doxology, it has quite another office and function. It has a baptifmal character, from its connection with the Creed, and is ufed rather, in its Prime or Compline pofition, in reference to the needs of the coming day or night, than to the remainder of the Office.

The direction* to fay the Pater Nofter with the "*clara vox*" is to abolifh the practice of faying it *fecreto*, at leaft in this place and others where the like rubrical order occurs.

---

* In ancient times the LORD's Prayer was faid fecretly, except in the two laft claufes,[1] "And lead us not," &c. "But deliver us," &c. which were repeated as verficle and refponfe with the ufual cadences.

[1] According to the Sarum ufe the *Et ne nos* and *Sed libera* were reiterated after the *Pater Nofter* and *Amen*, (faid *fecreto*,) had been finifhed. See Seager's Ed. of | Brev: Sarifbur. Fafc. i. fol. xv. and Chambers' Tranflation of the Sarum Pfalter, p. 14, note w.

141. *The Preces.*

"Then the Priest* standing up shall say."

THE Preces follow the rule of the Versicles, but the Officiant *stands junctis manibus*. The direction for the Priest to stand while saying the suffrages is a continuation of the rubric in the Sarum † Office.

The Preces‡ have an apparent reference to, and are in fact a short summary of, all that is contained in the Collect and Prayers, or in the Collect and Litany.

---

* The Rubric directs that the suffrages after the Creed should be said, "*the Priest standing.*" When a *Deacon* says prayers, he may kneel.

This Rubric was first inserted in the Second Book of Edward VI, (1552). The following is its Rationale. In the First Book of Edward VI, immediately after the *Benedictus* came the Lesser Litany, Apostles' Creed, *Paternoster* and *Preces*. The last clause of the Lord's Prayer, "But deliver us from evil, Amen," forming the first "answer" of the *Preces*, which went on as at present with "O Lord, show Thy mercy upon us,"—the Dominus Vobiscum and its "answer" forming the concluding pair of versicles. It would seem from the Rubric before the three collects which conclude the Office, that the Officiant, contrary to the Catholic use, knelt at the Preces though of course he stood at the Creed. But in the Second Book of Edward VI, the Creed was removed from its place after the Lesser Litany to its present position after the second lesson, only the Canticle intervening, followed by a direction for all to kneel devoutly at the Lesser Litany which succeeded the Creed, during which of course all stood, and as the Rubric infers at the *Dominus vobiscum*, which had been removed from the end of the Preces to the beginning of the Lesser Litany and *Paternoster*. It therefore became necessary to order the Officiant, who had been kneeling since the Oremus, to stand at the Preces in accordance with Catholic tradition, which, strangely enough, in this instance had been departed from in the First Book.

† "Finito Psalmo solus sacerdos erigat se et ad gradum cho. accedat ad mat. et ad vesperas tunc dicendo hos usus."—(ad Laudes) Brev. Sarisb. Psalt. Fol. xxii. p. 2. Paris, 1556.

"Ita tamen quod immediate post psalmum erigat se sacerdos sic dicens."—(Preces complet.) Brev. Sarisb. Psalt. Fol. lvii. p. 2. Paris, 1556.

See also Sparrow (in loc.) "It is noted that the Priest in the Holy Offices is appointed sometimes to *kneel*, sometimes to stand. The Priest being a man of like infirmities with the rest of the congregation, and so standing in need of grace and pardon, as well as the rest, in all confessions of sins and penitential prayers, such as the Litany is, is directed to beg his pardon and grace upon his knees. He being moreover a Priest of the Most High God, that hath received from Him an office and authority, sometimes *stands* to signify *that his office* and authority . . . and in all these acts of authority, such as teaching, baptizing, consecrating the Holy Eucharist, absolving the penitent, which he does in the Name and Person of Christ, he is to stand."—Rationale, 77—8. Ed. 1657.

‡ See Comber, Cosin, Freeman, Jebb, Palmer, Wheatley, in loc.

The firſt and two laſt petitions, "Grant us Thy ſalvation;" "Give peace, &c.;" "Take not Thy HOLY SPIRIT, &c.," correſpond with the three Collects which are reſpectively for ſalvation, peace, and grace. The intermediate three anſwer to the prayers for the Queen,* the Clergy, and for all conditions of men.

Theſe ſix Preces, followed by various Collects, and among them, that for the Clergy and people, and on occaſions at leaſt, if not always, one for the King, were uſed† every Sunday and Feſtival, according to the uſe of ſome Engliſh dioceſes.

142. *The Orationes.*

AT MATINS.	AT EVENSONG.
"Then ſhall follow three Collects; The firſt of the Day, which ſhall be the ſame that is appointed at the Communion; The ſecond for Peace; The third for Grace to live well. And the two laſt Collects ſhall never alter, but daily be ſaid at Morning Prayer throughout all the Year, as followeth; all kneeling.";‡	"Then ſhall follow three Collects; The firſt of the Day; The ſecond for Peace; The third for Aid againſt all Perils, as hereafter followeth: which two laſt Collects ſhall be daily ſaid at Evening Prayer without alteration."

---

* "The order in which the temporal powers and the clergy were prayed for was here, as elſewhere in the old Weſtern forms, the reverſe of that which we now have, both in theſe petitions and in the longer prayers, and which has often been ſeverely commented on as a note of Eraſtianiſm.[1] It is however the old Eaſtern order, both in Liturgies[2] and ordinary offices:[3] and indeed we may ſay, it is the order preſcribed by S. Paul himſelf."[4]—Freeman in loc.

† For examples, ſee Rev. H. O. Coxe's Forms of Bidding Prayer, p. 11, (Dioceſe of Worceſter, 1349): p. 29, (Liber Feſtivalis, 1483).

‡ The words "*all* kneeling," were inſerted at the final Reviſion in 1661. In the Firſt Book of Edward VI, the rubric concluded thus:

"*The Prieſt ſtanding up and ſaying,*
Let us pray.
Then the Collect for the Day."

It would therefore ſeem that the Prieſt ſaid the Collect ſtanding, according to the ancient uſe. In the Second Book this portion of the rubric was omitted, and Officiant and faithful probably both knelt as they generally do at preſent. But it appears that as there is no expreſs direction for the Prieſt to kneel, he may continue ſtanding, as, indeed, is the practice in ſome churches for him to do until the Anthem.

[1] See "Loſs and Gain." Compare Tracts for the Times, 86.
[2] Viz. S. Mark's; Syriac S. James'; and S. Baſil's Liturgies. The Greek S. James' does not mention "kings:" S. Chryſoſtom's and the Armenian have the Weſtern order.
[3] See the Eaſtern Lauds, Neale, pp. 915—916.
[4] 1 Tim. ii. 1, 2.

The Order for Morning and Evening Prayer.

HE first Collect connects the Ordinary with the Eucharistic Office, and is a reflection of the mind and spirit of the Epistle and Gospel, and presents the appointed variation of the Liturgy for the current week. The Collect for the Day and those immediately following should be said by the Priest standing.

"The Second Collect for Peace." | "The Second Collect at Evening Prayer."

The second collects at Morning and Evening, both entitled "for Peace," have a peculiar and deeply interesting origin. In the old English Lauds and Vesper Offices, certain "memorials" were introduced on week days varying with the season. Besides these were one or two fixed "memorials," used daily. One of these was of the HOLY SPIRIT, another of Peace. Of the Collects on the latter subject, one (our evening Collect for Peace) was used at Lauds and Vespers, the other (our Morning Collect) at Lauds only. They were from a special Eucharistic Office on the subject of Peace. These Collects represent a whole Communion Office, and are designed like that to embody and appropriate, though of course in a far lower way than the HOLY OBLATION ITSELF, our LORD'S Eucharistic promises of peace.

"The Third Collect for Grace." | "The Third Collect for Aid against all Perils."

The third Collects at Matins and Evensong are found in the Sacramentaries or Collect-books of Gelasius and S. Gregory. The third Morning Collect is based on Psalms xc. 1, 2, 3, 12, and 17; and xci. 11—16. The third Evening Collect on Psalms xiii. 4; xviii. 28; and xxi. 1—6: and in virtue of the latter reference associates us with our LORD in His commendation of His Spirit into the hands of GOD.

The intercessory part of the Office is said throughout *junctis manibus*.

143. *The Anthem.*

"In Quires and Places where they sing, here followeth the Anthem."*

HE choice of the Anthem ought to be a matter of deliberate and religious study. It should harmonize with some portion of the service of the day, the Lessons, or the Collect, or the Psalms, or the Epistle and Gospel. At each of the particular

---

* The word Anthem is a corruption of the ancient word Antiphona. It originally meant anything sung antiphonally. In the Breviary it has several significations. It is ordinarily applied to a short sentence, generally from Scripture, sung before and after one or more psalms

seasons of the year, as Lent, Advent, the Octaves of the great Festivals, and indeed the whole season from Easter to Trinity Sunday inclusive, it would be well to have a fixed rule as to the Anthems from which a selection should *invariably* be made; and on the greater Festivals the particular anthem should be designated.

Where Hymns are used, this is a proper place for them, in cases where the Anthem* cannot conveniently be sung.

---

of the day. The same name is given to the prayers or ejaculations in the commemoration used at the end of various Services; and also to the metrical hymns at the end of Compline and other Offices. In the present English Office the rubric relating to the Anthem dates from the final Revision of the Book of Common Prayer in 1661. The place of its performance seems suggested by that which the antiphons occupy in Commemorations and concluding parts of the Service of the Breviary. In respect to the Anthem in connection with the Litany,[1] we find in the time of S. Gregory the Great, that the Service (Litany) during the procession consisted in chanting a number of Anthems.

* *The Greater Antiphons of Advent.* Our Church by retaining "O Sapientia" in her Calendar on the 16th of December evidently intends that these Antiphons should be sung as formerly at the Magnificat at Vespers every day forward, except on the Feast of S. Thomas, until Christmas Eve.

Dec. 16. Antiphon. *O Sapientia.*

O Wisdom, which camest out of the mouth of the Most High, reaching from one end to another, mightily and sweetly ordering all things: Come and teach us the way of understanding.

Dec. 17. Antiphon. *O Adonai.*

O Lord, and Ruler of the house of Israel, Who appearedst to Moses in a flame of fire in the bush, and gavest him the Law in Sinai: Come and deliver us with an outstretched arm.

Dec. 18. Antiphon. *O Radix Jesse.*

O Root of Jesse, Which standest for an ensign of the people, at Whom kings shall shut their mouths, Thou to Whom the Gentiles shall seek: Come and deliver us now, tarry not.

Dec. 19. Antiphon. *O Clavis David.*

O Key of David, and Sceptre of the house of Israel, Thou that openest and no man shutteth, and shuttest and no man openeth: Come and bring the prisoners out of the prison-house, and him that sitteth in darkness and in the shadow of death.

Dec. 20. Antiphon. *O Oriens.*

O Orient, Brightness of the Everlasting Light, and Son of righteousness: Come and enlighten them that sit in darkness and in the shadow of death.

Dec. 22. Antiphon. *O Rex Gentium.*

O King and Desire of all nations, Thou Corner-stone, Who hast made both one: Come and save man, whom Thou formedst from the clay.

Dec. 23. Antiphon. *O Emmanuel.*

O Emmanuel, our King and Lawgiver, Hope of the Gentiles, and their Saviour: Come and save us, O Lord our God.

---

[1] See Procter, p. 227, where this note occurs:—"S. Gregor. *Antiphonarius*. In 'Litania majore ... ad processionem Antiphonæ;' 47 Anthems are given. Greg. M. *Opp.* iii. 689."

Hymns.—The singing of hymns has ever formed a part of Christian worship. Those formed on the ancient Catholic model, e. g. those in the "Hymnal Noted," assist very much in giving variety to our Services, and bring out objectively the great truths of the Gospel. The ancient melodies too are far superior to modern psalm tunes. The notice of what is to be sung should be given out by one of the Clergy officiating, and without any such preface as "Let us sing," &c.

Here the Office Book of Matins and Evensong ended till the Revision of 1662;* and does so still, when the Litany is said at a later hour, in which case the five prayers are omitted. It is permissible to add one or more of the Collects from those appended to the Communion Office.

In many places where the Holy Eucharist follows Matins it is customary after the anthem to omit the prayer following, and to end with the Prayer of S. Chrysostom and "The Grace,"—a custom quite worth following, as it tends to shorten the service, and does not weary people before the Holy Sacrifice is commenced.

144. *The Five Prayers.*

"Then these five Prayers following are to be read here, except when the Litany is read; and then only the two last are to be read, as they are there placed."

HE remainder of our present Office consists almost entirely of Intercessory Prayers. But though the conclusion of the Service is of so late an introduction as 1661, it belongs to a time when ancient customs were well understood. Our intercessions thus not only have their counterpart in the former phase of our ordinary Office, but follow the pattern of the Communion Office.

"A Prayer for the Queen's Majesty."†

---

* The Rubric ordering the Anthem was then first inserted.

† The Scotch Liturgy (1604) has the following rubric: "After this prayer ended, followeth the Litany; and if the Litany be not appointed to be said or sung that morning, then shall next be said the prayer for the King's Majesty, with the rest of the prayers following at the end of the Litany, and the benediction." See Keeling, p. 24.

Although the following prayers (viz. prayers for the Queen, Royal Family, Clergy and People, of S. Chrysostom, and the Benedictory Prayer) have long been used in the Church of England, yet they were not placed in their present position till the year 1661, having been previously repeated at the end of the Litany. The appellation of "prayers," which is given to these collects, in itself marks their introduction into the Divine Office at a different period

"A Prayer for the Royal Family."
"A Prayer for the Clergy and people."*
"A Collect or Prayer for all Conditions of men, to be used at such times when the Litany is not appointed to be said."

It is not necessary to give notice of such persons as desire the prayers of the Church before the Prayer for all Estates of Men, as the congregation are advertised of the fact in the Prayer itself.

"A General Thanksgiving."

It is customary to introduce the General Thanksgiving *daily* in this place; but there is no rubrical authority for its continual use, which rests on purely voluntary grounds. Some ritualists hold that its interpolation interrupts, as it certainly lengthens the Service. Others that it perfects

---

to the collects. The Rubric before the collect for the day says, "Then shall follow three *collects*." That before the collect for the king, "Then these five *prayers* following." Had these prayers been all introduced at the same time, they would all have been called "collects" or "prayers." (See Keeling, pp. 24, 25, 48, 49, for the dates of the changes in the position of these prayers in our service book). In fact there are now six collects after the collect for the day, besides the benedictory prayer. According to the ancient English Offices, these collects would be termed *memoriæ* or commemorations, *de Pace, de Gratia, pro Reginâ*,[1] &c. But see Palmer, *in loco*, vol. i. p. 248.

The *earliest form* of this prayer that has yet been discovered occurs in two little books, from the press of Berkelet, the king's printer, at the end of the reign of King Henry VIII. and the beginning of Edward VI. In the Prayer Book of Edward VI. this prayer was not put in the morning or evening service, it was, however, placed in the Primer (1553) as "*the fourth collect for the King*" at morning prayer; and another and shorter form, "*Prayer for the King*," was added to the collects "*for Peace*" and "*for aid against all Perils*" at evening prayer. In Elizabeth's time this prayer for the Queen was altered and shortened and together with the prayer for the clergy and people was placed before the "*Prayer of Chrysostome*" at the end of the Litany, where it remained till the rubric of 1661 placed it in its present position.

See Procter, pp. 218—220. Keeling, 24, 25, 48, 49. "Liturgies of Edward VI, and other documents," pp. 393—406. Ed. Park. Soc.

The prayer itself was approved if not composed by Archbishop Whitgift, and appears for the first time after the revision by King James on his sole authority. The place it then occupied was among the collects at the end of the Litany. See Cardwell's Conf. p. 235. Procter, p. 220. Keeling, pp. 24, 45, 50.

The prayers for the Queen, &c. are placed in precisely the same situation they would have occupied, had they been repeated in the Ordinary Office by the English Church in ancient times. See Palmer, *in loc*. vol. i. p. 218.

* "O omnipotens sempiterne Deus, qui facis mirabilia magna solus: prætende super famulos tuos pontifices, et super cunctas congregationes illis commissas, spiritum gratiæ salutaris: et ut

[1] Brev. Sar. Psalt. fol. xxii. Memoriæ Communes ad Laudes.

the Euchariſtic analogy of the Office, holding as it does a parallel poſition to the "Gloria in excelſis" in the Liturgy. Its uſe or diſuſe daily, or otherwiſe, muſt be left entirely to the direction of the Officiant.

"A Prayer of S. Chryſoſtom."*

The Prayer of S. Chryſoſtom ſums up in a reverſe or retroſpective order the features of the foregoing Office, deſiring firſt the fulfilment of our *petitions*; ſecondly, *knowledge* of GOD's truth; thirdly, life everlaſting, the occupation of which will be endleſs *praiſe*. And though this was perhaps not contemplated in appointing it, it is at leaſt ſignificant, that in its ancient Eaſtern poſition it was part of a *prelude* (the prayer of the ſecond antiphon to the hymn "Only-begotten") to the Holy Communion.

The Benedictory Prayer.†
"2 Cor. xiii."

---

in veritate tibi complaceant, perpetuum eis rorem tuæ benedictionis infunde."—Brev. Sariſ. Pſalt. fol. lx. p. 2. Paris, 1556.

This collect is as old as the fifth century, being found in the Sacramentary of Gelaſius, A. D. 494. Gelaſii Sacramentar. Muratori, tom. i. p. 719. (quoted from Palmer).

This was originally one of the prayers after the Litany, and was alſo in the Scotch Service Book (1637), though ſlightly altered. See Keeling, 50, 51. There has been an Engliſh verſion of it in the Primer ſince the fourteenth century. See Maſkell, Mon. Rit. vol. ii. p. 107.

* This prayer is found in the Liturgies of SS. Baſil and Chryſoſtom; and although the compoſition of it cannot be traced to either of thoſe fathers, the prayer has been very anciently uſed in the Liturgies which bear their names. This prayer was placed at the end of the Litany when that Service was reviſed by Cranmer in 1544, and at the concluſion of the Daily Matins and Evenſong in 1661, according to the rubric of the Prayer Book for Scotland (1637).—See Procter, *in loc.* p. 222.

† This prayer is derived from the Liturgies of the Eaſtern Churches,[1] in which it has been probably uſed from the moſt primitive times. It is a common form of bleſſing uſed by S. Paul at the cloſe of his epiſtles, turned into a benedictory prayer. The benediction appointed in the Breviary at the concluſion of the prayers at Prime was nothing more than the ordinary commencement of a religious action, "In the Name of the FATHER, and of the SON, and of the HOLY GHOST." This was omitted in the Reformed Offices, but nothing was ſubſtituted until our preſent precatory form was placed at the concluſion of "the Litany uſed in the Queen's Chapel." The words are ſomewhat altered from what they are in the text whence they are taken. For 1. The firſt perſon is put for the ſecond, ſo that the Officiant ſhares in them: 2. The word "evermore" is added. By the former of theſe alterations the form is turned from a benediction into a prayer. It is alſo expreſsly called a "prayer" in the rubric before the Prayer for the Sovereign. There is therefore no direction for the Officiant to ſtand whilſt he utters it, as there would have been had it been a benediction,—he remains kneeling as in the other prayers.—See Procter, p. 222, and Stephens, Ed. of Book of Common Prayer, *in loc.*

[1] The form occurred in the Liturgies of Antioch, Cæſarea, Conſtantinople, and Jeruſalem.—Goar. Euchol. pp. 75—165.

The Prayer which concludes our Office ſtands related in ſeveral ways to the ancient ritual. It repreſents firſt, the cloſing Prime and Compline benedictions, of which the former was in the Name of the FATHER, SON, and HOLY GHOST. Again, it was the ſhort chapter uſed at Terce, or Nine a.m. Office, on Sundays throughout the Weſt; and as ſuch, and not merely as a ſuitable apoſtolic benediction, found its way to its preſent poſition. But the ſelection of it for that hour on the firſt day of the week, (ſaid to be due to S. Ambroſe), doubtleſs aroſe from the fact that it formed throughout the greater part of the Eaſt, the introductory benediction to the more ſolemn part of the Communion Office; for the celebration of which Nine a.m., the hour of the deſcent of the HOLY SPIRIT, was more eſpecially ſet apart.

The chief excellence accordingly of this concluſion is, that while it breathes the preſent peace of old apoſtolic bleſſing, it is nevertheleſs not an abſolute concluſion at all, but points onward ſtill to ſome better thing hoped for; and ſo leaves the ſpirit, which has moſt faithfully yielded up itſelf to the joys of this lower ſervice, in the attitude of one unſatisfied ſtill, and expecting a higher conſolation.

"Here endeth the Order for Morning Prayer throughout the Year."

145. *Manner of leaving the Choir.*

THE Clergy and choriſters leave the chancel and return to the ſacriſty in exactly the ſame order in which they entered it, (ſee Par. 119, 120), the people ſtanding in like manner as when the proceſſion entered the nave before the beginning of the Office.

N. B.—After Office the Service Books ſhould be placed in their covers by the Sacriſtan.*

---

* "Be they (viz. the Service Books and Bible) well and fairly bound and emboſſed? and at end of Divine Service are they claſped or well tied up with fair ſtrings, to keep out duſt and ſoil, and to prevent tearing of the leaves?"—Bp. Montague's Viſitation Articles, p. 49, No. 3.

The Order for Morning and Evening Prayer.

146.

THE ORDER FOR EVENING PRAYER,
DAILY THROUGHOUT THE YEAR.

THE rules for Evensong mainly follow those for Matins. On great occasions when there are many clergy present, and the stalls are all filled, and solemn Vespers are being sung, the Officiant, vested in cassock, surplice, and cope of the colour of the day, attended either by two Clergy in albs and dalmatics, also of the colour of the day, or by two Acolytes, may occupy a position with his attendants on the south side of the sanctuary—not in the sedilia proper, but on stools or forms placed in front of the sedilia, thus:—

| North. | Holy ✠ Altar. | South. |

All facing the North.
{ Deacon or Acolyte.
Priest Officiant at Vespers.
Deacon or Acolyte. }

147. *The Magnificat.*

IT was formerly the old English custom to use incense at the Magnificat.

"While the antiphon of the 'Benedictus' or 'Magnificat' was being sung, the Priest, who had retired during the last verse of the hymn, returned with his silken cope, Taper-bearers, and Thuribles; and the boy having offered him the Thurible, he filled it with incense and blessed it; and bowing to the altar, censed it in the middle, then the right, then the left, then the reliquary of the church; then bowing at the lowest step of the altar, he returned to his stall. Then the boy censed the Priest himself, then the Rulers of the Choir, then the Dignitaries in order, beginning with the Dean's side and ending on the Precentor's side: bowing to each as he did so." From the Arlyngham MSS. at Vespers. Chambers' Sarum Psalter, p. 65.

144 The Order for Morning and Evening Prayer.

On Sundays and Festivals incense should be used at Evensong, during the singing of the *Magnificat*, and additional tapers may be lighted. This canticle—a daily memorial of the Incarnation—being its special feature; some of those who are taking part in the service should indicate this by gathering together in front of the Altar while it is being chanted, taking up, for the time being, such a position as that described here:—

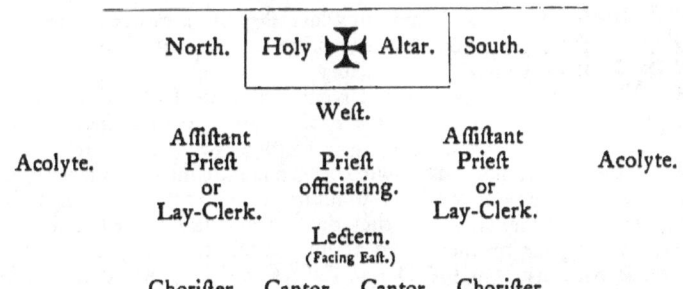

The officiating Priest, having had the thurible and incense-boat brought to him by two Acolytes, may silently bless the incense in the following terms: "Vouchsafe, we beseech Thee, O Almighty God, to bless ✠ and sanctify ✠ this incense, and grant that we who are permitted to worship Thee in Thy courts on earth, may hereafter adore Thee for ever in heaven. Amen," and then proceed to incense the Altar. He should incense the Cross first with three swings of the thurible: then the Gospel, and after that the Epistle side of the Altar. He then incenses the Altar from end to end, beginning at the Epistle corner, going on to the Gospel corner and returning to the centre, where, swinging the thurible from side to side for a few moments, he again incenses the Cross, and then returns the thurible to the thurifer, who will proceed to incense (1) the Priest Officiant at Vespers, (2) the assistant Clergy, and (3) each side of the choir, and lastly, (4) the congregation, first towards the north and finally towards the south side.

At the conclusion of the Evening Service—after the Sermon—if there be any Hymns sung, collections made, collects said, or blessing given, the same positions as those indicated in the above diagram may again be taken up by the Priest officiating and his assistants.

The Order for Morning and Evening Prayer. 145

148.

CAUTIONS AND DIRECTIONS.

Caution to officiant and choir in recitation of the Divine Offices.

THE officiant and choir should rather use a *monotoned* rendering of the confession than any other, as its position in the Divine Office is merely introductory.

The Creeds in the Divine Office are said *junctis manibus* throughout. The members of the choir should be instructed to stand upright, and not to lean slovenly against either the back or front of the stalls. They should not look about them, nor stare down the church, but should be intent on the work of praising Almighty GOD. When they kneel, care should be taken that they do so reverently, in order, and in a formal and regular manner. All should kneel down together, and all should rise together. In the Divine Offices the choir should turn to the east at the *Glorias*, and during Evensong, at the *Magnificat*, i. e. if it be the custom of the Church to do so. No individual member of the choir should introduce any practices which have not had the sanction and approval of the Priest of the church and of the appointed master of the ceremonies. During the collects and prayers the choir should kneel *junctis manibus*. During the Lessons and Sermon, they should be careful to sit upright, and not to lounge nor look about. They should not sit cross-legged, and their hands should be placed in the lap. They will make the sign of the cross at the beginning and ending of each Office, and in other parts of Divine Service when and where it is the custom to do so.

149. *The Cope.**

IT is proper and quite in accordance with the terms of the rubric of Edward VI's First Prayer Book, to wear a Cope of the proper colour at Solemn Vespers, viz. on the Evensong—both First and Second—of Sundays and Festivals.

---

* Copes were worn at Durham till lately. See Hierurgia Anglicana; Table of Contents, p. xvii.

U

150. *The Collects.*

OTH Sarum, Roman and Greek Offices order the Collects, properly so called, to be said *standing*. Our present rubric at Evensong, placed at the head of the Versicles and Responses, does the same. Notwithstanding custom to the contrary, it is undoubtedly right—following the ancient tradition of the Church of England—that the Collects be said standing. At the commencement of each Collect the Officiant's hands should be slightly extended; they should be joined, however, during the singing or saying of the Collect itself.

151. *Reading.*

HE way in which many pronounce, or rather mispronounce *o* is a growing defect in reading, viz. it is pronounced more like the Italian or French long *a*, or like our *au;* whereas it should have a round sound.

152. *A Collection after Office.*

F a "Collection" is made after Office, a Hymn, Metrical Litany or Anthem should be sung, during which the Alms should be collected by deacons, acolytes, or other fit persons habited in cassock and surplice. The alms bags will be reverently presented to the Priest, who will place them on the altar.

153. *Dress of the Preacher after Office.*

CASSOCK, surplice, hood or tippet, and stole.

154.

CREED OF S. ATHANASIUS.

Quicunque vult.

AT MORNING PRAYER.

" Upon thefe Feafts; *Chriftmas-day*, the *Epiphany*, Saint *Matthias*, *Eafter-day*, *Afcenfion-day*, *Whitfunday*, Saint *John Baptift*, Saint *James*, Saint *Bartholomew*, Saint *Matthew*, Saint *Simon* and Saint *Jude*, Saint *Andrew*, and upon *Trinity Sunday*, fhall be fung or faid at Morning Prayer, inftead of the Apoftles' Creed, this Confeffion of our Chriftian Faith, commonly called The Creed of Saint *Athanafius*, by the Minifter and people ftanding."

IT will be feen from the Rubric that the Athanafian Creed, or as it has been called the Pfalm *Quicunque vult*, is ordered on all Feafts of our LORD; on that of the HOLY GHOST; on that of the ever-bleffed TRINITY; on that of the Forerunner; and on that of every Apoftle *whofe eve is fafted*, with two exceptions, SS. Peter and Thomas; in the firft inftance, becaufe it has already been faid five days previoufly; in the other, becaufe it will be faid four days fubfequently. With the occafion then of repeating the Creed, the repetition is dropped, and this is perfectly in analogy with Catholic ufe in other points.

It fhould be remembered that the Creed of S. Athanafius is fung or faid upon certain *Feafts*, and when thofe Feafts are *only commemorated by the ufe of the Collect as a memorial*, the Pfalm *Quicunque vult* is not to be ufed. For inftance, when Advent Sunday falls on S. Andrew's Day, the Sunday takes precedence of the Saint's Day, being its fuperior, and confequently the Service for the Sunday is ufed, the Saint's Day fimply commemorated by its collect, and the Athanafian Creed is *not faid*. This Creed fhould never be fung when the Service for the Feaft on which it is ordered to be faid is not ufed.

In fome churches the Athanafian Creed is ftrangely enough the only portion of Matins which is faid colloquially—not even monotoned; but this is moft anomalous, and arifes from the current notion that Creeds are not Hymns, contrary to the univerfal acceptation of the Church.

148 The Order for Morning and Evening Prayer.

155.

THE LITANY.

"Here followeth the Litany, or General Supplication to be sung or said after Morning Prayer upon *Sundays, Wednesdays* and *Fridays*, and at other times, when it shall be commanded by the Ordinary."

156. *Vestments.*

CASSOCK, surplice and hood; or cassock, alb* and tippet.

157. *Position of the Litany-desk.*†

THE small desk for the Litany should be placed, as the Sarum Processional directs, in the midst of the choir, viz. between the east end of the choir and the altar. While some ritualists hold that the desk should be placed in front of the gates of the Rood-screen at the east end of the nave; the ancient English use seems preferable. If it be at all in the way at other times, it may be removed; especially for a great function.

---

* In the Sarum Rite, the rubric specifies the alb as the proper vestment. "The Priests and their Ministers in albs without the Cross."[1] See Chambers' Sarum Psalter, p. 466.
On Easter Eve, *when alone* the Litany was actually incorporated in the Mass; the Priest put off his chasuble and put on a red cope until the Litany was finished. See Chambers' Psalter, *ibid.*

† "Immediately before High Mass, the Priest with others of the choir, shall kneel in the midst of the church,² and sing or plainly say the Litany which is set forth in English, with all the suffrages following."—Injunctions of Edward VI. 1547. Sparrow's Collection, p. 8.
"Immediately before the time of Communion of the Sacrament, the Priests, with others of the choir, shall kneel in the midst of the church, and sing or say plainly and distinctly the Litany which is set forth in English with the suffrages following."—Injunctions of Elizabeth, 1559. Sparrow's Collection, p. 72.
"The Priest goeth from his seat into the body of the church, and at a low desk before the chancel door .... kneels, and says or sings the Litany. See the Prophet Joel, speaking of a place between the porch and the altar, where the priest and the prophet were commanded to weep and to say, '*Spare Thy People*, O LORD,' &c. at the time of a fast."—Bishop Andrewes' notes in Nicholls' Commentary, p. 23, second Edition.

[1] Probably the Processional Cross.
[2] i. e. In the midst of the *nave*.

158.

WO Priests, or a Priest attended by two choirmen, or two acolytes, can sing the Litany. If the Priest be unable to sing himself, the Cantor or Precentor may take the Priest's part. When the Litany is used as a distinct Service, the Canon requires that warning shall be given to the people by tolling of a bell.*

159.

"LL manner of persons then present shall reverently kneel upon their knees, when the . . . *Litany* and other Prayers are read." Canon xviii. 1603.

160. *Notice of Persons who desire the Prayers of the Church.*

WHEN persons in sickness desire the prayers of the Church, notice should always be given (though not by name after the first time) at the commencement of the Litany in these words, "The Prayers of the Church are desired for A. B."

"That it may please Thee to preserve all that travel by land or by water, all women labouring of child, all sick persons, and young children; and to show Thy pity upon all prisoners and captives;"

After the words "sick persons" a pause should be made for the offering up of special prayer; but no clause should be inserted such as "especially for those," &c.

161.

WHEN the Holy Communion is to follow the Litany—the Clergy and Choir may return to the Sacristy to vest, in the same processional order as at Matins.

---

* Canon XV. of 1603¼.
Archbishop Grindal was the first who ordered the Morning Prayer, Litany, and Communion Office to be celebrated at the same time. Thus a Protestant innovation was introduced, which has produced much mischief, and needs to be vigorously set aside.

162.

HE Litany ought never to be said on Wednesdays or Fridays, if a Festival occurs on those days; because, of course, the Office of the Feast takes the place of the Office of the *Feria*. And if a Festival of a higher character than an ordinary Sunday occurs on Sunday, the Service being that of the Feast and not of the Sunday, the Litany will be omitted.

163.

THE OCCASIONAL PRAYERS.

PRAYERS AND THANKSGIVINGS UPON SEVERAL OCCASIONS,

To be used before the two final Prayers of the Litany, or of Morning and Evening Prayer.

PRAYERS.

"In the Ember Weeks, to be said every day, for those that are to be admitted into Holy Orders."

HE second Ember Collect seems most suited for Saturday, the other for the previous days in Ember-week.

"A Prayer that may be said after any of the former."

See Par. 114, p. 107.

"A Prayer for the High Court of Parliament, to be read during their Session."

If the Houses adjourn themselves for a fortnight or longer time, it is still the *same Session*, and consequently this prayer is to be used. It should not be used, if they are prorogued for a shorter time, because that period is not reckoned part of the Session, they not being empowered to do business, as upon adjournment they are.

"A Collect or Prayer for all Conditions of men, to be used at such times when the Litany is not appointed to be said."

Bishop Gunning, the reputed author of this prayer, would never suffer it to be read in the chapel of his college at Evensong. Its use must be left to the discretion of the Officiant.

THANKSGIVINGS.

"A General Thankfgiving."

See *supra*, Par. 144, p. 140.

164.

THE COLLECTS, EPISTLES, AND GOSPELS,
TO BE USED THROUGHOUT THE YEAR.

"Note.—That the Collect appointed for every Sunday, or for any Holy-day that hath a Vigil or Eve, shall be said at the Evening Service next before."

Sundays before Advent.

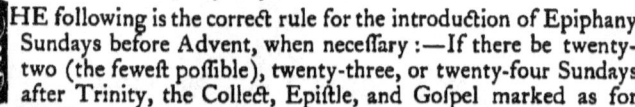HE following is the correct rule for the introduction of Epiphany Sundays before Advent, when necessary :—If there be twenty-two (the fewest possible), twenty-three, or twenty-four Sundays after Trinity, the Collect, Epistle, and Gospel marked as for the twenty-fifth Sunday are to be said on the Sunday next before Advent, to the omission of the others. If there be twenty-six, on the twenty-fifth are to be said the Collect, Epistle, and Gospel of the sixth Sunday after Epiphany. If there be twenty-seven (the greatest number possible), on the twenty-fifth the Collect, &c. of the fifth; and on the twenty-sixth, those of the sixth after Epiphany. And the Collect, Epistle, and Gospel marked as for the twenty-fifth Sunday after Trinity, are always to be said on the Sunday next before Advent.*

The First Sunday in Advent.

"This Collect is to be repeated every day, with the other Collects in Advent until Christmas Eve."

" With the other Collects," that is, as a " memorial" after the Collect for the day and other memorial Collect if there be one.

The Epiphany.

The Rubric after the Circumcision is as follows :—

" The same Collect, Epistle, and Gospel shall serve for every day after unto the Epiphany."

Acting by analogy, the Collect, Epistle, and Gospel serve for every day after unto the Sunday after Epiphany. At Saturday Evensong the Collect for the Sunday will, of course, be used instead of that for the Epiphany.

The Ascension Day.

On the days between this Feast and the Sunday after, the same rule will, of course, be followed.

---

* There are Lessons given for twenty-six Sundays. For the Twenty-seventh, when it occurs, the Lessons must be taken from the Monthly Calendar.

The Occasional Offices.

165.

THE MINISTRATION OF
PUBLIC BAPTISM OF INFANTS,
TO BE USED IN THE CHURCH.

OR Holy Baptifm fhould be fecured—
(1.) The integrity of the matter.
(2.) The integrity of the form.
(3.) The contact of the matter with the perfon.
(4.) The effential unity of the action in combination of matter and form together.

"The people are to be admonifhed, that it is moft convenient that Baptifm fhould not be adminiftered but upon Sundays and other Holy-days, when the moft number of people come together: as well for that the congregation there prefent may teftify the receiving of them that be newly baptized into the number of CHRIST's Church; as alfo becaufe in the Baptifm of Infants, every man prefent may be put in remembrance of his own profeffion made to GOD in his baptifm. For which caufe alfo it is expedient that baptifm be adminiftered in the vulgar tongue. Neverthelefs (if neceffity fo require), children may be baptized upon any other day.

"And note, that there fhall be for every male-child to be baptized two godfathers and one godmother: and for every female, one godfather and two godmothers.*

"When there are children to be baptized, the parents fhall give knowledge thereof over night, or in the morning before the beginning of Morning Prayer to the curate. And then the

---

* In a council held at York, in 1195, it is decreed:—"Statuimus ne in baptifmate plures quam tres fufcipiunt puerum de facro fonte; mafculum duo mares, et una mulier; fœminam duæ fœminæ, et unus mas." A fimilar order was made in a council at Durham. (Wilkins' Conc. Vol. i. p. 576) A.D. 1220. And again at a Synod of Worcefter (*Ibid.* Vol. i. p. 667) in 1240. The Canon (XXIX.) which forbids parents to be fponfors for their own children, is in ftrict conformity with the Sarum rubric:—"Similiter pater vel mater non debet proprium filium de facro fonte levare, nec baptizare, nifi in extremæ neceffitatis articulo." This, however, does not feem to have been always obferved. In Leofric's Miffal we find the

The Public Baptism of Infants.

godfathers and godmothers, and the people with the Children, muſt be ready at the font, either immediately after the laſt Leſſon at Morning Prayer, or elſe immediately after the laſt Leſſon at Evening Prayer, as the curate by his direction ſhall appoint. And the Prieſt coming to the font (which is then* to be filled with pure water) and ſtanding there, ſhall ſay,"

If Baptiſm be adminiſtered after the Second Leſſon at Evenſong, the choir and Prieſt ſhould go in proceſſion to the font. On either ſide of the Prieſt an Acolyte ſhould walk, one with the Service Book, and the other with the Baptiſmal ſhell and napkin. If ſeveral children are to be baptized, the Acolyte or pariſh clerk ſhould inſtruct the people with male children to ſtand on the Prieſt's right (facing eaſt,) and thoſe with females on his left.† Care ſhould be taken, for the ſake of order and ſo that no delay be cauſed, that thoſe in charge of the children be directed to give them into the Prieſt's arms with their heads towards his left ſhoulder. The males will be baptized firſt, and then the females.

Veſtments: caſſock, ſurplice, two ſtoles, one of violet and one of white ſilk. The violet to be worn till the Interrogations, when the white one is aſſumed.

The ancient Sarum uſe was to wear a violet ſtole in the firſt part of the Office, and to lay it aſide for a white one before the Interrogations and the "Ego te baptizo," &c. The Roman uſe‡ is the ſame.

The names of the Sponſors ſhould always be ſent in with the notice of a Baptiſm that is deſired to take place; and they ſhould be made to anſwer the queſtions one by one.

"It appertaineth to the Office of a Deacon, in the Church where he ſhall be appointed to ſerve, in the abſence of the Prieſt to baptize infants." Ordinal.

---

words, "Et accipiat preſbyter eos a parentibus eorum," which, explained by a further order given in the Bangor Pontifical, that the ſame parties who give the child to the prieſt ſhould take it back from his arms, would neceſſarily imply that parents might be admitted to anſwer for their own children. Our own rule forbids the father, but allows the *mother* to be ſponſor. See Canon XXIX.

* In ſome churches it is the practice for an acolyte to fill the font with pure water, (for which purpoſe a large latten veſſel ſhould be provided), in the preſence of the congregation immediately before the adminiſtration of Holy Baptiſm.

† "Maſculus autem ſtatuitur a dextra ſacerdotis; mulier vero a ſiniſtris." Manuale ad uſum percelebris eccleſiæ Sariſ. 1554; Ordo ad ſac. cat. In Leofric's Miſſal, "Baptizantur *primi* maſculi, deinde fœminæ."

‡ "Tunc Sacerdos indutus ſuperpelliceo et ſtola violacei coloris," &c. Rituale Angl. Bangor, MSS. "Hic deponit ſtolam violaceam, et ſumit aliam albi coloris." Rit. Rom. Lutetiæ Pariſiorum, 1665. (De Sac. Bap.)

x

It is defirable always to have at leaft one lay clerk or chorifter in attendance, habited in caffock and fhort furplice, or cotta, to hold the fervice book, and fhell (if the Prieft ufe one), and to make the refponfes, &c.

A napkin of fine linen, marked with a fmall crofs, fhould always be prepared for ufe at the font, e. g. to wipe the Prieft's fingers before taking the Service Book into the hand again.

It is proper for the Prieft, in celebrating this Sacrament, to make the fign of the crofs (" Hic dividat facerdos aquam manu fua dextra in modum crucis."—Ritual. Sarifb.) in the water at the words, " Sanctify this water," in the Prayer of Benediction. He alfo makes the fign of the crofs on the child's forehead, as the rubric directs. It fhould be made with the thumb of the right hand. He ought to ftand throughout according to the Sarum ufe, " verfus orientem."[*]

The cuftom of the Weftern Church, Englifh as well as Roman, is to pour the water in baptifm thrice[†]—once at the name of each perfon of the ever-Bleffed TRINITY—on the head of the recipient (which fhould always be uncovered for that purpofe).[‡] Sprinkling is not recognized by the rubric of the Englifh Church.[§] By the Canon law, confirmed by the Ecclefiaftical Courts, baptifm, although adminiftered by a woman or even by a heretic or fchifmatic, ought not, if the proper form and matter have been ufed, to be iterated, conditionally or otherwife.

With regard to names given to children, the Prieft has the power of

---

[*] Sarif. Manuale.

[†] " In the ancient Church the child to be baptized, was thrice dipped in the font, in the name of the FATHER, and of the SON, and of the HOLY GHOST; femblably is he to be thrice afperfed with water on his face, (if for fear of danger, not dipped, as the Book of Common Prayer appointeth) the Prieft ufing thofe facramental words ; after which act doth he receive the child into his arms, unto CHRIST's flock, and then fet the badge of Chriftianity upon him, figning him with the fign of the Crofs." Bifhop Montague's Vifitation Articles, p. 72, No. 7.

[‡] The ancient Englifh form of Baptifm is as follows:—" Deinde accipiat facerdos infantem per latera in manibus fuis, et interrogato nomine ejus, baptizet eum fub trina immerfione, tantum Sanctam Trinitatem invocando ita dicens, *N. et ego baptizo te in nomine Patris;* et mergat eum femel verfa facie ad aquilonem, et capite verfus orientem : *et Filii;* et iterum mergat femel verfa facie ad meridiem : *et Spiritus Sancti; Amen.* Et mergat tertio recta facie verfus aquam." At the fame time affufion was allowed according to our prefent practice. The practice of figning the infant with the chrifm followed immediately on the baptifm. In our formulary the announcement of its public reception into the Church takes the place of this ceremony, and of that of putting on the chrifom. Hence the fign of the crofs is made upon the child's forehead with the *thumb*.[1]

[§] Immerfion is the rule of the Englifh Church with permiffion to ufe affufion.

[1] "Hic liniat infantem de ipfo chrifmate cum pollice in vertice in modum crucis, dicens." Manuale Sarifbur. fol. xiii.

Private Baptism of Children.

altering them if they seem to him improper. It is well to give the godfathers and godmothers, in such a case, time to change the proposed name. It is a constitution of Archbishop Peckham,* A.D. 1281, which directs the Clergy to take care not to allow wanton names to be imposed on infants, especially those of the female sex. After a Baptism, the water should be let off immediately, otherwise it would be often consecrated over again.

166.

THE MINISTRATION OF
PRIVATE BAPTISM OF CHILDREN
IN HOUSES.

"The curates of every parish shall often admonish the people, that they defer not the baptism of their children longer than the first or second Sunday next after their birth, or other Holy-day falling between, unless upon a great and reasonable cause, to be approved by the curate.

"And also they shall warn them, that without like great cause and necessity they procure not their children to be baptized at home in their houses. But when need shall compel them so to do, then baptism shall be administered on this fashion:

"First, let the Minister of the parish (or in his absence, any other lawful Minister that can be procured) with them that are present call upon GOD, and say the LORD's Prayer, and so many of the Collects appointed to be said before in the Form of Public Baptism, as the time and present exigence will suffer. And then, the child being named by some one that is present, the Minister shall pour water upon it, saying these words:

"N. I baptize thee in the Name of the FATHER, and of the SON, and of the HOLY GHOST. Amen.

"Then, all kneeling down, the Minister shall give thanks unto GOD, and say,

"We yield Thee hearty thanks, most merciful FATHER, that it hath pleased Thee to regenerate *this Infant* with Thy Holy SPIRIT, to receive *him* for Thine own child by adoption, and to incorporate *him* into Thy holy Church. And we humbly beseech Thee to grant, that as *he* is now made *partaker* of the death of Thy SON, so *he* may be also of His resurrection; and that finally, with the residue of Thy Saints, *he* may inherit Thine everlasting kingdom; through the same Thy SON JESUS CHRIST our LORD. *Amen.*"

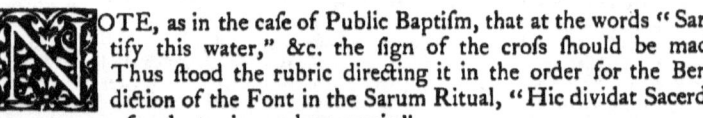OTE, as in the case of Public Baptism, that at the words "Sanctify this water," &c. the sign of the cross should be made. Thus stood the rubric directing it in the order for the Benediction of the Font in the Sarum Ritual, "Hic dividat Sacerdos aquam manu sua dextra in modum crucis."

---

* Lyndwood, Lib. 3, tit. 24. "Attendant sacerdotes, ne lasciva nomina, quæ scilicet, mox prolata, sonent in lasciviam, imponi permittant parvulis baptizatis, sexus præcipue fœminini." But see Stephens' edition of Book of Common Prayer, vol. ii. fol. 1286.

For private baptifm it is convenient for the parifh Prieft to have a baptifmal bafket, containing an Office Book, in fmall quarto: a fmall brafs veffel* marked with a crofs and facred monogram, and lined with lead—the material of the veffel itfelf being latten; a furplice, two ftoles—one of violet, the other of white filk; two linen napkins—one to fpread on the table, and the other to wipe the fingers, both marked with a red crofs; and a baptifmal fhell. The proper prayers to ufe are, the LORD'S Prayer; "Almighty and immortal GOD;" "Almighty and everlafting GOD, heavenly FATHER;" "Almighty everliving GOD."

The water, of which it is well, therefore, only to blefs a fmall quantity, fhould be taken into the church, and poured into the font and allowed to run away through the drain.

"And let them not doubt, but that the child fo baptized is lawfully and fufficiently baptized and ought not to be baptized again. Yet neverthelefs, if the child, which is after this fort baptized, do afterwards live, it is expedient that it be brought into the church, to the intent that, if the Minifter of the fame parifh did himfelf baptize that child, the congregation may be certified of the true Form of Baptifm, by him privately before ufed: In which cafe he fhall fay thus,

"I Certify you, that according to the due and prefcribed order of the Church, *at fuch a time*, and *at fuch a place*, before divers witneffes I baptized this child."

The Prieft having certified the faithful of the true form of Baptifm will then proceed to admit the child into the Church, beginning the Office provided for that purpofe, (fee the Miniftration of Private Baptifm of Children in houfes. Book of Common Prayer), at the Gofpel.

"But if the child were baptized by any other lawful Minifter;† then the Minifter of the parifh where the child was born or chriftened, fhall examine and try whether the child be lawfully baptized, or no. In which cafe, if thofe that bring any child to the church, do anfwer that the fame child is already baptized, then fhall the Minifter examine them further, faying,"

---

* The veffel ufed in private baptifms feems anciently to have been of fufficient fize for the practice of immerfion, as may be gathered from a glofs of Lyndwood's (Lib. 3, tit. 24), who fpeaking of an order that the veffel employed as above fhould be burnt or fet afide for the ufe of the Church, explains this to mean fuch ufes as to wafh veftments in, "vel poffunt talia vafa verti ad ufum prælati ecclefiæ in aliquo minifterio honefto."

† The term "lawful minifter" with regard to the Sacrament of Baptifm includes under certain circumftances not only perfons clerical but lay. But even if it meant an "ordained" minifter only, it would fimply act as a difcouragement to lay and fchifmatical Baptifms, for which purpofe it was introduced in the Book of 1604, as treating them as *irregular* but *valid*, and therefore not to be reiterated conditionally or otherwife, for the proper matter and form are alone effential to this Sacrament, "a lawful (ordained) minifter is *not*." See Mafkell's Holy Baptifm, c. ix. Procter, p. 361. Cardwell's Hift. of Conf. c. iii.

The best plan which can be adopted in uniting the two Baptismal Offices for Infants, is to cause the child (or children) that is about to be admitted into the Church to stand in a separate position (the sponsors of such child remaining with the other sponsors) and then to proceed with the Service as though it were an ordinary baptism till after the benediction of the water; and this done, to call up the child *and receive it into the Church before the others are baptized*. In this way there is no real awkwardness in the Service, provided that the sponsors of the child to be admitted can be made to understand that *they are not to answer the third question*— "Wilt thou be baptized in this faith?"

THE MINISTRATION OF
BAPTISM TO SUCH AS ARE OF RIPER YEARS,*
AND ABLE TO ANSWER FOR THEMSELVES.

"When any such persons, as are of riper years, are to be baptized, timely notice should be given to the Bishop, or whom he shall appoint for that purpose, a week before at the least, by the parents, or some other discreet persons; that so due care may be taken for their examination, whether they be sufficiently instructed in the Principles of the Christian Religion; and that they may be exhorted to prepare themselves with Prayers and Fasting for the receiving of this holy Sacrament.

"And if they shall be found fit, then the Godfathers and Godmothers (the people being assembled upon the Sunday or Holy-day appointed) shall be ready to present them at the Font immediately after the second Lesson, either at Morning or Evening Prayer, as the Curate in his discretion shall think fit.

"And standing there, the Priest shall ask, whether any of the persons here presented be baptized or no: If they shall answer, No; then shall the Priest say thus."

167. *Immersion and Affusion.*

"Then shall the Priest take each person to be baptized by the right hand, and placing him conveniently by the Font, according to his discretion, shall ask the Godfathers and Godmothers the name; and then shall dip him in the water, or pour water upon him, saying,"

* "Si baptizandus non poterit loqui; vel quia parvulus, vel quia mutus, vel quia ægrotans aut aliunde impotens, tunc debent patrini pro eo respondere ad omnes interrogationes in baptismo. Si autem loqui poterit, tum pro seipso respondeat ad singulas orationes nisi ad interrogationes sui nominis tantum, ad quas semper patrini sui respondeant pro eo." Manuale Sarisbur. De Baptismo, fol. xlvi.

Some Priests make the determination which Service should be used to depend on whether or no the child is of an age to be confirmed. At twelve or thirteen a child may very well be confirmed, and therefore should answer the questions for itself.

THE Prieſt may either immerſe the head of the adult in the water, or pour water upon it. In ſome caſes, where the adult has required total immerſion, a bath or ſome large veſſel has been brought into the church; but there is no ſpecific authority for this uncommon practice. The water muſt be placed in the Font and nowhere elſe. It ſhould be pointed out to a perſon wiſhing for total immerſion that dipping does not neceſſarily imply the ſubmerſion of the whole body, but rather the immerſion of a part thereof (viz. the head), and even if it did imply total ſubmerſion, the adult, from whatever cauſe, is phyſically incapable of being ſo dipped in a Font conſtructed for the immerſion of infants (and of theſe probably only the partial immerſion was contemplated, as is evident from the directions as to Trine immerſion in the ancient Rubric, and from the Rubric in the Firſt Book of Edward VI), and that the word "dip" is retained in the Office for adults as a proteſt that the Church only contemplates Infant Baptiſm, and uſes the word to the adult which was more conveniently applied in the caſe of infants.*

168. *Cautions and Directions.*

THE Prieſt during the entire Service will *ſtand facing eaſt* on the platform of the Font, in order not only to perform the function conveniently, but to be ſeen of the people in the action of pouring the water.

Immediately after the child is baptized, and without deſcending from the ſtone platform of the Font, the Prieſt will proceed with the Collect of Reception,—he will thus be ſeen by the faithful when he makes the ſign of the Croſs on the child's forehead. The prayer ſhould be ſaid without the uſe of the Service Book. After the prayer he will (without leaving the platform) deliver the child to the perſon in charge of it.

The whole function ſhould be moſt carefully performed.

---

* It is very ſtrange that ſo good a ritualiſt and theologian as Johnſon (ſee *The Clergyman's Vade Mecum*, p. 21) ſhould ſuggeſt that Fonts ſhould be made large enough for the ſubmerſion of adults; a practice which would have gone far to diſcourage the Church's Rule of Infant Baptiſm, and in behalf of which the word "dip," (whether taken to mean total or partial immerſion), in the Rubric, in "The Miniſtration of Baptiſm to ſuch as are of riper years," affords no ground to argue in favour of total immerſion of adults whether in Fonts conſtructed for that purpoſe or in unauthorized veſſels.[1]

[1] The editor [of the firſt Edition] knows an inſtance of a bath having been brought into the church for an adult Baptiſm in the Dioceſe of Ely, and has heard of ſome recent caſes where the demand has been made.

169. *The Rochet.**

A SHORT surplice with close sleeves (*Rochet*) is far more convenient for the administration of this Sacrament than the ordinary surplice, which is apt to get soaked in the sleeves.

170. *Parents not to Baptize their own children.*†

IF a Priest or Deacon may not be had, in an urgent case of private Baptism (the speedy death of the child being apprehended) the parents had better get some male friend to baptize the child. If such cannot be procured, the father must administer the Sacrament; the mother may only do so if the father knows not the Sacramental words,‡ or some other impediment exists.

---

* Winchelsea's Constitution, A.D. 1305, in force by virtue of 25 Henry VIII. c. 19, orders, amongst other ornaments and furniture to be provided for Divine Service by the parishioners, one rochet ("*unum Rochetum*"). The following is Lyndwood's Gloss: "The rochet differs from the surplice, because the surplice has hanging sleeves, but the rochet is *without sleeves*, and is ordered for the clerk who serves, or perhaps for the work of the Priest himself in baptizing infants, lest his arms be hindered by the sleeves." See Gibson's Codex, fol. 225. The rochet, however, may be either with or without sleeves. See Pugin's "Glossary of Ecclesiastical Ornament." Art. Surplice. If with sleeves, they should be rather tighter from the elbow to the wrist, and somewhat more full at the shoulder (decreasing towards the elbow) than those of the alb. A rochet with sleeves is most convenient for Baptisms, as it protects the cassock sleeve, and as in point of fact, a rochet is a *cotta* with the sleeves diminished, closed and gathered round the wrist; it answers to the description of "a decent and comely surplice with sleeves." LVIIIth Canon of 1603. Not that the Canon can limit the Rubric which orders the ornaments of the second year of Edw. VI.

† The following are the old English Rubrics on the subject:—"Non licet laico vel mulieri aliquem baptizare nisi in articulo necessitatis. Si vero vir et mulier adessent ubi immineret necessitatis articulus baptizandi puerum, et non esset alius minister ad hoc magis idoneus præsens: vir baptizet et non mulier, nisi forte mulier bene sciret verba sacramentalia, et non vir: vel aliud impedimentum subesset." "Similiter pater vel mater non debet proprium filium de sacro fonte levare nec baptizare, nisi in extremæ necessitatis articulo: tunc enim bene possunt sine præjudicio copulæ conjugalis ipsum baptizare, nisi fuerit aliquis alius præsens qui hoc facere sciret et vellet." Manuale Sarisbur. fol. xlv.

‡ The sacramental words (= "form") are: "N. I baptize thee in the Name of the FATHER, and of the SON, and of the HOLY GHOST." The "matter" of course pure water. The water should be poured upon the head of the infant, *and the contact thereof should be plainly seen.* Sprinkling is not only contrary to the rule of the Church, but in a case of private Baptism by a lay person, it might happen if the fingers were dipped into the water, that not even a drop

171.

THE ORDER OF CONFIRMATION,

OR LAYING ON OF HANDS UPON THOSE THAT ARE BAPTIZED AND COME TO YEARS OF DISCRETION.*

"Upon the day appointed, all that are to be then confirmed, being placed, and standing in order, before the Bishop; he (or some other Minister appointed by him) shall read this Preface following."

N the sacristy the proper vestments† should be prepared for the Bishop, viz. a rochet, an amice, a surplice, a white stole, a white cope, a gold embroidered (*aurifrigiata*) mitre, and pastoral staff; and the usual surplices and cottas, for the Priests and assistants. These latter wear white stoles. The pastoral staff may be carried in the Bishop's hand, or else borne before him by his chaplain. If the Litany is sung or said previously, a kneeling-stool should be prepared for the Bishop before the episcopal throne, which should be placed a little distance from the altar, against the north wall, facing the south. At the administration of this Sacrament‡ the throne should be adorned with white

---

in the hurry of the moment might come in contact with the child's person, in which case it would die unbaptized. The water ought to be seen evidently to *run* upon the child's person (not its clothes): laics should be careful to pour plenty of water upon the child.

Two corollaries seem to follow here:—α. that the Priest should use some instrument like a shell for holding the water. (See Parr. 165, 166). β. that the cap should be removed from the infant before it is given into the hands of the Priest.

* The preparation of persons to receive the grace of Confirmation by the laying on of the hands of the Bishop, consists in these two things, viz.: 1, instruction in the Catechism; and 2, examination of conscience according to the promises made at Baptism. In the latter, the parish Priest must do all he can to assist the candidates individually. The rite itself consists in the laying on of hands. The question asked before is intended to satisfy *the congregation* that the candidate is in earnest. The first Book of Edward VI. does not contain the renewal of Baptismal vows.

† "Whensoever the Bishop shall . . execute other public ministration, he shall have upon him beside his rochette, a surplice or albe, and a cope or vestment, and also his pastoral staff in his hand, or else borne or holden by his chaplain." Edw. VIth's first Prayer Book. The Roman Pontifical does not order both the rochet and surplice. The rochet is ordered, unless the Bishop be a religious, in which case he wears the surplice instead.

‡ "Therefore, neither it (Absolution) nor any other Sacrament else, be such Sacraments as Baptism and Communion are."—Second volume of Homilies, of Common Prayer and Sacraments.

"Confirmation is a *Sacrament* of no mean character, though the Church does not place it

Solemnization of Matrimony.

hangings, and the arms of the diocese may be suspended behind. Seats and kneeling-desks should be prepared for the chaplains, one on each side of the throne. The altar should be vested in white, and vases of white flowers should be placed upon the super-altar. In the ancient English Church the lights on the altar were burning.

At the actual time of Confirmation a chair should be placed facing westwards, before the centre of the altar, as at Ordinations.

The candidates when about to be confirmed are led up in order by the parish Priest, either singly (which is the most correct mode) or in batches, as may be arranged, and kneel either at the footstep of the Sanctuary; or —so that the Service may be both seen and heard better—at the step of the chancel. When only a few are to be confirmed, they may be taken one by one to the Bishop, who confirms them, sitting in his chair.

It is a Catholic custom for females to be dressed in white, and to wear veils without caps.

172.

THE FORM OF
SOLEMNIZATION OF MATRIMONY.*

N the sacristy should be prepared a surplice and white stole for the Priest, and also the Eucharistic vestments (*white*), surplices or cottas, for the clerks and servers, together with the Service book and the books of registration.

The altar should *always* be prepared for the celebration of the Holy Sacrament, in the event of the parties desiring to meet the LORD in His

---

among the two Sacraments (Baptism and the LORD's Supper) which are necessary to every one for his own salvation. Where there is no Bishop to confirm, it cannot be done, no one else *can* do it."—Bishop of Chichester; apud Newland's Confirmation and First Communion, p. 215.

* " Have any been married in the times wherein marriage is by law[1] restrained, without lawful licence, viz. from the Sunday next before Advent Sunday until the fourteenth of January; and from the Saturday next before Septuagesima Sunday until the Monday next after Low Sunday; and from the Sunday before the Rogation week until Trinity Sunday?" Bp. Montague's Visitation Articles, p. 74, No. 17.

[1] Solemnizatio non potest fieri a prima Dominica Adventus usque ad octavas Epiphaniæ exclusive; et a Dominica lxx. usque ad primam Dominicam post Pascha inclusive; et a prima die Rogationis usque ad septimum diem Pentecostes inclusive; licet quoad vinculum his diebus contrahi possit. Lyndwood's Gloss apud Gibson's Codex, fol. 518. See also Stephen's Edition of Book of Common Prayer, fol. 1502.

fulleſt manifeſtation of grace; or, if they have not deſired it, as a teſtimony, that the Prieſt is ready to adminiſter it, and wiſhes to do ſo.

The antependium ſhould be white, and vaſes of flowers may be placed on the ſuper-altar. The deacon or ſacriſtan will, of courſe, be careful to ſee that everything is prepared for the celebration. If there be a celebration, the chaſuble and maniple for the celebrant, and tunicles for the deacon and ſub-deacon, and maniple for the deacon may be laid upon a table in the Sacriſty.

The Office for Holy Matrimony conſiſts of three parts, viz. the Addreſs to the Congregation, the Betrothal,* both of which the Rubric orders to take place in the nave,† (in which will be prepared the faldſtool,) and the more ſacramental part, imploring the graces needful for the married ſtate, which is ſaid at the altar. In pronouncing the firſt Benediction, the Prieſt ſhould lay his hands on the heads of the man and woman. The Pſalm (which except the woman be "paſt child-bearing" ſhould always be the 128th, *Beati omnes*) is to be ſaid in proceſſion.

"It is convenient that the new-married perſons ſhould receive the holy Communion at the time of their Marriage, or at the firſt opportunity after their Marriage."

If the notice has been given to the Prieſt that a celebration is deſired, he ſhould wear an alb‡ inſtead of a ſurplice and alſo an amice, in which caſe he will not wear a hood, but may ſubſtitute a white cope.

The aſſiſtant Miniſters will wear albs and amices. They may wear, as well as the Prieſt, white copes during the function.

The celebrant and aſſiſtant Miniſters will veſt§ themſelves with the ex-

---

* The words of Betrothal, and indeed great part of the Rite, are *verbatim* from the old Sarum Form. The old Rubric provided that the ring ſhould be placed on the thumb of the woman's left hand at the name of the FATHER, on the forefinger at that of the SON, on the third at that of the HOLY GHOST, and on the fourth at the Amen. Some trace of this is found in our preſent Rubric which ſays, "the man *leaving* the ring upon the fourth finger of the woman's left hand," &c. and, indeed, the cuſtom ſtill prevails in ſome places.

† "The perſons to be married ſhall come into the *body of the church*."¹—Rubric of Book of Common Prayer.

‡ The Heref. Miſſale even ordered the maniple to be worn—in violation of the rule that it was not to be worn at any ſervice but the Holy Euchariſt.—"*Coram preſbytero amictu, alba, fanone, et ſtola veſtito.*"

§ According to Catholic cuſtom only the Deacon wears the ſtole (ſee p. 2, note †); both Deacon and Sub-deacon wear the maniple. In the old Engliſh Ordinals (ſee Pont. Sariſb. apud Maſkell. Mon. Rit. iii. 182; and Pont. Exon. apud Barnes, p. 84) the maniple was given to

¹ But outſide the chancel—the Prieſt will ſtand on the ſtep in front of the ſcreen gates.

ception of their maniples, and then proceed to veſt the celebrant, after which they will put on their maniples.

Only the bride and bridegroom and their immediate friends communicate.

Kneeling ſtools ſhould be prepared for them before the altar. The man will be communicated before the woman, and previous to the act of communion, if it be the cuſtom, or be thought deſirable, two acolytes ſhould ſpread the communion or houſelling cloth over the top of the kneeling ſtool.

A deacon ſhould never venture to adminiſter the Sacrament of Matrimony.

The perſon occupying the place of "father" (it is a great miſtake that this is not ordinarily the actual father), when the Prieſt inquires, "Who giveth this woman?" ſhould himſelf place her hand in that of the Prieſt.*

173. *Poſition of Aſſiſtant Miniſters, &c.*

URING the betrothal the clerks and acolytes will range themſelves in order on either ſide, a little eaſtward of the Prieſt in the body of the church. The Prieſt ſhould be attended by at leaſt two acolytes, who ſhould be provided with a diſh or almsbag, for the reception of the accuſtomed duty to the Prieſt and clerk, after it has been laid upon the ſervice book.

When the Prieſt goes to the altar, the aſſiſtant Miniſters (if there be any) will occupy their reſpective ſteps as goſpeller and epiſtoler on the ſouth ſide of the Sanctuary, and the acolytes on either ſide beyond the aſſiſtants—all ſtanding laterally, till the Introit of the Communion Office begins. If there be no aſſiſtant Miniſters, the Prieſt is attended by the acolytes.

If there be no Sermon, which may be delivered inſtead of the addreſs, or in the proper place in the Communion Office, the Exhortation may be read by the deacon or ſub-deacon as directed by the Prieſt.

---

the Sub-deacon as a diſtinctive badge—thence the cuſtom of epiſtoler and goſpeller both wearing maniples; and the latter the ſtole.

* The old Engliſh and preſent Roman uſe is for the father to place the hand of the woman in that of the man, without delivering her to the Prieſt. Our preſent rite ſeems preferable, as being more ſymbolical.

174.

THE ORDER FOR

THE VISITATION OF THE SICK.*

HE object of the Office for the Visitation of the Sick is to prevent the departure of any baptized person out of the world without the Church's blessing. Should the sick person be already in a state of grace, and in the habitual use of the privileges which the Church provides, he will be of course at once entitled to it. If not, the business of the Priest is, after the manner here laid down, to effect his reconciliation. The Office should not be repeated.

The Priest should be vested in cassock, surplice, and *purple* stole. †

The Preface to the "Visitatio Infirmorum" (London: Masters,) contains some careful instructions on this head; but the most valuable manual, which can be strongly recommended, is the "Priest's Prayer Book," (third edition, London: Masters,) edited by the Rev. Dr. Littledale and the Rev. J. E. Vaux.

The accustomed form for making a confession (as the sick are to be moved to do) is as follows:‡ "In the Name of the FATHER, and of the SON, and of the HOLY GHOST. Amen. I confess to GOD the FATHER Almighty, to His only-begotten SON JESUS CHRIST our LORD, to GOD the HOLY GHOST, and before the whole company of heaven, and to thee, Father, that I have sinned exceedingly in thought, word and deed, through my fault, through my fault, through my most grievous fault, [here comes in the confession.] For these and all my other sins which I cannot now remember I humbly beg pardon of Almighty GOD and grace to amend; and of thee, Father, I ask penance, counsel, and absolution. And therefore I beseech GOD the FATHER Almighty, His only-begotten SON JESUS CHRIST, and GOD the HOLY GHOST, to have mercy upon me, and thee, Father, to pray for me."

---

* "The Spirit of the Church" (London: Masters,)—a collection of articles from the "Ecclesiastic"—contains a most valuable paper on "The Visitation of the Sick." The concluding observations with reference to the care of the body after death are very important. If they were followed, "the laying out" would be a pious and dutiful Christian office, instead of the ghastly and shocking process it has degenerated into only too often.

† "Inprimis se sacerdos superpellicio cum stola." Man. Sar. Ordo ad Vis. Infirm. fol. lxxxv. The surplice, however, *may* be omitted; all that is *essential* as far as ritual is concerned is the stole.

‡ Not kneeling, of course, if the sick person be a clinic.

In pronouncing the Absolution it is proper either to lay the right hand, or hands, upon the head of the person, or else to raise the right hand. The imposition of hands is the usual custom in the English Church. In either case the sign of the Cross should be made over the penitent.

175.

THE COMMUNION OF THE SICK.

"Forasmuch as all mortal men be subject to many sudden perils, diseases, and sicknesses, and ever uncertain what time they shall depart out of this life; therefore, to the intent they may be always in a readiness to die, whensoever it shall please Almighty God to call them, the Curates shall diligently from time to time (but especially in the time of pestilence, or other infectious sickness) exhort their Parishioners to the often receiving of the holy Communion of the Body and Blood of our Saviour Christ, when it shall be publicly administered in the Church; that so doing, they may, in case of sudden visitation, have the less cause to be disquieted for lack of the same. But if the sick person be not able to come to the Church, and yet is desirous to receive the Communion in his house; then he must give timely notice to the Curate, signifying also how many there are to communicate with him (which shall be three, or two at the least), and having a convenient place in the sick man's house, with all things necessary so prepared, that the Curate may reverently minister, he shall there celebrate the holy Communion, beginning with the Collect, Epistle, and Gospel, here following."

ESTMENTS:* cassock, alb, chasuble, &c. of the colour of the day.†

For the Communion of the Sick the Priest should take with him the elements required, together with a chalice, paten and cruets.

---

* The following are the ancient English Rubrics on the subject:—"Interim sacerdos præparet se omnibus sacerdotalibus indumentis, præter casulam." Ordo ad Comm. Infirm. Bangor Pontifical apud Maskell. Mon. Rit. vol. i. p. 66. "Induat se superhumerali, alba, et stola, cum phanone, atque planeta, si affuerit; sin alias casula non induatur." English Order of the ninth century. *Ibid*. p. 68. "In primis induat se episcopus superpellicio cum stola." Pont. Sarisf. *Ibid*. p. 69. "Sacerdos præter casulam indutus aut stola pro necessitate." Manuale Ebor. *Ibid*. The present Roman Rubric prescribes a surplice and stole, and white cope. "Sacerdos indutus superpellicio et stola, et si haberi posset, pluviali albi coloris." Rit. Rom. De Sac. Euch. p. 94. As with us there is no reserved Sacrament, the Sacrificial Vestments must be used; in accordance also with the old English practice which existed in times when the Eucharist was reserved for the sick.

† The Priest will send a server, or other fit person, with the vestments he uses at *Low* Service.

There is ample authority for the use of a portable altar of stone,* marble, or alabaster. The use of portable stones was enjoined by many early English Canons and visitation articles.† These were formed of a thin stone or piece of marble, set in a wooden frame, either plain or ornamented with gold, and silver, and jewels. They were sometimes employed in churches or oratories, which possessed only wooden altars, being placed upon the *mensa* to hold the paten and chalice. Their‡ size was about one foot long by six inches across, and about two inches high. It was the custom for Bishops to consecrate many of them to be distributed, not only to persons who had private chaplains and oratories of their own, but to guilds and brotherhoods and parish priests, that thus the Holy Eucharist might be celebrated with great reverence even in unconsecrated places.

It seems also desirable to provide (besides altar linen, pall, chalice veil, and veil of linen and lace) a cross or crucifix, and a pair of small candlesticks, all of which add greatly to the solemnity of the Function, and tend to impress those present with the necessity of a reverent demeanour,—so much to be wished.

The Priest should be served by an assistant, who will previously have made the requisite preparations, and must be vested in cassock and surplice.

It is highly desirable to administer the Holy Communion in the morning—that being the universal practice of the Catholic Church. If, however, this be impracticable, it is only seemly for the Priest to have been fasting at least for some hours previously.§

N.B.—Should the sick person, in accordance with the command in the fifth chapter of the General Epistle of S. James, desire the Priest to "pray over him, anointing him with oil in the Name of the Lord;" the proper place will be after the Collect which follows the Absolution in the "Visita-

---

* Its size should be one foot by six inches, and it should be marked with the usual five crosses.

† See Rock: Church of our Fathers. Vol. i. pp. 247, sqq.

‡ Super-altar, for Communion of Sick. Bede tells us of two Priests, who "Quotidie Sacrificium Deo victimæ salutaris offerebant, habentes secum vascula sacra, et tabulam altaris vice dedicatam." Hist. Ecclesiast. Bedæ, lib. v. cap. x.

§ The old rubrics permit the sick man to communicate after eating in extreme cases, and hence a Priest may be allowed to celebrate in case of extreme urgency after eating, under present circumstances of our not being allowed to reserve the Blessed Sacrament. If a Priest went to a sick person after eating his usual meal, and found him dying, he would be justified in returning to get the Sacramental vessels and Eucharistic vestments, &c. to *celebrate, because* we have no reserved Sacrament. But except in the like emergencies there is no justification—(*save on the plea of ill-health*)—to warrant celebration after eating.

tion," just before the "Communion of the Sick," as the sick person will, in this case, probably be visited, and communicate "all at one time." If at different times—the anointing will be ministered immediately after the Prayer—"The Almighty GOD who is a most strong tower," &c. in the Office for the Visitation of the Sick.

The Priest should use the Office in the first Book of Edward VI.* given below.

" But if a man, either by reason of extremity of sickness, or for want of warning in due time to the Curate, or for lack of company to receive with him, or by any other just impediment, do not receive the Sacrament of CHRIST's Body and Blood, the Curate shall instruct him, that if he do truly repent him of his sins, and steadfastly believe that JESUS CHRIST hath suffered death upon the Cross for him, and shed His Blood for his redemption,

---

* "¶ *If the sick person desire to be anointed, then shall the Priest anoint him upon the forehead or breast only, making the sign of the cross, saying thus:—*
" As with this visible oil thy body outwardly is anointed: so our heavenly FATHER, Almighty GOD, grant of His infinite goodness, that thy soul inwardly may be anointed with the HOLY GHOST, who is the Spirit of all strength, comfort, relief, and gladness: and vouchsafe for His great mercy (if it be His blessed will) to restore unto thee thy bodily health and strength to serve Him; and send thee release of all thy pains, troubles, and diseases, both in body and mind. And, howsoever His goodness (by His divine and unsearchable providence) shall dispose of thee; we, His unworthy ministers and servants, humbly beseech the Eternal Majesty to do with thee according to the multitude of His innumerable mercies, and to pardon thee all thy sins and offences, committed by all thy bodily senses, passions, and carnal affections: who also vouchsafe mercifully to grant unto thee ghostly strength, by His Holy Spirit, to withstand and overcome all temptations and assaults of thine adversary, that in no wise he prevail against thee, but that thou mayest have perfect victory and triumph against the devil, sin, and death, through CHRIST our LORD: Who, by His death, hath overcome the prince of death, and with the FATHER, and the HOLY GHOST, evermore liveth and reigneth GOD, world without end. *Amen. Usque quo, Domine.* Psalm xiii." First Book of Edward VI, *Order for the Visitation of the Sick.*

The holy oil stock should be made of silver, or at least of latten. It should be shaped like a cruet. The holy oil stock should have a case of purple silk, and may be preserved in the aumbry on the gospel side of the altar, or if there be not one, in some convenient place in the sacristy, or in the house of the Priest if he resides far from the church.

The Priest will anoint the sick person by making the sign of the most holy cross upon the forehead with his right thumb,[1] steeped in the holy oil. He will then cleanse his thumb with a particle of bread, which he will have brought with him for that purpose, and at the end of the function wipe the unction from the sick person's forehead with a piece of cotton stuff. The Priest will be careful to take the particle and cotton so used to the sacristy, there to be burnt in the accustomed place.

[1] " Dum dicitur prædictus Psalmus a choro vel a clerico, accipiat interim sacerdos oleum infirmorum super pollicem dextrum: et sic cum illo pollice tangat infirmum cum oleo, signum sanctæ crucis faciens, super utrumque oculum incipiendo ad dextrum, et dicat sacerdos hoc modo." Man. Sarisb. fol. xciv.

" Deinde intincto pollice in oleo sancto in modum crucis ungit infirmum." Rit. Rom. de Ex. Unc.

earneftly remembering the benefits he hath thereby, and giving Him hearty thanks therefore, he doth eat and drink the Body and Blood of our SAVIOUR CHRIST profitably to his foul's health, although he do not receive the Sacrament with his mouth."

The very fame provifion occurs in the pre-Reformation Service Books. * "*Deinde communicetur infirmus nifi prius communicatus fuerit, et nifi de vomitu vel alia irreverentia probabiliter timeatur: in quo cafu dicat facerdos infirmo:* Frater, in hoc cafu fufficit tibi vera fides, et bona voluntas: tantum crede et manducafti." Manuale Sarif. de Extrema Unctione, fol. xcvii.

176.

THE BURIAL OF THE DEAD.†

VESTMENTS: Prieft—furplice, black ftole, black cope, and birretta.

‡ Clerks—caffocks and furplices.

It is very defirable that the Burial Office fhould be celebrated chorally, and gloominefs avoided in all the arrangements. The coffin, which ought to have nothing black about it, fhould be placed on a bier in church *before* the mourners, and covered with a purple (or for young unmarried perfons a white) pall, with a crofs of red or white. The people fhould be inftructed to ftand during the Pfalm,§ and to fing or fay the alternate verfes. The laft prayer is called "the Collect," becaufe it is to be ufed as fuch in the Communion Office, which fhould form a part of this Office as well as of that for Holy Matrimony.

The moft proper place for the Prieft and clerks to fay the Pfalm appears to be in the middle of the chancel, half-way between the choir-doors and the lower ftep of the altar, where a fmall lectern fhould be placed for the Office-book. A clerk might ftand on either fide the Prieft, all of whom fhould face eaftward. The Leffon fhould be read from the lectern outfide

---

* "Mox autem ut eum viderint ad exitum propinquare, communicandus eft de facrificio fancto; etiam fi comediffet ipfa die." Rubric, Leofric. MS. apud Mafkell. Mon. Rit. vol. i. p. 89.

† At the burial of infants, who have died after baptifm under feven years of age, the Prieft will wear a white ftole, and if there be a celebration, white veftments.

‡ Clerks are not Priefts and Deacons, but *Minifters*, acolytes, or lay clerks (properly fo called).

§ The firft is more fuitable for the young; the other for old perfons.

the chancel screen. If the Holy Eucharist be celebrated, it should commence immediately after the Lesson when the Priest and sacred Ministers will vest themselves for the altar function either at a table placed in the chancel, or in the Sacristy; and after the blessing, the Priest will uncross his stole, and resume the black cope and birretta, as preparatory to going towards the grave.

Holy Eucharist at funerals:—
    Vestments: black.
        Introits: Psalm xliii. *Judica me, Deus.*
                Psalm cxxx. *De profundis.* Sometimes the *Dies Iræ* is sung as an Introit.
    Collect: "O merciful God," &c. Burial Service.
    Epistle: 1 Thess. iv. ver. 13 to end.⎫ Edw. VIth's first Prayer Book.*
    Gospel: S. John vi. ver. 37 to 40. ⎭

Bishops, Priests, and other clerics, are each buried in vestments proper to their order. It was an ancient custom to place a chalice and paten of inferior metal into the hands of Priests and a pastoral staff into the left hand of Bishops; examples which it would be well to follow where practicable now-a-days.

Both in the procession from the churchyard gate to the church, and afterwards from the church to the grave, a cross should be borne before the corpse, (α) as symbolizing the faith in which the deceased died, and (β) also as showing forth the truth that by the Cross alone salvation is looked for.†

The altar should be vested in black. The sanctuary hangings, if there be any, may be of purple or violet. The Service Book should be put into a cover of black silk or velvet, and no flower vases should remain on the altar—nothing but a plain cross or crucifix and two lights. If a coloured pede-cloth be in ordinary use, a black or violet carpet should, if possible, be substituted for it. The coffin should be placed in a bier outside the chancel screen or in the usual place, with the head towards the west; except in the case of ecclesiastics, when it may be brought into the chancel, and should be placed with the head towards the east. If there be a funeral sermon, the pulpit will be hung with black drapery. (*Vide Funerals and Funeral Arrangements.* London: Masters.)

---

* If the Epistle and Gospel for the day are used, the Collect for the day must be used also, followed by the Collect from the Burial Service.

† Processional tapers, carried in lanterns on staves, were anciently used; and it would be well should the opportunity occur to re-introduce this Catholic and symbolical practice.

In Heylyn's Hiftory of the Reformation (London, 1660; p. 119), where he treats of the obfequies of the French King, celebrated at S. Paul's cathedral, by Parker, Barlow, Scorey, &c. we find—"a *communion* was celebrated by the Bifhops then attired in *copes* upon their furplices."

The purpofe for which of old the corpfe was brought into the church was to have the Euchariftic Sacrifice offered in the prefence and on behalf of the dead. Our own practice is a ftanding proteft againft the neglect of the Holy Sacrament, and it is in conformity alike with ancient precedent and modern directions that the altar Service fhould commence after the Leffon: the coffin ftanding before the congregation in the nave.

When there is a celebration of the Holy Euchariſt in the prefence of the deceafed, "the Collect," *O merciful* GOD, *the* FATHER *of our* LORD JESUS CHRIST, which occurs at the end of the Order of the Burial of the Dead as if it were an occafional prayer, is to be ufed in the Communion Office inftead of the Collect for the day—it is, of courfe, not to be repeated afterwards. When there is no celebration, "the Collect" is a kind of link between the Burial of the Dead and the Euchariftic Office, and alfo the Church's proteft for a celebration on behalf of the foul of the deceafed perfon.

If there is to be a Funeral Sermon it will, of courfe, be delivered in the appointed place before the Offertory, if there is a celebration; if there is not, it will be preached after the Leffon. In the former cafe, if the celebrant is preacher, he will do fo in his full Euchariftic veftments either from the altar or from the pulpit. If one of the affiftant Minifters preach he will do the fame. If another Prieft he will be vefted in furplice or cotta and black ftole.

Funeral palls fhould be made of a violet colour, ornamented with pink or white croffes. For children or young people they fhould be of a white material. If adorned with infcriptions, the following, from the beft authorities, are recommended:—

"Bleffed are the dead that die in the LORD."

"JESU Mercy."

"LORD of mercy, JESU bleft, Grant them Thine eternal reft."

"The fouls of the righteous are in the hands of GOD."

"Eternal reft give to them, O LORD, and let perpetual light fhine upon them."

"The LORD grant that they may find mercy of the LORD in that day."

Wilkins, i. p. 180. Laws of Kenneth, 840 A.S.: "Let every tomb be efteemed facred, adorn it with the fign of the crofs, and beware that you trample not upon it with your feet."

The Churching of Women. 171

N.B.—The altar lights should be lighted by an acolyte in cassock and *cotta* immediately after the lesson.

It is an ancient custom to have three lights burning on each side of the bier,* and for a mourner holding a lighted taper to kneel on each side facing the chancel gates.

All the candles should be of unbleached wax.

177.

THE THANKSGIVING OF WOMEN AFTER CHILDBIRTH,†

COMMONLY CALLED

THE CHURCHING OF WOMEN.‡

"The Woman, at the usual time after her Delivery, shall come into the Church decently apparelled, and there shall kneel down in some convenient place, as hath been accustomed, or as the Ordinary shall direct: And then the Priest shall say unto her,"

HE Priest should be vested in surplice and white stole, and should be attended by at least one lay clerk or chorister in surplice. The Service Book should be prepared in the sacristy beforehand.

---

* "The funeral tapers (however thought of by some) are of the same humble import (viz. Gospel lights). Their meaning is to show that the departed souls are not quite put out, but having walked here as children of light, are now gone to walk before GOD in *the light of the living*." Gregorie's Works, p. 169.

† "If she be an unmarried woman, the form of thanksgiving shall not be said for her, except she hath either before her childbirth, done penance for her fault, or shall then do it at her coming to be churched, by appointment of the Ordinary. Abp. Grindal's¹ Art. for Cant. Prov. 1576." "It is to be done immediately before the Communion Service." Bp. of Norwich, 1536. "If there be a Communion she is to receive It." Bp. Cosin's Works, vol. v. Notes and Collections on the Book of Common Prayer.

‡ "The Order for the Purification of Women." Edw. VIth's First Book. In Latin, "Purificatio post Partum" or "Purificatio Mulierum." Manuale Sarisbur.

¹ "Whether your parson, vicar, curate, minister, or reader do church any unmarried woman who hath been gotten with child out of lawful marriage, and say for her the Form of Thanksgiving of Women after Childbirth, except such an unmarried woman have either, before her childbirth, done due penance for her fault to the satisfaction of the congregation, or at her coming to give thanks do openly acknowledge her fault before the congregation, at the appointment of the minister, according to order prescribed to the said minister by the Ordinary or his deputy; the same churching to be always on some Sunday or Holy Day, and upon no other day." Articles, &c. within Prov. of Canterbury. Art. 22, Grindal's Remains, p. 164.

It is proper to have a kneeling-ſtool and portable rails placed near the church door* for the woman who is to be churched.

The right time for women to return thanks after childbirth is juſt *before* the ſervice in which they are going to take part, whether Morning or Evening Prayer; moſt fitly of all before the celebration of the Holy Euchariſt, in which the Rubric directs them to partake.† The addreſs "Foraſmuch" ſhould be ſaid to the woman near the door. The Pſalm—the firſt if before Holy Communion, the ſecond at other times—ſhould be ſaid by the Prieſt ſtanding near to the woman, who follows him *ſecreto*. The Pſalm is not proceſſional. When ended, the Prieſt may lead the woman by her right hand‡ to the altar rails, and complete the Function at the altar.§ The ſervice completed, the woman ſhould make her offering, placing it in an alms-bag to be held by an acolyte. If there is not a celebration the Prieſt will place the woman's offering‖ on the altar, and then paſs to his place in the choir. If there be a celebration the offering ſhould be given through the Offertory.

---

* "Ordo ad purificandum mulierum poſt partum ante oſtium eccleſiæ." Man. Sariſ.

† "If there be a Communion it is convenient that ſhe receive the Holy Communion." Book of Common Prayer.

‡ "Deinde inducat eam ſacerdos per manum dextrum in eccleſiam dicens." Man. Sariſ.
"Et ipſa ingreſſa genuflectit coram Altari et orat, gratias agens Deo de beneficis ſibi collatis: et ſacerdos dicat." Rit. Rom. De Benedic. Mul. p. Partum.

§ "Tunc ſurgat et eat ad locum ubi ſedere debeat, uſque poſt miſſam. Peractaque miſſa ſurgat et reveniat ad eundem locum ubi prius, videlicet, ad gradum altaris: et ibi genuflectens ut ſumat et recipiat abſolutionem a ſacerdote. Hoc modo dicat ſacerdos. Miſereatur, etc." Man. Ebor. apud Maſkell.

‖ The uſe of the chriſm¹ which was put on the child at Baptiſm was difuſed in 1532. And in 1561 we find amongſt the Biſhop's interpretations of the Royal Injunctions the following directions: "To avoid contention, let the curate have the value of the chriſm, not under the value of fourpence, and above as they may agree, and as the ſtate of the parents may require." This appears to be a rule for the amount of the offering at Churching. See Stephen's Book of Common Prayer in loc. fol. 1762.

¹ "The Miniſter ſhall put upon him his white veſture, commonly called the chriſm." Rub. 1ſt Book Edw. VI. This preceded the anointing. The ſame Book of Edw. VI. orders, that "the woman who is purified muſt offer her chriſm and other accuſtomed offerings."

178.

A COMMINATION,

OR DENOUNCING OF GOD'S ANGER AND JUDGEMENTS AGAINST SINNERS.

With certain Prayers, to be used on the first Day of Lent, and at other times, as the Ordinary shall appoint.

"After Morning Prayer, the Litany ended according to the accuſtomed manner, the Prieſt ſhall, in the reading-pew or pulpit, ſay,"

ESTMENTS: the ſame as at Matins.
The Commination Service is to be regarded as a proteſt againſt the abeyance of that Godly diſcipline by which the Church has never reſted till her ſinning members are brought to confeſs their ſins, and to ſeek reconciliation.

The word "reading-pew" in the Rubric prefixed to this Office is merely an ancient expreſſion for "reading-ſtall,"* i.e. the ſtall in the chancel from which the ancient "Lections" were read, which was uſually one of thoſe placed againſt the chancel ſcreen; ſuppoſing then, that the chancel be uſed as in olden times, this is the place from which to read the addreſs, "Brethren, &c." Or, as the Rubric aſſerts, the pulpit may be uſed.

"Then ſhall they all kneel upon their knees, and the Prieſts and Clerks kneeling (in the place where they are accuſtomed to ſay the Litany) ſhall ſay this Pſalm."

Miſerere mei, Deus. Pſal. li.

The Litany ſtool ſhould be placed between the choir and the altar: that is, at the eaſtern end of the ſtalls, at the commencement of the Sanctuary.

---

* This may be ſeen from any old church-wardens' account book: the expreſſion is found in uſe more than a century prior to the erection of Puritan "dozing-pens."

The Ordinal.

"Homo imponit manum, Deus largitur gratiam: facerdos imponit fupplicem dexteram, Deus benedicit potenti dextera."—*S. Ambrose.*

179.

THE FORM AND MANNER OF*

MAKING, ORDAINING, AND CONSECRATING OF

BISHOPS, PRIESTS, AND DEACONS,†

ACCORDING TO THE ORDER OF THE UNITED CHURCH OF ENGLAND AND IRELAND.

THE PREFACE.

T is evident unto all men diligently reading the Holy Scripture and ancient Authors, that from the Apoftles' time there have been thefe Orders of Minifters in CHRIST's Church; Bifhops, Priefts, and Deacons. Which Offices were evermore had in fuch reverend eftimation, that no man might prefume to execute any of them, except he were firft called, tried, examined, and known to have fuch qualities as are requifite for the fame; and alfo by public Prayer, with Impofition of Hands, were approved and admitted thereunto by lawful authority. And therefore, to the intent that thefe Orders may be continued, and reverently ufed and efteemed, in the United Church of *England* and *Ireland;* no man fhall be accounted or taken to be a lawful Bifhop, Prieft, or Deacon in the United Church of *England* and *Ireland,* or fuffered to execute any of the faid Functions, except he be called, tried, examined, and admitted thereunto, according to the Form hereafter following, or hath had formerly Epifcopal Confecration, or Ordination.‡

---

* "Et bene femper caveatur ab omni intitulacione, et nimia deformitate membrorum in facris, ne fint gibbofi, vel neri, vel alias corpore vitiati, propter fcandalum ecclefiæ et cleri evitandum : præmuniantur omnes ordinandi quod non recedunt ante finem miffæ." Pont. Exon.

"Et bene caveatur de omni mutilatione membrorum ordinandorum in facris. Ne fint etiam gibbofi, vel manfi, vel alias corpore vitiati, propter fcandalum cleri et ecclefiæ evitandum." Pont. Sarif.

† Bifhops are confecrated before the Offertory, Priefts after the Gofpel, and Deacons before it: according to the rule of the Univerfal Church.

‡ On this principle a Prieft coming from the Greek or the Roman Church is received without re-ordination. A Lutheran or Calvinift Minifter cannot exercife any Sacerdotal Functions till he has been ordained, and is treated in every refpect as a mere layman, for fuch he is.

Ordering of Deacons. 175

"And none shall be admitted a Deacon, except he be twenty-three years of age, unless he have a faculty. And every man which is to be admitted a Priest shall be full four-and-twenty years old. And every man which is to be ordained or consecrated Bishop shall be fully thirty years of age.

"And the Bishop, knowing either by himself, or by sufficient testimony, any person to be a man of virtuous conversation, and without crime; and, after examination and trial, finding him learned in the Latin tongue, and sufficiently instructed in Holy Scripture, may at the times appointed in the Canon, or else, on urgent occasion, upon some other Sunday or Holy-day, in the face of the Church, admit him a Deacon, in such manner and form as hereafter followeth."

THE FORM AND MANNER OF
MAKING OF DEACONS.*

"When the day appointed by the Bishop is come, after Morning Prayer is ended, there shall be a Sermon or Exhortation, declaring the duty and office of such as come to be admitted Deacons; how necessary that Order is in the Church of CHRIST, and also, how the people ought to esteem them in their Office."

EPISCOPAL Vestments: purple cassock,† amice, rochet, alb, stole, tunicle, dalmatic, maniple, chasuble, mitre, gloves, episcopal ring, sandals,‡ buskins,‡ gremial, and pastoral staff. The Bishop will enter the Cathedral Church vested in purple cassock, rochet, chimere,§ episcopal ring, zucchetto, and birretta. If he do not vest in the sacristy he will receive his vestments from the altar. The faldstool or seat must be placed near the epistle corner for this purpose.

---

* The Synod of Exeter, A.D. 1287, expressly forbids Deacons to hear confessions; "firmiter inhibemus, ne diaconi confessiones audiant, pœnitentiasve injungant, vel sacra ministrant, aut aliqua officia exerceant, quæ solis sacerdotibus sunt concessa." Wilkins' *Conc.* tom. 2, p. 145.

† The Bishop's cassock has a train which is looped up, till he vests for the function.

‡ These are put on in the sacristy by the Bishop's domestic servant—not dressed in the episcopal livery.

§ The Bishop's chimere answers to the *Mantelletum*[1] of the west. The Priest's hood corresponds to the Mozzetta[2] in form. The Roman Pontifical prescribes that the Bishop shall come to the church vested in a cope.[3]

[1] "Induet aliam vestem breviorem apertam, ut per scissuras brachia extrahi possint, quod genus vestis Mantelletum vocant. Vestes autem hujusmodi erunt, vel ex lana, vel ex camelotto coloris violacei, nullo autem modo sericæ." Cær. Epis. Lib. i. cap. 1.

[2] The *Mozzetta* is not unlike a properly shaped academical hood, except the *caputium* (cowl) is much smaller. The Cardinal's cape has no hood attached. And such is the proper shape of the tippet of the Canons.

[3] "Et demum, cum tempus ordinationis instat, hora competenti, Pontifex cappa magna indutus, capelano illam post eum deferente, venit ad Ecclesiam ubi ordinationes fieri debent," &c. Rub. de Ord. Conf. Pont. Rom. There is no difference between the *cappa* and *pluviale*—they both mean a cope. See Gavant. Thes. Liber i. Pars. i. Tit. xix.

The Bishop bearing his pastoral staff, unless it be carried by his chaplain, will proceed from the sacristy to the altar preceded by the choir, acolytes, deacons, priests, and ministers of the altar, in their proper vestments, in the accustomed processional order. The persons to be ordained will remain with the Archdeacon in the sacristy. On reaching the faldstool the Bishop will remove his birretta and deliver it to the Deacon, who will hand it to the Sub-deacon, who in his turn will deliver it to an acolyte. He will wear the zucchetto till the assumption of the mitre. The master of the ceremonies will distribute the episcopal vestments amongst the clerks, commencing with the amice, according to the usual order. The gloves will be carried on a salver. The vestments will be received by the Deacon from the acolyte in the accustomed order, and with the assistance of the Sub-deacon he will vest the Bishop therewith.

The Bishop on being vested with the dalmatic sits down, and the Deacon removes the episcopal ring, and hands it to the Sub-deacon to place on a salver, held by an acolyte for that function. The gloves are then presented on a salver, and should be so arranged that the right may lie at the side of the Deacon and the left on that of the Sub-deacon. In putting on the gloves the Deacon assists at the right, the Sub deacon at the left. The Bishop having put on his gloves rises and is vested in the chasuble, and again sits down. Whilst he is assuming the chasuble the assistant Priest, who should be the highest dignitary of the choir, puts on a cope and reverently places the ring on the annular finger of the Bishop. The Deacon then puts upon him the orphreyed mitre which the Sub-deacon has brought from the gospel corner. The Deacon throughout the function is principally intrusted to assist with the mitre. The mitre being placed on the Bishop's head, the Deacon and Sub-deacon pass to his left, having previously made an inclination to him. They then, with the assistance of the acolytes, put on their maniples. The Bishop then leaves his faldstool, which the acolytes place in front of the midst of the altar, and seats himself on his throne on the north side fronting the south. He then delivers his pastoral staff to his chaplain, who either holds it or places it in its stand on the left of the throne. The Deacon and Sub-deacon will stand on the right and left of, and nearest to, the throne. The assistant Priest and Clergy will take their position west of the throne facing the south, the acolytes theirs on the south side. The Canons, who should wear the almyss instead of the hood, will sit on benches north and south of the Sanctuary. The altar-rails, if temporary, should be removed, as they would interfere with the ceremony. Other clerics specially not engaged in the rite, will sit in the chancel stalls.

Ordering of Deacons.

The Archdeacon, vested in surplice and cope,* will then come forth from the sacristy followed by the persons about to be ordained, (the Deacons, if there be any to be ordained Priests, to take precedence of the laics to be admitted into the order of Deacons), and will conduct them to their place in the choir. The most eastern stalls on either side should be reserved for them.

Matins will then commence, and a sermon will follow; which being ended, the Bishop, bearing his pastoral staff in his left hand, will take his seat on the chair in front of the altar; the Deacon and Sub-deacon standing on his right and left, the other clerics and acolytes on either side facing north and south.

The Archdeacon will then signify (by an acolyte) that the persons to be ordained are to come out of the stalls and take their places in front of the Sanctuary. They will advance two by two *in plano*, and taught by the Archdeacon will, in succession, bow reverently to the Bishop and gradually arrange themselves in a semicircle before the episcopal chair.† After the presentation by the Archdeacon, who will then kneel at a faldstool fronting the north prepared for him on the south side at the extremity of the *corona* of persons to be ordained, the Bishop (having delivered his pastoral staff to his Chaplain, who will stand on the left of the Sub-deacon) will sing the Litany at the faldstool with his face to the east, the Deacon passing to his right, the Sub-deacon to his left,—both kneeling. If the Bishop delegates the singing of the Litany to an inferior cleric, as it appears he may from the remarkable introduction of the word "Priest" in the latter portion of the Litany,—"Then shall the *Priest*," &c. the Litany desk must either be previously moved within the Sanctuary, or else the *corona* of persons to be ordained must open out into two lines, north and south, facing each other. In either case the Bishop will still kneel before his chair, as directed above. The old English custom is for the Bishop to rise at the petition,‡—" That it may please Thee to bless these Thy servants, now to be admitted into the order of Deacons (or *Priests*)," or " our brother elected," if a Bishop

---

* " Archidiaconus capa indutus humiliter respiciens in episcopum cum his verbis alloquatur." Rubric Sarisbur. Pont.

† " Et si sint multi, stent in circuitu." Rub. Sarif. Pont. "Ad Pontificem accedunt, et coram eo in modum coronæ se disponunt." Rub. de Ord. Presb. Pont. Rom.

‡ " Hic surgat episcopus et sumat baculum in manu sua, et conversus ad ordinandos dicat: Ut electos istos bene✠dicere digneris. Te rogamus," &c. Sarif. Pont. Cf. Pont. Exon. apud Barnes, p. 84. "Tunc surgat confecrator et ad confecrandum se vertens, baculum pastoralem in manu sinistra tenens, dicat primo: Ut hunc præsentem electum benedicere ✠ digneris. Chorus: Te rogamus audi nos." Pont. Exon. Conf. Epif.

or Archbishop, &c. and taking his pastoral staff, which his chaplain will deliver to him, in his left hand to turn him to those about to be ordained, and make the sign of the Cross over them. This done, the Bishop delivers his staff to his chaplain and again kneels as before.

N. B.—The Bishop wears the mitre throughout the function, except at (the first verse of the *Veni Creator* at the ordination of Priests and consecration of an Archbishop or Bishop), the Collects, Gospel, and intonations of the Creed.

The maniple is not placed on the altar with the other vestments, but in the Service Book, in the place of the Gospel for the day. It is put on *last** of all the vestments. An acolyte will remove the maniple from the Service Book and present it to the Sub-deacon. The Deacon will retire a little behind to give place to the Sub-deacon. The Sub-deacon then vests the Bishop with it.

The gloves and ring are taken off at the Offertory by the Deacon and Sub-deacon; the Deacon taking off the ring and right glove, the Sub-deacon the left. After the Washing the Deacon places the ring on the Bishop's annular finger. The gloves are not put on again, but are placed upon a salver on the credence. Consequently they are worn at the laying on of hands.†

The Bishop will place both hands upon the heads of the persons to be ordained, he sits in his chair‡ each person kneeling before him in succession. All those to be ordained kneel immediately after the Interrogations.

---

* According to the Roman Rite the Bishop's maniple is not put on till the "Confiteor." But as in the English Rite the Confession has been removed from the *Præparatio ad missam*, which before the revision of our Services in the reign of Edw. VI. preceded the *Introit*, to the Ordinarium missæ,[1] it seems most convenient, and accordant with Liturgical propriety for the Bishop to vest with maniple as directed in the text.

† In the old English Ordinal there were two layings on of hands; at the first, the Bishop *stood* and laid his *right* hand on the heads severally of each person to be ordained, the Priests doing likewise. At the second laying on of hands he places his *hands* (both hands) it would seem from the rubrics, *standing*, on the heads of those to be ordained. The Roman Pontifical directs the Bishop to stand during the first, and to sit during the second Imposition. Between the two layings on of hands the Unction formerly took place, for which purpose the gloves were removed, the ring being retained. The gloves were resumed, according to the rubric in the Exeter Pontifical, immediately before the second imposition. It is therefore proper to retain the gloves throughout the function, with the exceptions given in the text. See Maskell's Mon. Rit. Vol. iii. pp. 204, 212, 219, and Exon. Pont. apud Barnes, pp. 37, 91.

‡ See note †. As our rubric combines the two impositions, it is proper for the Bishop to sit, considering the position that the laying on of hands occupies in the function. At the

[1] In the First Book of Edward VI. the Confession was remanded to the *Canon missæ*.

Ordering of Deacons. 179

The celebration will be, of course, solemn or high service, especially as it is "Pontifical."* The lights will be lighted by an acolyte immediately before the Communion Service, and the incense ignited in a thurible on the credence.

180. *Vestments for those to be Ordained Deacons.*

"First, the Archdeacon, or his Deputy, shall present unto the Bishop (sitting in his† chair near the holy table) such as desire to be ordained Deacons, (each of them being decently habited,) saying these words."

A girded alb,‡ or a surplice, over a cassock.

181. *The Bishop's Chair or Faldstool.*

SHOULD be in front of the altar,§ facing west, below the Subdeacon's step of the altar.

182. *The Litany.*

THE Litany as said by the Bishop in the Ordinal is so done in *full* Eucharistic Vestments, because in the Ordering of Priests and Deacons, he is vested as "Pontifex" and celebrant, throughout the Function: not that the Litany is part of the Communion Office, but a prelude to it. If the Bishop delegates the singing of it to an assistant Priest or Priests, they will be vested in amices, girded albs, and white copes, or at least in surplices and white copes. But

---

second imposition the Sarum Pontifical directed the *hands* of the Bishop to be imposed. The Exeter directed the gloved right hand, the mitre to be worn, and the stole to be held in the left hand. See Maskell and Barnes as above.

* When a Bishop celebrates at *Low* Service, he should always vest at the altar. He does not wear the tunic, dalmatic, or mitre, nor use his pastoral staff. The maniple is not put in the book, but laid on the gospel side. He is served by two servers, vested in cassock and *cotta,* one of whom ought properly to be in Deacon's orders at the least.

† "*Episcopus sedens cum mitra.*" Pont. Sarif. et Exon.

‡ "Every one of them that are present having upon him a plain alb."—Ordination Offices, published by Grafton, 1549. Abp. Sancroft's Collections.

§ "Tunc sedeat episcopus ante medium altaris et introducantur omnes ordinandi et stent similiter ante episcopum." Rubric from Bp. Lacy's Pontifical.

Ordering of Deacons.

in the Confecration of an Archbifhop or Bifhop the Litany is *interpolated* into the Liturgy, and confequently muft be faid by the Confecrator in his full Archi-epifcopal and Euchariftic veftments. If he delegates it to be fung by the Affiftant Bifhops, (the Gofpeller and Epiftoler,) they are already vefted in the veftments proper to the function. If, however, the Affiftant Priefts have been directed by the Archbifhop to fay it, they will be vefted in girded albs, amices, and white copes.

183. *The colours of veftments for the Communion Office.*

HE Veftments of the altar and the minifters thereof will be of the colour of the day.* Clerics not miniftering at the altar will wear caffocks, furplices, and hoods.

"Then one of them, appointed by the Bifhop, fhall read the Gofpel."†

The Deacon appointed to read the Gofpel will be previoufly vefted in amice, girded alb, and maniple. He will carry his ftole in his left hand, and his dalmatic over his left arm. An acolyte will affift him, before reading the Gofpel, to veft in the ftole and dalmatic; as he fhould perform the function of a Deacon in the full diaconal veftments required by the rubric.

An acolyte, while the Deacon is vefting, will replenifh the thurible (with a fpoon) from the incenfe-boat.

"And here it muft be declared unto the Deacon, that he muft continue in that Office of a Deacon the fpace of a whole year (except for reafonable caufes it fhall otherwife feem good unto the Bifhop) to the intent he may be perfect, and well expert in the things appertaining to the Ecclefiaftical Adminiftration. In executing whereof if he be found faithful and diligent, he may be admitted by his Diocefan to the Order of Priefthood, at the times appointed in the Canon, or elfe, on urgent occafion, upon fome other Sunday, or Holy-day, in the face of the Church, in fuch manner and form as hereafter followeth."

---

* In the Latin Church, in the "Miffa pro eligendo Summo Pontifice," the colour is *red*. "In Confecratione Summi Pontificis, . . . et electionis et confecrationis epifcopi," *white*. See *Rub. Gen. Miff. Rom.*

† "Putting on a tunicle, fhall, &c." Ordinal of 1549.

THE FORM AND MANNER OF
ORDERING OF PRIESTS.

" When the day appointed by the Bifhop is come, after Morning Prayer is ended, there fhall be a Sermon or Exhortation, declaring the Duty and Office of fuch as come to be admitted Priefts; how neceffary that Order is in the Church of CHRIST, and alfo how the people ought to efteem them in their Office."

184. *Habits of thofe who are to receive the Order of Priefthood.*

" Firft, the Archdeacon, or, in his abfence, one appointed in his ftead, fhall prefent unto the Bifhop (fitting in his chair near to the holy table) all them that fhall receive the Order of Priefthood that day (each of them being decently habited) and fay,"

ASSOCK, amice, girded alb,* maniple, and ftole (worn over left fhoulder and tied on right fide under the arm), and maniple. The folded chafuble may be carried on the left arm.
N. B.—When there are perfons to be ordained Deacons, as well as Priefts, the former ftand on the epiftle fide laterally, the latter in a femicircle before the Altar. The rubric directs the Ordination of Deacons to precede that of Priefts. But the Priefts are to be communicated before the Deacons.

The proper Introit to the Communion is according to the Ordinal of 1549, " *Expectans expectavi Dominum,*" Pf. xl; or elfe this Pfalm, " *Memento, Domine, David,*" Pf. cxxxii; or elfe this Pfalm, " *Laudate Nomen Domini,*" Pf. cxxxv.

185. *Veni Creator Spiritus and Ordination.*

HE Bifhop fings the firft verfe kneeling, without his mitre, turned to the altar. He then refumes the mitre and fits in his chair.† The next prayer following is faid without the mitre, ftanding before the chair and facing the Deacons to be ordained. The Bifhop's Deacon will kneel before him and hold the Service Book.

N. B.—The Priefts who join in laying on of hands *ftand* on either fide of the Bifhop who *fits* in his chair, the Deacons in turn kneeling before him—all the Deacons to be ordained Priefts kneeling in a femicircle. The Archdeacon fhould take each candidate by the right hand and lead him up to the Bifhop.

---

* " Every one of them having upon a plain alb." Ordinal of 1549.
† Cf. Rub. Pont. Rom. de Ord. Prefb.

186. *Pauſe during ſilent Supplication.*

"After this, the congregation ſhall be deſired, ſecretly in their prayers, to make their humble ſupplications to God for all theſe things; for the which prayers there ſhall be ſilence kept for a ſpace."

RETHREN, let us all join in one prayer, that he, who is choſen for the help and furtherance of your ſalvation may, by God's merciful gift, obtain the bleſſing of the prieſthood, ſo that he may never be found unfit for his ſtation; but that by the privilege of his office he may receive the gift and virtues of the HOLY GHOST, through JESUS CHRIST our LORD. Amen."—*Old Gallican Form of Prayer for thoſe about to be Ordained Prieſts.*

187.

"Then the Biſhop ſhall deliver to every one of them kneeling, the Bible into his hand, ſaying,"*

" And if on the ſame day the Order of Deacons be given to ſome, and the Order of Prieſthood to others; the Deacons ſhall be firſt preſented, and then the Prieſts; and it ſhall ſuffice that the Litany be once ſaid for both. The Collects ſhall both be uſed; firſt, that for Deacons, then that for Prieſts. The Epiſtle ſhall be *Epheſ.* iv. 7--13, as before in this Office. Immediately after which, they that are to be made Deacons ſhall take the Oath of Supremacy, be examined, and Ordained, as is above preſcribed. Then one of them having read the Goſpel (which ſhall be either out of *S. Matt.* ix. 36—38, as before in this Office; or elſe *S. Luke* xii. 35—38, as before in the Form for the Ordering of Deacons,) they that are to be made prieſts ſhall likewiſe take the Oath of Supremacy, be examined, and Ordained, as in this Office before appointed."

Caution.

 DEACON will of courſe, during his diaconate, have profoundly ſtudied every the minuteſt detail of the Communion Office, and will have been careful to perfect himſelf in the duties of his ſpecial function, for his habitual attendance on the Prieſt in offering the Holy Sacrifice, is the beſt of all preparation for the day when he ſhall be privileged to offer it himſelf.† A careful ſtudy

---

* "The Bible in the one hand, and the chalice or cup with the bread in the other hand, and ſay." Ordination Offices, 1549.

† "His expletis, et eis ad ordinem ſuum reverſis Pontifex ſedens cum mitra, et baculo, admonet eos, dicens: quia res, quam tractaturi eſtis, ſatis pericuſoſa eſt, filii dilectiſſimi, moneo

of the ancient Liturgies together with the Sarum Rite, the Roman Miffal, and this *Directorium*, will enable the newly-ordained Prieft to celebrate with reverence and propriety.

THE FORM OF ORDAINING OR CONSECRATING OF AN
ARCHBISHOP OR BISHOP;

WHICH IS ALWAYS TO BE PERFORMED UPON SOME SUNDAY OR HOLY-DAY.

" When all things are duly prepared in the church, and fet in order, after Morning Prayer is ended, the Archbifhop (or fome other Bifhop appointed) fhall begin the Communion Service."*

188. *The Veftments.*

PISCOPAL veftments. In addition to the ufual epifcopal veftments the Archbifhop will wear over his chafuble the pall,† and the crozier will be borne by one of his chaplains, chofen to act as crofs-bearer or "croyfer."

The veftments of the altar, of the confecrator, and of the holy Minifters will be white. For the other arrangements and pofition the directions regarding the making of Deacons and Priefts fhould be confulted.

The altar lights will be lighted before the Archbifhop arrives at the altar.

The two affiftant Bifhops will wear rochets, white copes,‡ and plain mitres, and though they act as epiftoler and gofpeller, they will not wear the maniple nor the ftole.

The mitre given to the elected Bifhop is *mitra fimplex.*

---

vos, ut diligenter totius Miffæ ordinem, atque Hoftiæ confecrationem, ac fractionem, et communionem, ab aliis jam doctis Sacerdotibus difcatis, priufquam ad celebrandum Miffam accedatis." Pont. Rom. De Ord. Prefb.

* " Then fhall the Pfalm for the Introit and other things at the Holy Communion be," &c. Ordination Offices, 1549.

" The Pfalm for the Introit at the Communion as at the Ordering of Priefts." Ordination Offices, 1549.

† The Englifh Archbifhops affume the pall, as belonging to their fees. It is never worn over any veftment but the chafuble.

‡ " Duo epifcopi, capis induti, deducant electum." Pont. Sarifb. Two Bifhops (being alfo *in furplices and copes, and having their paftoral ftaves in their hands*). Ordination Offices, 1549.

189. *Habit of the Elected Bishop.*

"After the Gospel, and the *Nicene* Creed, and the Sermon are ended, the elected Bishop (vested with his rochette*) shall be presented by two† Bishops unto the Archbishop of that province (or to some other Bishop appointed by lawful commission) the Archbishop sitting in his chair near the holy table, and the Bishops that present him saying,"

A ROCHET, which is worn under a girded alb with its appendages, viz. amice, maniple, stole crossed, and over all a cope. The colour white.

During the Litany‡ the Archbishop will kneel at his faldstool with his face to the altar; the two assistant Bishops on each side. The elected Bishop will kneel at a faldstool placed for him below the platform of the altar. For further directions, episcopal and otherwise, in singing the Litany, see the detailed directions regarding the ordering of Priests.

The *Veni Creator* ended, the Archbishop will stand, served by the senior Bishop with the book.

---

* "Consecratio episcoporum semper agenda est die dominica, et examinatio et professio eorum ante missarum solemnia. *Electus vero sacerdotalibus indumentis induatur præter casulam, pro qua induatur capa solempni* et sic comprovinciales episcopi deducent eum per manus eorum, consecratore sedente super faldistorium, *in medio magni altaris, dorso verso ad altare,* sedilia episcoporum in modum coronæ a dextris et a sinistris electi. Tunc consecrator dicat." Rubric from Bishop Lacy's Pontifical (Consecratio Episcoporum). "The elected Bishop having upon him a *surplice and a cope* shall," &c. Ordination Offices, 1549.

† "Ut sine tribus episcopis nullus episcopus ordinetur." Council of Arles.

"Electus ducatur ad locum suum; acoliti induant illum sandalia, tunicam, dalmaticam et casulam, postquam consecrator dixerit," &c. Bp. Lacy's Pontifical, Consecratio Episcoporum. The mitre is given somewhat later, but immediately before the delivery of the "codex evangeliorum."

‡ "Cum Litania; et prosternat se ordinator simul cum electo et cæteris episcopis ante altare super faldistoria; episcopus electus desuper stramenta ad basim altaris; et dicatur litania sicut in ordinibus, et cum ventum fuerit ad versum qui pro domino episcopo cantatur, surgat consecrator, et dicat conversus ad electum sic:
"Ut hunc electum bene✠dicere digneris,
Resp. Te rogamus," &c.
—Pont. Sarisb. Consf. Elec. in Episf.

190. *Assumption of the rest of the Episcopal habit.*

"Then shall the Bishop elect put on the rest of the Episcopal habit; and kneeling down, *Veni, Creator Spiritus*, shall be sung or said over him, the Archbishop beginning and the Bishops, with others that are present, answering by verses, as followeth."

HE two assistant Bishops will then vest the elected Bishop with the tunic, the dalmatic, the gloves, the chasuble, and episcopal ring, and put the plain white mitre upon his head, the elected Bishop kneeling in front of the Archbishop.

191. *The Consecration proper or laying on of hands.*

HE elected Bishop will kneel, without his mitre, before the Archbishop, who has resumed his mitre, sitting in his chair before the midst of the altar.* The assistant Bishops will *stand* on either side the chair, the senior on the right, the junior on the left hand of the Archbishop. The Consecrator and assistant Bishops will touch the head of the elected Bishop with both hands, and all three will say the words " Receive the HOLY GHOST."

An assistant Priest vested in cassock and *cotta* will kneel at the right of the Archbishop with the Book, which should be of folio size, as more convenient for the Consecrator to read from, the assistant Bishops continuing to stand on each side the chair as before. If the Archbishop, following an ancient custom,† lays the Bible on the neck of the Bishop before delivering it to him, he will, on receiving it from the senior assistant Bishop, stand and lay the book open upon the Bishop's neck. The lower part of the book will touch the nape of the neck, and the junior assistant Bishop will support the (reversed) book with his two hands. This is done in silence. The Archbishop will then sit in his chair, and receive the Bible from the senior assistant Bishop, and deliver it closed to the consecrated Bishop, who will lay his right hand upon it, whilst the senior assistant Bishop supports the

---

* The following is the old English rubric :—"Consecratore sedente super faldistorium, in medio majoris altaris, dorso verso ad altare, sedilia episcoporum in modum coronæ a dextris et a sinistris electi." Rub. Liber Pont. Exon. Con. Epis.

† The old English rubric at the laying the " evangeliorum codex" on the Bishop's neck is, " Et duo episcopi ponant et teneant evangeliorum codicem super cervicem ejus et scapulas clausum." When the book is *delivered* later in the Service the rubric is "dat ei evangeliorum codicem." Pont. Sarif. et Exon. The direction in the text combines the two rubrics.

book by holding it on the right fide, and the junior affiftant Bifhop on the left, places his right hand under the book.

192. *The Delivery of the Bible.*

"Then the Archbifhop fhall deliver him the Bible, faying,"*

IVE heed unto reading, exhortation, and doctrine. Think upon the things contained in this Book. Be diligent in them, that the increafe coming thereby may be manifeft unto all men. Take heed unto thyfelf, and to doctrine, and be diligent in doing them: for by fo doing thou fhalt both fave thyfelf and them that hear thee.† Be to the flock of CHRIST a fhepherd, not a wolf; feed them, devour them not. Hold up the weak, heal the fick, bind up the broken, bring again the outcafts, feek the loft. Be fo merciful, that you be not too remifs; fo minifter difcipline, that you forget not mercy; that when the chief Shepherd fhall appear you may receive the never-fading crown of glory; through JESUS CHRIST our LORD. *Amen.*"

At the words, "Be to the flock of CHRIST a Shepherd," &c. the fenior affiftant Bifhop, receiving the Paftoral Staff from the junior Bifhop, may place the Paftoral Staff with the crook turned towards the Confecrator in the hands of the Bifhop, who receives it between his joined hands.

The newly-confecrated Bifhop does not re-affume his mitre till the clofe of the Service, when if it is his own Cathedral he fhould be conducted to the Epifcopal throne. If in the Cathedral of the province, or other Church, he will go to the facrifty and unveft.

The Confecrator will unveft at the faldftool.

193. *Number of Chaplains to be "occupied" at Ordinations.*

IGHT at Confecration of Bifhops;‡ Six at Ordination of Priefts and Deacons.

---

* "Then the Archbifhop fhall lay the Bible upon his neck, faying, &c." Ordination Offices, 1549.

† "Then fhall the Archbifhop put into his hand the Paftoral Staff, faying, Be to the Flock," &c. Ordination Offices, 1549.

‡ "Provided always, that every Archbifhop, becaufe he muft occupy eight chaplains at confecration of Bifhops, and every Bifhop, becaufe he muft occupy fix chaplains at giving of orders and confecration of churches, may, every one of them, have two chaplains over and above to the number limited unto them (viz. four)," &c. 21 Hen. VIII. c. xiii. f. 24, A.D. 1529. *Statutes at large.*

APPENDIX.

Appendix.

I.—ADDITIONAL CAUTELS.

The Bread.

F the ordinary wafer-breads, so eminently convenient, which are commonly used in the Western Church be not provided, it is very desirable that the bread or wafers should be made in the Priest's own household. Doubtless some of our Sisterhoods would gladly prepare the breads for the use of the Church. They may be either leavened or unleavened. The former is the more primitive custom, and is still that of the Eastern Church; the latter is more convenient, and is according to the usage of the West. Wafers are preferable as they do not crumble. If ordinary bread be used, it should be cut up into small squares in the sacristy, and the crumbs cleared away before being placed on the credence. The Priest's own bread should be much larger than the squares for the laity. Should ordinary bread be used, it ought to be new, as in that case it is not so likely to crumble.

The Wine.

REAT care should be taken about the wine, to get it as pure as possible.* Tent wine is the tradition of the English Church; and *when it can be had genuine* is to be preferred. But this is rarely the case. The editor [of the First Edition] is convinced of this both from chemical analysis, and from information

---

* The Rev. J. Purchas, of Orwell Rectory, suspecting that even the sacramental cup was not exempt from adulteration, procured a sample of Tent from a London wine merchant, which he sent for analysis. The result was given by the chemical referee as follows:—Rev. Sir—Having completed the examination of the wine you sent me, I beg to submit the following analysis:—Litmus Paper indicated much acidity. Evaporated, it yielded 25 P.C. of a

derived from wine merchants themselves. The wine used in many college chapels in Cambridge, is half good sound port, and half as pure a Tent wine as can be procured. A wine so prepared is sufficiently pure, of the required colour,* and its taste is removed from ordinary associations. The editor, since he caused "a first-class sample" of tent to be analysed, has used a cruet of three parts sherry and one part Tent.† The colour is dark and reddish, and the taste pleasanter than the mixture of Port and Tent. Claret and Asmenhausser are also pure wines of the required colour. The former was till lately used in the Royal Chapels, except in the German Chapel, where white wine is still used. White wine is also used very generally in the West, being considered most convenient, as it does not stain the altar linen. Red wine (Malaga) is used on feast days in the Latin Church in some countries. Where there is a daily celebration it might be expedient to use white wine on ferial days and red on festivals. It is greatly to be desired that more care should be taken in preparing the oblations.

It is believed that the careful study of the Cautels of the English Church used in times of old (which have already been given) will be the means of wakening many priests to a sense of what is due on the score of reverence in so great a mystery. It should also be remembered that very nearly the whole of the Cautels are to be found in the Provisions of the Canons and Constitutions of the Church of England passed before the sixteenth century, and that such of them as are consistent with the structure of our Service Book have the force of statute law in virtue of 25 Henry VIII. c. 19, § 7, and 35 Henry VIII. c. 16, § 2.

---

thick syrupy substance, consisting almost entirely of treacle; which substance, when ignited, left 0.78 per cent of ash, differing both in quantity and chemical composition from the ash of the genuine grape juice. It does not, however, owe its colouring matter to the ordinary substances used for colouring dark wines, such as logwood, brazilwood, elderberries, or mulberries. From the result of my examination, I am of opinion that the sample of wine you sent me was a compound of treacle, spirits of wine, water, and a small quantity of a genuine but very sour wine.—*Monthly Domestic Circular.*

* "Is the wine for the communion white, or reddish, which should resemble blood, and doth more effectually represent the LORD's Passion upon the crosse?"—Bp. Montague's Articles of Inquiry. Tit. iii. § 14.

† "Tent" is ordinarily a mixture of the lees of sherry and treacle. But many of the compounds sold under the name of "Tent" have only so very small a quantity of wine (and that bad) in their composition as not to be *wine* at all.

Cautels.

Of the Veiling of the Cross and Pictures, &c. at Passion-tide.

ROM the Evensong of the Saturday before Passion Sunday, or the *fifth* Sunday in Lent (i. e. on its first vespers), the altar cross and other crosses, images of the saints, and pictures should be covered* till the *Celebration* on the morning of Easter Eve. They are then re-covered until evensong—the first vespers of Easter Day.

The veils used for this purpose should be either of black or purple stuff, having neither emblems of the Passion nor figures worked on them.

Of the Folded Chasuble.

N† the celebration of the Holy Eucharist the celebrant *always* wears the vestment (chasuble) over the alb. The celebrant never uses the cope‡ except at the *Missa sicca* (which should never be used except on Good Friday).

---

* They remain veiled, even should the feast of the saint to whom the church is dedicated, or the feast of the dedication of the church, occur.

† In the First Book of Edw. VI. the celebrant is ordered to wear "a vestment or cope."[1] The chasuble was *always* called, by way of excellency, "the vestment." It has been thought that the allowance of the cope refers to the case of a *Missa sicca*, which ought never to take place except in the instance in the text. A large number of examples of the use of copes at the Eucharist have been already provided by the Editor of *Hierurgia Anglicana*. They were worn it appears at Lichfield, Salisbury, Exeter, Wells, Durham, Ely, Hereford, S. Paul's, London, and Westminster Abbey. More than thirty years ago a crimson cope was commonly used at a parish church in Leicestershire, in the presence and with the approbation of the late Bishop Ryder of Lichfield.

‡ In the west the *cappa magna* is quite distinct from the *pluviale* (*cappa pluvialis*) or *cope*. The former is now no longer a large cope, but a rich dress worn by certain Canons, Bishops, and Cardinals. There used also to be a distinction between the *cappa choralis* (the quire cope) and the *cappa pluviale* (the processional cope),—the former being the richer vestment. There is now no difference.

[1] "In these Injunctions, &c. (viz. the Injunctions and Advertisements of Elizabeth as well as the Canons of 1603), the 'Principal Minister' with the 'Epistler and Gospeller' are directed to wear copes. And although copes have been worn in the English Church at the Coronations to this day, and in some cathedrals, as at Durham, to the reign of George III; it is probable that the term included the chasuble with the tunicles, which, in both Eastern and Western Churches, were the correct vestments for the Administration of the Lord's Supper, the cope being more of a Processional Vestment. The word Cappa (cope) which as well as Casula, was formerly used to signify the Chasuble, may have given rise to this confusion of the Cope with the Vestment. 'Presbyter, si responsorium cantat in missa, vel quæcunque agat, *cappam* suam n..n tollet; si Evangelium legat, super humeros ponat.' (Theodor. lib. de Pœnit.) 'This *cappa* is evidently our chasuble.' See Rock's Church of our Fathers, vol. i. p. 382. It may be here added that the cope is worn by the Archbishop of Rheims at the coronation of the French King." Cleaver's edition of Bp. Wilson's "Short and Plain Instructions for the better understanding of the Lord's Supper."—P. 267.

The folded* chafuble (*planeta plicata*) fhould be worn by the Deacon and Sub-deacon inftead of the dalmatic and tunic, throughout Advent and Lent, except on the Sundays *Gaudete* and *Lætare*, viz. the third Sunday of Advent and fourth Sunday in Lent, when purple ornaments of more than ordinary coftlinefs fhould be ufed; and on other fafts, except they be vigils of Saints' Days. It is alfo worn on the vigil of Whitfun-Day *before* the Celebration and on the Ember Days at Whitfuntide. The chafuble is folded before the breaft on thefe occafions, taken off at the reading of the Gofpel, and then placed (folded) over the left fhoulder, over the ftole: or in its ftead a wide purple ftole is ufed in form of a folded chafuble; after communion the Deacon refuming his chafuble as before. The Sub-deacon in like manner puts off his folded chafuble at the reading of the epiftle, which he does in his alb and maniple only; after this he refumes his chafuble (*planeta*) as before.

The broad purple ftole is not unfrequently fubftituted altogether for the folded chafuble (*planeta*), but this is not fo correct.

Where neither the *planeta* nor broad purple ftole are ufed, the Deacon fhould wear only the alb, ftole and maniple, and the Sub-deacon the alb and maniple.

Of the Preparation of the Altar and its Ornaments for the Holy Communion.

THE Altar fhould be duly vefted before fervice, and the ornaments placed on the fuper-altar.

The brafs book-ftand will be placed at the north fide.

At Solemn Service the Book is placed open on the ftand: at Low Service the Book is placed clofed on the ftand, as it is then opened by the Prieft at the altar.

When the Book is on the north fide it fhould be placed corner-wife, fo that the Prieft faces north-eaft. When it is on the fouth fide, it fhould be placed fquare with the altar, fo that the Prieft reads facing eaftwards.

When the Prieft ftands in the midft of the altar, the Service Book fhould be on his left hand (*ad latus evangelii*) a *little* flanted that he may read without difficulty. As he ftands facing eaftwards, it cannot be placed im-

---

* The colour of *planeta* is purple except on the Whitfuntide Ember days, when it is red. The chafubles are ufually folded outfide and not turned up underneath.

mediately in front of the celebrant, as it would interfere with the corporal and chalice.

At Solemn Service the chalice should be placed upon the altar before Service, at Low or Plain Service the celebrant carries it himself when he goes to the altar.

The Sign of the Cross.

HEN the celebrant himself blesses with the Cross he places his left hand upon his breast, and makes the sign with his right hand. In blessing anything upon the altar the left hand is laid upon the *mensa;* while if such blessing takes place during the Celebration of the Holy Eucharist, the left hand is to be laid *outside* the corporal if before the consecration of the elements,—*upon* the corporal if afterwards.

Directions for the Celebrant.

HE Celebrant should keep his head and body erect, but his eyes bent downwards even when turned towards the faithful, so as to avoid distraction. When he turns to the people, he turns from left to right, that is, standing in front of the altar facing eastwards, he turns round towards the south or right side, (epistle corner); when he turns again to his Normal Position at the altar with his face eastwards, he turns in the same way, i. e. from left to right.

When the hands are "elevated," they are raised with the palms fronting each other, so that the tips of the fingers can be just seen above the shoulders.

The Collects are said with "extended and elevated hands," but the hands are "joined" again at the close, " through our LORD," &c.

The Nicene Creed is said according to the ancient English use, simply "junctis manibus." In the West the hands are elevated and extended at the intonations and then joined.

The celebrant* *first* stands humbly before the steps of the Altar, he then ascends to the midst of the Altar, after which he takes up his position at the *north-side.*

---

* See the *Ecclesiastic*, vol. xx. p. 193, for a very valuable article (which has also been reprinted and published in a separate form) on "The Position of the Priest at the Altar."

As there is in the minds of fome an unaccountable confufion between the north-*fide* of the altar and the north *end** thereof, it may be well to define exactly what is evidently meant by the term north-fide. It is difficult to conceive how any one moderately acquainted with the ancient and the mediæval Liturgies, in neither of which is anything ever ordered to be done at the end (or fhort fide) of the altar, fhould conceive that the north-fide ever meant the north end. Dr. Littledale's remarkable pamphlet on this fubject fhould be carefully ftudied.

The parts of the Altar.

THE *old* Englifh rule was for the Prieft *at firft*, i. e. at the "*Aufer a nobis*," &c. after the *Præparatio* which was faid "*ante gradum Altaris*," to ftand *in medio*† *altaris*, and *before* the Introit to ftand "*in dextro cornu altaris*," where everything (except only the *Gloria in excelfis* which was fung in the midft of the Altar with extended hands) was faid before the Epiftle. The Gofpel was faid or fung "*in finiftro cornu altaris.*" The Creed and everything after it "*in medio altaris.*" As the Prieft ftood in front of the altar facing the eaft, the gofpel corner or north fide would be on his left, the epiftle or fouth fide on his right. None of the old Rubrics fpeak of anything to be done at the *end* of the altar. When the Reformers tranflated and re-arranged the old Service Books, they ordered in Edward VIth's Firft Book, the Prieft to begin the Celebration, "ftanding humbly before the midft of the Altar;" but in the Book of 1552‡ the part of the Communion

---

* The ftrange practice of ftanding at the north *end* of the altar did not begin to be general till about a hundred years ago. It originated, however, with the Nonjurors: probably from a mifapprehenfion of the terms north and fouth *fides* in the ancient Liturgies. Before the time of the Nonjurors, whenever "end" was ufed, it was fimply as the Englifh tranflation of *cornu*, and not the end, or fhort fide, of the *menfa*. It is fo ufed in Laud's Book, "the Prefbyter ftanding at the north fide or end thereof," viz. ad latus feptentrionale, vel, ad cornu Evangelii. See "The parts of the Altar," p. 167.

† "*North-fide.*) Antiquitas vero ad medium Divini Altaris adftitit." Eccl. Hier. cap. 3.¹

‡ About this time it became the unfeemly practice of the Puritan party to fet the Altar table-wife, in which cafe, if the Prieft ftood as of old, *in dextro cornu*, his Service Book, &c. would hide the chalice, which the Puritans defired fhould be feen throughout the whole function, therefore the north fide was fubftituted for the fouth fide. It would alfo prevent the

---

¹ "καὶ νιψάμενων τὰς χεῖρας ὕδατι τοῦ ἱεράρχου καὶ τῶν ἱερῶν, ὁ μὲν ἱεράρχης ἐν μέσῳ τοῦ θυσιαστηρίου καθίσταται. S. Dionyf. Areop. de Eccl. Hierarchia, cap. 3, Op. p. 188, A." Cofin's Works, vol. v. p. 308.

Office which was said by the Priest in the unrevised service *at the south side* (*in dextro cornu*), and in the Book of 1549 "afore the middes of the Altar," was directed to be said "*at the north side*" (*in sinistro cornu*). Had they intended the Priest to stand at the *north end* facing the south they would have said so, and would not have used a technical term (*north-side*) which every Priest knew to mean the part of the altar on the left of the midst thereof. But *strictly* speaking, the north or gospel "side" and gospel or left "corner" are *not* synonymous (see the Illustration of the Diagram of the *Mensa* of an Altar). The north "corner" is the *extreme point*, so to speak, of the front of the altar, going northwards—thence to the middle is the "north-side." As a collateral proof the present Roman Missal may be quoted as to the technical meaning of "side" and "corner" as opposed to "end." This is quite plain in the Rubrics about incensing, as e.g. "procedendo thurificat *aliud latus altaris* triplici ductus *usque ad cornu Evangelii.*" Rit. Cel. Miss. Tit. iv. § 4. But practically the two phrases are often interchanged in the Roman Missal.

The north and south sides and corners of the altar are called Gospel and Epistle sides and corners, in reference to the reading of the Gospel and Epistle therefrom, and left* and right sides and corners in reference to the position of the celebrant standing with his face to the altar.

In the Creed the Priest genuflects† at "was incarnate .... made man." During the singing of the Creed (*after the Intonations*) the celebrant may sit between the Deacon and Sub-deacon at the south side.

If the Priest deputes the Epistoler and Gospeller to say the Exhortation and Invitatory, he himself remains in his Normal Position.

At the Sursum Corda he raises his hands, the palms facing each other breast high.

In consecrating the elements the Hereford Missal has the following rubric immediately before the words of Consecration, "inclinet se ad hostiam, et distincte dicat." The traditional manner of this *inclination* is to rest the elbows on the Altar, inclining moderately. The Blessed Sacrament should be held between the finger and thumb of both hands. The Priest then

---

Priest, when the Altar was table-wise arranged, from standing on the south of the Sacrarium with his face to the north, as was the custom of some puritan ecclesiastics.

* In the Roman Missal the Epistle side is called the *left*, and the Gospel the *right* side, but this with reference to the crucifix on the altar. This arrangement, in the west, dates from 1485, when it was laid down as a rule in the Roman Pontifical, published at Venice. See Maskell's Anc. Lit. p. 19, note 19, 2nd Edition.

† This is the only genuflection before the Consecration.

stands erect and elevates It. The same form is observed with the chalice, which is held by the knob with both hands. When the Priest *first* takes the chalice into his hand, he holds it in his left hand beneath the bowl.

After the Consecration, the Priest's forefinger and thumb having once touched the Blessed Sacrament, are not separated, save to touch it in communicating himself or others, in blessing or such-like necessity, until after the ablutions. The thumb and forefinger are kept closed,* in case any particle of the Blessed Sacrament should rest upon either, and so be lost or desecrated. The celebrant kneels and adores after the consecration of each species.

The celebrant on communicating the faithful should hold the pyx, paten, or ciborium in his left hand, and standing in the midst of the Altar† with his right hand should make the sign of the cross over them. He then goes to the Epistle corner and begins to communicate them, making again over each the sign of the cross.

If the Priest has to *duplicate*, i. e. to celebrate twice in one day, he must not drink the ablutions, which must be poured into a chalice and left for him to consume at the second celebration. For to drink the ablutions would be to break his fast.

When the Priest is about to return to the sacristy, he ought to resume his *birretta*.

Additional Notes for Deacon and Sub-deacon.

(a)

HE Deacon and Sub-deacon having preceded the Celebrant as far as the sanctuary, ascend with him, the Deacon on his right, the Sub-deacon on his left. They pause and stand in humble adoration before the steps of the altar. When the Celebrant

---

* Et ex tunc illos digitos cum quibus levavit corpus Christi teneat junctos usque ad ablutionem, nisi cum necesse fuerit. Post hæc cum aliis digitis, discooperiat calicem, et teneat eam per medium et dicat : Simili modo posteaquam cœnatum est. Hereford Missal.

† The Priest may here say, *secreto*, "*Ecce agnus Dei, ecce qui tollit peccata mundi,*" and then, "*Domine, non sum dignus, ut intres sub tectum meum, sed tantum dic verbo, et sanabitur anima mea.*" The Priest will be careful to teach young persons at Confirmation, on preparing for their first Communion, how to take the Holy Sacrament, viz. thus—the right hand should be extended flat, quite clear of the body, and resting on the left for a support at right angles, so as to make the shape of the cross, and to say Amen at the first clause of the words used in delivering the Sacrament. See "Guide to the Eucharist." London : Masters.

Directions for Deacon and Sub-deacon.

advances to the centre of the altar, the Deacon afcends to his right hand, the Sub-deacon to his left.

(*b*) When the Introit is fung the Prieft goes to the Book on the *north-fide* (*ad latus Evangelii*) while the Deacon ftands on his right on the fecond ftep, and the Sub-deacon on the right of the Deacon on the third ftep.

(*c*) At the recitation of the Ten Commandments the Deacon paffes to his ftep on the *fouth-fide* (*ad latus Epiftolæ*) and the Sub-deacon to his ftep behind the Deacon, to his right, both ftanding facing the eaft, with hands joined before the breaft—the ufual pofition of the hands of Affiftant Minifters.

(*d*) They remain in this pofition till the Collects, when they ftand in rotation behind the Celebrant.

(*e*) At the reading of the Epiftle the Deacon moves the Celebrant's Book to the Epiftle corner, and ftands on his right to ferve the Book whilft the celebrant reads the Epiftle *fecreto*, the Sub-deacon paffes to his own ftep on the Epiftle fide, an acolyte hands him the Book of the Epiftles, and he reads the Epiftle to the faithful.

(*f*) The Epiftle ended, the Sub-deacon moves the Celebrant's Book to the gofpel fide neareft to the midft of the altar, whilft the Deacon advances to the place for reading the Gofpels on the fecond ftep at the north-fide ; the Sub-deacon then receives the Book of the Gofpels from an acolyte near the credence, and takes it to the Deacon, who reads the Gofpel, the Sub-deacon holding the Book before him, the upper part refting on his forehead.* The Gofpel is moft correctly read towards the north, but moft ufually towards the weft. The Gofpel ended, the Sub-deacon returns the Book to the acolyte.

(*g*) As the Celebrant begins the Creed the Deacon ftands behind him and the Sub-deacon behind the Deacon ; after the Intonations they ftand on each fide the Celebrant, all facing the eaft. They genuflect, together with the Celebrant, at the " was incarnate . . . . made man," and each make the fign of the crofs at the words " The refurrection of the body."

(*h*) During the Offertory the Deacon and Sub-deacon ftand on their refpective fteps, facing eaftwards. When the alms are brought to the fanctuary, an acolyte will receive them in the alms-difh, (which the Sub-deacon, having received from the Deacon, will have delivered to him at the commencement of the Offertory), and will hand them to the Sub-deacon, who hands them to the Deacon, to give them to the Prieft to offer.

---

* If the book is placed on a lectern the Sub-deacon ftands in front of it facing the Deacon.

After they are offered the Deacon will remove the alms-diſh from the altar and hand it to the Sub-deacon, who will give it to an acolyte to place upon the credence. When, before the Offertory, the perſons appointed to collect the alms come to the ſanctuary for the alms-bags, it is the Sub-deacon's place to deliver them to the acolytes to diſtribute.

(*i*) At the Exhortation and Invitatory (if read by the Celebrant) they remain ſtanding facing the eaſt.

(*j*) When the Deacon makes the confeſſion both he and the Sub-deacon kneel. They both kneel during the Abſolution.

(*k*) They then ſtand in their normal poſition on their reſpective ſteps till the Preface, when they ſtand in rotation behind the Celebrant.

(*l*) At the ſinging of the *Sanctus* the Deacon paſſes to the right, the Sub-deacon to the left of the Celebrant.

(*m*) At the Prayer of Humble Acceſs they kneel with him before the Altar.

(*n*) At the Prayer of Conſecration the Deacon goes to the *left* of the Celebrant to ſerve him with the Book, and will then ſtand a little to his *right;* the Sub-deacon ſtands behind the Celebrant. During the Conſecration proper, the Deacon will kneel at the right of the Prieſt, riſing to raiſe the chaſuble at the lifting up of the Bleſſed Sacrament, and to cover and uncover the chalice. The Sub-deacon during this time, i. e. after the firſt Conſecration, kneels on his own ſtep behind the Celebrant. After Conſecration and adoration, the Deacon and Sub-deacon ſtand, the latter aſcends to the left of the Celebrant, and the former to his right, and uncovers the chalice. They both ſtand inclining before the Altar, whilſt the Prieſt is communicating.

(*o*) During the communion of the faithful,* when the Sub-deacon† is not engaged, he ſhould ſtand upon his ſtep in his place, with hands joined before his breaſt, laterally, facing the ſouth.

---

* In communicating the people it is an ancient cuſtom for the Sub-deacon to follow the Deacon (who bears the chalice) with a veſſel of wine and water in his right hand and a purificator in his left. The wine and water is for the faithful to drink after communicating, that no particle of the Bleſſed Sacrament may adhere to the teeth or gums, the purificator is carried in the left hand,[1] as a badge of office.

† The Sub-deacon may carry a ſecond chalice if neceſſary, but this will hardly, at leaſt *ought not* to, be the caſe at the midday Solemn Celebration, as the faithful ſhould as a rule communicate at the early Low Celebration that they may do ſo *faſting*, in accordance with the invariable practice of the Univerſal Church.

[1] It was formerly uſed to cleanſe the mouth of communicants.

(*p*) At the "Veiling of the Blessed Sacrament," an acolyte hands the linen veil to the Sub-deacon, who gives it to the Deacon. They then take their places, the Deacon on the right, the Sub-deacon on the left of the celebrant, in the midst of the Altar facing the east.

(*q*) At the Blessing they ascend to the edge of the platform, where they kneel. *Immediately* after the Blessing they stand, and the Deacon passes to the left, the Sub-deacon to the right hand of the Celebrant for the consumption and purification.

Whenever the Celebrant sits, the Deacon and Sub-deacon raise the chasuble over the back of the seat, or so arrange it that it be not crumpled in the sedilia. If there be no constructional sedilia in the Church, the seat for the Sacred Ministers should be a bench covered with green cloth—with purple in Lent and Advent—and with black on public fasts *et de missis de requiem*.

N.B.—The Sacred Ministers having occasion to pass from one side of the Altar to the other, before Consecration bow reverently* in the centre, but after the Consecration they genuflect at the Celebrant's side. They must observe never to place their hands on the Altar.

Solemn Service in the Absence of a Sub-deacon.

N many churches there are only two clerics; in this case at Solemn Service, it is proper for the Deacon to do the Sub-deacon's part as well as his own, the celebrant confining himself to his own part. A layman, however, in a cassock and surplice (without, of course, the tunic and maniple), may act as Sub-deacon, so as to put one person on each side of the Priest. The Deacon could in this case read both Epistle and Gospel; the layman holding the book of the Gospels and Epistles whilst he is doing so.

When a layman acts as Sub-deacon, there should be in addition at least two acolytes and two thurifers. They will wear the cotta, and the layman acting as Sub-deacon, a surplice or alb.

---

* The reason of this is—that no genuflection is to take place till our Blessed Saviour is present. The only exception being at the "was incarnate . . . . made man," in the Creed.

Appendix.

Directions for Acolytes or Lay Assistants.

 QUARTER of an hour before Service the two acolytes, who should be, if possible, of equal height, having vested themselves in cassock and cotta, go to the Altar and assist the Deacon or Sacristan to prepare what is needed; they then assist the Deacon and Sub-deacon to vest. They light the candles on the Altar (unless this function is performed by the Sacristan, or by some other fit person appointed to do it), the one on the one side, the other on the other. If only one acolyte lights them he begins on the Epistle side; in extinguishing them he begins on the Gospel side. A reed with a wax taper, and an extinguisher attached to the top, should always be kept for this especial purpose.

In the procession to the Altar the acolytes precede the Deacon and Sub-deacon. They walk abreast with heads uncovered, both hands joined before the breast. The first acolyte on the right, the second on the left.

On reaching the steps of the Altar, they divide for the celebrant and the Sacred Ministers to pass between them, and whilst the Priest, Deacon, and Sub-deacon ascend to the platform and take their places before the midst of the Altar, the acolytes kneel facing the east, the one on the Gospel the other on the Epistle side. At the singing of the Introit, and indeed normally, they stand facing the Altar. They stand throughout the function, except at the Confession, at the Prayer of Humble Access, and at the Consecration. They stand during the Communion.

For the Epistle, the acolyte who is near the Epistoler or Sub-deacon hands to him the Book of Epistles, opened at the proper place. For the Gospel, the acolyte who is near the Gospeller or Deacon hands the Book of the Gospels, opened at the proper place, to the Sub-deacon, who, passing across to the Gospel side, holds the lower part of the book with both hands towards the Deacon. The acolytes stand laterally, i.e. facing respectively north and south at the Epistle and Gospel.

When the Sacred Ministers sit down, the acolytes raise the dalmatic and tunic, and arrange them so that they be not injured; during this function, if they have occasion to pass before the Celebrant, they make an inclination.

During the Sermon they sit on stools upon the Altar-steps on either side of the Sanctuary.

At the Blessing they kneel in their places, rising *immediately* after the Blessing to fulfil their office at the purifications.

Acolytes hold their hands joined (*junctis manibus*) before their breasts. When one hand is occupied, the other should be laid on the breast.

In choir, when a reverence is to be made, it is usual to make it first on the Gospel side, then on the Epistle side, always commencing with the highest dignitary.

Position of Acolytes.

Holy ✠ Altar.

Priest.
Sub-deacon.   Deacon.
Acolyte.   Acolyte.
Assistant Priest.
Acolyte.   Acolyte.
Ceremoniarius.

Thurifers,
with Incense Boat-bearer.

Directions for Servers.

AT Plain Service (i.e. when the Service is said) the Celebrant is assisted by one server, who should be vested in cassock and cotta* at least a quarter of an hour before Service.

He will assist at the lavatory,† when the Priest washes his hands before vesting. He will then stand on the left of the Priest and assist him to vest. He should be careful to see that the alb hangs equally on all sides, about an inch from the ground; and that the stole is crossed in the middle near the lower part of the neck, and folded so as to remain covered by the chasuble, but so that the ends may be visible below. The chasuble should be so arranged that the Priest may put it on himself; yet, if he desire it, the Server may vest him with it. Before Service he will have placed the elements and cruets, &c. on the credence, and have lighted the Altar lights, if this be not done by the Sacristan.

* Servers never use the birretta.
† Every sacristy ought to be provided with a lavatory.

In leaving the facrifty he will precede the Prieft and carry the Service Book, taking care not to difplace the markers, which the Prieft has placed therein. He will carry the book with both hands, ftraight before the breaft, the opening towards his left. He will bow and ftand before the loweft ftep on the Epiftle fide when the Prieft afcends to the midft of the Altar, and will receive his birretta from him as he paffes. He will firft place the Prieft's birretta on the credence, and then place the Service Book *clofed* on the ftand, on the north fide (it fhould be placed cornerwife with its back to the north-eaft), with the opening of the book towards the Prieft.

The Server, while the Prieft privately fays the Introit, ftands upon the firft ftep on the right of the Prieft.

When the Book is on the Gofpel fide the Server kneels on the Epiftle fide of the celebrant; when the Book is on the Epiftle fide the Server kneels on the Gofpel fide. When the Prieft is in the midft of the Altar the fame rule holds, and the Server is on the Epiftle fide.

Throughout the Service the Server fhould be in uniformity with the Prieft in making the fign of the crofs, bowing, &c. and he fhould be careful never to leave the Prieft alone at the Altar.

At the Offertory, the Server will bring the elements from the credence; firft the breads, then the cruets—the wine in his right hand and the water in his left; and, where it is cuftomary, the veffel for the Prieft to wafh his fingers, together with a towel or napkin, which, folded, may hang over the acolyte's left arm. He will afterwards place the alms-difh on the credence after it has been offered. He then returns to his place, and kneels on the Epiftle fide.

At the Prayer of Humble Accefs the Server kneels immediately behind the Prieft. At the Prayer of Confecration he kneels *throughout* on the platform, not behind the Prieft, but a little on the Epiftle fide. At the elevation he will take the chafuble in his left hand, juft lifting it when the Prieft elevates the paten and the chalice; when the Prieft genuflects the chafuble is not held. At the Elevation he will bow down in profound adoration. The Server does not rife till after the Communion of the Prieft.

During the Communion of the faithful the Server fhould continue to kneel.

He will ftand on the lower ftep facing the eaft at the *Gloria in excelfis*, and kneel down there when the Prieft gives the Bleffing. *Immediately* after the Bleffing he rifes and goes to the credence to have the cruets in readinefs for the purifications. Taking the wine cruet in his right hand, he pours (1) a little wine into the chalice, then (2) a little wine and water from the cruet in his left hand over the fingers of the Prieſt, and finally (3) a little water.

When the Celebrant has deſcended to the ſanctuary platform with the chalice, the Server will take his birretta from the credence and hand it to him with his right hand, in ſuch a manner that it may be conveniently taken. He will then take the Service Book from the deſk and precede the Prieſt to the ſacriſty.

On reaching the ſacriſty the Server will ſtand a little aſide, and as the Prieſt paſſes him will make a reverence. Having laid down the Service Book, he will aſſiſt him to unveſt. In receiving the alb, he will be careful not to trail it on the ground. If the Prieſt ſhould waſh his hands, as is moſt likely, the ſerver will aſſiſt at the lavatory. When all is done, he will make a final reverence to the Prieſt. He will then, with the proper extinguiſher, return to the altar and put out the candles, firſt the light on the Goſpel ſide, then that on the Epiſtle ſide. They ſhould always be put out with the extinguiſher, and never left ſmoking. The lights are ſometimes extinguiſhed by the ſerver while the Prieſt is going to the ſacriſty.

N. B.—(α.) Whenever the Server paſſes the altar, he will bow to the croſs, crucifix, or picture of our LORD JESUS CHRIST on the Croſs.

(β.) After the conſecration, in paſſing before the Bleſſed Sacrament, the Server will be eſpecially careful always to genuflect with great reverence.

(γ.) The Server will ſee when the Service Book is on the ſtand at the Goſpel ſide that it be placed corner-wiſe, ſo that the Prieſt faces north-eaſt. When it is on the Epiſtle ſide, it ſhould be placed ſquare with the altar, ſo that the Prieſt faces eaſtwards.

(δ.) When the Prieſt takes his poſition finally at the midſt of the altar at the creed, the Book is placed a little on the Goſpel ſide of the centre of the altar, only *juſt ſo much ſlanted* as to enable the Prieſt to read eaſily as he ſtands with his face due eaſt.

(ε.) After the celebration is over, if the Sacriſtan be not at hand, the Server will aſſiſt the Prieſt to waſh and carefully put by the ſacred veſſels.

(ζ.) He will then carefully fold and put by the veſtments, and place the ordinary cover of green ſilk on the top of the altar.

(η.) He ſhould remember that the veſſels have touched CHRIST, that the ſacred veſtments have been very near to HIM, that he himſelf "has been with JESUS"—and ſo he will perform theſe pious duties with a reverent cheerfulneſs and an earneſt care, doing them with all his might as unto the

LORD and not unto man, and he will find his service acceptable to our LORD.

(θ.) When there are great numbers to communicate, a Priest (or Priests) could put a surplice and stole (pendent) over his cassock and leave his place in the choir for the ministering of the chalice. This is quite necessary when there are many communicants. The Priest (or Priests) may if he please wear the surplice from the beginning of the service, so long as he keeps his place in choir and does not advance to the sanctuary, till it is the time of communion, if he is going to communicate, or if not, he will receive the chalice, (or chalices), from the Priest to communicate the faithful.

Directions as to Chalices and Patens.

More than one Chalice not to be placed upon the Altar. The mode of using a second Chalice if necessity requires.

WHEN there are a very large number of communicants expected, the Celebrant had better consecrate two or more large chalices for the communion of the faithful. And it is well in addition to the breads on the corporal and Paten to consecrate a large number in a Ciborium, from which either the Paten may be replenished, or the faithful may be directly communicated.

Sometimes the wine is consecrated in a large Flagon* or Cruet, and the Chalices are supplied from the Cruet at the time of communion. If so, the Cruet will be prepared with water in the same manner as a Chalice at the Offertory.

The first usage is much to be preferred.

"*Calices plures in altari non ponendi.*—A.D. 731, Greg. III. ad Bonifacium, Tom. ii. Conciliorum, constituit, ne in Missarum solemniis, duo vel tres Calices in altari ponerentur, quoniam id parum Christi institutioni conveniret, qui de uno et eodem Calice omnes communicasset. Unde colligere licet, sanguinem non fuisse sacratum in Calicibus ministerialibus, sed in alio quodam, et ex illo deinde transfusum in ministeriales, ad usum populi." Jo. Ste. Durantus de Ritibus Ecclesiæ. Lib. i. cap. vii. sec. 5, p. 70. Paris, 1632.

---

* " And here he is to lay his hand upon every vessel (be it chalice or flagon) in which there is any wine to be consecrated." Rubric, Book of Common Prayer.

This manner of communicating large numbers of the faithful in an expeditious manner, ſhould always be adopted at the early Plain Service on the great feſtivals, &c. It *ought* not to be neceſſary at the mid-day Solemn Celebration, when it is ſuppoſed there will be fewer communicants, though a larger congregation; for the faithful ſhould have communicated at the early celebration, and ought to be preſent ſimply for purpoſes of worſhip and Euchariſtic adoration at mid-day.

Solemn Euchariſtic Service ſung in preſence of a Biſhop aſſiſting pontifically.

THE Biſhop ſhould on the great Feſtivals aſſiſt at Solemn Service, veſted in amice, rochet, ſtole, paſtoral croſs, cope, and mitre. He will occupy the throne, and be aſſiſted by two Prieſts, if poſſible Canons, and two Deacons in ſurplice and amyſs. Unleſs the Biſhop aſſiſts at the throne veſted in the ſacred veſtments he does not uſe the paſtoral ſtaff.

The Biſhop at firſt proceeds to the midſt of the altar with his aſſiſtants, who then retire behind. Having given up the paſtoral ſtaff and mitre, he goes to the north ſide of the altar, accompanied as above by the Celebrant and Sacred Miniſters, and the Introit will begin, which ended, the Biſhop will ſing the *Pater Noſter, Collect for Purity,* and the Ten Commandments. The Biſhop does not ſing any other part of the Service, except the abſolution—which is pronounced ſtanding up and turning to the people—until the final bleſſing. The Book of the Goſpels is brought by the Subdeacon to be bleſſed by the Biſhop.

The Biſhop is ſerved throughout with a Service Book by one of his Aſſiſtant Prieſts.

In giving the pax and bleſſing, he ſtands with his aſſiſtants on either ſide facing the ſouth-weſt. At the pax he extends his arms, and at the bleſſing holds in his left hand the paſtoral ſtaff, making the ſign of the croſs over the people with his right.

Appendix.

A FORM* of Confecration, or Dedication of Churches and Chappels, according to the Ufe of the Church of IRELAND.†

¶ The Patron, or the Chief of the Parifh where a new Church is erected, is to give timely Notice to the Bifhop of the Diocefs, and humbly defire him to appoint a convenient time, fome Lord's-Day, or other great Feftival of the Church, for performance of the Solemnity.

¶ At the Day appointed, the Bifhop, with a convenient Number of his Clergy, (of which the Dean or Archdeacon to be one) and the Chancellor of the Diocefs, and his Regifter fhall come between the Hours of Eight and Ten in the Morning; and when they are near, the Bell is to ring till they be entered into the Church appointed to be confecrated.

¶ Firft, the Bifhop and his Clergy, together with the Patron or his Deputy, fhall go round about the Cœmetery or Churchyards; which done the Bifhop and his Clergy fhall enter into the Church at the Weft Door, the Patron and People ftanding without, while the Bifhop and Prieft do veft‡ themfelves in their refpective Ecclefiaftick Habits.

¶ When they are vefted, they fhall kneel down in the Body of the Church, with their Faces to the Eaft, and fay together.

OUR Father, which art in heaven, Hallowed be thy Name; thy kingdom come; thy will be done in earth, as it is in heaven: Give us this day our daily bread, and forgive us our Trefpaffes, as we forgive them that trefpafs againft us; and lead us not into temptation, but deliver us from evil. *Amen.*

¶ Then the Bifhop fhall pray.

Prevent us, O Lord, in all our doings with thy moft gracious favour, and further us with thy continual help, that in all our works begun, continued, and ended in thee, we may glorifie thy holy Name, and finally by thy mercy obtain everlafting life; through Jefus Chrift our Lord. *Amen.*

¶ Then rifing up, they fhall go together to the Weft Door, and the Dean or Archdeacon on one Hand, and the Chancellor on the other, fhall bring the Patron to the Threfhold of the Weft Door, and prefent him to the Bifhop; who fhall thus fay to him:—

SIR,—I am come hither at your defire; I afk therefore for what intent you have defired my coming?

¶ The Patron fhall anfwer; or fome of the Clergy at his requeft and appointment fhall anfwer for him.

---

* The typographical arrangement, capital letters, &c. are accurately reproduced from the original edition.

† From "the Book of Common Prayer, and Adminiftration of the Sacraments, and other Rites and Ceremonies of the Church, according to the Ufe of the Church of Ireland, &c. Dublin: printed by and for George Grierfon in Effex Street. 1736."

‡ This order to veft in church does not imply that they were without furplices before, but only refers to the fpecial veftments.—Ed. D. A.

A Form of Consecration of Churches.

He hath, [or *mutatis mutandis*,] I have caused a House to be built for the service of God, and the publick Ministries of Religion, and separated a burying place for [his or] my dead; and [his or] my humble desire is, that it may be set apart from all common and prophane uses, and dedicated to the honour of God by your Prayers and holy Ministries, according to the Word of God, and the Laws and Customs of this Church.

¶ Then shall the Bishop say,

Whiles it remained, was it not thine own? and before it is given to God, was it not in thine own power? but when once you give it to God, it can never be recalled; but is in his propriety for ever.

¶ The Patron or his Deputy shall answer.

I humbly desire he will be graciously pleased to accept it, and that it may remain his own for his service and his honour for ever.

¶ Then shall the Patron kneel down and receive the Bishop's blessing in the words following.

¶ The Bishop laying his hand upon, or lifting it over the Patron's head, shall say,

The Lord bless you and prosper you; the Lord make his face to shine upon you, and be merciful unto you. Remember thy servant, O God, concerning this also; accept his gift, sanctifie his heart, purifie his intentions, reward his loving-kindness, and spare him according to the greatness of thy mercies. Enrich him and his family with all blessings of thy Spirit and thy Providence for ever, through Jesus Christ our Lord. *Amen.*

And now in the Name of God, and to the honour of our Lord Jesus Christ, let us perform this Ministry.

¶ Then the Patron arising, the Bishop shall call for the Instrument of Donation, which the Bishop receiving from the hands of the Patron, shall deliver to the Register, to be read publickly in that place.

¶ Which being done, all may enter into the Church: then shall the Bishop, attended by his Clergy, kneel in the body of the Church, before the Chancel door, at a Convenient distance upon a foot-step raised higher than the floor, and shall say,

Let us pray.

I.

1 Chron. xxix. 10, &c.

Blessed be Thou, O Lord God, Father of our Lord Jesus Christ for ever and ever. Thine, O Lord, is the greatness, and the power, and the glory, and the victory, and the Majesty: All that is in the heavens, and in the earth is thine. Thine is the Kingdom, O Lord, and thou art exalted as head over all. Both riches and honour come of thee, and thou reignest over all; and in thine hand is power and might, and in thine hand it is to make great, and to give strength unto all. Now therefore, our God, we thank thee, and praise thy glorious Name, that thou hast put it into the heart of thy servants to build a house for the honour of thy Name, and the service of thy Majesty. O Lord our God, What are we, and what is thy people, that from thy servants anything should be given and offered unto thee by us? All things come of thee, and of thy own we give unto thee. But we know also, O God, that thou trieſt the hearts, and haſt pleaſure in uprightneſs. O Lord God of our fathers, God of mercy, and Father of Men and Angels, keep this, and all thankfulneſs and piety, and devotion in the imagination of the thoughts of the hearts of thy ſervants for ever; and proſper thou the work of our hands unto us, O proſper thou our handy work. Confirm this thing which thou haſt wrought in us, from thy holy Temple, which is in Jeruſalem, which is from above, and is the Mother of us all. And for ever be pleaſed to imploy us in thy ſervice, to ſtrengthen us in all obedience, to lead us in the way everlaſting, and to accept us in thoſe religious duties which we ſhall perform by thy commandment, and by the aſſiſtances of thy holy Spirit, through Jeſus Chriſt our Lord. *Amen.*

II.

O Almighty and Eternal God, Who by thy Immenſity filleſt all places both in heaven and earth, and canſt not be limited nor circumſcribed in any: Thou art the moſt High, and dwelleſt not, as we do, in houſes made with hands; for Heaven is thy Throne, and the earth is thy Footſtool; and what houſe can we build for thee? And what is the place of thy reſt, that we can furniſh out for thee? Surely every place is too little and too low for thee, who dwelleſt on high, and thy glory is above the heavens: And yet thou humbleſt thyſelf to behold the things that are in heaven and earth, and thy delight is to be with the ſons of men. Thou ſpeakeſt out words, thou complieſt with our weakneſſes, thou accepteſt our ſervices, and wilt be worſhipped and ador'd according to what thou haſt put into our power. Thou therefore haſt been pleaſ'd in all ages to meet with thy ſervants in places ſeparate for thy worſhip and for the invocation of thy holy Name. In Paradiſe there was a proper place which thy ſervant *Moſes* called *The preſence of the Lord;* and thy ſervant *Abraham* called on thy Name in the *place of the Altar,* [Gen. xiii. 4]. And thou didſt meet the Patriarch *Jacob* at *Bethel,* and he conſecrated a ſtone for thy memorial, and it became dreadful and venerable, the houſe of God, and the Gate of Heaven, [Gen. xxviii. 17]. And *Rebekah* had a proper place whither ſhe went to enquire of the Lord. Thou alſo didſt fill the Tabernacle with thy preſence, and the Temple with thy glory; and when the fulneſs of time was come, thou, by thy moſt holy Son, didſt declare that thou wilt be preſent in all places, where two or three are gathered together in thy Name; and that amongſt all Nations for ever thy houſe ſhall be called the houſe of prayer; and by thy Apoſtle haſt ſignified to us, that our dwelling-houſes are to eat and drink in, but that we muſt not deſpiſe the Churches of God. For thou art a jealous God, and wilt not endure that thy Temples ſhould be defiled. Our God is a conſuming fire, and he that defiles a Temple him will God deſtroy.

Therefore, in confidence of thy goodneſs, in expectation of thy favours, in full aſſurance of thy promiſes, in obedience to the manifold declaration of thy pleaſure, and in imitation of the piety of thy ſervants, who in all generations of the world have ſeparated places and houſes for thy ſervice, and left great monuments of their piety for our comfort and example, that we may come together into one place,* and by a join'd prayer, wreſtle with thee for bleſſings, and not depart thence till thou haſt bleſſed us: We thy ſervants walking in the ſteps of their moſt holy faith, partakers of the ſame hope, fellow Citizens with the Saints, and of the houſehold of God, are this day met together in thy fear and love, to dedicate a houſe to thee, and to the glories of thy Name, that we may not neglect the aſſembling of ourſelves together, but meet here to implore thy mercies, to deplore our ſins, to deprecate thy anger, to magnifie thy goodneſs, to celebrate thy praiſes, to receive thy Sacraments, to bleſs thy people, and to perform all Miniſtries of Salvation.

* Πάντες ἐπὶ τὸ αὐτὸ, πάντες ἐπὶ τὸν ναὸν τοῦ Θεοῦ. S. Ignatius, *Epiſt. ad Magneſ.*

A Form of Consecration of Churches.

Be pleased, therefore, most gracious Lord and Father, to accept the devotion and oblation of thy servants: admit this place and house into a portion of thine own inheritance: Let it be a resting-place for thy feet, and the seat of thy graciousness. Depute thy holy Angels to abide here, to defend thy servants, and to drive away all the power of the Enemy. Place thy Mercy-seat among us also: Let thine eyes and thine ears be open towards this house night and day, and hear the prayers of thy people which they shall make unto thee in this place; granting to them all the graces which they shall need and ask: And whensoever in humility and contrition they shall confess their sins unto thee, be thou more ready to hear than they to pray: forgive them all their sins: encrease and perfect their repentances, remove thy judgments far from them, and let them feel and rejoice in thy mercies and lovingkindnesses for ever and ever. Grant this for his sake, who is the King of the Saints, and the Head of the Church, the great lover of souls, and our High Priest, who continually makes intercession for us, our blessed Lord and Saviour Jesus. *Amen*.

III.

O Almighty God, who art the Father of the faithful, and a gracious God to all that call upon thee in truth and love; thou hast taught us by thy holy Apostle, that everything is sanctified by the word of God and prayer: Attend this day and ever to the prayers of thy servants: be present with thy grace in all our Ministries of the Sacraments, and Sacramentals; and bless all the labours and accept all the religious duties, and satisfie all the holy desires of them who in this thy house shall make their supplications before thee. And let the dew of thy divine blessing descend and abide for ever upon this house, which by invocation of thy holy Name, and to the honour of the Lord Jesus, and the Ministries of thy servants, we, though unworthy, consecrate, and dedicate unto thee.

Spare all the penitents, relieve the distressed, comfort the comfortless, confirm the strong, and strengthen the weak; Ease the afflicted, heal the wounded and the sick; provide for the widows, and be a father to the fatherless; and unto all them whose consciences being accus'd for sin, come with confidence to the Throne of Grace, give help in all the times of their need, that whensoever thy Name is called upon thy blessings may certainly descend. Let thy eternal peace be to this house, and to them who in this house come to thee to be eased and refreshed.

Here let thy Priests be cloathed with righteousness, and let thy Saints sing with joyfulness. Here let thy people make their prayers, and perform their vows, and offer their free-will offerings with a holy worship. Here let the weight of their sins that so easily besets them be laid aside: here let the chains of their corruptions, and the cords of vanity be broken. Let the lapsed be restored, let the sick be cured, let the blind eyes and hearts be enlightened with the lanthorn of thy Word and the lights of thy Spirit. Here let the power of Satan be lessened and destroyed; and let thy servants find a cure for all their wounds; a comfort for all their sorrows; a remedy to all their inconveniencies: that all who shall enter this house now dedicated to thy service may obtain all their desires and triumph in the Name of the Lord our God, who hath performed all their petitions. Preserve their souls from sin, their eyes from tears, and their feet from falling, for Jesus Christ his sake; to Whom with Thee, O Father, and thy most Holy Spirit, be all honour and glory, praise and thanksgiving, love and obedience, for ever and ever. *Amen*.

¶ Then the Bishop and the Congregation arising from their knees, the Bishop attended by his Clergy, shall go in procession round about the church within, and say this hymn alternately,

Hymn I.

Ex Pfalmis 127, 84.

1. Except the Lord build the houfe, they labour in vain that build it: except the Lord keepeth the city, the watchman waketh but in vain.
2. Bleffed is the man whofe ftrength is in thee, in whofe heart are thy ways.
3. They go from ftrength to ftrength: every one of them in Zion appeareth before God.
4. How amiable are thy tabernacles, O Lord of Hofts!
5. My foul longeth, yea, even fainteth for the courts of the Lord, my heart and my flefh crieth out for the living God: whence fhall I come and appear before the prefence of God?
6. The fparrow hath found her an houfe, and the fwallow a neft for herfelf, where fhe may lay her young, even thy altars, O Lord of Hofts, my King and my God.
7. Bleffed are they that dwell in thy houfe: they will be always praifing thee.
8. For a day in thy courts is better than a thoufand: I had rather be a door-keeper in the houfe of my God, than to dwell in the tents of wickednefs.
9. For the Lord God is a Sun and a Shield: the Lord will give grace and glory, and no good thing will he withhold from them that walk uprightly.
10. O Lord of hofts: bleffed is the man that trufteth in thee.

Glory be to the Father, and to the Son, and to the Holy Ghoft:
As it was in the beginning, is now, and ever fhall be, world without end. *Amen.*

¶ Then fhall the Bifhop go to the vault appointed in the church for the burial-place (in cafe there be any), or elfe ftanding in the moft open pavement of the church, the Archdeacon fhall read this leffon.

¶ The Leffon in the Coemetery.

And when the inhabitants of Jabefh-Gilead heard of that which the Philiftines had done to Saul; all the valiant men arofe, and went all night, and took the body of Saul and the bodies of his fons from the wall of Bethfhan, and came to Jabefh, and burnt them there. And they took their bones, and buried them under a tree at Jabefh, and fafted feven days. 1 *Sam.* xxxi. 11—13.

And they told David, faying, that the men of Jabefh-Gilead were they that buried Saul. And David fent meffengers unto the men of Jabefh-Gilead, and faid unto them, Bleffed be ye of the Lord, that ye fhewed this Kindnefs unto your lord, even unto Saul, and have buried him. 2 *Sam.* ii. 4, 5.

And the fon of David, King Solomon, faid, If a man beget an hundred children, and live many years, fo that the days of his years be many, and his foul be not filled with good; and alfo that he hath no burial; I fay, that an untimely birth is better than he. *Ecclef.* vi. 3.

And fo I faw the wicked buried, who had come and gone from the place of the Holy, and they were forgotten in the city where they had fo done. *Ecclef.* viii. 10.

But let a man remember the days of darknefs, for they fhall be many. *Ecclef.* xi. 8.

For the duft fhall return to the earth as it was, and the Spirit fhall return unto God that gave it. *Ecclef.* xii. 7.

¶ Then the Bifhop ftanding in the fame place fhall pray.

O Almighty God, with whom do live the fpirits of them that die in the Lord, grant unto all thy fervants whofe bodies fhall be buried in this Dormitory, that they may lie down with

A Form of Consecration of Churches.   211

the righteous, and their souls may be gathered to their Fathers in the bosom of Christ, and their bodies may rest in peace unto the latter day; and when thy holy Son shall come to judge both the quick and the dead, they may hear the sentence of the right hand, and may have their perfect consummation and bliss in their eternal and everlasting glory, through Jesus Christ our Lord. *Amen.*

¶ Then the Bishop, with the Clergy attending, shall go to the Font, and the Verger or Clerk presenting pure water to him, he shall pour the water into the Font.

¶ Then shall the Senior Priest read this Lesson.

¶ The Lesson at the Font.

And Jesus came and spake unto them, saying, All power is given unto me in heaven and in earth. Go ye therefore, and teach all nations, baptizing them in the Name of the Father, and of the Son, and of the Holy Ghost: teaching them to observe all things whatsoever I have commanded you: and, lo, I am with you alway, even unto the end of the world. *Amen.* Matt. xxviii. 18—20.

¶ Then shall the Bishop pray.

O Eternal God, fountain of all purity, bless and sanctifie the waters which thou hast ordained and constituted for the mystical washing away of sin: and grant unto all them who shall come hither to be presented unto thee, and to be washed in this Lavatory, that they may receive the baptism of the Spirit, and may have a title and portion in repentance, remission of sins, and all the promises of the Gospel, that they may not only have the washing of the filth of the flesh, but the answer of a good conscience towards God; that they dying unto sin and being buried with Christ in his death, may live unto righteousness, and become thy disciples in an unreprovable faith and a perfect obedience, and at last may partake of the Resurrection of thy Son to eternal life, through the same Jesus Christ our Lord. *Amen.*

¶ Then shall the Bishop go attended as before, to the Pulpit, and laying his hand upon it, shall appoint one of the Priests to read the following Lesson.

¶ The Lesson at the Pulpit.

I charge thee therefore before God, and the Lord Jesus Christ, who shall judge the quick and the dead at his appearing and his Kingdom, preach the Word, be instant in season, and out of season, reprove, rebuke, exhort with all longsuffering and doctrine: for the time will come when they will not endure sound doctrine; but after their own lusts shall they heap to themselves teachers, having itching ears. 2 *Tim.* iv. 1—3.

This is a faithful saying, and these things I will that thou affirm constantly, that they which have believed in God might be careful to maintain good works: these things are good and profitable unto men. But avoid foolish questions, and genealogies, and contentions, and strivings about the Law, for they are unprofitable and vain. *Titus* iii. 8, 9.

But let the man of God watch in all things, endure afflictions, do the work of an Evangelist, and make full proof of his Ministry. 2 *Tim.* iv. 5.

¶ Then shall the Bishop pray.

O Almighty God, who by thy Word, and by thy Spirit, dost instruct thy servants and teach them all truth, and lead them in the way of salvation; Grant that this place may be always filled with wife and holy persons, who may dispense thy word faithfully according to the ability thou givest, and the charge which thou imposest and the duty thou requirest; giving to every one their portion in due season, and feeding the flock of God, not of constraint or of necessity, but willingly and chearfully; not for filthy lucre's sake, but readily and of a good mind. O send faithful labourers into thy harvest; and grant that all the people which from this place shall hear thy word, may not receive it as the word of man, but as the good word of God, able to save their souls: and let thy holy Spirit for ever be the Preacher, and imprint thy word in their minds, opening their hearts, convincing their understandings, overruling their wills, and governing their affections, that they may not be hearers of the Word only, but doers of good Works; that they by their holy lives adorning the Gospel of God, and seeking for glory and honour, and immortality, may attain eternal life, through Jesus Christ our Lord. *Amen.*

¶ Then the Bishop and Clergy shall go towards the Chancel, the doors of which being shut, he shall stand there, and with the Priests recite this Hymn alternately.

Hymn II.

1. Open to me the gates of righteousness, I will go into them, and praise the Lord:
2. This is the gate of the Lord, into which the righteous shall enter.
3. The stone which the builders refused, is become the head stone of the corner.
4. This is the Lord's doing, and it is marvellous in our eyes.
5. This is the day which the Lord hath made: we will rejoyce and be glad in it.
6. Save now, I beseech thee, O Lord: O Lord, I beseech thee, send us now prosperity.
7. Blessed be he that cometh in the Name of the Lord: we have blessed you out of the house of the Lord.
8. God is the Lord which hath showed us light: bind the sacrifice with cords, even to the horns of the altar.
9. O Lord, open thou my mouth: and my lips shall show forth thy praise.
10. For thou desirest not sacrifice, else would I give it thee: but thou delightest not in burnt-offerings.
11. The sacrifices of God are a broken spirit: a broken and a contrite heart, O God, thou wilt not despise.
12. Do good in thy good pleasure unto Sion: build thou the walls of Jerusalem.
13. Then shalt thou be pleased with the sacrifice of righteousness, with burnt-offerings and whole burnt-offerings: then shall they offer bullocks upon thine altar.
14. Whoso offereth praise, glorifieth me, and to him that ordereth his conversation right will I show the salvation of God.

Glory be to the Father, and to the Son, and to the Holy Ghost;
As it was in the beginning, is now, and ever shall be, world without end. *Amen.*

¶ Then the doors being opened, the Bishop with his Clergy shall enter and ascend to the Communion Table, and sitting in a Chair on the south side of it, shall appoint the Dean or Archdeacon to read this Lesson.

¶ The Lesson at the Communion Table.

I speak as to wise men, judge what I say. The cup of blessing which we bless, is it not the communion of the blood of Christ? The bread which we break, is it not the communion of the body of Christ? For we being many are one bread, and one body, for we are all par-

A Form of Consecration of Churches. 213

takers of that one bread. Ye cannot drink the cup of the Lord, and the cup of Devils: ye cannot be partakers of the Lord's table, and the table of Devils. Do we provoke the Lord to jealousie? are we stronger than he? Whether therefore ye eat, or drink, or whatsoever ye do, do all to the glory of God. 1 *Cor.* x. 15—17, 21, 22, 31.

We have an altar, whereof they have no right to eat which serve the tabernacle. Wherefore Jesus also, that he might sanctifie the people with his own blood, suffered without the gate. Let us go forth therefore unto him, bearing his reproach. For here we have no continuing city, but we seek one to come. By him therefore let us offer the sacrifice of praise to God continually, that is, the fruit of our lips giving thanks to his name. But to do good and to communicate forget not: for with such sacrifices God is well pleased. *Heb.* xiii. 10, 12—16.

¶ Then the Bishop arising from his chair shall kneel before the Altar, or Communion Table, and say,

¶ Let us pray.

O Eternal God, who in an infinite mercy to mankind, didst send thy holy Son to be a sacrifice for our sins, and the food of our souls, the Author and finisher of our faith, and the great Minister of eternal glory; who also now sits at thy right hand, and upon the heavenly altar perpetually presents to thee the eternal Sacrifice, a never ceasing prayer, be present with thy servants, and accept us in the dedication of a ministerial altar, which we humbly have provided for the performance of this great Ministry, and in imitation of Christ's eternal Priesthood, according to our Duty and his Commandment. Grant that all the gifts which shall be presented on this table may be acceptable unto thee and become unto thy servants a favour of life unto life. Grant that all who shall partake of this table may indeed hunger after the bread of life, and thirst for the wine of elect souls, and may feed upon Christ by faith and be nourished by a holy hope, and grow up to an eternal charity. Let no hand of any that shall betray thee be ever upon this table; let no impure tongue ever taste of the holy body and blood which here shall be sacramentally represented and exhibited. But let all thy servants that come hither to receive these mysteries come with prepared hearts, and with penitent souls, and loving desires, and indeed partake of the Lord Jesus, and receive all the benefits of his Passion. Grant this for his sake, who is the Priest and the Sacrifice, the Feeder and the Food, the Physician and the Physic of our souls, our most blessed Lord and Saviour Jesus. Amen.

¶ Then the Bishop arising shall return to his Chair, and sitting covered, some persons by the Patron's appointment shall bring the Carpet, the Communion cloath, and Napkins, the Chalice, Paten, and other Vessels, Books, and Utensils for the Communion; and humbly presenting them on their knees to God, the Bishop shall receive them severally, and deliver them to the Deacon, to be laid orderly on the Communion Table; excepting only the Chalice and the Paten, which two Priests shall (when the Table is covered) humbly on their knees lay upon it. Then the Bishop returning to the Altar, shall with reverence and solemnity (his face being Eastward) lay his hands upon the Plate, and say this Prayer standing:

What are we, O God, and what is this people, that we should be able to offer so willingly after this sort? For all things come of thee, and of thine own we have given thee. Accept the Oblation of thy servants, who in the uprightness of their hearts have willingly offered these things, and give unto them a perfect heart to keep thy Commandments, thine Ordinances, and thy Sacraments; and be pleafed to grant to them a greater ability, an enlarged heart, and an increafing love to ferve thee with their fouls and bodies, with all their time, and all their goods, that thou may'ft be honoured with all their heart and with all their ftrength; and grant that thefe gifts may be received into the lot of God and of Religion, and the Donors be continued for ever in the lot of thine inheritance: that by thy grace, accepting thefe gifts, they may in all their other Poffeffions be bleffed, and by the ufe of thefe gifts in the Miniftries of thy holy Religion, they may be fanctified, and by a guard of Angels they may be preferved from all evil, and by the perpetual prefence of thy holy Spirit they may be led into all good, and accepted to pardon, and preferved in peace, and promoted in holinefs, and conducted certainly to life eternal, through Jefus Chrift our Lord. *Amen.* 1 *Chron.* xxix. 14.

¶ Then the Bifhop fhall go to the North end of the Holy Table, and turning to the People, fhall fay,

The Lord be with you.
Anfwer. And with thy fpirit.

Let us pray.

I.

O Moft Glorious and eternal God, who makeft all things by thy power, and adorneft all things with thy bounty, and filleft all things with thy goodnefs, and fanctifieft the hearts and gifts of thy fervants by thy Spirit, we worfhip and adore thy glories, who filleft all the world by thy Prefence, and fuftaineft it by thy Almightinefs: We love and magnify thy mercies, that thou haft been pleafed to enable and admit thy fervants [*to build an houfe to thee,* *and*] out of thine own ftore to give gifts to thee, who giveft all that we poffefs. We humbly pray thee by the Death and Paffion, by the Refurrection and Afcenfion, and by the glorious Interceffion of our Lord, that thou wouldeft vouchfafe to fanctifie [*this houfe and*] thefe gifts to thy fervice, by the effufion of thy holinefs from above. Let the Sun of Righteoufnefs for ever fhine here, and let the brighteft illumination of the Spirit fill [*this place, and fill*] all our hearts for ever with thy glorious prefence: That which we have bleffed, do thou blefs; that which we offer, do thou accept; that which we place here, do thou vifit gracioufly and for ever, through Jefus Chrift our Lord. *Amen.*

II.

Let this houfe be for the religious ufes of thy fervants; let it be the abode of angels; let it be the place of thy Name, and for the glory of thy grace, and for the mention and honour, and the memorial of the Lord Jefus. Let no unclean thing ever enter here: Drive from hence all facrilegious hands, all fuperftitious Rites, all prophane Perfons, all proud and unquiet Schifmaticks, all mifbelieving Hereticks. Let not the powers of darknefs come hither, nor the fecret arrow ever fmite any here. Let no corrupt air, and no corrupt communication, no bloodfhed, and no unclean action ever pollute this place dedicated to thy holinefs.

By the multitudes of thy mercies and propitiations, to the vifitors of this place coming with devotion and charity, let there be peace and abundance of thy bleffings. Hear them that fhall call upon thee, fanctifie their Oblations, let the good Word of God come upon them and difpenfe thy good things unto them. Let the title of this Church abide until the fecond coming of Chrift, and let thy Holy Table ftand prepared with the bleffings of a Celeftial Banquet.

A Form of Consecration of Churches.

Bleſs the gifts and the givers, the dwellers and the dwelling, and grant unto us here preſent, and to all that ſhall come after us, that by the participation of thy heavenly graces, we may obtain eternal life, through Jeſus Chriſt our Lord. *Amen.*

III.

O Eternal God, who art pleaſed to manifeſt thy preſence amongſt the ſons of men by the ſpecial iſſues of thy favour and benediction, make our bodies and ſouls to be temples pure and holy, apt for the entertainments of the Holy Jeſus, and for the inhabitation of thy holy Spirit. Lord, be pleas'd with the powers of thy grace to caſt out all impure luſts, all worldly affections, all covetous deſires, from theſe thy Temples, that they may be places of prayer and holy meditation, of godly deſires, and chaſte thoughts, of pure intentions, and great zeal to pleaſe thee, that we alſo may become Sacrifices, as well as Temples, eaten up with the zeal of thy glory, and even conſumed with the fires of thy love; that not one thought may be entertained by us, but ſuch as may be like perfume exhaling from the Altar of Incenſe; and not a word may paſs from us, but may have the accent of heaven in it, and found pleaſantly in thy ears.

O deareſt God, fill every faculty of our ſouls with the impreſſes of Religion, that we loving thee above all things in the world, worſhipping thee with frequent and humbleſt adorations, continually feeding upon the apprehenſions of thy divine ſweetneſs, and living in a daily obſervation of thy Divine Commandments, and delighted with the perpetual feaſt of a holy Conſcience may, by thy Spirit, be ſeal'd up to the day of Redemption, and the fruition of thy glories in thine everlaſting Kingdom, through Jeſus Chriſt our Lord; to whom with thee, O Father of mercies, Father of our Lord Jeſus Chriſt, and with thee, O bleſſed and eternal Spirit the Comforter, all honour and power be aſcribed from generation to generation for ever and ever. *Amen.*

¶ Then add the Prayer of S. Clement.

God, the beholder and diſcerner of all things, the Lord of ſpirits and all fleſh, who hath choſen our Lord Jeſus, and us through him to be a peculiar people, grant unto every ſoul that calleth upon his glorious and holy Name, faith and fear, peace and patience, longſuffering and temperance, with purity and wiſdom, to the well pleaſing of his Name, through our High Prieſt and Ruler, by whom unto Him be glory and Majeſty, both now and to all ages evermore. *Amen.*   *Clement. 1 Epiſt. ad Corinth. in fine.*

¶ Then the Biſhop ariſing ſhall ſit in his Chair at the ſouth end of the Holy Table, and being covered, ſhall cauſe the Chancellor to read the inſtrument of Conſecration, and give command that it be entred into the Regiſtry and an Act made of it *in perpetuam rei memoriam:* A Duplicate of which Inſtrument atteſted under the Regiſter's hand and ſeal of the Office, is to remain with the Patron or Founder, and the Original with the Biſhop.

¶ After which the Anathematiſm ſhall be read by him and his Clergy alternately, all ſtanding up.

¶ The Anathematiſm.

Ex Pſalmis 79, 83, 129.

1. Keep not thou ſilence, O God: hold not thy peace, and be not ſtill, O God.
2. Let not thine Enemies make a tumult, and they that hate thee lift up their head.
3. Let them not come into thine inheritance to defile thy holy temple, leſt they lay waſte thy dwelling places, and break down the carved work thereof with axes and hammers.
4. Make their Nobles like Oreb and Zeeb: yea, all their princes like Zeba and Zalmunna.

5. Who say, let us take to ourselves the houses of God in possession.
6. O my God, make them like unto a wheel, as the stubble before the wind.
7. As the fire burneth the wood, and as the flame setteth the mountains on fire.
8. So persecute them with thy tempest, and make them afraid with thy storm.
9. Fill their faces with shame, that they may seek thy Name, O Lord.
10. That men may know, that thou, whose Name is Jehovah, art the most High over all the earth.
11. For the Lord is righteous, he will cut asunder the cords of the wicked.
12. Let them all be ashamed that hate Sion.
13. Let them be as the grass upon the house-tops, which withereth before it groweth up.
14. Wherewith the mower filleth not his hand: nor he that bindeth sheaves his bosom.
15. Neither do they which go by say, The blessing of the Lord be upon you: we bless you in the Name of the Lord.

The Bishop.

Glory be to God on high.
Answer. And on earth peace to men of good will.
Bishop. Amen.
Answer. Amen.

¶ Then shall the Bishop conclude with this Εὐφημισμός, or Acclamation, the Clergy answering alternately.

¶ The Bishop first saying,

Seeing now, dearly beloved in the Lord, that by the blessing of God and his gracious favour, we have dedicated to God [*this House of Prayer, and*] these gifts for the Ministries of Religion, let us give hearty thanks to Almighty God for these benefits, and say,

Ex Psalmis 150, 68, 87, 99, 100.

1. Praise ye the Lord: praise God in his sanctuary, praise him in the firmament of his power.
2. Blessed be the Lord, who daily loadeth us with benefits: even the God of our salvation.
3. He that is our God, is the God of salvation; and unto God the Lord belong the issues from death.
4. The chariots of God are twenty thousand, even thousands of Angels: the Lord is among them as in Sinai, in the holy place.
5. They have seen the goings of God, even the goings of my God, my King in the sanctuary.
6. The singers went before, the players on Instruments followed after: amongst them were the damsels playing with the timbrels.
7. Bless ye God in the congregation: even the Lord from the fountains of Israel.
8. Thy God hath commanded thy strength: strengthen, O God, that which thou hast wrought in us.
9. O God, thou art terrible out of thy holy places; the God of Israel is he that giveth strength and power unto his people. Blessed be God.
10. His foundation is in the holy mountains: the Lord loveth the gates of Sion more than all the dwellings of Jacob.
11. Glorious things are spoken of thee, O thou city of God; and of Sion it shall be said, This and that man was born in her, and the Highest himself shall establish her.

A Form of Consecration of Churches.

12. Exalt ye the Lord our God: and worship at his footstool, for he is holy.
13. Moses and Aaron among his Priests: and Samuel among them that call upon his name: they called upon his name and he answered them.
14. Thou answeredst them, O Lord our God: Thou wast a God that forgavest them, though thou didst take vengeance of their inventions.
15. Exalt the Lord our God, and worship at his holy hill: for the Lord our God is holy.
16. Enter into his gates with thanksgiving and into his courts with praise: be thankful unto him, and bless his name.

¶ Then shall All together say,

For the Lord is good, his mercy is everlasting, and his truth endureth to generations.
Bishop. Worship Jesus.
Answer. *We worship and adore the great King of heaven and earth, the blessed Saviour of the World.*
Bishop. Holy is our God.
Answer. *Holy is the Almighty.*
Bishop. Holy is the Immortal.

All together.

Holy, Holy, Holy, Lord God of Sabaoth; blessed be thy Name in Heaven and Earth for ever and ever. *Amen. Amen.*

So ends the Office of Consecration.

¶ Then the Bell tolling a little in the interval, the Bishop shall appoint the Dean to read the Morning Prayer, or first Service, in the reading desk.
¶ The Psalms appointed for the day. Psalm 122, 125, 132.
¶ The first Lesson is Genesis 28, 10 unto the end. Or else 1 Kings 8, 10 unto 62 exclusively.
¶ The second Lesson is St. Matt. 21, verse 1 unto 17, inclusively.
¶ At the end of the Litany the Bishop shall confirm such persons as can be conveniently brought to him, fitted for that purpose.
¶ The Bishop shall read the second Service and administer the Communion.
¶ The Epistle is taken out of the third of the Acts, verse 1 unto verse 16, inclusively.
¶ The Gospel is S. Luke 7, verse 1 to the 10th, inclusively.
¶ The Collect to be said at Morning Prayer, and the Communion, together with the Collect of the day.

O Almighty God, who dwellest among thy Saints and hast plac'd thy Tabernacle in the hearts of thy servants, give thy heavenly blessings and encrease to the place where thine honour dwelleth, that what is founded by thy Providence and built according to thy Commandment, may be established for ever and blessed in all things by thy eternal goodness, through Jesus Christ our Lord. *Amen.*

Appendix.

*An Office to be used in the Restauration of a Church.**

¶ When the Fabrick of a Church is ruined, and a new Church is built upon the same Foundation; the Bishop attended by his Clergy, shall enter into the Churchyard, and go in Procession round about the Church new built; and recite alternately Psalm 74.

I.

GOD, wherefore art thou absent from us so long: why is thy wrath so hot against the sheep of thy pasture?

2. O think upon thy congregation: whom thou hast purchased, and redeemed of old.

3. Think upon the tribe of thine inheritance: and mount Sion, wherein thou hast dwelt.

4. Lift up thy feet, that thou mayest utterly destroy every enemy: which hath done evil in thy sanctuary.

5. Thine adversaries roar in the midst of thy congregations: and set up their banners for tokens.

6. He that hewed timber afore out of the thick trees: was known to bring it to an excellent work.

7. But now they break down all the carved work thereof: with axes and hammers.

8. They have set fire upon thy holy places: and have defiled the dwelling-place of thy Name, even unto the ground.

9. Yea, they said in their hearts, Let us make havoc of them altogether: thus have they burnt up all the houses of God in the land.

10. We see not our tokens, there is not one prophet more: no, not one is there among us, that understandeth any more.

11. O God, how long shall the adversary do this dishonour: how long shall the enemy blaspheme thy Name, for ever?

12. Why withdrawest thou thy hand: why pluckest thou not thy right hand out of thy bosom to consume the enemy?

13. For God is my King of old: the help that is done upon earth he doeth it himself.

14. Thou didst divide the sea through thy power: thou brakest the heads of the dragons in the waters.

15. Thou smotest the heads of Leviathan in pieces: and gavest him to be meat for the people in the wilderness.

16. Thou broughtest out fountains and waters out of the hard rocks: thou driedst up mighty waters.

17. The day is thine, and the night is thine: thou hast prepared the light and the sun.

18. Thou hast set all the borders of the earth: thou hast made summer and winter.

19. Remember this, O Lord, how the enemy hath rebuked; and how the foolish people hath blasphemed thy Name.

20. O deliver not the soul of thy turtle-dove unto the multitude of the enemies: and forget not the congregation of the poor for ever.

---

* Consecration should take place whenever the site of the Altar is changed, so as to be on new ground, not otherwise.—Ed. Direct. Anglic.

21. Look upon the covenant : for all the earth is full of darkness, and cruel habitations.

22. O let not the simple go away ashamed : but let the poor and needy give praise unto thy Name.

23. Arise, O God, maintain thine own cause : remember how the foolish man blasphemeth thee daily.

24. Forget not the voice of thine enemies : the presumption of them that hate thee increaseth ever more and more.

¶ Then entering into the Church, the Bishop and Clergy shall vest themselves; which being done, and the people in their places, the Bishop shall kneel down in the body of the Church, on a footstool raised above the floor and say,

Our Father, which art in Heaven, hallowed be thy Name; thy kingdom come; thy Will be done in earth, as it is in Heaven; Give us this day our daily Bread; and forgive us our Trespasses, As we forgive them that trespass against us; and lead us not into Temptation, but deliver us from evil.

℟ The Clergy and people repeating after him every petition.

℣ Then shall the Bishop say,

Prevent us, O Lord, in all our doings with thy most gracious favour, and further us with thy continual help, that in all our works begun, continued, and ended in thee, we may glorifie thy holy Name; and finally, by thy mercy obtain everlasting life; through Jesus Christ our Lord. *Amen.*

¶ Then the Bishop standing up with his Face to the People, shall pray in the words of *Ezra, paucis mutatis, ut sequitur.*

O Lord our God, we are asham'd, and blush to lift up our faces unto thee, O God; for our iniquities are increased over our heads, and our trespasses grown up unto the heavens. Since the days of our fathers have we been in a great trespass unto this day; and for our iniquities have we, our Kings, and our Priests, been delivered unto the hands of our enemies, to the sword, to the spoil, and to confusion of face, as it is this day. And now for a little space hath grace been showed to us from the Lord our God, to leave us a remnant to escape, and to give us a nail in his holy place, that our God may lighten our eyes, and give us a little reviving from our afflictions. For our God hath not forsaken us, but hath extended mercy to us in the sight of our enemies, to give us a reviving, to set up the house of our God, and to repair the desolations thereof. And now, O our God, what shall we say after this? For we have forsaken thy Commandments which thou hast commanded us by thy Servants the Prophets. And after all that is come upon us for our evil deeds, and for our great trespasses, seeing that thou our God hast punished us less than our iniquities deserve, and hast given us such a deliverance as this, should we again break these Commandments? Wouldst not thou be angry with us till thou hadst consumed us? *Ezra 9.*

O Lord God of heaven and earth, thou art righteous and just and true; thou art also good and gracious, and of great mercy, and of loving-kindness; and though thou hast punished us for our inventions, yet thou hast forgiven our misdeeds, and restor'd us to a rejoycing this day. O give unto us abundance of thy grace, that we may no more provoke thee to anger, or to jealousie; that we may never force thee to severity, and to pour forth thy heavy Judgments upon us; but give us thy holy Spirit to lead us in the ways of righteousness, and to prepare us for thy mercies for ever. Defend thy Church, and bless thine inheritance; feed them, and set them up for ever. So shall we thy people give thee thanks in the congregations of thy redeemed ones, and rejoyce in giving thee praises for the operations of thy hands, who hast mightily delivered thy sons and servants, through Jesus Christ our Lord. *Amen.*

¶ Then shall be said or sung *Psalm* 144, alternately.

1. Blessed be the Lord my strength: who teacheth my hands to war, and my fingers to fight;
2. My hope and my fortress, my castle and deliverer, my defender in whom I trust: who subdueth my people that is under me.
3. Lord, what is man, that thou hast such respect unto him: or the son of man that thou so regardest him?
4. Man is like a thing of nought: his time passeth away like a shadow.
5. Bow thy heavens, O Lord, and come down: touch the mountains, and they shall smoke.
6. Cast forth thy lightning, and tear them: shoot out thine arrows, and consume them.
7. Send down thine hand from above: deliver me, and take me out of the great waters, from the hand of strange children;
8. Whose mouth talketh of vanity: and their right hand is a right hand of wickedness.
9. I will sing a new song unto thee, O God: and sing praises unto thee upon a ten-stringed lute.
10. Thou hast given victory unto kings: and hast delivered David thy servant from the peril of the sword.
11. Save me, and deliver me from the hand of strange children: whose mouth talketh of vanity, and their right hand is a right hand of iniquity.
12. That our sons may grow up as the young plants: and that our daughters may be as the polished corners of the temple.
13. That our garners may be full and plenteous with all manner of store: that our sheep may bring forth thousands and ten thousands in our streets.
14. That our oxen may be strong to labour, that there be no decay: no leading into captivity, and no complaining in our streets.
15. Happy are the people that are in such a case: yea, blessed are the people who have the Lord for their God.

¶ After which the Bishop, attended with the Clergy, shall go to the Font, and use the same Office as is appointed for the Consecration or Dedication of Churches: and so to the end: Omitting the word [*place*, or *places*] because the place was consecrated before and so was the Cœmitery. In other things proceed without change.
¶ The first Lesson at Morning Prayer shall be *Haggai* i.
¶ The second Lesson, *Luke* 12, beginning at verse 32 to the end.
¶ The Collect, the same as is used in Morning Prayer in the Office of Consecration.

A Short Office for Expiation and Illustration of a Church defecrated or prophaned.

¶ If a Church hath been defecrated by Murther and Bloodshed, by Uncleanness, or any other sort of prophanation, the Bishop attended by two Priests at least, and one Deacon, shall enter into the Church, which shall be first prepared by cleansings and washings, &c.

An Office for a Defecrated Church.

¶ The Bishop and his Clergy being vested, shall go in Procession about the Church on the inside, saying alternately the Seventh Psalm, and the Ninth Psalm.
¶ After which the Bishop, with his Clergy, shall go to the Holy Table and there kneeling down shall pray.

ALMIGHTY God, Who art of pure eyes and canst not behold impurity, behold the Angels are not pure in thy sight, and thou hast found folly in thy Saints; have mercy upon thy servants, who with repentance and contrition of heart, return unto thee, humbling ourselves before thee in thy holy place. We acknowledge ourselves unworthy to appear in thy glorious presence, because we are polluted in thy sight, and it is just in thee to reject our prayers, and to answer us no more from the place of thy Sanctuary; for wickedness hath reached unto the Courts where thy holy feet have trod, and have defiled thy dwelling-place, even unto the ground, and we by our sins have deserved this calamity. But be thou graciously pleased to return to us as in the days of old, and remember us according to thy former lovingkindnesses in the days of our Fathers. Cast out all iniquity from within us, remove the guilt of that horrible prophanation that hath been committed here, that abomination of desolation in the holy place, standing where it ought not; and grant that we may present unto thee pure Oblations; and may be accepted by the gracious interpellation of our High Priest, the most glorious Jesus. Let no prophane thing enter any more into the lot of thine inheritance; and be pleased again to accept the prayers which thy servants shall make unto thee in this place. And because holiness becometh thine house for ever, grant to us thy grace to walk before thee in all holiness of conversation; that we becoming a royal Priesthood, a chosen Generation, a people zealous of good works, thou mayest accept us according to thine own lovingkindness, and the desires of our hearts. O look upon thy most holy Son, and regard the cry of his blood, and let it on our behalf speak better things than the blood of *Abel*.

O let that sprinkling of the blood of the holy Lamb, who was slain from the beginning of the world, make this place holy and accepted, and purifie our hands and hearts, and sanctifie our prayers and praises, and hallow all our Oblations, and preserve this house, and all the places where thy Name is invocated from all impurity and prophanation for ever; and keep our bodies, and souls, and spirits, unblameable to the coming of our Lord Jesus. Thus, O blessed Father, grant that we being presented unto thee without spot or wrinkle, or any such thing, may be cloathed with the righteousness of Saints, and walk in white with the Lamb in the Kingdom of our God for ever and ever. Grant this, O Almighty God, our most gracious Father, for Jesus Christ his sake, to whom with thee and the Holy Spirit, be all worship, and love, and honour, and glory, from generation to generation for ever. *Amen.*

¶ Then the Bishop and Clergy arising from their knees shall say the Anathematism unto the Εὐφημισμὸς, or Acclamation, as in the Form of Consecration : After which, kneeling down, shall be said the Third Prayer placed in that Office a little before the Anathematism. And next to that the Second Prayer which is immediately before that; and then the Prayer of S. Clement.
¶ After which, arising from his knees, the Bishop shall say,

Seeing now, dearly beloved in the Lord, we have by humble prayer implored the mercy of God and his holy Spirit, to take from this place, and from our hearts, all impurity and prophanation, and that we hope by the mercies of God in our Lord Jesus Christ, he hath heard our prayers, and will grant our desires, let us give hearty thanks for these mercies, and say,

Appendix.

¶ Then shall be said the Εὐφημισμὸς, or Acclamation, as at the end of the Office of Consecration of Churches, &c.
¶ Then shall the Priest, whom the Bishop shall appoint, begin Morning Prayer.
¶ The Psalms for the day are *Psalm* 18 and *Psalm* 30.
¶ The first Lesson is *Zechariah* i.
¶ The second Lesson, *Mark* xi. unto verse 26 inclusively.
¶ The Collect is the same with that at Morning Prayer in the Consecration of Churches.
¶ If any Chalice, Paten, Font, Pulpit, or any other Oblation or Utensil for the Church, be at any time newly to be presented, the Bishop is to use the Forms of Dedication of those respective Gifts which are particularly used in the Dedication; and this is to be done immediately after the *Nicene Creed*, at the time of the Communion; ever adding the Anathematism and Acclamation.

Te decet Hymnus.

The following Services, which were each formally sanctioned by the Right Rev. Dr. Suther, one of the bishops in the Episcopal Church of Scotland, are thought worthy of being reprinted here, as fair models for imitation, by several who have considered them in their original form.

*Service for Blessing and Laying the Foundation-Stone of S. Mary's Church, Aberdeen.**

¶ The Bishop, attended by his Chaplains and the Incumbent, and preceded by the Choir and Clergy—all duly vested—shall proceed in order to the site of the New Church. During which shall be sung:—

PSALM LXVIII. *Exurgat Deus.* (8th Tone, 2nd Ending).

¶ The Bishop having taken his place near the Foundation-Stone, and the Clergy and Choristers being duly ranged in a semicircle on either side, the Bishop shall say,

In the Name of the Father, and of the Son, and of the Holy Ghost, Amen.

    V. Our help is in the Name of the Lord.
    R. Who hath made Heaven and Earth.
    V. Lord, hear our prayer.
    R. And let our cry come unto Thee.
    V. The Lord be with you.
    R. And with thy spirit.
    Let us pray.

REVENT us, O Lord, in all our doings, with Thy most gracious favour, and further us with Thy continual help, that in all our works, begun, continued, and ended in Thee, we may glorify Thy Holy Name, and finally, by Thy Mercy, obtain everlasting life, through Jesus Christ our Lord. R. Amen.

Antiphon.—Place, O Lord, the Sign of Salvation here: that the destroying angel may not enter herein. (Exodus xii. 23.)

---

* Sanctioned by me, Thomas George Bishop of Aberdeen, June 2, 1862.

Blessing and Laying a Foundation-Stone.

PSALM LXXXIV. *Quam dilecta.* (8th Tone, 2nd Ending).

O how amiable are Thy dwellings: thou Lord of hosts!

My soul hath a desire and longing to enter into the courts of the Lord: my heart and my flesh rejoice in the living God.

Yea, the sparrow hath found her an house, and the swallow a nest where she may lay her young: even Thy altars, O Lord of hosts, my King and my God.

Blessed are they that dwell in Thy house: they will be alway praising thee.

Blessed is the man whose strength is in thee: in whose heart are Thy ways.

Who going through the vale of misery use it for a well: and the pools are filled with water.

They will go from strength to strength: and unto the God of gods appeareth every one of them in Sion.

O Lord God of hosts, hear my prayer: hearken, O God of Jacob.

Behold, O God our Defender: and look upon the Face of thine Anointed.

For one day in thy courts: is better than a thousand.

I had rather be a door-keeper in the house of my God: than to dwell in the tents of ungodliness.

For the Lord God is a light and defence: the Lord will give grace and worship, and no good thing shall He withhold from them that lead a godly life.

O Lord God of Hosts: blessed is the man who putteth his trust in thee.

Glory be to the Father, &c. As it was in the beginning, &c.

Antiphon.—Place, O Lord, the Sign of Salvation here: that the destroying angel may not enter herein. (Exodus xii. 23.)

¶ Then the Bishop shall say,

Let us pray.

O Lord God, Whom the heaven of heavens cannot contain, and Who yet vouchsafest to have a house here upon earth, wherein Thy Name may be constantly invoked, look down, we beseech Thee, with benign countenance upon this place, and by Thy grace cleanse it from all defilement, and evermore preserve it inviolate; and, as Thou didst fulfil the holy purpose of Thy servant David in the work of his son Solomon, so vouchsafe to accomplish our desires in this work, and let all spiritual wickedness flee far from hence, through Jesus Christ, Thine only Son, our Lord, Who liveth and reigneth with Thee, in the unity of the Holy Ghost, One God, world without end. R. Amen.

After which the following shall be said or sung,

V. Our help is in the Name of the Lord.
R. Who hath made Heaven and Earth.
V. The Lord's Name be praised.
R. Henceforth, world without end.
V. The Stone which the builders rejected.
R. The same is become the Head of the Corner.
V. This is the Lord's doing.
R. And it is marvellous in our eyes.
V. Glory be to the Father, &c.
R. As it was in the beginning, &c.

Appendix.

Let us pray.

Lord, have mercy upon us.
Christ, have mercy upon us.
Lord, have mercy upon us.
Our Father, &c.

O Lord Jesus Christ, Son of the Living God, the Brightness of the Father's glory, the express Image of His Person, and Life Everlasting, Who art the Corner Stone cut out of the mountain without hands, and the Immutable Foundation, Who, in the beginning, didst lay the foundation of the earth; vouchsafe, we beseech Thee, to bless, stablish, and make sure this Stone now to be placed in Thy Name. Be thou, O Lord, the beginning, the increase, and the ending of this work which we have undertaken to the praise and glory of Thy Sacred Name, Who, with the Father and the Holy Ghost, livest and reignest, ever One God, world without end. R. Amen.

Then the Bishop, touching the Foundation-Stone, shall say,

O Lord, Holy Father, Almighty, Everlasting God, vouchsafe to bless and consecrate this Stone for the foundation of a Church in honour of the Blessed Virgin Mary, and grant that whosoever, with pure mind, shall assist in the building of the same by the work of his hands, or the offering of his substance, may obtain health of body and grace to the soul, through Jesus Christ, our Lord. R. Amen.

Antiphon.—And Jacob rose up early in the morning, and took the stone that he had put for his pillow: and set it up for a pillar, and poured oil upon the top of it. (Genesis xxviii. 18.)

Psalm cxxvii. *Nisi Dominus.* (8th Tone, 2nd Ending).

Except the Lord build the house: their labour is but lost that build it.
Except the Lord keep the city: the watchman waketh but in vain.
It is but lost labour that ye haste to rise up early, and so late take rest, and eat the bread of carefulness: for so he giveth his beloved sleep.
Lo, children and the fruit of the womb: are an heritage and gift that cometh of the Lord.
Like as the arrows in the hand of the giant: even so are the young children.
Happy is the man that hath his quiver full of them: they shall not be ashamed when they speak with their enemies in the gate.

Glory be to the Father, &c. As it was in the beginning, &c.

Antiphon.—And Jacob rose up early in the morning, and took the stone that he had put for his pillow: and set it up for a pillar, and poured oil upon the top of it. (Genesis xxviii. 18.)

¶ Here followeth the Lesson, Revelation xxi. Verse 9 to the end of the Chapter.

¶ Then the person selected, assisted by the builder, shall lay the Foundation-Stone in its appointed place, and touching it shall say,

In the Faith of Jesus Christ our Lord we lay this Foundation-Stone; In the Name of the Father, and of the Son, and of the Holy Ghost, that here true faith, with the fear of God and brotherly love, may for ever flourish and abound; and that this place may be a House of

Blessing and Laying a Foundation-Stone.

Prayer for all time to come, to the glory and praise of the great Name of our Blessed Lord and Saviour Jesus Christ, Who, with the Father and the Holy Spirit, liveth and reigneth, ever One God, world without end. *R.* Amen.

Antiphon.—O thou afflicted, tossed with tempest and not comforted: behold, I will lay thy stones with fair colours, and lay thy foundations with sapphires. And I will make thy windows of agates, and thy gates of carbuncles: and all thy borders of pleasant stones. And all thy children shall be taught of the Lord: and great shall be the peace of thy children. (Isaiah liv. 11, 13.)

PSALM LXXXVII. *Fundamenta ejus.* (6th Tone).

Her foundations are upon the holy hills: the Lord loveth the gates of Sion more than all the dwellings of Jacob.

Very excellent things are spoken of thee: thou City of God.

I will think upon Rahab and Babylon: with them that know me.

Behold ye the Philistines also: and they of Tyre, with the Morians; lo, there was he born.

And of Sion it shall be reported that he was born in her: and the most High shall stablish her.

The Lord shall rehearse it when he writeth up the people: that he was born there.

The singers also and trumpeters shall he rehearse: All my fresh springs shall be in thee.

Glory be to the Father, &c. As it was in the beginning, &c.

Antiphon.—O thou afflicted, tossed with tempest, and not comforted: behold, I will lay thy stones with fair colours, and lay thy foundations with sapphires. And I will make thy windows of agates, and thy gates of carbuncles: and all thy borders of pleasant stones. And all thy children shall be taught of the Lord: and great shall be the peace of thy children. (Isaiah liv. 11, 13.)

¶ Then shall the Bishop address the people, and say,

Dearly beloved, let us now ask Almighty God, of His infinite mercy, to bless, sanctify, and consecrate the House which is to be built in this place, to His greater honour and glory.

Let us pray.

O Almighty and Everlasting God, Who in every place of Thy dominion art wholly present, wholly operating, and Who yet dost hallow the places dedicated to Thy Name, pour forth Thy grace upon the house of prayer here to be built, that it may be raised up a temple to Thy honour, and remain for ever inviolable. And as Thou art the Founder of this house, be Thou also its Protector. Here let no malice of Thine enemy prevail; no perverse desire, no contentious thought divide those whom One Fold contains, and One Shepherd rules; but through the powerful aid of Thy Blessed Spirit, mayest Thou always be worshipped in this place, in faith and charity, in purity and true devotion: and grant that all who shall here seek Thee, may ever find the light of Thy countenance, and be filled with the abundance of Thy heavenly grace, through Christ our Lord. *R.* Amen.

Antiphon.—The rain descended, and the floods came, and the winds blew, and beat upon that House: and it fell not, for it was founded upon a rock. (St. Matthew vii. 25.)

Psalm CXXII. *Lætatus sum.* (5th Tone, 1st Ending).

I was glad when they said unto me: We will go into the house of the Lord.
Our feet shall stand in thy gates: O Jerusalem.
Jerusalem is built as a city: that is at unity in itself.
For thither the tribes go up, even the tribes of the Lord: to testify unto Israel, to give thanks unto the name of the Lord.
For there is the seat of Judgment: even the seat of the house of David.
O pray for the peace of Jerusalem: they shall prosper that love thee.
Peace be within thy walls: and plenteousness within thy palaces.
For my brethren and companions' sakes: I will wish thee prosperity.
Yea, because of the house of the Lord our God: I will seek to do thee good.

Glory be to the Father, &c. As it was in the beginning, &c.

Antiphon.—The rain descended, and the floods came, and the winds blew, and beat upon that House: and it fell not, for it was founded upon a rock. (St. Matthew vii. 25.)

¶ Then shall the Bishop, or the Incumbent, being deputed by him, say,

Let us pray.

O Lord God Almighty, Who art the Author and Source of all wisdom, we give thee hearty thanks for all our friends and benefactors, and for all those through whose charity the walls of this Thine House are about to arise. Remember this to them, O Lord, for good. Bless them in their going out and coming in, in mind and in body, in spirit, soul, and estate. Be with them in the hour of death, and in the day of judgment, and at last take them to Thyself for ever, for His sake Who died and was buried, and rose again, Jesus Christ our only Mediator and Advocate. *R.* Amen.

O God, who art the Shield and Defence of all Thy people, be ever at hand, we beseech Thee, to succour and protect the builders of this House, that so this work which, through Thy great mercy, hath now begun, may be continued and ended in Thee, and under Thy protection, through Jesus Christ our Lord. *R.* Amen.

O Almighty God, Who hast built Thy Church upon the foundation of the apostles and prophets, Jesus Christ Himself being the Head Corner Stone, grant us so to be joined together in unity of spirit by their doctrine, that we may be made an holy temple acceptable unto Thee, through Jesus Christ our Lord. *R.* Amen.

¶ Then shall be sung the Hymn, *Veni Creator Spiritus*, in English.

Come, O Creator, Spirit Blest,
And in our souls take up Thy Rest,
Come with Thy grace and heavenly aid
To fill the hearts which Thou hast made.

Great Paraclete; to Thee we cry;
O highest gift of God most high!
O Fount of life! O fire of love!
And sweet anointing from above!

Thou in Thy seven-fold gifts art known;
Thee, Finger of God's Hand we own;

Blessing and Laying a Foundation-Stone.

    The promise of the Father Thou!
    Who dost the tongue with power endow.

    Kindle our senses from above,
    And make our hearts o'erflow with love;
    With patience firm, and virtue high,
    The weakness of our flesh supply.

    Far from us drive the foe we dread,
    And grant us Thy true peace instead;
    So shall we not, with Thee for Guide,
    Turn from the path of life aside.

    Oh, may Thy grace on us bestow,
    The Father and the Son to know,
    And Thee, through endless times confess'd,
    Of Both th' Eternal Spirit blest.

    All glory, while the ages run,
    Be to the Father, and the Son,
    Who rose from death; the same to Thee,
    O Holy Ghost, eternally. Amen.

¶ Then the Incumbent, addressing the Bishop, shall say,

Right Reverend Father, before we leave this place, I desire your blessing upon the work which we have this day begun, upon those who are waiting its issue, and upon all of us who are now assembled together.

¶ Then the Bishop shall say,

    V. The Lord's Name be praised.
    R. Henceforth, world without end.
    V. The Lord be with you.
    R. And with thy spirit.

The Blessing of God Almighty, the Father, the Son, and the Holy Ghost, be amongst you, and remain with you always. R. Amen.

In returning from the site of the New Church *Te Deum* shall be sung.

SERVICE FOR HOLY COMMUNION.

    Introit: Psalm lxxxvii. *Fundamenta ejus*.
    Proper Collect. That for SS. Simon and Jude.

    For the Epistle: 1 Kings v. 13—18.
    The Gospel: S. John xii. 1—8.
    Offertory: Exodus xxxv. 21, 22.

Service for the Solemn Blessing and Opening of S. Mary's Church, Aberdeen.

¶ The Bishop, attended by his Chaplains and by the Clergy of S. Mary's, and preceded by the Choir and Clergy, duly veiled and ordered, shall proceed through the west door of the Church to their appointed places in the Chancel. During which shall be sung,

PSALM LXVIII. *Exurgat Deus.* (8th Tone, 2nd Ending).

LET God arise, and let His enemies be scattered: let them also that hate Him flee before Him.

2 Like as the smoke vanisheth, so shalt Thou drive them away: and like as wax melteth at the fire, so let the ungodly perish at the presence of God.

3 But let the righteous be glad and rejoice before God: let them also be merry and joyful.

4 O sing unto God, and sing praises unto His Name: magnify Him that rideth upon the heavens, as it were upon an horse; praise Him in His Name JAH, and rejoice before Him.

5 He is a father of the fatherless, and defendeth the cause of the widows: even God in His holy habitation.

6 He is the God that maketh men to be of one mind in an house, and bringeth the prisoners out of captivity: but letteth the runagates continue in scarceness.

7 O God, when Thou wentest forth before the people: when Thou wentest through the wilderness.

8 The earth shook, and the heavens dropped at the presence of God: even as Sinai also was moved at the presence of God, Who is the God of Israel.

9 Thou, O God, sentest a gracious rain upon thine inheritance: and refreshedst it when it was weary.

10 Thy congregation shall dwell therein: for Thou, O God, hast of thy goodness prepared for the poor.

11 The Lord gave the word: great was the company of the preachers.

12 Kings with their armies did flee, and were discomfited: and they of the household divided the spoil.

13 Though ye have lien among the pots, ye shall be as the wings of a dove: that is covered with silver wings, and her feathers like gold.

14 When the Almighty scattered kings for their sake: then were they as white as snow in Salmon.

15 As the hill of Basan, so is God's hill: even an high hill, as the hill of Basan.

16 Why hop ye so, ye high hills? this is God's hill, in the which it pleaseth Him to dwell: yea, the Lord will abide in it for ever.

17 The chariots of God are twenty thousand, even thousands of angels: and the Lord is among them, as in the holy place of Sinai.

18 Thou art gone up on high, Thou hast led captivity captive, and received gifts for men: yea, even for thine enemies, that the Lord God might dwell among them.

19 Praised be the Lord daily: even the God Who helpeth us, and poureth His benefits upon us.

20 He is our God, even the God of Whom cometh salvation: God is the Lord, by Whom we escape death.

---

* Sanctioned by me, Thomas George Bishop of Aberdeen, Feb. 11, 1864.

Blessing and Opening a Church.

21 God shall wound the head of His enemies: and the hairy scalp of such a one as goeth on still in his wickedness.

22 The Lord hath said, I will bring My people again, as I did from Basan: Mine own will I bring again, as I did sometime from the deep of the sea.

23 That Thy foot may be dipped in the blood of Thine enemies: and that the tongue of Thy dogs may be red through the same.

24 It is well seen, O God, how Thou goest: how Thou, my God and King, goest in the sanctuary.

25 The singers go before, the minstrels follow after: in the midst are the damsels playing with the timbrels.

26 Give thanks, O Israel, unto God the Lord in the congregations: from the ground of the heart.

27 There is little Benjamin their ruler, and the princes of Judah their counsel: the princes of Zabulon, and the princes of Naphthali.

28 Thy God hath sent forth strength for thee: stablish the thing, O God, that Thou hast wrought in us.

29 For Thy temple's sake at Jerusalem: so shall kings bring presents unto Thee.

30 When the company of the spear-men, and multitude of the mighty are scattered abroad among the beasts of the people, so that they humbly bring pieces of silver: and when He hath scattered the people that delight in war;

31 Then shall the princes come out of Egypt: the Morians' land shall soon stretch out her hands unto God.

32 Sing unto God, O ye kingdoms of the earth: O sing praises unto the Lord;

33 Who sitteth in the heavens over all from the beginning: lo, He doth send out His voice, yea, and that a mighty voice.

34 Ascribe ye the power to God over Israel: His worship, and strength is in the clouds.

35 O God, wonderful art Thou in Thy holy places: even the God of Israel; He will give strength and power unto His people; blessed be God.

Glory be to the Father, and to the Son: and to the Holy Ghost;
As it was in the beginning, is now, and ever shall be: world without end. Amen.

¶ The Bishop, having taken his appointed place on the north side of the sanctuary, the Incumbent of S. Mary's shall approach his Lordship, and say,

In the name, and on behalf of the clergy and congregation of S. Mary's, I request your Lordship to bless and formally open this building for the worship of Almighty God.

¶ The Bishop shall reply,

I am willing to do so, the Lord being my helper.

¶ Then, proceeding to the midst of the sanctuary, attended by his chaplains, the Bishop shall say,

In the Name of the Father, and of the Son, and of the Holy Ghost. Amen.

V. Our help is in the Name of the Lord.
R. Who hath made Heaven and Earth.
V. Lord, hear our prayer.
R. And let our cry come unto Thee.
V. The Lord be with you.
R. And with thy spirit.

Appendix.

Let us pray.

Prevent us, O Lord, in all our doings with Thy most gracious favour, and further us with Thy continual help, that in all our works begun, continued, and ended in Thee, we may glorify Thy Holy Name, and finally, by Thy mercy, obtain everlasting life, through Jesus Christ our Lord. R. Amen.

¶ Then the Bishop shall return to his appointed place, and the Litany shall be sung, as it stands in the Book of Common Prayer, with the following suffrage introduced after the words " bless and keep all Thy people :"—

That it may please Thee to bless and sanctify this building which we are about to dedicate to Thy service.
We beseech Thee to hear us, good Lord.

¶ At the conclusion of the Litany, the Hymn, *Veni Creator Spiritus*, shall be sung in English.

> Come, O Creator, Spirit Blest,
> And in our souls take up Thy Rest,
> Come with Thy grace and heavenly aid
> To fill the hearts which Thou hast made.
>
> Great Paraclete; to Thee we cry;
> O highest gift of God most high!
> O Fount of life! O fire of love!
> And sweet anointing from above!
>
> Thou in Thy seven-fold gifts art known;
> Thee, Finger of God's Hand we own;
> The promise of the Father Thou!
> Who dost the tongue with power endow
>
> Kindle our senses from above,
> And make our hearts o'erflow with love;
> With patience firm, and virtue high,
> The weakness of our flesh supply.
>
> Far from us drive the foe we dread,
> And grant us Thy true peace instead;
> So shall we not, with Thee for Guide,
> Turn from the path of life aside.
>
> Oh, may Thy grace on us bestow,
> The Father and the Son to know,
> And Thee, through endless times confess'd,
> Of Both th' Eternal Spirit blest.
>
> All glory, while the ages run,
> Be to the Father, and the Son,
> Who rose from death; the same to Thee,
> O Holy Ghost, eternally. Amen.

Blessing and Opening a Church.

☞ After which, the Bishop, attended by his Chaplains, and the Clergy of the church, shall proceed to that part of the chancel immediately fronting the choir gates, where shall be said or sung the following,

V. Our help is in the Name of the Lord.
R. Who hath made Heaven and Earth.
V. The Lord's Name be praised.
R. Henceforth, world without end.
V. Lord, we have loved the habitation of Thy House.
R. And the place where Thine Honour dwelleth.
V. O come let us worship and fall down.
R. And kneel before the Lord our Maker.
V. Glory be to the Father, &c.
R. As it was in the beginning, &c.

Let us pray.

Lord, have mercy upon us.
Christ, have mercy upon us.
Lord, have mercy upon us.
Our Father, &c.

O Lord God, Whom the heaven of heavens cannot contain, and Who yet vouchsafest to have a house here upon earth, wherein Thy Name may be constantly invoked, look down, we beseech Thee, with benign countenance upon this place, and by Thy grace cleanse it from all defilement, and evermore preserve it inviolate; let all spiritual wickedness flee far from hence, through Jesus Christ, Thine only Son, our Lord, Who liveth and reigneth with Thee, in the unity of the Holy Ghost, One God, world without end. R. Amen.

O Almighty and Everlasting God, Who in every place of Thy dominion art wholly present, wholly operating, and Who yet dost hallow the places set apart to Thy Name, pour forth Thy grace upon this House of Prayer, dedicated in honour of the Blessed Virgin Mary, that it may be accepted as a temple of Thine, and remain for ever inviolable. And as Thou art the Founder of this house, be Thou also its Protector. Here let no malice of Thine enemy prevail; no perverse desire, no contentious thought divide those whom One Fold contains, and One Shepherd rules; but through the powerful aid of Thy Blessed Spirit, mayest Thou always be worshipped in this place, in faith and charity, in purity and true devotion; and grant that all who shall here seek Thee, may ever find the light of Thy countenance, and the joy of Thy love, and be filled with the abundance of Thy heavenly grace, through Jesus Christ our Lord. R. Amen.

☞ Then the Bishop, attended by his Chaplains, &c. shall proceed to the Baptiltry, where standing near the Font, and placing his right hand upon it, he shall say the following prayer of dedication,

Bless, O Lord, and sanctify this Font, and grant that whosoever shall be here dedicated to Thee by Baptism, may be renewed by the Holy Ghost, delivered from Thy wrath and eternal death, and, being thus made a living member of Thy church, may ever remain in the number of Thy faithful and elect children, through Jesus Christ our Lord. R. Amen.

¶ While the Bishop and clergy are returning to the chancel, the choir shall sing the following:—

There is a River, the streams whereof shall make glad the City of God, the holy place of the tabernacles of the Most High. God is in the midst of her; she shall not be moved: God shall help her, and that right early. (Psalm xlvi. verses 4, 5. *Bible version*.)

¶ At the chancel steps, the Bishop shall then say these prayers,

Grant, O Lord, that they who in this place shall in their own persons renew the promises and vows made for them by their sureties at their baptism, and thereupon be Confirmed by the Bishop, may continue Thine for ever, and daily increase in Thy Holy Spirit more and more, until they come to Thine everlasting kingdom. *R.* Amen.

Grant, O Lord, that they who shall be joined together in this place in the Holy Estate of Matrimony may faithfully perform and keep the vow and covenant betwixt them made, and remain in perfect love and peace together unto their lives' end. *R.* Amen.

Grant, O Lord, that those who shall here confess their sins, and seek of Thee, the God of all consolation, mercy, and pardon, peace and quietness, may ever find Thee in the fulness of Thine abundant charity. *R.* Amen.

Grant, O Lord, that by Thy Holy Word, which shall be read and preached in this place, the hearers thereof may both perceive and know what things they ought to do, and also may have grace and power faithfully to fulfil the same. *R.* Amen.

¶ While the Bishop and his Chaplains are returning to their places, the choir shall sing the following:—

O pray for the peace of Jerusalem: they shall prosper that love Thee. Peace be within thy walls, and plenteousness within thy palaces. (Psalm cxxii. verses 6, 7.)

¶ Then the Bishop, standing at the Altar, and placing his right hand upon it, shall say the following prayer,

Regard, we beseech Thee, O Lord, the supplications of Thy people, sanctify this Thy Holy Table, and grant that they who shall here offer the Sacrifice of Praise and Thanksgiving, may find and feel that with such sacrifices Thou art well pleased. *R.* Amen.

Adding those that follow,

And grant us, gracious Lord, in the Holy Sacrament of Thy love, so to eat the Flesh of Thy dear Son, Jesus Christ, and to drink His Blood, that our sinful bodies may be made clean by His Most Sacred Body, and our souls washed through His Most Precious Blood, and that we may evermore dwell in Him and He in us. *R.* Amen.

And be pleased, O Lord, as Thou didst accept the offering of Solomon, to receive and accept the varied gifts here presented for Thy service. Bless those who have given of their substance towards raising and furnishing this House of Prayer. Remember this to them, O Lord, for good. Bless them in their going out and coming in, in mind and in body, in spirit, soul and estate. Be with them in the hour of death and in the day of judgment, and at last take them to Thyself for ever, for His sake, Who died and was buried, and rose again, Jesus Christ, our only Mediator and Advocate. *R.* Amen.

Blessing and Opening a Church.

¶ Then the Donor of the Altar Vessels shall advance with them to the Bishop, and say,

Right Reverend Father in God, I desire to present these Vessels for the celebration of the Holy Eucharist in this Church, and ask you, in the Name of God, to set them apart and bless them for that holy service.

¶ The Bishop, receiving them and placing them on the Altar, shall say,

I am willing to do so, the Lord being my Helper.

And shall proceed saying.

V. Our help is in the Name of the Lord.
R. Who hath made Heaven and Earth.
V. Lord, hear our prayer.
R. And let our cry come unto Thee.
V. The Lord be with you.
R. And with thy spirit.

Let us pray.

Almighty and Everlasting God, Who, under the old law, willedst that gold and silver should be set apart for Thine honour and worship, vouchsafe, we beseech Thee, to bless, sanctify, and consecrate, these Vessels for the ministration of the Eucharist of Thy dearly-beloved Son, Who for our salvation, offered Himself a sacrifice on the Altar of the Cross, and now—pleading the same sacrifice—liveth and reigneth with Thee and the Holy Ghost, ever One God, world without end. R. Amen.

¶ Then the choir shall sing the following:—

Thine, O Lord, is the greatness, and the power, and the glory, and the victory, and the majesty: for all that is in the heaven and in the earth is Thine: Thine is the Kingdom, O Lord, and Thou art exalted as Head over all. (1 Chronicles xxix. 11.)

¶ Then shall be sung the following Psalms·

Antiphon.—Upon Thy Right Hand did stand the Queen in a vesture of gold, wrought about with divers colours.

PSALM XLV. *Eructavit cor meum.* (8th Tone, 2nd Ending.)

1 My heart is inditing a good matter: I speak of the things which I have made unto the King.

2 My tongue is the pen: of a ready writer.

3 Thou art fairer than the children of men: full of grace are Thy lips, because God hath blessed Thee for ever.

4 Gird Thee with Thy sword upon Thy thigh, O Thou most Mighty: according to Thy worship and renown.

5 Good luck have Thou with Thine honour: ride on, because of the word of truth, of meekness, and righteousness; and Thy right hand shall teach Thee terrible things.

6 Thy arrows are very sharp, and the people shall be subdued unto Thee: even in the midst among the King's enemies.

7 Thy seat, O God, endureth for ever: the sceptre of Thy kingdom is a right sceptre.

8 Thou hast loved righteousness, and hated iniquity: wherefore God, even Thy God, hath anointed Thee with the oil of gladness above Thy fellows.

H H

9 All Thy garments smell of myrrh, aloes, and cassia: out of the ivory palaces whereby they have made Thee glad.

10 Kings' daughters were among Thy honourable women: upon Thy right hand did stand the Queen in a vesture of gold, wrought about with divers colours.

11 Hearken, O daughter, and consider, incline thine ear: forget also thine own people, and thy father's house.

12 So shall the King have pleasure in thy beauty: for He is thy Lord God, and worship thou Him.

13 And the daughter of Tyre shall be there with a gift: like as the rich also among the people shall make their supplication before Thee.

14 The King's daughter is all glorious within: her clothing is of wrought gold.

15 She shall be brought unto the King in raiment of needle-work: the virgins that be her fellows shall bear her company, and shall be brought unto Thee.

16 With joy and gladness shall they be brought: and shall enter into the King's palace.

17 Instead of thy fathers thou shalt have children: whom thou mayest make princes in all lands.

18 I will remember Thy Name from one generation to another: therefore shall the people give thanks unto Thee, world without end.

Glory be to the Father, and to the Son: and to the Holy Ghost;

As it was in the beginning, is now, and ever shall be: world without end. *Amen.*

Antiphon.—Upon Thy Right Hand did stand the Queen in a vesture of gold, wrought about with divers colours.

Antiphon.—How dreadful is this place! This is none other but the House of God, and this is the gate of Heaven! (Genesis xxviii. 17.)

PSALM XLVI. *Deus noster refugium.* (8th Tone, 2nd Ending).

1 God is our hope and strength: a very present help in trouble.

2 Therefore will we not fear, though the earth be moved: and though the hills be carried into the midst of the sea.

3 Though the waters thereof rage and swell: and though the mountains shake at the tempest of the same.

4 The rivers of the flood thereof shall make glad the city of God: the holy place of the tabernacle of the Most Highest.

5 God is in the midst of her, therefore shall she not be removed: God shall help her, and that right early.

6 The heathen make much ado, and the kingdoms are moved: but God hath shewed His voice, and the earth shall melt away.

7 The Lord of Hosts is with us: the God of Jacob is our refuge.

8 O come hither, and behold the works of the Lord: what destruction He hath brought upon the earth.

9 He maketh wars to cease in all the world: He breaketh the bow, and knappeth the spear in sunder, and burneth the chariots in the fire.

10 Be still then, and know that I am God: I will be exalted among the heathen, and I will be exalted in the earth.

11 The Lord of Hosts is with us: the God of Jacob is our refuge.

Glory be to the Father, and to the Son, and to the Holy Ghost;

As it was in the beginning, is now, and ever shall be: world without end. *Amen.*

Blessing and Opening a Church.

Antiphon.—How dreadful is this place! This is none other but the House of God, and this is the gate of Heaven. (Genesis xxviii. 17.)

Antiphon.—The light of the moon shall be as the light of the sun, and the light of the sun shall be sevenfold, as the light of seven days, in the day that the Lord bindeth up the breach of His people, and healeth the stroke of their wound. (Isaiah xxx. 26.)

PSALM XLVIII. *Magnus Dominus.* (5th Tone, 1st Ending).

1 Great is the Lord, and highly to be praised : in the city of our God, even upon His holy hill.
2 The hill of Sion is a fair place, and the joy of the whole earth : upon the north side lieth the city of the great King; God is well known in her palaces as a sure Refuge.
3 For lo, the kings of the earth : are gathered, and gone by together.
4 They marvelled to see such things : they were astonished, and suddenly cast down.
5 Fear came there upon them and sorrow : as upon a woman in her travail.
6 Thou shalt break the ships of the sea : through the east wind.
7 Like as we have heard, so have we seen in the city of the Lord of Hosts, in the city of our God : God upholdeth the same for ever.
8 We wait for Thy lovingkindness, O God : in the midst of Thy temple.
9 O God, according to Thy Name, so is Thy praise unto the world's end : Thy right hand is full of righteousness.
10 Let the mount Sion rejoice, and the daughter of Judah be glad : because of Thy judgments.
11 Walk about Sion, and go round about her: and tell the towers thereof.
12 Mark well her bulwarks, set up her houses: that ye may tell them that come after.
13 For this God is our God for ever and ever: He shall be our guide unto death.
Glory be to the Father, and to the Son : and to the Holy Ghost;
As it was in the beginning, is now, and ever shall be: world without end. *Amen.*

Antiphon.—The light of the moon shall be as the light of the sun, and the light of the sun shall be sevenfold, as the light of seven days, in the day that the Lord bindeth up the breach of His people, and healeth the stroke of their wound. (Isaiah xxx. 26.)

Antiphon.—For from the rising of the sun, even unto the going down of the same, My Name shall be great among the Gentiles; and in every place Incense shall be offered unto My Name, and a Pure Offering: for My Name shall be great among the heathen, saith the Lord of Hosts. (Malachi i. 11.)

PSALM LXXXIV. *Quam dilecta!* (8th Tone, 2nd Ending).

1 O how amiable are Thy dwellings : Thou Lord of hosts!
2 My soul hath a desire and longing to enter into the courts of the Lord : my heart and my flesh rejoice in the living God.
3 Yea, the sparrow hath found her an house, and the swallow a nest where she may lay her young : even Thy altars, O Lord of hosts, my King and my God.
4 Blessed are they that dwell in Thy house : they will be alway praising Thee.
5 Blessed is the man whose strength is in Thee : in whose heart are Thy ways.
6 Who going through the vale of misery use it for a well : and the pools are filled with water.

7 They will go from strength to strength: and unto the God of gods appeareth every one of them in Zion.
8 O Lord of hosts, hear my prayer: hearken, O God of Jacob.
9 Behold, O God, our Defender: and look upon the face of Thine Anointed.
10 For one day in Thy courts: is better than a thousand.
11 I had rather be a door-keeper in the house of my God: than to dwell in the tents of ungodliness.
12 For the Lord God is a Light and Defence: the Lord will give grace and worship, and no good thing shall He withhold from them that live a godly life.
13 O Lord God of hosts: blessed is the man that putteth his trust in Thee.
Glory be to the Father, and to the Son: and to the Holy Ghost;
As it was in the beginning, is now, and ever shall be: world without end. *Amen.*

Antiphon.—For from the rising of the sun, even unto the going down of the same, My Name shall be great among the Gentiles; and in every place Incense shall be offered unto My Name, and a Pure Offering: for My Name shall be great among the heathen, saith the Lord of Hosts. (Malachi i. 11.)

¶ Then shall follow the Lesson. Revelation xxi.

And I saw a new heaven and a new earth: for the first heaven and the first earth were passed away; and there was no more sea. And I John saw the holy city, new Jerusalem, coming down from God out of heaven, prepared as a bride adorned for her husband. And I heard a great voice out of heaven, saying, Behold, the tabernacle of God *is* with men, and He will dwell with them, and they shall be His people, and God Himself shall be with them, *and be* their God. And God shall wipe away all tears from their eyes; and there shall be no more death, neither sorrow, nor crying, neither shall there be any more pain: for the former things are passed away. And He that sat upon the throne said, Behold, I make all things new. And He said unto me, Write: for these words are true and faithful. And He said unto me, It is done. I am Alpha and Omega, the beginning and the end: I will give unto him that is athirst of the fountain of the water of life freely. He that overcometh shall inherit all things; and I will be his God, and he shall be my son. But the fearful, and unbelieving, and the abominable, and murderers, and whoremongers, and sorcerers, and idolaters, and all liars, shall have their part in the lake which burneth with fire and brimstone: which is the second death. And there came unto me one of the seven angels which had the seven vials full of the seven last plagues, and talked with me, saying, Come hither, I will shew thee the bride, the Lamb's wife. And he carried me away in the spirit to a great and high mountain, and shewed me that great city, the holy Jerusalem, descending out of heaven from God, Having the glory of God; and her light *was* like unto a stone most precious, even like a jasper-stone, clear as crystal; And had a wall great and high, *and* had twelve gates, and at the gates twelve angels, and names written thereon, which are *the names* of the twelve tribes of the children of Israel: On the east, three gates; on the north, three gates; on the south, three gates; and on the west, three gates. And the wall of the city had twelve foundations, and in them the names of the twelve apostles of the Lamb. And he that talked with me had a golden reed to measure the city, and the gates thereof, and the wall thereof. And the city lieth four-square, and the length is as large as the breadth. And he measured the city with the reed, twelve thousand furlongs. The length and the breadth and the height of it are equal. And he measured the wall thereof, an hundred *and* forty *and* four cubits, *according to* the measure of a man, that is, of the angel. And the building of the wall of it was of jasper; and the city was pure gold, like unto clear glass. And the foundations of the wall of the city were garnished with all manner of precious stones. The first foundation was jasper; the second, sapphire; the third, a chalcedony; the fourth, an emerald; the fifth, sardonyx; the sixth, sardius; the seventh, chrysolite; the eighth, beryl; the ninth, a topaz; the tenth, a chrysoprasus; the eleventh, a jacinth; the twelfth, an amethyst. And the twelve gates were twelve pearls; every several gate was of one pearl; and the street of the city was pure gold, as it were transparent glass. And I saw no temple therein; for the Lord God Almighty and the Lamb are the temple of it. And the city had no need of the sun, neither of the moon, to shine in it; for the glory of God did lighten it, and the Lamb is the light thereof. And the nations of them which are saved shall walk in the light of it: and the kings of the earth do bring their glory and honour into it. And the gates of it shall not be shut at all by day; for there shall be no night there. And they shall bring the glory and honour of the nations into it. And there shall in no wise enter into it any thing that defileth, neither *whatsoever* worketh abominations, or *maketh* a lie; but they which are written in the Lamb's book of life.

¶ Then shall be sung the following:—

Antiphon.—Thus saith the Lord, I am returned unto Zion, and will dwell in the midst of Jerusalem: and Jerusalem shall be called a city of truth, and the mountain of the Lord of Hosts the holy mountain. (Zechariah viii. 3.)

Benedictus. S. Luke i. 68. (1st Tone, 1st Ending).

Blessed be the Lord God of Israel: for He hath visited and redeemed His people.
And hath raised up a mighty salvation for us: in the house of His servant David;
As He spake by the mouth of His holy Prophets: which have been since the world began;
That we should be saved from our enemies: and from the hands of all that hate us;
To perform the mercy promised to our forefathers: and to remember His holy Covenant;
To perform the oath which He sware to our forefather Abraham: that He would give us;
That we being delivered out of the hand of our enemies: might serve Him without fear;
In holiness and righteousness before Him: all the days of our life.
And thou, Child, shalt be called the Prophet of the Highest: for thou shalt go before the face of the Lord to prepare His ways;
To give knowledge of salvation unto His people: for the remission of their sins,
Through the tender mercy of our God: whereby the Day-Spring from on high hath visited us;
To give light to them that sit in darkness, and in the shadow of death: and to guide our feet into the way of peace.
Glory be to the Father, and to the Son: and to the Holy Ghost;
As it was in the beginning, is now, and ever shall be: world without end. *Amen.*

Antiphon.—Thus saith the Lord, I am returned unto Zion, and will dwell in the midst of Jerusalem: and Jerusalem shall be called a city of truth, and the mountain of the Lord of Hosts the holy mountain. (Zechariah viii. 3.)

¶ After which the following shall be said or sung:—

The Lord be with you.
And with thy spirit.

Appendix.

Let us pray.

Lord, have mercy upon us.
Christ, have mercy upon us.
Lord, have mercy upon us.
Our Father, &c.
V. O Lord, shew Thy mercy upon us.
R. And grant us Thy salvation.
V. O Lord, save the Queen.
R. And mercifully hear us when we call upon thee.
V. Endue thy ministers with righteousness.
R. And make Thy chosen people joyful.
V. O Lord, save Thy people.
R. And bless Thine inheritance.
V. Give peace in our time, O Lord.
R. Because there is none other that fighteth for us, but only Thou, O God.
V. O God, make clean our hearts within us.
R. And take not Thy Holy Spirit from us.

We beseech Thee, O Lord, pour Thy grace into our hearts; that as we have known the Incarnation of Thy Son Jesus Christ by the message of an angel, so by His Cross and Passion, we may be brought unto the glory of His Resurrection, through the same Jesus Christ our Lord. *R.* Amen.

Almighty God, Who through Thine only-begotten Son Jesus Christ hast overcome death, and opened unto us the gate of everlasting life: we humbly beseech Thee, that as by Thy special grace preventing us, Thou dost put into our minds good desires, so by Thy continual help we may bring the same to good effect, through Jesus Christ our Lord, Who liveth and reigneth with Thee and the Holy Ghost, ever one God, world without end. *R.* Amen.*

O Lord Jesus Christ, Who saidst unto Thine apostles, My Peace I leave with you, My Peace I give unto you, regard not our sins but the faith of Thy Church, and grant Her that Peace and Unity which is agreeable to Thy Will, who livest and reignest God, for ever and ever. *R.* Amen.

¶ Here shall be sung the following Hymn.—

  Christ is made the sure Foundation
   And the precious Corner-stone,
  Who, the two-fold walls surmounting,
   Binds them closely into one;
  Holy Sion's help for ever
   And her confidence alone.

  All that dedicated city,
   Dearly loved by God on high,
  In exultant jubilation
   Pours perpetual melody;

---

* The Church was to have been blessed on the (transferred) Feast of the Annunciation of our Lady, during the Easter season,—hence the use of these Collects.

Blessing and Opening a Church.

>   God the One and God the Trinal
>   Singing everlastingly.
>
> To this Temple, where we call Thee,
>   Come, O Lord of Hosts, to-day;
> With Thy wonted loving-kindness
>   Hear Thy people as they pray;
> And the fullest benediction
>   Shed within its walls for aye.
>
> Here vouchsafe to all Thy servants
>   That they supplicate to gain,
> Here to have and hold for ever
>   Those good things their prayers obtain.
> And hereafter, in Thy Glory,
>   With Thy blessed ones to reign.
>
> Laud and honour to the Father,
>   Laud and honour to the Son,
> Laud and honour to the Spirit,
>   Ever Three and ever One;
> Consubstantial, co-eternal,
>   While unending ages run.   Amen.

Assist us mercifully, O Lord, in these our supplications and prayers, and dispose the way of Thy servants towards the attainment of everlasting salvation: that, among all the changes and chances of this mortal life, they may ever be defended by Thy most gracious and ready help; through Jesus Christ our Lord.   R. Amen.

The Grace of our Lord Jesus Christ, and the Love of God, and the Fellowship of the Holy Ghost, be with us all evermore.   R. Amen.

Service for Holy Communion.

Missa de Angelis.   (Published by Novello).

Introit:—Psalm cxxii.   *Lætatus sum.*   (5th Tone, 1st Ending).

Proper Collect, Epistle, and Gospel:—Those for the Feast of the Annunciation, B. V. M. (with commemoration of Easter).

Offertory: In process of time.   (Scottish Office).

Hymn: O Word of God above.

At the conclusion of the Service, the Hymn, *Te Deum*, in English, to the Ambrosian Chant.

During the Octave.

Proper Psalms—Morning: xlv, xlvi, lxxxiv, xlviii.
    Evening: xci, cxxii, cxlix, cl.

Antiphons: as on the day of opening.

Proper Leſſons—Morning: 1ſt, 1 Kings viii. 22—62.
2nd, S. John i. 1—14.
Evening: 1ſt, Ezra vi. 16 to end.
2nd, Revelation xxi.

Ad Majorem Dei Gloriam.

Office for the Benediction of a Dwelling-Houſe.*

IN THE ORATORY.

‘ The Prieſt ſhall begin by ſaying,

EACE be to this houſe and all who dwell in it.
V. Our help ſtandeth in the Name of the Lord.
R. Who hath made Heaven and Earth.
Glory be to the Father, &c.
As it was in the beginning, &c.
Let us give thanks unto the Lord for He is gracious.
And His mercy endureth for ever.

HYMN.

Chriſt the Chief and ſure Foundation,
 As our Corner-ſtone is laid,
Who each wall of ſeparation
 One United Whole hath made.
Sion is His ſacred ſtation,
 And on Him her truſt is ſtayed.

In this dwelling, God Supremeſt!
 Now at theſe our prayers appear;
Of Thy wonted loving-kindneſs
 Here unto our vows give ear;
With the riches of Thy goodneſs
 This our earthly ſojourn cheer.

Here with ſure and conſtant favour
 Grant us each devout requeſt;
Of Thy gifts in plenteous meaſure
 Make us with Thy Saints poſſeſſed,
Till in Thy Paradiſe of Pleaſure
 We attain our final reſt.

---

* This Service, for which the Editor of the Second Edition of the *Directorium Anglicanum* is indebted to John D. Chambers, Eſq. (who tranſlated and arranged the ſame), is taken from two or three old forms to be found in the Sarum and other Breviaries, and in *Martene, de Antiq. Eccleſ. Ritibus.* The Editor tenders his thanks for permiſſion to place it here.

Benediction of a Dwelling-House.

>Glory be to God and Honour
>In the Highest, as is meet,
>To the Son as to the Father,
>And the Holy Paraclete,
>Whose is boundless Praise and Power
>Throughout ages infinite. Amen.

V. Blessed are they that dwell in Thy House, O Lord!
R. They shall be alway praising Thee.

Psalm xci. *Qui habitat.*

Whoso dwelleth under the defence of the most High : shall abide under the shadow of the Almighty.

I will say unto the Lord, Thou art my Hope and my Stronghold : my God, in Him will I trust.

For He shall deliver thee from the snare of the hunter : and from the noisome pestilence.

He shall defend thee under His wings, and thou shalt be safe under His feathers : His faithfulness and truth shall be thy shield and buckler.

Thou shalt not be afraid of any terror by night : nor for the arrow that flieth by day ;

For the pestilence that walketh in darkness : nor for the sickness that destroyeth in the noon day.

A thousand shall fall beside thee, and ten thousand at thy right hand : but it shall not come nigh thee.

Yea, with thine eyes shalt thou behold : and see the reward of the ungodly.

For Thou, Lord, art my hope : Thou hast set Thine house of defence very high.

There shall no evil happen unto thee : neither shall any plague come nigh thy dwelling.

For He shall give His Angels charge over thee : to keep thee in all thy ways.

They shall bear thee in their hands : that thou hurt not thy foot against a stone.

Thou shalt go upon the lion and adder : the young lion and the dragon shalt thou tread under thy feet.

Because he hath set his love upon Me, therefore I will deliver him : I will set him up because he hath known My Name.

He shall call upon Me, and I will hear him : yea, I am with him in trouble, I will deliver him and bring him to honour.

With long life will I satisfy him : and shew him My salvation.

Glory be to The Father, &c.

As it was in the beginning, &c.

Antiphon.—Other foundation can no man lay but that which is laid ; Christ the Lord.

Psalm cxxi. *Levavi oculos.*

I will lift up mine eyes unto the hills : from whence cometh my help.

My help cometh even from the Lord : Who hath made Heaven and Earth.

He will not suffer thy foot to be moved : and He that keepeth thee will not sleep.

Behold, He that keepeth Israel : shall neither slumber nor sleep.

The Lord Himself is thy keeper : the Lord is thy defence upon thy right hand.

So that the Sun shall not burn thee by day : neither the Moon by night.

The Lord shall preserve thee from all evil : yea, it is even He that shall keep thy soul.

The Lord shall preserve thy going out and thy coming in : from this time forth for evermore.
Glory be to The Father, &c.
As it was in the beginning, &c.

Antiphon.—Thou that rulest Israel, look down upon this house! Thou Who leadest Joseph like a sheep, pour upon it Thy benediction! Thou Who fittest above the Cherubim, hear our prayers!

PSALM CXXV. *Qui confidunt.*

They that put their trust in the Lord shall be even as Mount Syon : which may not be removed, but standeth fast for ever.
The hills stand about Jerusalem : even so standeth the Lord round about His people from this time forth for evermore.
For the rod of the ungodly cometh not into the lot of the righteous : lest the righteous put their hand unto wickedness.
Do well, O Lord : unto those that are good and true of heart.
As for such as turn back unto their own wickedness : the Lord shall lead them forth with the evil-doers; but peace shall be upon Israel.
Glory be to the Father, &c.
As it was in the beginning, &c.

Antiphon.—Let this building receive of God the Grace of blessing and mercy from Christ Jesus.

PSALM CXXXIII. *Ecce quam bonum.*

Behold how good and joyful a thing it is : brethren, to dwell together in unity!
It is like the precious ointment upon the head, that ran down unto the beard : even unto Aaron's beard, and went down to the skirts of his clothing.
Like as the dew of Hermon : which fell upon the hill of Syon.
For there the Lord promised His blessing : and life for evermore.
Glory be to The Father, &c.
As it was in the beginning, &c.

Antiphon.—Bless, O Lord ! this house now completed ; let Thine Eyes be open upon it day and night.

V. O Lord ! defend this habitation.
R. And let Thine Angels guard its walls.

Responsory.—O Lord ! forgive the sins of them that pray unto Thee in this place, and shew them the good way wherein they should walk, and give glory to Thy great Name.
R. In it may all who ask receive, who seek find ; and to him that knocketh may it be opened.
And give glory to Thy great Name.

CHAPTER. Luke xix.

And Jesus entered and passed through Jericho ; and behold there was a man named Zacchæus, and he sought to see Jesus, and ran before and climbed up into a sycamore tree to see Him. And when Jesus came to the place He looked up and saw him, and said unto him,

"Zacchæus, make haste and come down, for to-day I must abide in thy house." And he made haste and came down, and received Him joyfully.

    Thanks be to God.
   V. O Lord! shew Thy mercy upon us.
   R. And grant us Thy salvation.
   O Lord! hear my prayer.
   And let my crying come unto Thee.
   The Lord be with you.
   And with thy spirit.
     Let us pray.

Be present, O Lord! with our supplications, and enlighten this dwelling with the serene Eyes of Thy Goodness. May the Grace of Thy Goodness and the fulness of Thy Benediction descend upon those that dwell in and who may visit it; and may all adversity and iniquity be driven far away from them by the power of Thy Majesty, through Christ our Lord. *Amen.*

Bless, O Lord! this edifice, and this place, that Health, Sanctity, Chastity, Virtue, Strength, Purity, Humility, Gentleness, Kindness, the keeping of Thy laws, obedience and thanksgiving to God the Father, and Son, and Holy Spirit may ever abide therein; and may the fulness of Thy benediction ever rest upon this abode, and all who are therein; that with piety inhabiting this house made with hands, they may be also evermore dwelling-places for Thine Holy Spirit, through Christ our Lord. *Amen.*

O Almighty God! Who hast built Thy Church upon the foundation of the Apostles and Prophets, Jesus Christ Himself being the Head Corner Stone; grant us so to be joined together in unity of spirit by their doctrine, that we may be made an holy temple acceptable unto Thee, through Christ our Lord. *Amen.*

For the Oratory.

Bless, O Lord! we beseech Thee, and sanctify this place of prayer, that our supplications may be set forth in Thy sight as the incense and the lifting up of our hands be as an Evening Sacrifice. Drive far away from us, O Lord! all worldly cares and distractions, that we serving Thee with fear and devout hearts may at last attain to Thy glorious presence, through Christ our Lord. *Amen.*

In a Sitting Room.

O Almighty God! Who hast knit together Thine Elect in one Communion and fellowship in The Mystical Body of Thy Son Christ our Lord; grant us grace so to follow Thy Blessed Saints in all virtuous and godly living, that we may come to those unspeakable joys which Thou hast prepared for them that unfeignedly love Thee, through Christ our Lord. *Amen.*

O most gracious God! the Giver of all good gifts, we beseech Thee to send Thine Holy Spirit on these rooms, and all that shall live therein. Bless them, O Lord! in their going out and coming in, in their studies and recreations, in their food and rest, in their conversation and in their silence; and grant that the words of their mouths, and the meditations of their hearts may alway be acceptable in Thy sight, and that all may be to Thine Honour and Glory, through Christ, our Lord. *Amen.*

In a Bed Chamber.

Bless, O Lord! we beseech Thee, these bed-chambers, and all who shall lie down to sleep therein, that they may repose in Thy peace, and abide in Thy will; and going on from strength to strength, and increasing in length of days, may finally attain to Thine Everlasting Kingdom, through Christ our Lord. *Amen.*

Return to the Oratory.

PSALM V.

Ponder my words, O Lord: consider my meditations.

O hearken Thou unto the voice of my calling, my King and my God: for unto Thee will I make my prayer.

My voice shalt Thou hear betimes, O Lord: early in the morning will I direct my prayer unto Thee, and will look up.

For Thou art the God that hast no pleasure in wickedness: neither shall any evil dwell with Thee.

Such as be foolish shall not stand in Thy sight: for Thou hatest all them that work vanity.

Thou shalt destroy them that speak leasing: the Lord shall abhor both the bloodthirsty and deceitful man.

But as for me, I will come into Thine House, even upon the multitude of Thy mercy: and in Thy fear will I worship toward Thy Holy Temple.

Lead me, O Lord! in Thy righteousness, because of mine enemies: make Thy way plain before my face.

For there is no faithfulness in his mouth: their inward parts are very wickedness.

Their throat is an open sepulchre: they flatter with their tongue.

Destroy Thou them, O God! let them perish through their own imaginations: cast them out in the multitude of their ungodliness, for they have rebelled against Thee.

And let all them that put their trust in Thee rejoice: they shall ever be giving of thanks because Thou defendest them. They that love Thy name shall be joyful in Thee.

For Thou, Lord, wilt give Thy blessing unto the righteous: and with Thy favourable kindness wilt Thou defend him as with a shield.

Glory be to the Father, &c.
As it was in the beginning, &c.
The Lord be with you.
And with thy spirit.

Let us pray. (*Kneeling.*)

O God! Father Almighty! we Thy suppliants intreat Thee, on behalf of this house and its occupiers, that Thou wouldest vouchsafe to bless and sanctify, and enlarge them in all good things. Bestow upon them, O Lord! abundance of Thy celestial dew and plenteousness of the fatness of the Land of the living and of Thy compassion: and bring to good effect all their desires and vows. At this our prayer be graciously pleased to bless and hallow this abode, as Thou didst vouchsafe to bless and hallow the House of Abraham, Isaac, and Jacob. May Angels of Light ever dwell within its walls, and guard it and its inhabitants from all evil, through our Lord Jesus Christ Thy Son, Who with Thee liveth and reigneth in the Unity of the Holy Ghost, God world without end. *Amen.*

The Lord be with you.
And with thy spirit.
Bless we the Lord.
Thanks be to God.

The Grace of our Lord Jesus Christ, and the Love of God, and the Fellowship of the Holy Ghost, be with us all evermore. *Amen.*

Various Benedictions.

(TRANSLATED FROM THE EXETER PONTIFICAL.)

Form of Blessing the Holy Water.

The Exorcism of the Salt.

EXORCISE thee, creature of salt, by the living GOD, ✠ by the true GOD, ✠ by the holy GOD, ✠ by the GOD Who by the Prophet Eliseus, commanded thee ✠ to be cast into the water that the barrenness of the water might be healed, that thou mightest be salt exorcised for the spiritual health of believers, and be to all who take thee health of soul and body, that all delusion and wickedness, or crafty deceit of the devil, and every unclean spirit, may flee and depart from the place in which thou art sprinkled, adjured by Him, Who will judge the quick and the dead and the world by fire. R. Amen.

Benediction of the Salt.

Almighty and Everlasting GOD, we implore Thy great mercy, that Thou wouldest deign of Thy lovingkindness to bless ✠ and sancti✠fy this creature of salt which Thou hast given for the use of the human race, that it may be to all who take it health of mind and body, that whatever is touched or sprinkled by it may be freed from all uncleanness and may be defended from all attacks of ghostly wickedness, through our LORD JESUS CHRIST. R. Amen.

Exorcism of the Water.

I exorcise thee, creature of water, in the Name of GOD the FATHER Almighty, and in the Name of JESUS CHRIST HIS SON our LORD, and in the virtue of the HOLY GHOST, to become water exorcised to chase away all power of the enemy, and to be able to uproot and overthrow the enemy himself and his apostate angels ; by the virtue of the same LORD JESUS CHRIST Who will come to judge the quick and dead and the world by fire. R. Amen.

Benediction of the Water.

GOD, Who for the salvation of the human race, hast hidden even Thy greatest Sacraments in the substance of water; mercifully hear our supplications, and pour upon this element, prepared by divers purifications, the virtue of Thy Bless✠ing, that Thy creature obeying Thee in Thy mysteries, may by divine grace be effectual for casting out devils and for driving away diseases, that whatever in the houses or places of the faithful this water has sprinkled, may be cleansed from all uncleanness, and be freed from bale, that there the breath of pestilence, and the destroying blast shall not abide ; that all snares of the enemy who lies in wait may be dispersed, and that whatsoever does despite to the safety and quietness of Thy servants may flee by the sprinkling of this water, that health may be sought by the invocation of Thy Holy Name, and may be defended from all assaults, through our LORD JESUS CHRIST. R. Amen.

Then shall the Consecrator cast the salt into the water, and shall say,

This mixture of salt and water together is done in the Name of the FATHER, and of the SON, and of the HOLY GHOST. R. Amen.

Then shall follow the Benediction of Salt and Water together in this wise.

   V. The Lord be with you.
   R. And with thy spirit.
     Let us pray.

O Almighty God, the Author of victorious power, King of all kings, magnificent conqueror, Who crushest the strength of adverse rule, Who overcomest the bondage of the enemy, Who vanquishest all hostile wickedness; suppliant and trembling we beseech and implore Thee, O Lord, mercifully to accept this creature of salt and water, and of Thy lovingkindness to illuminate and sancti✠fy it with the dew of Thy blessing, that wherever it shall be sprinkled, by the Invocation of Thy Holy Name, all malice of the unclean spirit may be driven away, and the terror of the venomous serpent be chased far hence, and that the presence of the Holy Spirit may be vouchsafed to us in every place when we ask Him of Thy tender mercy, through our Lord Jesus Christ Thy Son, Who liveth and reigneth with Thee in the unity of the same Spirit, one God world without end. R. Amen.

  (Translated from a MS. in the possession of the Rev. Frederick G. Lee.)

     Of a Chalice and Paten.

   V. Our help standeth in the Name of the Lord.
   R. Who hath made Heaven and Earth.
   V. Lord, hear our prayer.
   R. And let our cry come unto Thee.
   The Lord be with you.
   And with thy spirit.

     Let us pray.

Almighty and Everlasting God, Who under the old law willedst that gold and silver should be set apart for Thine honour and worship, vouchsafe, we beseech Thee, to bless ✠, sanc✠tify, and con✠secrate this chalice and paten for the ministration of the Eucharist of Thy dearly beloved Son Jesus Christ, Who for our salvation offered Himself a Sacrifice on the Altar of the Cross, and now—pleading the same sacrifice—liveth and reigneth with Thee and the Holy Ghost, ever one God, world without end. R. Amen.

     Of a Corporal.

   V. Our help standeth in the Name of the Lord.
   R. Who hath made Heaven and Earth.
   V. Lord, hear our prayer.
   R. And let our cry come unto Thee.
   The Lord be with you.
   And with thy spirit.

O Almighty God, we humbly beseech Thee graciously to bless ✠, sanc✠tify, and con✠secrate this Corporal for the use of Thine Altar, on which is presented to Thee the Sacrifice of Thy dearly beloved Son Jesus Christ, and grant that all who assist at these sacred Mysteries may receive here the virtue of that Sacrament and hereafter everlasting life, through the same Jesus Christ our Lord. R. Amen.

Of a Chalice-veil.

Almighty and Everlasting God, Whose most blessed Son Jesus Christ willed not only to die for our sins, but also to feed us with His most Blessed Body and Blood, bless ✠ and sanc✠tify, we beseech Thee, this Chalice-veil for the use of Thine Altar, and grant that we who by faith know Thine only-begotten Son here, may hereafter behold Him face to face, through the same Jesus Christ our Lord. R. Amen.

Of an Alb or Surplice.

O God, the Creator and Sanctifier of all things, vouchsafe, we beseech Thee, to bless ✠, sanc✠tify, and con✠secrate this Alb (*or Surplice*) that they who wear it for Thy glory, may have grace to wash their robes and make them white in the blood of the Lamb, and at last be found meet to worship Thee in heaven for ever, through Jesus Christ our Lord. R. Amen.

Of a Maniple or Girdle.

Hear us, Almighty God, and vouchsafe to bless ✠, sanc✠tify, and con✠secrate this Maniple (or *Girdle*) prepared for the use of Thy Ministers, for the sake of Jesus Christ our Lord. R. Amen.

Of a Stole.

O Lord Jesus Christ, Son of the living God, Who hast said with Thine own blessed and holy Lips, "Come unto Me, all ye that labour and are heavy laden, and I will give you rest. Take My yoke upon you, for My yoke is easy and My burden is light;" grant that all who wear this Stole—which do Thou vouchsafe to bless✠, sanc✠tify, and con✠secrate—may follow Thee in all humility, and at last find eternal rest for their souls, through Thee, O Blessed Saviour of the world, Who with the Father and the Holy Ghost livest and reignest one God world without end. R. Amen.

Of a Chasuble or Vestment.

O Almighty God, vouchsafe, we beseech Thee, to bless✠, sanc✠tify, and con✠secrate this Vestment for the ministry of Thy Holy Altar, and grant that those who use it may gain the graces bought by the Sacrifice of Thy dear Son, through Him Who liveth and reigneth with Thee and the Holy Ghost ever one God world without end. R. Amen.

A General Benediction.*

Vouchsafe, we beseech Thee, O Almighty God, to bless✠, sanc✠tify, and con✠secrate this ———— for Thy service, and grant that we who are permitted to worship Thee in Thy courts below may hereafter adore Thee for ever in heaven, through Jesus Christ Thine only Son our Lord. R. Amen.

※ After each and every Benediction the thing blessed should be reverently sprinkled with holy water.

✠
A.M.D.G.
✠

---

* It is convenient to use this Form for the Blessing of Bells, &c.

Old Vestments to be burnt.

LTARIS pallæ, cathedræ, candelabrum, et velum, si fuerint vetustate consumpta, incendio dentur; quia non licet ea, quæ in sacrario fuerint, male tractari; sed incendio universa tradantur. Cineres quoque eorum in baptisterium inferantur, ubi nullum transitum habeat; aut in pariete, aut in fossis pavimentorum jactentur, ne introeuntium pedibus inquinentur." Corpus Juris Can. Vol. i. p. 960.

And again: " Ligna Ecclesiæ dedicatæ non debent ad aliud opus jungi, nisi ad aliam Ecclesiam, sed igni sunt comburenda." (*Ibid.*) *Apud* Harrington.

Under the law the old Vestments were made up into wicks for the great candlestick in the Holy Place and the lamps in the Temple.

Reconsecration and Reconciling of Churches.

F the Altar be taken away, let the church be consecrated anew. If the walls only are altered, let it be reconciled with salt and water. If it be violated with murder or adultery, let it be most diligently cleansed and consecrated anew." Excerptions of Ecgbriht.

See also Harrington on the Consecration of Churches, pp. 44, 96, 98, 140.

The Oil of Chrism, the Oil of the Sick, and Holy Oil.

HESE oils were formerly consecrated by the Bishop on Maundy Thursday. The Chrism is a mixture of oil and balsam; the other two are pure oils. The Chrism was used in Baptism, Confirmation, Orders, also at the consecration of Churches, and at the Coronation of the Sovereign. The other two oils were used for the anointing of the Sick, and for the admission of catechumens.

The Chrism ought still to be used in the consecration of churches.

In the Form of Coronation holy oil has been used since the sixteenth century. The form used in consecrating it has not been published. See Mon. Rit. Vol. III. xxii. This oil as well as the chrism was used at Baptisms; hence called also the holy oil of the catechumens.

The holy oil of the sick under the First Book of King Edward VI. was consecrated by the Bishop of the diocese according to the rite in the English Pontifical. Since that period it has mostly been the custom of the English Priests to consecrate things used in the service of the Church for themselves. The fact is, that all such matters as licensing Penitentiaries, receiving Vows, or using Benedictions of various kinds, were merely as matter of convenience and discipline reserved to the Bishop in mediæval times. But they are not, nor were ever held to be, essentially parts of his Office. Our Bishops do not claim to do any of these. Consequently they revert to the Priest as inherently within his province. It is a mere matter of order, not of right. A Priest has an inalienable *power* to *consecrate*—for he performs the highest sacerdotal act when he says " Hoc EST CORPUS MEUM," and is therefore fully empowered to execute the Priest's Office whether in respect of Absolution, receiving brothers or sisters, or using sundry Benedictions.

The Sacrament of Absolution.

IN administering the Sacrament of Penance or Absolution (as the Homily calls it), the Priest will wear a surplice, violet[*] stole, and either zucchetto or birretta. The penitent will kneel beside the faldstool, or seat on which the Priest sits. At the Form of Absolution, " I absolve thee from all thy sins," &c. the Priest should stand up and make the sign of the cross towards the penitent, and lay his right hand on the head of the penitent according to the English tradition; or else he should, according to the usage of the West, make the sign of the cross, and then raise the right hand to the height of the shoulder, with the fingers extended and palm towards the penitent.

"Deinde dextera versus pœnitentem elevata dicit." Rub. de Sac. Pœn. Rom. Rit.

It seems preferable in absolving to put the right hand or hands upon the head. The sign of the cross should always be made. See Cope and Stretton's "Visitatio Infirmorum," for instances of imposition of hands in the case of sick persons—Introduction, p. xciv.

---

[*] "Superpelliceo et stola violacei coloris utatur, prout tempus, vel locorum feret consuetudo." Rubric. de Sacram. Pœnitent. Rom. Rit.

Appendix.

The Blessing should also be given at the same time in this form:— "GOD the FATHER, GOD the SON, GOD the HOLY GHOST, bless, preserve, and keep thee: the LORD mercifully with His favour look upon thee, and bring thee to everlasting life. Amen."

A Form for the Admission of a Chorister.*

¶ At a convenient time before Morning or Evening Prayer, all the members of the choir assemble in the vestry, robed in their proper ecclesiastical habits; and range themselves on their respective sides, "Decani" and "Cantoris," except that the position of the officiating Priest is at the upper end of the room and facing the choir. The boy to be admitted remains outside; all present kneeling down, the Priest shall say:—

REVENT us, O LORD, in all our doings with Thy most gracious favour, and further us with Thy continual help; that in all our works begun, continued, and ended in Thee, we may glorify Thy holy Name, and finally by Thy mercy obtain everlasting life; through JESUS CHRIST our LORD. *Amen.*

Our FATHER, &c.

¶ Then, as previously instructed, the two senior choristers go out, and bring in the Probationer, who vested in cassock coming in, and guided by them, stands in front of the Priest officiating.

¶ Then there shall be read the Lesson.

    1 Samuel iii. 1—10; and ii. 18, 19.

  ¶ The Lesson being ended the Priest shall proceed thus, saying:—

    V. Our help is in the Name of the LORD:
    R. Who hath made Heaven and Earth.
    V. Blessed be the Name of the LORD:
    R. Henceforth, world without end.

¶ And then taking the Boy by the right hand, the Priest shall admit him, using this form, the Boy kneeling:—

N. I admit thee to sing as a chorister in ———— In the Name of the FATHER, and of the SON, and of the HOLY GHOST. Amen.

¶ Then shall he pronounce this admonition, at the same time presenting him with the Prayer Book, Psalter, and Hymnal, he will use in the choir:—

See what thou singest with thy mouth, thou believe in thine heart, and what thou believest in thine heart, thou prove by thy works.

---

* Reprinted by the permission of the compiler, the Rev. F. G. Lee, F.S.A. London: Masters.

Admission of a Chorister.

¶ Then putting the surplice on the new chorister, he shall say:—

I clothe thee in the white garment of the surplice, and see that thou so serve God, and sing His praises, that thou mayest hereafter be admitted into the ranks of those who have washed their robes, and made them white in the Blood of the Lamb, and are before the throne of God, and serve Him day and night continually.

¶ Then laying his hand upon the new chorister's head, the Priest shall pronounce the Benediction, the boy still kneeling:—

The Lord bless thee, and keep thee, and make His Face to shine upon thee and be gracious unto thee, the Lord lift up His countenance upon thee and give thee peace now and for ever. Amen.

¶ The newly-admitted Boy then rising, retires and takes his place among the choristers, upon which the following Psalms are chanted:—

Psalm lxxxiv. *Quam dilecta.*
Psalm cxxii. *Lætatus sum.*
Psalm cxxxiv. *Ecce nunc.*

¶ After which these prayers shall be said, all kneeling, the Priest first pronouncing:—

V. The Lord be with you:
R. And with thy spirit.

¶ Priest. Let us pray.

Lord, have mercy upon us.
Christ, have mercy upon us.
Lord, have mercy upon us.
Our Father, &c.

¶ Then the Priest standing up shall say:—

V. O Lord, save Thy servant:
R. Who putteth his trust in Thee.
V. O Lord, send him help from Thy holy place:
R. And evermore mightily defend him.
V. Be unto him a tower of strength:
R. From the face of his enemy.
V. Lord, hear our prayer:
R. And let our cry come unto Thee.
The Lord be with you:
And with thy spirit.

¶ Priest. Let us pray.

Let Thy merciful ears, O Lord, be open to our prayers, and be pleased to bless this Thy Servant, on whom we have placed the garments of Religion in Thy name, that by Thy Grace he may remain devoted to his work in Thy Church, and may inherit everlasting life. O Lord Jesu, bless him with all abilities of mind and body, that he may daily increase in his learning: but above all bless him with wisdom from above, and give him Thy Holy Spirit to assist and enlighten him: that as he grows in age he may daily grow in grace, and in the knowledge of Thee, and in favour with God and man, and every day become more and more conformable to Thy unsinning and divine example, Who livest and reignest with the FATHER and the HOLY GHOST, one GOD world without end. *Amen.*

Almighty and Everlasting GOD by whose SPIRIT the whole body of the Church is governed and sanctified; receive our supplications and prayers, which we offer before Thee for all estates of men in Thy holy Church, that every member of the same in his vocation and ministry, may truly and Godly serve Thee, through our LORD and SAVIOUR JESUS CHRIST. *Amen.*

Priest.

The Grace of our LORD JESUS CHRIST, and the Love of GOD, and the Fellowship of the HOLY GHOST be with us all evermore. *Amen.*

¶ Then all rising, the whole choir enter the church in procession. After Service the name of the new Boy shall be inscribed on the Register belonging to the church, of the boys approved and admitted to sing as choristers therein. And no Boy shall be admitted by this form until he has passed some time in probation, and the Priest is fully satisfied of his good conduct and aptness for the office.

Floral Decorations.

GREAT caution should be exercised in the use of natural flowers for temporary decorations. As a general rule their use is questionable in any position in which they cannot be kept in water, as it is impossible to prevent their speedy fading and decay,—the appearance, and not unfrequently the smell of which is as actually offensive, as the idea is itself indefensible.

The best means, therefore, of employing fresh flowers is in vases upon the super-altar, (as previously prescribed on festivals and other occasions), and in other positions, e. g. the top of the rood-screen, parcloses, &c. and growing naturally in flower-pots, by a tasteful arrangement of which in the sanctuary, and especially in the immediate vicinity of the Altar,* a most chaste and dignified form of decoration is attained,—the general effect of which is pleasing in the extreme. The number of vases upon an altar may of course be regulated by circumstances, but the circumstances are rare in which the symmetry is not impaired by the use of more than four: that

---

* One of the most common, and at the same time satisfactory, dispositions of pot flowers is in groups at the corners of the altar, shelving thence to the edge of the foot-pace; and again in a circular group round the bases of standard candlesticks. Small pieces of oil-cloth should be used to place under the pot and saucer, both of which, if not of an ecclesiastical pattern, should be ornamented with moss.

number harmonizing best with the other ornaments of an altar arranged for the English rite. The cross is, of course, central; the candlesticks should be distant from the cross two-thirds of the whole distance between it and the corners of the altar, and the vases should be placed one on each side of each candlestick. No other arrangement either of more or less gives such unity and dignity to the grouping of the altar.

Though, however, the present English use adheres to the ancient rule of two lights only upon the altar, and though four vases of flowers only are admissible without giving an idea of poverty to the whole arrangement; this necessity by no means prevents the use of as many vases of flowers and lights, as are desired on a series of receding shelves, or *retables*—temporary or otherwise—behind, and separate from the altar. The employment of this means of decoration is very desirable in the arrangement of our chancels. The necessity of a passage behind the altar has recently been insisted on by both ritualists and architects, and this passage would sufficiently dissever the super-altar from the additional shelves or platforms here recommended. This separation is of course desirable to avoid the appearance of a desire to conceal any supposed paucity in the "ornaments" of an Anglican Altar, which, when arranged as here prescribed and within the limits suggested, yield to the accessories of no other rite in their severe dignity and beauty.

These, then, are the only means of employing natural flowers wholly free from objection, and such employment of them is by no means incapable of general application as many are apt to suppose. Vases of flowers, and even flower pots, judiciously disposed may be placed in windows, on a rood-loft, in doorways, on steps, and in most parts of a church, where they produce an effect to which no unnatural twisting of mixed flowers into ropes, sheaves or festoons is in any way comparable, and without any of the disadvantage necessarily attending these latter forms of decoration.

Still there may be circumstances in which such a use of evergreens and flowers is the only one open to a sacristan, and to this use of them—as also in some degree to the arrangement of flowers in water or otherwise—the following remarks apply:—

Never mix flowers for church decoration quite indiscriminately, with reference, that is, solely to the collocation as it appears to yourself the decorator, standing in close proximity to your work, or you will certainly achieve nothing but what will appear at a distance *a confused dark mass*, occasionally relieved by a solitary red or white flower.

Aim at obtaining *masses* of colour so far as the materials of your decorations admit, and this is even the more neceſſary in the conſtruction of feſtoons and wall decorations, than in the arrangement of vaſes.

Never adhere ſtrictly to the lines of the architecture, as that ſyſtem of decoration profeſſes which makes holly and laurel run like ivy and vine along horizontal ſtring-courſes and round the hood-mouldings of windows. Such an unnatural abuſe of foliage only exaggerates and renders painful the lines it profeſſes to illuſtrate and relieve. Arches and windows are difficult features to treat ſuccefsfully with extempore decorations, and in thoſe caſes where they have any conſtructional or other colours, it is better to leave their proper beauty unmoleſted. In any caſe evergreens are beſt employed in ſpiral bands* round pillars, by which they are evidently ſupported, rather than in arduous ſtruggles to follow impoſſible lines which afford them no viſible ſupport, and conſequently are perpetually threatening to fall, as they frequently do.

Spandrils, between the arches of an arcade, may be very appropriately filled with banners, either ſupported on poles fixed into the wall, or hung flat againſt it. Similarly ſhields emblazoned with religious devices—the emblems of the Paſſion for example—either with or without decoration of foliage, or even plain wreaths, or devices, honeſtly nailed up againſt the wall, may be employed very preferably to thoſe impracticable coils, which only fill the beholder with wonder as to the means by which they attained their poſition, and by which they are ſuſtained in it.

A large extent of wall, e. g. that of a ſanctuary, or chancel may be effectively decorated by a continuous feſtoon, depending upon nails or pegs at intervals in the wall; or better ſtill from rods reſting upon the pavement, or even from regulated points in a horizontal rod, ſuch as thoſe which ſupport ſanctuary curtains. It is on the conſtruction of theſe feſtoons that ſome remark ſeems neceſſary :—

It is indiſpenſable for any effect that flowers of the ſame kind and colour be grouped together; as for inſtance a feſtoon might be arranged in compartments (ſay ſix inches) of RED (roſes or geraniums, &c.), then of WHITE (lilac, pinks, candytuft, or lilies), then of YELLOW (daffodils, furze-bloſſom, &c.), and ſo on, bordered with a narrow band of green leaves, and varied of courſe at the taſte of the decorator. One chief advantage ariſing from this plan will be found to be that the gradual fading of the flowers will not be ſo apparent, when they are bound in compact maſſes of ſimilar form and

---

* If box is uſed, the branches may be tied together upon a piece of wire, with the leaves in one direction; if laurel, the leaves ſhould be ſewn with taſte upon a ground of green calico.

colour, as when they are promiscuous and isolated. Still, decorations by natural flowers, not placed in water, should never be carried out to such an extent as to preclude the substitution of fresh festoons at intervals, if the decorations are required for any length of time. Nothing is so unseemly or unsightly, or in extreme cases so positively offensive, as decaying vegetation in a church. Evergreens even should not be so extensively used as they frequently are, if the decorators are not prepared to take the trouble of renewing them during the long intervals between Christmas and Candlemas, or the still longer period between Easter and Corpus Christi.

These suggestions on the grouping of flowers apply, as has been said, to the arrangement of flowers in vases.

Still the fundamental difference in the position they are respectively designed to occupy must be borne in mind. Thus, while juxta-position of colour is as necessary for effect in one as in the other, yet the stiffness and conventional treatment, which is a direct advantage in the one case in consequence of the abnormal and unnatural position which the festoons are required to occupy, is to be avoided in the other, in which as much appearance of ease is to be aimed at as is possible.

The practice of fastening upon small pieces of stick the flowers which are subsequently placed in the altar vases, without their having the benefit of the water, which it is the sole purpose of vases to supply them, cannot be too strongly condemned. If it be difficult to form bouquets for the altar of a sufficient size, it is easy to place a tall and narrow vase inside the metal one which stands upon the altar, which will then give the required height.

With a view, then, of producing the effect of one or two prominent colours in an altar vase, it is desirable to use for the purpose flowers entirely of the same kind and colour according to particular seasons or festivals. A list of appropriate flowers will be found below.

Before leaving the subject it is necessary to add some brief remarks upon the employment of artificial flowers:

The writer is fully aware that a great prejudice exists amongst many against their use in church; but he cannot conceive it to be otherwise than to a great extent groundless.* In many places in particular seasons it is quite impossible to obtain natural flowers, and the attention of the sacristan —desirous of seeing the altar and the sanctuary of the church under his care present that beautiful appearance which it usually wears—becomes

---

* The employment of artificial flowers is common in the churches of France and Belgium, as well as in portions of the Eastern Church.

occasionally turned to them for adoption in purposes of decoration. White and crimson roses, without leaves, will be found the most effective, which should be fastened by the wire by which the stem is made to small branches of the box tree, which is by far the most beautiful evergreen for use upon the altar. These, placed with taste in vases or fixed to the upper portion of standard candlesticks or round coronas, will give a most beautiful appearance to a church, and may be used in village churches during the depth of winter, or at other times, when out-door or greenhouse plants cannot be obtained.

Wax flowers likewise may be pressed into the service of the church—representations of the *Lilium Candidum* being very especially effective.

The following list of red and white Flowers, compiled with great care, and with the assistance of a practical gardener, is appended in the hope that it may be found useful in indicating what flowers—making allowance for the variableness of the seasons—may be obtained for the different Feasts of the Church:—

January.

WHITE. Christmas rose. *Helleborus niger.*
Laurustinus.
Snowdrop. *Galanthus nivalis.*
Wall speedwell. *Veronica arvensis.*
RED. Common maidenhair. *Asplenium trichomanes.*
Bearsfoot. *Helleborus fœtidus.*

February.

WHITE. Dwarf bay. *Daphne mezereon.*
White crocus. *Crocus albus.*
Herb S. Margaret. *Bellis perennis plena.*
RED. Common primrose. *Primula verna.*
Persian cyclamen. *Cyclamen Persicum.*
Cloth of gold. *Crocus Susianus.*

March.

WHITE. Early daffodil. *Narcissus pseudonarcissus.*
Great scented jonquil. *Narcissus lætus.*
Common marygold. *Calendula officinalis.*
Wood anemone. *Anemone nemorosa.*
RED. Upright chickweed. *Veronica triphyllos.*
Sweet tulip. *Tulipa suaveolens.*

April.

WHITE. White violet. *Viola odora alba.*
Cypress narcissus. *Narcissus orientalis albus.*
RED. Red polyanthus. *Primula polyantha purpurea.*
Borage. *Borago officinalis.*
Herb S. Robert. *Geranium Robertianum.*
Crimson currant. *Ribes sanguinea.*
Crown imperial. *Corona imperialis rubra.*

May.

WHITE. White stock gilliflower. *Matthiola incana alba.*
Apple-blossom. *Pyrus mala.*
Lily of the valley. *Convalaria Maialis.*
Solomon's seal. *Convalaria polygonatum.*
White star of Bethlehem. *Ornithogalum umbellatum.*
RED. Standard tulip. *Tulipa Gesneri.*
Red campion. *Lychnis dioica rubra.*
Cross flower. *Polygala vulgaris.*
Common peony. *Pæonia officinalis.*
Meadow lychnis or ragged robin. *Lychnis flos cuculi.*

Floral Decorations.

June.

WHITE. Indian pink. *Dianthus Sinensis.*
White dog-rose. *Rosa arvensis.*
Garden ranunculus. *Ranunculus Asiaticus.*
S. John's wort. *Hypericum pulchrum.*
Jasmine (white). *Jasminum officinalis.*
RED. Rose (moss). *Rosa muscosa.*
Rose de Meux. *Rosa provincialis.*
Barbary. *Berboris vulgaris.*
S. Barnaby's thistle. *Centaurea solstitialis.*
Prince's feather. *Amaranthus hypochondriacus.*
Sweet S. William. *Dianthus barbatus.*
Red mallow. *Malope grandiflora.*

July.

WHITE. Our Lady's lily. *Lilium candidum.*
Upright virgin's bower. *Clematis flammula.*
African lily. *Agapanthus umbellatus.*
White mullien. *Verbuscum lychnitis.*
RED. Corn poppy. *Papaver rhæus.*
Red centaury. *Erythræa centaurea.*
Nasturtium. *Tropeolum majus.*
Red sweet-pea. *Lathyrus odoratus.*
Herb S. Christopher. *Actæa spicata.*
Scarlet blood flower. *Hæmanthus coccinæus.*
Musk flower. *Scabiosa atropurpurea.*

August.

WHITE. Common thorn apple. *Datura stramonium.*
Harvest bells (or S. Dominic's bells). *Campanula rotundifolia.*
Egyptian water lily. *Nelumbo Nilotica.*
Fleur de S. Louis. *Iris bistora.*
Rosa lily. *Nerine Sarniensis.*
RED. Tiger lily. *Lilium tigrinum.*
Hollyhock. *Althea rosea.*
China after. *Aster Chinensis.*
Herb S. Timothy. *Phleum pratense.*
S. Bartholomew's star. *Helianthus annuus.*
S. John's wort. *Hypericum ascyron.*

September.

WHITE. Laurustinus. *Vibernum tinus.*
Myrtle.
Verbena.
Candy tuft. *Iberis sempervirens.*
Michaelmas daisy. *Aster tradescanti.*
Guernsey lily. *Amaryllis Sarniensis.*
RED. Passion flower. *Passiflora incanata.*
Fuschia.
Salvia.
Bignonia.
Stocks.

October.

WHITE. S. Remy's lily. *Amaryllis humilis.*
Soapwort. *Saponaria officinalis.*
Indian chrysanthemum. *Chrysanthemum Indicum.*
Sweet milfoil. *Arbillaca aggeratum.*
Beautiful starwort. *Aster pulcherrimus.*
RED. Indian fleabane. *Mula Indica.*
Starlike Silphicum. *Silphicum asteriscus.*
China rose.

November.

WHITE. Sweet bay. *Laurus nobilis.*
Glaucous aletris. *Veltheiruca glauca.*
Snowy coltsfoot. *Tussilago nivea.*
Large-flowered wood-forrel. *Oxalis grandifolia.*
RED. Common strawberry-tree. *Arbutus unedo.*
Trumpet-flowered wood-forrel. *Oxalis tubiflora.*
Sweet butter-bur. *Tussilago fragrans.*
S. Andrew's cross, or Ascyrum. *Crux Andreæ.*
N.B.—If All Souls' Day is observed, the church may be decorated with yew, *Taxus baccata*, and cypress, *Cypressus sempervirens.*

December.

WHITE. Indian tree. *Euphorbia Trincalli.*
Arbor vitæ. *Thuja occidentalis.*
Mistletoe berries.
RED. Holly berries. *Ilex bacciflora.*
Chinese arbor vitæ. *Thuja orientalis.*
Sparrow wort. *Erica passerina.*

(*Vide, also, flowers for January.*)

Altars and Dossels of Village Churches.

IN the arrangement and decoration of the altar of a village church, where but small sums of money can be expended, it is recommended that the altar cloth be of green colour, in the first instance, and afterwards that separate frontals of the other colours be obtained by degrees. The most important colour, and that which should be the most richly embroidered, should be the white frontal, as being used at all the principal feasts of our Blessed LORD. It is suggested that the best effect is obtained in embroidery, if gold be used upon green and crimson,—silver and scarlet upon white, and white upon violet or purple. It is better to use conventional flowers than crosses upon *altar frontals*, or diapers. If there be no constructional Reredos, behind and above the altar, a hanging of cloth, silk or damask should be placed. If it is changed according to the colours of the seasons, rings should be fastened to it, and it should hang upon a rod, but if not, it might be stretched on a frame, or affixed in any other way to the wall. If permanent, white, or white bordered with blue or scarlet is recommended, i.e. if the walls around are coloured; but if they are whitewashed, some colour, green or scarlet, should by all means be used. There should always be an altar-ledge. Its height should, if possible, never be less than eight inches. Upon it should stand two candlesticks with wax tapers, and between them a material cross, of oak, brass, or more precious metal. Flowers in vases should always be placed upon the super-altar.

Flowers on the Altar.

"ALTARE in solemnibus festis floribus seu veris seu fictis exornandum."
—Gavantus, tom. ii. par. 5.

Flower Vases.

FLOWER vases should be very carefully wiped out immediately after use, especially those of latten or other metal. They should be thoroughly cleaned before being put away in a dry cupboard, and should be occasionally rubbed with washleather. If they are enamelled great care should be taken in cleansing them.

Feasts of Obligation.

All the Sundays in the year.
*Christmas Day.
Circumcision.
Epiphany.

*Ascension Day.
S. Peter's Day, June 29.
All Saints, Nov. 1.
[Corpus Christi.]

Feasts of Devotion.

Feb. 2. Purification of B. V. M.
Feb. 24. S. Matthias.
March 25. Annunciation of B.V.M.
†April 23. S. George.
May 1. S. Philip and S. James.
†May 3. Invention of the Holy Cross.
June 24. S. John Baptist.
July 25. S. James.
†July 26. S. Anne, Mother of B. V. M.
August 10. S. Laurence.
August 24. S. Bartholomew.

†Sept. 8. Nativity of B. V. M.
Sept. 21. S. Matthew.
Sept. 29. S. Michael.
Oct. 28. S. Simon and S. Jude.
†Dec. 8. Conception of B. V. M.
Dec. 26. S. Stephen.
Dec. 27. S. John Evangelist.
Dec. 28. Holy Innocents.
Easter Monday.
Easter Tuesday.
Whitsun Monday.
Whitsun Tuesday.

N.B.—March 17, S. Patrick's Day, is peculiarly and especially observed in the sister communion of Ireland.

The following Festivals likewise are now specially commemorated by the English Church:—

Jan. 25. Conversion of S. Paul.
April 25. S. Mark.
June 11. S. Barnabas.

Oct. 18. S. Luke.
Nov. 30. S. Andrew.
Dec. 21. S. Thomas.

* These great Feasts have a proper preface, in addition to Easter Day, Whit Sunday, and Trinity Sunday, and with the exception of the last-named, are kept with an octave.
N.B.—The fifth Sunday in Lent is called Passion Sunday—the sixth, Palm Sunday.
† These Feasts have now no special Collect or Service.
N.B.—The anniversary festival of the dedication of a church, college, or religious house is kept with an octave as a feast of devotion, though under the patronage of a Saint not so commemorated.

Rules for a Sacristy or Vestry.

I.

STRICT silence should be observed, except a reasonable cause presents itself, and then whispering only is permitted.

II. The lay-clerks and choristers will take their cassocks and surplices in an orderly and becoming manner, having previously said the usual "Prayer before Service" and "On vestng with the surplice." On returning from the church they will carefully replace them from whence they were taken.

III. When the signal is given by the sacristan or master of the ceremonies, the clerks and choristers will arrange themselves in processional order so as to proceed to the choir.

IV. No boy should be allowed to vest with soiled hands, face, &c. or dirty shoes.

V. The Clergy should not proceed to vest for any function in soiled clothes or shoes. A brush should be kept in the sacristy, that when necessary they may clean their ordinary clothes before vesting. It is also convenient to have a well-stocked pin-cushion, which is often required for a deacon's stole, &c.

N.B.—There should always be an *inner* sacristy, into which alone enter the Priest, Sacred Ministers, acolytes, and ceremoniarius. It is the duty of the sacristan to close the door, so as to prevent the entrance of any one not authorized to be there. The choir will vest in the outer sacristy. No females should be admitted into the *inner* sacristy *on any plea whatever*. They may speak, on particular business, to the Priest or Sacristan in the *outer* sacristy, but as rarely and for as short a time as possible. Every inner sacristy should have a platform for the Priest to vest upon.

Cleansing of Church Furniture.

I.

ONCE every quarter the altar should be entirely stripped, so that everything about it may have the benefit of fresh air. And at the same time all the ornaments, linen, &c. connected with it should be well cleansed.

II. The altar vestments should be thoroughly dusted, and hung up in a

Cleansing of Church Furniture. 261

room to get fresh air, they should all be well brushed with a soft brush of feathers, care being taken that the embroidery, &c. be not injured in so doing.

III. The foot-pace and sanctuary should be swept at the least twice in a week.

IV. Candle-sticks, flower-vases, altar-crosses, &c. of metal should, if possible, not be touched with the bare hands, but with a piece of washleather or green baize. If the brass-work be lacquered it does not require the application of any powders or rubbing; dusting with a soft dry cloth being sufficient, with the occasional use of a little sweet oil. If unlacquered it is cleaned with polishing paste, and rubbed with washleather. Stains may be removed by a little oxalic acid (poison) dissolved in hot water.

V. Every six months the chalice and patens, &c. should be well washed in water, with soap and brush, and then two or three times in pure water. This should be done by one in Holy Orders, who will pour the water into the piscina. Silver or plated work is best cleaned with rouge, whitening, or spirits of wine, and afterwards well polished with washleather.

VI. The cruets should be washed out at least once a month, so that no incrustations be formed within them.

VII. The altar candles should be kept in a drawer by themselves, and care should be taken of the ends or refuse wax. Sperm or composition candles should on no account be used for the altar. Care should be taken that the wicks are ready for lighting, and that there are no wax excrescences at the top, otherwise the candles are liable to gutter and waste. If soiled by dirty fingers they may be cleaned with a cloth damped with spirits of wine.

VIII. Gilt wood or stone-work should only be dusted with a soft cloth or a feather brush. Frescoes, mural paintings, &c. should be very carefully dusted with an extremely soft brush.

IX. Encaustic tiles may be cleaned with milk, and rubbed with a dry coarse flannel.

X. Embroidered altar linen, corporals, &c. should be washed in lukewarm water with white soap. Wax droppings may be removed by carefully scraping them with a knife, and then soaking the part in spirits of wine. Wine stains may be removed by holding the stained portion in boiling milk.

XI. Damask, velvet, or silk hangings should be taken down every two months, and well shaken and dusted. They may afterwards be hung across a line in the air for an hour or two: but not when the sun is too hot, as otherwise they may lose their colours.

N.B.—If any of the Precious Blood fall upon a linen vestment, the part must be washed over a chalice, and the ablution reverently poured down the piscina; if It fall on a vestment of silk or stuff, the part must be cut out and burnt, and the ashes disposed of as above.

Processions.

THE following seems to be the most desirable order in which solemn religious processions—such for instance as at the Consecration of a Church, or the Benediction of a College, &c. should be marshalled:—

Verger and Churchwardens in gowns,
(*bearing staves or maces.*)
Choristers.*
Lay-Clerks.
Chorister *with Banner.*
Chorister *with Banner.* Deacons. Chorister *with Banner.*
Priests.
Lay-Clerk *with Banner.*
Rural-Deans.
Prebendaries.
Lay-Clerk *with Banner.* Canons. Lay-Clerk *with Banner.*
Archdeacons.
Deans.
Deacon *with Banner.* Cross-bearer. Deacon *with Banner.*
Chaplains. Bishops. Chaplains.
Priest *with Banner*,
With arms of the Archdiocese.
Chaplain. Archbishop. Chaplain.

If there chance to be many Priests or Deacons, they may be placed in pairs—care being taken that as near as possible they be of equal height, the juniors going first, either according to seniority or to the degree they possess. If the latter, the following list is correct:—

---

* The choristers should be arranged so as to stand equal in height. The same will apply to the lay-clerks.

I. Literates.
II. S.C.L.
III. B.A.
IV. M.A.
V. B.C.L. or LL.B.
VI. B.D.
VII. D.C.L. or LL.D.
VIII. D.D.

Oxford, by custom, takes precedence of Cambridge, Cambridge of Dublin, Dublin of Durham, and Durham of the Theological Colleges, e.g. King's, London; S. Bees', Cumberland, &c.

The same principle of arrangement should, as far as possible, be observed in all places where more than one cleric takes part in the Service. In a procession juniors should invariably precede seniors, and the *locus honoris* is, of course, always at the end. A procession should on no account leave the chancel in any other order than that in which it came. It is entirely wrong to reverse the arrangement in returning; the choristers and juniors should leave first; the seniors and more dignified last.

· N.B.—On no account should hats be worn in procession. The college cap, the skull-cap, or the birretta should be used. The first may be used with the academical hood, though the birretta seems preferable; the birretta should be used always with the cope, and is indeed to be preferred at all times to the academical cap.

The Clergy should take off their birretta whenever they stand up, whenever they are saluted by the Sacred Ministers, or others, who enter or leave the choir, and also on all occasions which require an inclination of the head. They should take off their zucchettos in the act of genuflecting, whilst the Deacon sings the Gospel, at the "was made man," and from the beginning of the Sanctus to the Communion of the Clergy. The birretta is removed in singing, but the zucchetto need not be removed.

The Master of the Ceremonies.

In all, especially solemn, functions a master or director of the ceremonies ought to be previously appointed, who should make himself well acquainted with ecclesiastical order and arrangement, and take time beforehand in learning what number and classes of the Clergy are likely to be present, and in considering the parts of the Service to be assigned to each, and the position each one is to occupy. If this is not done, disorder and irregularity are certain to prevail. This important Office is very frequently undertaken by the Sacriſtan, who will, of courſe, conſult the Prieſt as to the arrangements to be made.

The ceremoniarius ſhould be veſted in caſſock and cotta. His place is properly before the Sacred Miniſters; but no poſition is preciſely aſſigned to him unleſs under ſome particular circumſtances, ſince he ought to be wherever his preſence is moſt uſeful or neceſſary. When not engaged in his duties his place is in the centre of the chancel below the ſteps of the Sanctuary. On great occaſions he ſhould have two acolytes with him— one on either ſide—in caſe of his being required to communicate with the cantors, organiſt, croſs-bearer, verger, or other official.

Proceſſional Banners.

BANNERS are uſed to ſtimulate the devotion of the faithful, eſpecially of the poor, and conſequently ſhould have the devices and emblems worked upon them as clearly ſet forth as poſſible, in order that they may be eaſily underſtood. The ſtaves of theſe ſhould be ſurmounted by a ſmall croſs. When not in uſe they ſhould be detached from the ſtaves, and very carefully put away. Figures are far better than mere legends in mediæval letters, becauſe the former can be ſeen, whereas too frequently the latter cannot be read, and are almoſt unintelligible and puzzling. The following ſubjects are recommended for banners:—

1. The Banner of the Croſs. A white croſs on a crimſon or ſcarlet ground, called uſually St. George's Croſs.
2. A Figure of the Patron Saint of the church.
3. A Figure of our Bleſſed Lady, either bearing Her Holy Child in Her lap, or repreſented as crowned in glory.
4. The Banner of our Bleſſed LORD and SAVIOUR. He may be repreſented ſeated on a throne, with a rainbow round about the throne, and in the act of benediction.

The Verger and Churchwardens' Staves.

The Verger's ſtaff is uſually made of oak or ebony, bound with braſs or ſilver, ſurmounted by an emblem of the Patron Saint of the Church, or ſome other appropriate deſign, e.g. a Fleur-de-lys, &c. The Churchwardens' ſtaves may be made of a ſimilar pattern and material, though larger.

The Processional Cross or Crucifix.[*]

The Proceffional Crofs fhould be made of brafs, and fhould be borne before the Proceffion to the Altar at High Celebration every Sunday. On fpecial feftivals and particular occafions it will likewife be carried at the head of the proceffion before Evenfong. Cuftom likewife fanctions its ufe at Burials and upon other occafions.

Form for Bidding of Prayer.

YE fhall pray for CHRIST's Holy Catholic Church, particularly for that portion of it to which we belong, and herein as well for all Patriarchs and Archbifhops as for Bifhops, Priefts, and Deacons, more efpecially are we bound to pray for —— the Bifhop of this Diocefe and for all the Clergy under him, that they may fhine like lights in the world, and adorn the doctrine of GOD our SAVIOUR in all things; ye fhall alfo pray for our Sovereign Lady *Victoria* by the grace of GOD, Queen, of this realm, and for the reft of the Royal Family, for the Queen's moft honourable privy council, for all the nobility and magiftrates of this kingdom, (and for the great council of the nation now affembled in Parliament), that all and each of thefe in their feveral callings may ferve truly to the glory of GOD, and the edifying and well-governing of His people, remembering that folemn account they muft one day give before the judgment-feat of CHRIST. Finally, let us pray GOD to abfolve the fouls of all His fervants, who have departed this life in His faith and fear, from every bond of fin, befeeching Him to give us grace fo to follow their good examples, that finally we with them and they with us, may be made partakers of the glorious refurrection in life everlafting, through the merits of JESUS CHRIST our SAVIOUR. May their fouls reft in peace. Amen.

Our FATHER, &c.

---

[*] In Lent the crofs may be of wood, and fhould be painted red, according to the ancient Englifh ufe.

Palm Sunday.

INTRODUCTORY DIRECTIONS.

IT may be advisable under some circumstances not to bless the palms publicly in church, but to do so privately in an Oratory, or in the Sacristy, at the early celebration. The plan, however, being previously determined, the Parish Priest, together with the Sacristan and Ceremoniarius, should read very carefully, so as to make themselves thoroughly acquainted with the following office from the Sarum Rite, and provide everything necessary for the solemn and reverent performance of the ancient ceremonies therein set forth. If the benediction takes place in the church the cross and candlesticks should alone stand on the altar-ledge. Between the candlesticks, however, palm branches may be placed. The table for receiving the palms, &c. should be placed near the altar on the Epistle side, and be covered with a fair white linen cloth.

Form for Blessing the Palms before a Low Celebration on Palm Sunday.

The Lesson is read by* one of the Ministers, vested in an alb, on the altar-step at the south side, over the flowers and branches, saying thus:—

The Lesson is from the Book of Exodus. Chap. xv. 27—xvi. 1—10.

In those days, the children of Israel came to Elim, where were twelve wells of water, and threescore and ten palm-trees: and they encamped there by the waters. And they took their journey from Elim, and all the congregation of the children of Israel came unto the wilderness of Sin, which is between Elim and Sinai, on the fifteenth day of the second month after their departing out of the land of Egypt. And the whole congregation of the children of Israel murmured against Moses and Aaron in the wilderness: And the children of Israel said unto them, Would to GOD we had died by the hand of the LORD in the land of Egypt, when we sat by the flesh-pots, and when we did eat bread to the full; for ye have brought us forth into this wilderness, to kill this whole assembly with hunger. Then said the LORD unto Moses, Behold, I will rain bread from heaven for you; and the people shall go out and gather a certain rate every day, that I may prove them, whether they will walk in My law, or no. And it shall come to pass, that on the sixth day they shall prepare that which they bring in; and it shall be twice as much as they gather daily. And Moses and Aaron said unto all the children of Israel, At even, then ye shall know that the LORD hath brought you out from the land of Egypt: And in the morning, then ye shall see the glory of the LORD; for that He heareth your

---

* The Sub-deacon. The branches, &c. should be placed upon a small table, covered with a white linen cloth.

murmurings againſt the LORD: and what are we, that ye murmur againſt us? And Moſes ſaid, This ſhall be, when the LORD ſhall give you in the evening fleſh to eat, and in the morning bread to the full; for that the LORD heareth your murmurings which ye murmur againſt Him: and what are we? your murmurings are not againſt us, but againſt the LORD. And Moſes ſpake unto Aaron, Say unto all the congregation of the children of Iſrael, Come near before the LORD: for He hath heard your murmurings. And it came to paſs, as Aaron ſpake unto the whole congregation of the children of Iſrael, that they looked toward the wilderneſs, and, behold, the glory of the LORD appeared in the cloud.

The Goſpel follows immediately, and is read by the Deacon, in the accuſtomed place, turning to the eaſt. After he has received the benediction of the Prieſt, he ſays:—

℣. The LORD be with you.
℟. And with thy ſpirit.

The Holy Goſpel is written in the Goſpel according to S. John. Chap. xii. 12—19.

Glory be to thee, O LORD.

On the next day much people that were come to the feaſt, when they heard that JESUS was coming to Jeruſalem, Took branches of palm-trees, and went forth to meet Him, and cried, Hoſanna: Bleſſed is the King of Iſrael that cometh in the name of the LORD. And JESUS, when He had found a young aſs, ſat thereon; as it is written, Fear not, daughter of Sion: behold, thy King cometh, ſitting on an aſs's colt. Theſe things underſtood not His diſciples at the firſt: but when JESUS was glorified, then remembered they that theſe things were written of Him, and that they had done theſe things unto Him. The people therefore that was with Him when He called Lazarus out of his grave, and raiſed him from the dead, bare record. For this cauſe the people alſo met Him, for that they heard that He had done this miracle. The Phariſees therefore ſaid among themſelves, Perceive ye how ye prevail nothing? behold, the world is gone after Him.

The Goſpel being finiſhed, the bleſſing of the flowers and branches follows, by a Prieſt[*] veiled in a red ſilk cope, upon the third ſtep of the altar, and turning towards the eaſt; the palms and flowers[†] having been previouſly placed upon the altar for the clergy; but for the congregation upon the altar-ſtep on its ſouth ſide.

I exorcize thee, creature of flowers and branches; in the Name of GOD the FATHER ALMIGHTY, and in the Name of JESUS CHRIST His Son our LORD, and in the power of the HOLY GHOST: henceforth thou whole might of the adverſary, thou whole army of Satan, and whole power of the enemy, thou whole inroad of evil ſpirits, be rooted up and pulled out from theſe creatures of flowers and branches; that thou purſue not with thy wills the footſteps of thoſe haſtening to attain unto the grace of GOD. Through Him Who ſhall come to judge the quick and the dead and the world by fire. ℟. Amen.

Let us pray.

Almighty everlaſting GOD, Who amidſt the waters of the flood didſt, by the mouth of the

---

[*] The Prieſt ſhould be veſted in amice, alb, girdle, *red* ſtole, maniple, and cope. The ſtole is *violet* according to the Roman uſe.

[†] Up to this period they remain on the table already referred to.

dove bearing an olive-branch, announce to thy servant Noah the return of peace to the earth, we humbly beseech Thee, that Thy truth may hal✠low these creatures of flowers and branches and palm branches (or boughs of trees), which we offer before the face of Thy Glory; that Thy people devoutly receiving them in their hands, may be found worthy to obtain the grace of Thy blessing, through CHRIST our LORD. R. Amen.

Let us pray.

O GOD, Whose Son for the salvation of mankind came down from heaven to earth; and willed as the hour of His Passion drew near to enter into Jerusalem sitting upon an ass, to be hailed as King and to receive the praises of the multitude; increase, we beseech Thee, the faith of those who hope in Thee, and mercifully hear the prayers of those who call upon Thee. Let Thy blessing descend on us, O LORD, we beseech Thee; and vouchsafe to bl✠ess these branches of palms (and other trees), that all they who shall carry them may be filled with the gift of Thy Benediction. Grant, therefore, O LORD, that like as the Hebrew children crying Hosanna in the highest ran to meet the same Thy Son JESUS CHRIST our LORD with branches of palms, so also we, bearing branches, may run to meet CHRIST with good works, and attain to everlasting joy. Through the same CHRIST our LORD. R. Amen.

Let us pray.

O GOD, Who gatherest together the dispersed and preservest those who are gathered together; Who didst bless the people meeting CHRIST JESUS and bearing palm branches: bl✠ess also these branches of palms (and other trees), which Thy servants faithfully receive to the blessing of Thy Name: that into whatsoever place they shall be brought, all the dwellers of that place may receive Thy Blessing; so that all sickness and infirmity being driven away, Thy Right Hand may protect those whom It has redeemed. Through the same CHRIST our LORD. R. Amen.

Here the flowers and boughs are sprinkled with holy water and incensed.

Then is said:—

V. The LORD be with you.
R. And with thy spirit.

Let us pray.

O LORD JESUS CHRIST, Son of the living GOD, Maker and Redeemer of the world, Who for our deliverance and salvation didst vouchsafe to come down from the highest heavens, to take flesh and to meet Thy Passion; and Who, when drawing nigh of Thine Own Will to the place of this same Passion, didst ordain that the multitudes who met Thee in the way with palm branches should bless and praise Thee, and with a loud voice cry out, Blessed is the King that cometh in the Name of the Lord; accept now our praises and acknowledgments; and vouchsafe to bl✠ess and hal✠low these flowers and branches of palms and the other trees; that whosoever shall carry anything hence in the obedience of Thy power, may be sanctified with Thy heavenly blessing, and be found meet to obtain remission of sins and the reward of eternal life. Through Thee, JESUS CHRIST our Saviour, who livest and reignest with the FATHER and the HOLY GHOST, GOD for ever and ever. R. Amen.

This done, the palms are immediately distributed by the Celebrant among the Clergy, Clerks, and Choir, and then to the Congregation, to the men first, and afterwards to the women.

Palm Sunday.

[NOTE.—In diſtributing the palm branches, the Prieſt ſhould ſtand facing the people at the loweſt ſanctuary ſtep, with his aſſiſtants on either ſide. He will firſt, however, receive his own palm from the Deacon, who taking it from the altar with a reverence, kiſſes it and preſents it to the Prieſt. The Prieſt then gives palms to the Deacon, Sub-deacon, and other Clergy, and then to the Choir, who kneel before him in order, and kiſs the palm branch, and then the Prieſt's hand. Two Acolytes ſhould bring the palm and other branches to the Aſſiſtant Clergy, who will in regularity ſupply the Prieſt with the ſame. Thoſe of the congregation who receive the palms will come forward one by one in the ſame manner, kneeling before the Prieſt, to kiſs the palm branch and then the Prieſt's hand. The women will only kiſs the palm branch. During the diſtribution of the palms, the choir ſhould ſing the anthem, "Pueri Hebræorum."]

The Proceſſion.

The Proceſſion ſhould take place before the High Celebration. It will be ordered and arranged in the Sacriſty, and, if poſſible, thoſe forming it ſhould go through the outer door of the Sacriſty into the churchyard or church encloſure ; paſſing through which, they ſhould enter the church by the weſt or principal door. It will be arranged on the uſual model and in the cuſtomary order of proceſſions.* If it cannot paſs outſide the church, it ſhould go down one of the aiſles, and up the centre aiſle to the chancel. To the proceſſional croſs (veiled) a bleſſed palm ſhould be attached. All ſhould hold their palms with the right hand, pointing each palm over the right ſhoulder. The Hymn *Gloria, Laus,* &c. ſhould be ſung in Engliſh. If the Hymn be finiſhed before thoſe forming the proceſſion have taken their places, the laſt verſe may be repeated.

---

* *Firſt*, two thurifers, attended by the incenſe boat bearer ; *ſecond*, croſs-bearer, attended by two acolytes ; *third*, choir boys (two and two) ; *fourth*, choir men (two and two) ; *fifth*, the cantors ; *ſixth*, the ceremoniarius ; *ſeventh*, Deacon and Sub-deacon ; *eighth*, the Prieſt-Celebrant. If there be additional Prieſts, they will walk immediately before the ceremoniarius.

Appendix.

Ornaments of the Church.

Sacrarium or Sanctuary.

1. N Altar with a super-altar.
An altar cross or crucifix.
Two altar candlesticks.
Two standard candlesticks.
Candlesticks for additional steps or ledges behind the altar on great feasts.
One desk for service-book for celebrant.
One service-book for celebrant only.
Flower vases.
Antependia of the five "sacred" canonical or church colours.
A super-frontal which may always be red.
A fair white linen cloth.*
The corporal—enclosed in the Burse—or corporal case.
A paten.
A chalice.
One silk chalice veil and pall.

The Credence.

2. The cruets, viz.
One cruet or flagon for the wine.
One cruet for the water of mixture.
A canister for wafers or breads.
A spoon.
A perforated spoon.
One offertory basin or alms-dish.
Offertory bags.†
A chalice-cover of linen and lace for veiling the Blessed Sacrament.
A metal basin.
‡Ciborium, and a metal-plate.
Sundry maniples or napkins.

3. §Ampulla, (only used in the consecration of churches, and in anointing the sick, in which latter case it is called the Holy Oil Stock. The ampulla is

---

* It is well to have one more richly-worked in scarlet and blue for festivals.

† Of the colour of the season.

‡ The ciborium is sometimes used in communicating the people when the number of wafers or breads is too great to be laid upon the paten.

§ "On the morning upon the day of the Coronation early, care is to be taken that the Ampulla be filled with oil, and, together with the Spoon, be laid ready upon the Altar in the abbey church." First rubric in the Form and Order of the Service used in the Coronation of her Majesty Queen Victoria.

"Here the Archbishop lays his hand upon the Ampulla." *Ibid.* (Rubr. in Blessing of the Oil).

"The Queen will then sit down in King Edward's chair placed in the midst of and over against the Altar, with a faldstool before it, whereon She is to be anointed. Four Knights of the Garter hold over her a rich Pall of silk, or Cloth of Gold; the anthem being concluded, the Dean of Westminster taking the Ampulla and Spoon from off the Altar, holding them ready, pouring some of the Holy Oil into the Spoon, and with it the Archbishop anointeth the Queen in the form of a cross:

Ornaments of the Church. 271

also used in the Coronation Service).
4. *For the Piscina.**
   A ewer or large cruet.
   A basin of metal.
   Sundry maniples or napkins.
5. Sedilia, or, in absence thereof, a bench, or,
   Three stools, placed at the south wall of the sanctuary.
6. An aumbrye.
7. A reredos or a dossel.
8. A triptych.
9. Pede-cloth.
   † Three kneeling cushions.
   A Book of the Gospels.
   A Book of the Epistles.

Chancel.
10. Symbols of our Blessed Lord's Passion, &c.
11. Communion rails.‡
12. Houselling cloth or towel of silk.§
13. Corona.
    Branches for additional tapers on great Feasts.
14. Music and Prayer Books.
15. An organ, harmonium, or Regal.
16. Stalls.
17. Low desk for Litany.
18. An eagle desk.
19. A large-sized Bible.
    A Book of Occasional Offices.

"On the crown of the head [on the breast, *the orders for Kings Geo. II. and IV.*] and on the palms of both the hands, saying, Be thou anointed with Holy Oil, as Kings, Priests, and Prophets were anointed; and as Solomon was anointed king by Zadok the priest, and Nathan the prophet, so be you anointed, blessed, and consecrated Queen over this People, whom the Lord your God hath given you to rule and govern, in the Name of the Father, and of the Son, and of the Holy Ghost. Amen.

"Then the Dean of Westminster layeth the Ampulla and Spoon upon the Altar, and the Queen kneeleth down at the faldstool, and the Archbishop standing on the north side of the Altar, saith this prayer or blessing over her." *Ibid.* (The anointing).

Should any sick person urgently wish to be anointed with oil, in accordance with the Scriptural command (S. James v. 14, 15), the Priest would in paying a pastoral visit of this nature, take the oil in an ampulla. This would, of course, be done as a private work of mercy, and (not being at present expressly commanded by the Church of England) not as a portion of any Office in the Book of Common Prayer.

* The following utensils are placed on the credence.

† Not used at Plain Service, and, strictly speaking, not at Solemn Service, except when a Bishop celebrates.

When a cushion is used to support the Service-book, it should not be filled with feathers, but with wool or deer's hair. An altar-desk is, however, much to be preferred to an altar-cushion.

‡ Ordered by Abp. Laud to prevent desecration of the Altar; they are not necessary where there is a rood-screen, but should always be used in default thereof.

§ This is used to cover the communion rails, or to lay on the ground in front of communicants. It may be held by two assistants. "Whilst the king receives, the Bishop [Bishops Geo. II.] appointed for that service shall hold a towel of white silk, or fine linen, before him." Rubric from Coronation Order of Geo. IV.

· Several Books of Common Prayer.
20. A rood-screen,* with cross and lights.
Seat-covers.

For Nave.

21. A lectern.†
A pulpit, (with brass desk—no cushion).
22. A stone font.
A cover for the font.
A padlock for the same.
A baptismal shell, gold or silver-gilt, or,
A scallop shell.
A water bucket.
Several fair linen maniples.
A baptismal cruet.‡
23. Table of Commandments.§
24. Table of prohibited degrees.‖
25. Moveable rails for the solemnization of Holy Matrimony, and for the "Churching of Women," otherwise "kneeling rails," which latter should be near the entrance of the church.
26. An alms-chest.**
Three keys thereof.
27. Bells, *with ropes*.
28. Clocks and chimes, or Sundial.
29. A brazier, or Stove.
30. The Royal Arms of England, which should be placed in an unconspicuous place, and of small dimensions.
31. A bier.
32. Funeral palls of various colours.
A processional cross for the dead.
33. Funeral cloaks.
34. Paintings and images of our Lord, our Lady, the Angels and Saints.
35. Evergreens and flowers.
36. Table of benefactions.
37. Monumental brasses, &c.
38. Lights—sconces; branches, &c.
39. Hangings, tapestry.

The Sacristy, otherwise the Vestry.

40. The parish chest,†† with three locks and keys, containing,
A register of strange preachers.

---

* "Is there any partition between the body of the church and the chancel? and if not, when, and by whom, and by what authority was it taken down?" Cosin's Articles of Visitation, A.D. 1626. See also Hierurgia—Contents XV.

† There should be lectern-hangings of the sacred colours.

‡ This vessel is conveniently retained for private Baptisms, for carrying the water.

§ Canon 82 of 1603¼. See Ecclesiologist, Vol. III. p. 33, which rightly states that there is no authority for placing them east of the chancel. If, however, the table of Commandments is set up at the east of the chancel, it should be distempered in scrolls upon the wall, thus making no construction necessary for them, and allowing them to bear a part in the decorative colouring of the building. They should be as small as possible in size and quite undemonstrative.

‖ Canon 99 of 1603¼.   ** Canon 84 of 1603¼.

†† By statute law, 52 Geo. III. c. 146; by 6 & 7 Will. IV, c. 86; and 1 Victoria, c. 22,

Ornaments of the Church.

A register of baptisms.
  of banns.
  of marriages.
  of burials.
Copies of entries.
41. A chest for Communion plate* and *Instrumenta*.
42. Book registers of the sacred colours.
43. Chests for vestments.
  Book covers, of the sacred colours.
  Cases for service-books.
  Table, writing apparatus, benches, &c.
44. Lavatory.
45. A portable altar.
46. Altar bread-cutters.
  Altar bread-irons.
  Altar canister.
47. Processional candlesticks.
  Torches.
  Lanthorns, processional and otherwise.
  Candle lighters and extinguishers.
  Processional crosses and staves.†
  Cantoral staff.
  Flags, banners, and other decorations, &c.
  Vestry candlesticks.
48. The church-yard crosses, placed on north-side of church-yard.

". . Such ornaments of the Church and of the ministers thereof at all times of their ministration, shall be retained, and be in use, as were in this Church of *England*, by the Authority of Parliament, in the second year of the reign of King *Edward* the Sixth." Rubric, Book of Common Prayer.

Vestments of a Chorister.
49. Cassock.
  Surplice.
  Chorister's cap.

The Vestments of a Deacon. (*Eucharistic*).
50. Cassock.
  Amice.
  Alb.
  Maniple.
  Stole (over left shoulder and fastened under the right arm). Not worn by Epistoler (Subdeacon).
  Dalmatic.
  Tunicle; the Epistoler's (Subdeacon's) vestment.
  Zucchetto and birretta.

Canon 70 is overruled by statute law (52 Geo. III. c. 146, s. 5), which directs the register books to be kept in a dry well-painted iron chest, which shall be constantly kept locked in some dry, safe, and secure place within the usual place of residence of the rector, vicar, curate, or other officiating minister, if resident within the parish or chapelry, or in the parish church or chapel.

* If not kept in the aumbry: the proper position of which is on the Gospel side of the Altar.

† A cross of wood, painted red, should be used in Lent.

(*Choir*).
Caſſock.
Surplice.
Academical hood.
Birretta.
Tippet.*

The Veſtments of a Prieſt.
(*Euchariſtic*).
51. Caſſock.
Amice.
Alb.
Girdle.
Maniple.
Stole (croſſed).
Chaſuble.
Zucchetto and Birretta.

———

Cope (on Good Friday and proceſſions).

(*Choir*).
Caſſock.
Surplice.
Academical hood.
Birretta.
Grey amice (for rectors).
Tippet.

*The Veſtments and Inſignia of an
Archbiſhop or Biſhop.*
(*Euchariſtic*).
52. Buſkins.
Sandals.
Amice.

Alb.
Girdle.
Subcingulum, otherwiſe ſaſh or
  ſuccinctorium.
The pectoral croſs.
The ſtole, worn pendant, not
  croſſed.
The tunic.
The dalmatic.
The gloves.
The ring and guard.
The maniple (after the *Confiteor*,
  according to the Roman rite.
  See Maſkell's Anc. Lit. 150).
The chaſuble.
The mitre (of three ſorts: pre-
  tioſa, aurifrigiata, ſimplex).
The croſier (Archbiſhop), or,
  Paſtoral ſtaff (Biſhop).
The rochet.
The gremial.

———

The cappa magna.
The cope.
The ſurplice.
The pall (Archbiſhop).
The chimere.
The caſſock.

Veſtments of a Sacriſtan.

53. Caſſock.
Cotta or ſurplice.

---

* It would ſeem that literates may lawfully uſe ſtuff-tippets over their ſurplice in lieu of the academical hood, but never over their habit, viz. their "preaching gown," ſhould they uſe that robe. See canon 58. Graduates may uſe *ſilk* tippets over their gowns, the accuſtomed apparel of their degree, but *never* over the ſurplice when officiating. See canons 58 and 74 of 1603/4. When a graduate preaches in his gown he ſhould always wear the academical hood.

Ornaments of the Church.

The Vestments are divided into—

Eucharistic.		Processional.	
Amice.*	Maniple.†	Surplice.	Priest's cap.
Alb.	Stole.	Cope.‡	Academical hood.
Girdle.	Chasuble.	Amyss.	Cassock.

Besides these there are the vestments for the Sacred Ministers.
The dalmatic for the Gospeller.§
The tunic for the Epistoler.

The Sacred Vestments are "the Vestment" (chasuble), cope, stole, maniple, dalmatic, and tunic. The ordinary vestments are the alb, surplice, amice, girdle, hood, &c.

---

* "From the fact that the presence of the amice cannot be detected in our Anglo-Saxon manuscripts, the illuminations in which were done after the period when we know the Anglo-Saxons employed it, we may presume that here it was worn under the alb, and rather hung low upon the shoulders than about the neck, whilst elsewhere it was, and in some places, Milan and Lyons,¹ for example, still is, put on after and above the alb." Rock's Church of our Fathers, vol. i. p. 465.

The old English amice—the *statutable* amice—has a very rich apparel; the modern Roman amice has none, the want being supplied by the neck apparel of the vestment. The modern amice is most convenient, if not so strictly rubrical.

† According to the old English use the Bishop's maniple² was *not* put in the missal at the Gospel, and put on at the *Confiteor*, but the Bishop was vested in it from the beginning.

‡ The maniple and stole are not worn with the cope, which is a Processional and not an Eucharistic vestment. In the *Missa Sicca* on Good Friday he will wear a black stole crossed over his surplice and no maniple.

§ It would seem from the *ad degradandum sacerdotes*, from the Exeter Pontifical (Mask. III. p. 324,) that the dalmatic and tunic are among the Priest's vestments. They are numbered among the Priest's vestments, on the same principle that they are among the episcopal—the greater order including the lower one. It is to be observed, however, that though dalmatic or tunic are worn by a Bishop fully vested, they are not by a Priest, except when he officiates as a Deacon, and consequently lays aside the peculiar garment of a hierophant. The Bishop represents the Church's head, and therefore wears the insignia of *all* orders. The Priest is a consecrator, &c. but when to be degraded, he wears the diaconal vestures as well.

---

¹ "Missale Lugd. A.D. 1510, and a work in French, intituled, *La Recueil des Cérémonies de l'Eglise de Lyon*, l'an 1702. In the more scarce work *Rationale Cærimoniarum Missæ Ambrosianæ*, its author, P. Casola, a Canon of the Metropolitan Church of Milan, whilst describing the 'modus missam celebrandi,' says: Sacerdos præparando se ad missam celebrandum primo induit camisium dicendo . . . . . Dealba me, Domine, &c. . . . . Deinde accipiendo cingulum dicit: Percinge me, Domine, cingulo fidei, &c. . . . . . Accipiendo amictum dicit hunc versum; Pone, Domine, galeam, &c. ut *supra*, fig. *a*, iii."
The old English amice had a richly-embroidered apparel. See Illustration of Priest vested for Holy Communion. The modern Latin amice has no apparel, and therefore cannot be seen. If the former is used, it is most convenient to wear it over the alb; if the latter, under it.—Ed. D. A.

² "Postea exuat capam et induat amictum, albam, et stolam et reliquias circa collum, ac deinceps, tunicam, dehinc dalmaticam *et manipulum*, et tunc sedendo cirothecas manibus imponat et annulum pontificalem magnum, una cum uno parvo strictiore annulo ad tenendum fortius super imponat, et sudarium retortum in manu recipiat ad faciem extergendam . . . ." Exeter Pontifical.

The parishioners are responsible for what is *essential* to Divine Service; the Priest for "*other decent ornaments*," in addition to his liability to maintain " the principal chancel," i.e. the parish ought to provide the vestments for the Priest and the Sacred Vessels for the Sacrament of the altar, and other essential matters. But the canon law, which has *statutable* force, orders the Rector or Vicar not only to provide the other decent ornaments, viz. the altar-lights and altar-cross, but says, " he may be compelled " to do so, by the Ordinary. This then is a distinct answer to a common but erroneous notion—that the clergyman has nothing whatever to do with ordering the ornaments and furniture of the church. As to the "ornaments of the minister," if the churchwardens have not supplied them, they can be compelled to do so, but they can raise no legal objection if on their refusing to supply them, the Priest in his liberality shall furnish them himself ; or if any pious person present them *Deo et ecclesiæ*, the Priest may accept them, and the churchwardens are bound to keep and preserve them ; but ordinarily the views of the parochial Clergy and the churchwardens will doubtless coincide on these matters which pertain to the glory of GOD as much as to the edification of the faithful. See Lawful Church Ornaments, by the Rev. T. W. Perry, pp. 487, 488.

Extracts from Inventories of Church Goods,*

TAKEN IN THE REIGN OF KING EDWARD THE SIXTH,

In the Record Office, at Carlton Ride.

Name of Parish and Date of Inventory.	Crosses.	Candlesticks.	Altar Cloths.	Other Vestments.	Remarks.
S. PAUL'S CATHEDRAL, London, 1552, 6 Edward VI, more than two years after Ridley's Primary Visitation. N.B. It will be remembered that the law as	A precious cross of cristal, set in silver, and all gilt, with many precious stones about him on both sides, and a crown of silver and gilt, set with many and divers precious stones. A fair cross	Two great candlesticks, silver, and parcel gylte; 2 other candlesticks, silver, and parcel gilt; 2 candlesticks of silver, the shafts of cristal.	One rich front for high altar, full of perles; 1 hanging white damask, richly made, with needlework hanging of red velvet, with angels; another of blue silk, with goodly images; another of	241 copes of clothe of gold, silk, satin, velvet, embroidered in gold and colours; 76 tunicles, with gold and embroidery, and figures; 32 vestments, richly embroidered; 41 albes, 9	Several basons of silver. Five fyne towels for the communion. This Inventory is signed by Walter May, Dean, and 3 of the Canons.

* These extracts are selected from Mr. Chambers' Collection (containing an analysis of more than four hundred Inventories) to be found in the Appendix to his " Strictures, Legal and Historical, on the Judgment of the Consistory Court of London, in December, 1855, in the case of Westerton *versus* Liddell." London : Benning.

Extracts from Inventories of Church Goods.

Name of Parish and Date of Inventory.	Crosses.	Candlesticks.	Altar Cloths.	Other Vestments.	Remarks.
to ornaments had now just been altered by the 5 & 6 Edward VI, c. 1.	with the crucifix, and Mary and John, with two angels. A great large cross, with the crucifix enamelled. A plain cross, plated with silver, and gilt, and 4 red stones, set with pearls and stones. Two cristal crosses.		blue silk, with crucifix in midst. Hanging of red silk, with stripes of gold; another of white damask, with flowers of silk; another of red bawdkin, with a crucifix and flowers, with many other hangings and cloths.	corporal cases, and the linen.	
S. Martin Outwich, London, 16th of September, 1552.	A cross of silver, parcel gilt, weighing 45 ounces.	Two fair candlesticks of silver, both weighing 82 ounces.	Five table cloths, one plain, four of diaper. An altar cloth of russet velvet, and a crucifix of gold.	2 fair copes of cloth of gold, red and blue velvet. A vestment of white damask, cope of red velvet, with flowers.	A communion table with a frame.
S. Augustine's next Paul's, London, 1552.	Cross of latteen, another for Lent.	4 pairs of latteen candlesticks.	Upper and nether cloth of gold and red velvet; do. blue velvet flowered and embroidered; do. white velvet, do. white damask, and others; 21 of diaper, 8 plain.	6 old chasubles, 6 copes, 6 albes.	Diaper towels, corporal cases.
S. Botolph's, Aldersgate Street, London, 1552.	Cross, silver-gilt, lxxi. ozs.		Altar cloth, red bawdkin, cloth of gold, another red and blue velvet embroidered, another red and white satin of Bruges, and several others.	2 copes of cloth of gold. 2 red bawdkin, with crosses of gold. Several vestments, deacon and sub-deacon, cloth of gold, white damask, &c.	Cruets of silver. 5 corporal.
S. Nicholas, Cold Abbey, London, 6 Ed. VI.	A crozier staff, cross of silver and gilt, weighing 100 ounces.	2 candlesticks, copper and gilt, 2 candlesticks, silver and gilt, weighing 64 ounces, 2 great candlesticks of latteen.	8 altar cloths of green damask, with flowers, 6 hangings of green satin, 7 do. of white damask, with flowers, 8 altar cloths of white, with drops of blood for Lent, and others.	Cope of red cloth of gold, priest, deacon, sub-deacon; 3 other such. 2 do. with flower-de-luces, 2 copes, blue, with grapes of gold, and several others; vestment of crimson with angels of gold, of crimson with spangles of gold, of green cloth of gold, and	

Appendix

Name of Parish and Date of Inventory.	Crosses.	Candlesticks.	Altar Cloths.	Other Vestments.	Remarks.
S. Christopher, Brede Street, London, 1552.	Silver cross, parcel-gilt, 81 ounces	Pair of silver candlesticks up to 1552.	Three carpets for communion table.	roses of gold; green silk with swans of gold, and several others, some white and black damask and silk; 6 copes for children. Fourteen copes and vestments of silk, satin, &c. blue, green, white, some broidered; twenty vestments very rich.	Falcon of latteen to put Bible on.
Dry Drayton, Cambridgeshire.	2 crosses, copper.	2 great, 2 small candlesticks.	3 altar cloths.	Copes and vestments.	
Graveley, Cambridgeshire.	2 crosses, latteen.	2 candlesticks, silver.	4 altar cloths.	2 vestments, white satin, 2 others red and tawney, 2 copes of silk.	
Haddenham, Cambridgeshire.	Cross, latteen, and 2 cross staves, copper.	2 standards of latteen.	8 table cloths, 10 do.	Copes, vestments, in suits of green, red, &c. silk velvet.	Corporas cloths.
Putney, Surrey.	Cross of wood, plated.	2 great candlesticks.		Copes and chasubles.	
All Saints, Worcester.	Cross, silver and gilt.	2 standards of brass, and others.	9 altar cloths.	Suits of vestments and copes of blue, green, red, and white silk, embroidered, and chasubles do.	
S. Clement's, Worcester.	Cross of brass, cross staff of copper.	Pair of candlesticks, brass.	3 altar cloths, 3 table cloths.	Copes, vestments, with albes of blue, green, silk, velvet, &c.	Corporas cloths.
S. Andrew's, Worcester.	Crucifix, with Mary and John.	Wooden cross, silvered over.	Altar cloths.	Copes, and vestments, and chasubles, 1 blue and red, with albe; 1 with red cross; and two albes 1 red satin.	Corporas cloths.

See also for further lists, Perry's Lawful Church Ornaments, pp. 88—92, 94—108; and Appendix lxv—lxxiii; also Ecclesiologist, No. cxiv. p. 197; and Stephens' edition of B. C. P. Vol. I. fol. 352—365; which prove what most of the Ornaments of the second year were nominatim.

The Judgment of the Privy Council in the cafe of the Knightfbridge Churches.

The things complained of were nine in number:
1. An altar, or holy table, of ftone.
2. A credence table.
3. An altar-crofs.
4. A crofs on chancel fcreen.
5. Altar-lights.
6. Frontals of various colours.
7. Linen cloths edged with lace.
8. A chancel-fcreen and gates.
9. Decalogue not infcribed on eaft wall.

The Judgment of Dr. Lufhington, confirmed by Sir John Dodfon, only permitted Nos. 5 and 8, viz. altar lights and chancel-fcreen and gates.

The Judgment of the Privy Council permitted Nos. 2, 4, 6, 3, viz. the credence-table; the crofs on chancel-fcreen, and the unreftricted ufe of the crofs as a fymbol; frontals of various colours; and the altar-crofs, fo it be not fixed.

The Judgment forbad No. 1, i.e. the altar muft not be a ftructure of ftone, and the fair white linen cloth which covers the *menfa* at celebrations muft not be edged with lace or embroidery (No. 7).

As regards the ftone altar the Court of Appeal has done nothing more than re-affirm Sir H. Jenner Fuft's Judgment in the S. Sepulchre's cafe, while as regards the altar-crofs what is condemned is a *fixed* ftone or metal crofs, not as a crofs, but as part of the ftructure of the altar. What is not condemned is, e.g. a crofs of metal, ftone, or wood, ftanding on the fuper-altar.

The Judgment has authorized the following important principles:—

a. In the chancel and fcreen, the principle of choral worfhip and the feparation of orders in the congregation.

b. In the credence, the doctrine of an "Oblation in the Eucharift."

c. In the crofs on the altar and on the chancel-fcreen, the principle of fymbolical allufion, and adherence of the Church of England to hiftorical antiquity.

d. In the ufe of frontals of various colours, the facrednefs of the Chriftian year, and the ritual commemoration of faints and martyrs.

e. In the altar-lights, not only a fymbolical allufion of efpecial propriety, but what is far greater, a relative dignity as due to the place and time of the special Christian mystery, and a denaturalizing influence.

N.B.—The following comment* from the pen of an eminent Barrister, the Recorder of Salisbury, deserves a careful attention.

" To the Editor of the ' Union.'

" Sir,—As I have been requested by various persons to state in your columns the legal effect and bearing of the late 'Judgment' in the case of 'Westerton v. Liddell,' for the guidance of clergymen and churchwardens, I proceed to do so as shortly as I can. It will be convenient to divide the subjects into three classes: first—the things directed to be removed or altered; secondly—those directed to be retained; thirdly—those which remain yet in dispute; or about which the Court said nothing.

I.

" First, then, as to the things which the judgment orders to be removed or altered.

" 1. The 'fair white linen cloth' upon the table at the time of the celebration seems designated in the judgment by the terms, ' The embroidered linen and lace used on the communion table.' This then must be wholly white, and without any lace, embroidery, or other ornament; but, as the Court distinctly stated that they were 'not disposed in any case to restrict within narrower limits than the law has imposed the discretion which within those limits is justly allowed to congregations,' I conceive that fringes, borders, and interwoven patterns, may be used of the finest and most beautiful and delicate variety, so long as they are not attached or worked by hand, but are textile; only a part or a mere prolongation of the tissue of the linen cloth itself, and not additions thereto. Whether the 'fair linen cloth,' for covering over the remains of the Sacrament after use, and not directed to be white, is included in this prohibition, will be presently considered.

" 2. Next, as to the altar itself. Every stone altar or table, constructed of stone or of any other material but wood, of whatever shape it may be, is unauthorized; and may be removed, if already erected, by due course of law. It must be a structure of wood—'a table in the ordinary sense of the word, at which, or around which, the communicants might be placed in order to partake,' and moveable. I see no reason, however, why a small slab of stone may not be let into the surface at the place of consecration. There are no directions that the table shall be wholly of wood; and this small piece would not affect its moveability, or deprive it of the character of a table of wood.

" 3. As to the removal of stone altars already in existence, the Injunctions of Elizabeth declare that none are to be taken down except by authority. For the removal or alteration of any part of the church, it is well known that a faculty is required: hence it would be illegal for any incumbent or churchwarden to remove or change any stone altar without such faculty; nor has the Archdeacon any right to order the removal without such a faculty.

" 4. All ornaments *used for Divine Service*, other than those prescribed by the First Prayer Book of Edward VI. are unlawful; therefore the use of crosses in the service is excluded by the Book of Common Prayer: consequently, held the Council, crosses *affixed to communion tables* are unlawful [the conclusion is not supported by the premises]. Another reason given for the removal was, that such a cross was not consistent with the letter or spirit of the direction that the whole table be covered with the linen cloth, or that the table should be flat and moveable. How far moveable crosses placed on the table, or above it, are allowed, shall be presently considered.

---

* Reprinted by permission of the author.

II.

"Next with regard to those things which the Court refused to disturb or change, and which it therefore especially authorized as legal.

"1. 'A rood-screen of carved wood separating the chancel from the nave.'

"2. 'Two brazen gates attached to the rood-screen at the only point of communication with the chancel, which are ordinarily kept closed or locked, but open during Divine Service.'

"3. All 'crosses and other articles set up in churches being ornaments in the sense of decorations' and not used in the services. 'All crosses, not crucifixes, *used as mere emblems of the Christian faith*, and not as objects of superstitious reverence, may be lawfully erected as architectural decorations;' and, in particular, a wooden cross of large size set up in the middle of the chancel-screen is lawful. Under these words, I think that a moveable or fixed cross of metal, or any other material, set up on a super-altar or bracket or ledge, which is separated from and unconnected with the altar, although behind it—such cross being a reasonable distance above the altar so as not to appear used as a 'part of the service'—is lawful and unobjectionable.

"4. 'Two massive metal candlesticks of elaborate patterns upon the said altar, with candles therein, lighted only when required for the purpose of giving necessary light.' But this is a decision only of the Consistory Court, not of the Privy Council, for there was no appeal; and from the language of the Court above, as to the ornaments for worship, it is somewhat doubtful whether they would have been allowed to remain *on* the altar.

"5. A credence or side-table of wood or marble of any kind, without restriction of material or situation, as being 'consistent with, and subsidiary to, the service,' and 'properly an adjunct of the communion-table,' on the ground that—

"6. 'It is the true meaning of the rubric that, at a certain point of the Communion Service, the minister shall place the bread and wine on the communion table; but where it is to be placed before is nowhere stated. In practice they are usually placed on the communion table before the commencement of the service; but *this is not according to the order prescribed;*' so that the usual careless practice is expressly declared to be unlawful.

"7. Altar cloths of any colour, shape, variety, and material, with or without work or embroidery or gilding, subject to the discretion of the Ordinary. Those used at S. Barnabas' were all exhibited to the Privy Council; and, therefore, have express and the highest approval and sanction of the Supreme Ordinary of the kingdom. They were of white, red, violet, dark violet, and green; they were embroidered and highly decorated; were in several pieces with side-hangings, frontals, &c. They were used in a peculiar order of succession, which was expressly forbidden by Dr. Lushington; but, his decision being reversed, as expressly *permitted* by the Privy Council—viz. white, from Christmas Eve to the Octave of the Epiphany (except S. Stephen and the Holy Innocents); from Easter Eve to Vigil of Pentecost, on Trinity Sunday, and the Feasts relating to our Lady; Conversion of S. Paul, S. John Baptist, S. Michael, S. Luke, All Saints. Red, on the Vigil of Pentecost to the next Saturday; and on all other Feasts. Violet, during Lent and Advent, Ember-week in September. Dark violet, on Good Friday and funerals. Green, on all other days. On principle, however, any other colours, and any other succession of colours—as, for instance, the ancient English use of Sarum—is permissible; which, as I think, is more desirable and according to precedent and authority.

III.

"Next, as to those points which the judgment left unsettled.

"1. The shape of the Altar. The Consistory Court left that at S. Paul's, which is in the shape of an altar tomb, untouched, and therefore sanctioned it. There was no appeal from this decision: consequently, the Privy Council pronounced no decision nor intimated any opinion on the point, except the general direction that it must be a table, in the ordinary sense of the word, flat and moveable, and capable of being covered with a cloth. The east end or chancel was recognized as the proper place.

"2. The super-altar was sanctioned at S. Paul's by Dr. Lushington; and although no direct decision was, or could be, made upon this point by the Privy Council, as there was no appeal, yet I think it is clear the opinion of their lordships was that it ought not to be placed *on the* table itself, 'which must be flat, capable of being covered with a cloth, at or around which the communicants may be placed.' Besides the cross being affixed to the super-altar at S. Barnabas' was one of the reasons why it was to be removed. I therefore recommend that the super-altar should be a stone or marble ledge, supported on a solid plynth unconnected with the table; but placed immediately behind it, and reaching a reasonable height above it.

"3. The cross and candles may be placed on this ledge; and the cross may, I conceive, be moveable or fixed at pleasure; but fixed would be preferable, in order that it may assume the character of an architectural decoration.

"4. As to the 'fair linen cloth' to cover the remains of the Sacrament and the chalice, but not by the rubric directed to be white, and the chalice veils—complaint was made against 'the other articles of linen used at the time of the celebration;' but Dr. Lushington took no notice of this point, and his order (which is that now confirmed) entirely omits all reference to them (see pp. 22, 68, of printed case); and applies to coverings of the communion table only. This order is in these words, 'To take away all cloths at present used in the church for covering the structure as a communion table, and to substitute one only covering for such purpose of silk or other decent stuff; and, further, to remove any cover used at the time of the ministration of the Sacrament, worked or embroidered with lace, or otherwise ornamented; and to substitute a fair white linen cloth without lace or embroidery, or other ornament, to *cover the communion table* at the time of ministration.' Since this order clearly refers to coverings of the table only, and does not notice the others, I think that the 'fair linen cloth' may have lace or embroidery and colour as before, as well as the chalice veils.

"5. The Privy Council expressly laid down that the rubric in the First Book of Edward was the rule for ornaments and 'dresses' of the ministers; and since that directs that, 'at the time of the Holy Communion, the Priest that shall execute the holy ministry *shall* put upon him the vesture appointed for that ministration—that is to say, a white alb plain, with a vestment or cope'—and the assistant Priests and Deacons '*shall* likewise have upon them the vestures appointed for their ministry—that is to say, albs with tunicles;' since also the present rubric directs 'that such ornaments of the ministers at all times of their ministration *shall be* retained *and be* in use,' I have no hesitation in affirming that the use of a vestment or cope for the ministering Priest, and of albs with tunicles for the assistant Priests and Deacons at the celebration of Holy Communion, is obligatory on all Priests and Deacons of the Church of England. That a 'vestment' means a chasuble is evident from the inventories, which use the words indifferently; and because the only two vestments named are chasubles and copes.

"Lastly, with regard to lights. As to these there would be no difficulty, but that the Privy Council have, most culpably, refused to decide the point as to the parliamentary authority of the ancient Ecclesiastical Constitutions, Canons, and Common Law, which expressly required 'candles to be lighted while the solemnities of the mass were being performed.'

"Omitting, however, all reference to this question, I think it plain that *lights* at the celebration of Holy Communion are lawful, though not obligatory, for, amongst many others, the following reasons:—

"1. The cross was retained as a decoration, by the Privy Council, because 'an emblem of the Christian faith,' 'held in great repute and used by the early Christians,' 'used from the earliest period of Christianity,' 'not necessarily superstitious,' 'a memorial of the most momentous event of Christianity.' Now, Prudentius, in the fourth century, tells us that 'throughout all the churches in the East, at the Gospel, lights were brought forth at noon day,' under the type of corporal light to indicate that light—'Thy word is a lamp unto my feet and a light to my paths.' The fourth Canon of the Apostles mentions 'lamps at the Holy Offering.' Isidore of Seville speaks of the same thing—'This light signifies the light we read of in the Gospel.' Lyndewode also, commenting on Reynolds' Constitution, says—'The candles so burning signify CHRIST Himself, Who is the brightness of Eternal Light.' The lights before the Sacrament—(*i.e.* the *celebrated*, not the *reserved*, Sacrament, as may be easily proved)—of Edward's Injunctions, were 'for the signification that CHRIST is the true Light of the world.' Hence these lights were, like the cross, primitive; and had no relation to superstitions, and are used as 'emblems of the Christian faith.'

"2. Because candlesticks appear as part of the furniture of very numerous churches in the inventories, up to the end of Edward VIth's reign.

"3. Because the parliamentary authority of the Injunctions of Edward VI. requiring these lights 'to remain still,' was recognized by both the Superior Courts as in force in the second year of Edward VI. and has never been repealed.

"4. The express statement of Cosin that, *by virtue of this rubric and those Injunctions*, lights were in very general use during the reigns of Elizabeth and James I. and the statement of Fuller to the same effect, is strong historical evidence.

"5. Because the 'lights' are quite 'consistent with the present service,' like the credence; and with the idea of a feast and a table.

"6. Because other Protestant bodies use them, as the Lutherans do, and Luther did.

"7. Because, even regarding the 'high altar' as abolished, the place WHERE they are to be put is immaterial: they are adjuncts of 'the *Sacrament*'—not of the Altar.

"8. Because the declaration of the Court, that crosses are to be excluded from the service because not mentioned in Edward's First Book, cannot apply to 'lights,' which are in force by virtue of another and independent authority of Parliament co-existing in that second year, and not repealed by that book.

"9. That 'lights' are 'decorations,' not 'ornaments,' as interpreted by the Privy Council; and are not forbidden to be used at any time or any place.

"10. For reasons formerly given, and to avoid raising some of these questions, I should recommend these 'lights,' which may issue from candles or be of gas, should be placed on the ledge or super-altar now to be raised behind the table, and be some distance above it, or be in the shape of standards before the table.

"I am, Sir, yours faithfully,
"JOHN DAVID CHAMBERS.

"*Lincoln's-Inn, April* 2, 1857."

"*To the Editor of the 'Union.'*

"SIR,—I wish to make the following additions to my opinion on the 'Legal Effect of the Judgment in the Westerton case.'

"1. The statute 1 Mary, c. 3, still in force, subjects to imprisonment for three months 'any person who, of his own power or authority, pulls down or defaces *any altar or altars*, cross or crucifix, that now is, or hereafter may be, in any church or churchyard.' By Moone's case (1 Sir T. Jones, 159), it was decided this statute applied to the present office and services; and a similar decision was given 1 Glover *v.* Hynde, 1 Mod. 168.

"2. By this statute, coupled with the declarations of the Court of Privy Council, churchyard crosses are legalized and protected.

"3. With respect to 'Lights before the Sacrament,' an additional argument in their favour arises from the fact that the Injunctions of Edward are referred to as being law in a rubric at the end of the Communion Office of Edward's First Book.

"I am, Sir, yours,
"J. D. CHAMBERS.

"*Lincoln's-Inn, April* 15, 1857."

N.B.—In mediæval times the altar stood some way from the east wall, in front of a retable or small reredos, which was a wall built from the ground, between which and the east wall was generally the baldachin for reliquary and suspension of ciborium. This retable or reredos served as the super-altar of the present day, and on it were placed the candlesticks, and crucifix or cross.

The editor has seen this arrangement adopted, and it is very effective; but the super-altar is to be preferred for the cross and lights.

On the Music of the English Church.

THE authoritative directions of the English Church since the Reformation touching Church Music are few and vague.

The allusion to the singing of the "*Psalter or Psalms of David*," borne on the title-page of our present Prayer Book "*Pointed as they are to be sung or said in churches;*" certain rubrics in the body of the work;—the XLIXth of Queen Elizabeth's Injunctions; and the XIVth Canon of 1603-4, which begins thus,—"The Common Prayer shall be said or *sung* distinctly and reverently," are perhaps all the directions we can adduce as bearing the authority of written law upon this subject.

But the written law has all along been consonant with and explainable by certain musical traditions and customs, continued to a great extent in the actual uses of choirs, and noted in musical directions and collections of written or printed music.

The text-book prepared at the same time with Edward the Sixth's first Prayer Book by Marbeck, and printed the following year, 1550, bears evidence of the adoption by Archbishop Cranmer, and those who acted with him in settling the uses of the remodelled Services, of that species of music called *Plain Song*, which had been used in the Church Catholic from time immemorial, but had, it would seem, too generally given way, at least in the ordinary Services, attended by the people, to an "operose" and intricate style of harmonized music in which the people could neither take part, nor (even if they knew Latin) perceive the "sentence," or meaning of the words. In music, therefore, as in doctrine, the appeal was from modern innovations and corruptions of Catholic antiquity, to the uses of an earlier and purer age. Plain Song had been the music of the Church from the beginning: it was restored to more general use in the Reformed Church of England. What that Plain Song was—what were its rules, how copious, how diversified, may be learnt from the ancient books in use both before and at the time of the Reformation which have escaped the fanatical destruction of things sacred during the Great Rebellion, and the subsequent Usurpation. The Antiphonarium gave the Plain Song music for the ordinary daily Offices; the Gradual that for the Service of the Mass. The former included the chants for the Psalms, the Antiphons for all the year, as also the hymns, which (as is well known to ritualists) were as definitely appointed in their several places as the Canticles, Psalms, or Collects. The Gradual contained Introits, Sequences, Glorias, Credos, and all the musical portions of the Liturgy properly so called.

Thus (as has been satisfactorily shown by Mr. Dyce in the Preface to his Book of Common Prayer with plain-tune, after the model of Marbeck) Plain Song was "not an indeterminate kind of melody, but a mode of intonating, chanting and singing in the Church, which implies an adherence to certain rules, and to a great extent the use of certain well-known melodies, that are severally appropriated to particular parts of the Service."

Queen Elizabeth's XLIXth Injunction is entirely confirmatory of this view, enjoining "a modest and distinct song" to be "so used in all parts of the common prayers, that the same may be as plainly understanded as if it were read without singing," while at the same time permission is given for "the singing in the beginning or in the end of the Morning and Evening Prayer, of a hymn or such-like song to the praise of Almighty GOD in the best sort of melody and music that may be conveniently devised, having respect that the sentence of the hymn may be understanded and perceived." This permission was doubtless confirmatory of the use previously established and subsequently retained of singing under the title of Anthems more elaborate music by trained choirs in addition to the Plain Song of more wide and general application.

The difficulty of translating the ancient hymns into English verse, and the substitution of metrical translations of the Psalms after the example of Clement Marot, cir. 1540, in Paris, and of Beza in Strasburg (1545), frustrated the wishes of Archbishop Cramner that these most Catholic compofitions should be adopted to vernacular use in the Reformed Church of England: Sternhold and Hopkins in Edward VIth's reign, and Tate and Brady in that of William and Mary furnished the songs of most general adoption in this country, to the utter confusion of men's views and feelings. The Psalter pointed for singing came too generally to be used as, and called the *reading Psalms*, while the metrical versions had transferred to them both the phraseology and the interest which attached of old to the chanted Psalms, and thus the evangelical Hymns of S. Hilary, S. Ambrose, Prudentius, Sedulius, S. Eunodius, and S. Gregory, and those of the subsequent era of Venantius Fortunatus, Venerable Bede, Adam of S. Victor, and still later of Santolius Victorinus, were entirely lost to the people. And if the natural craving of the renewed nature in any case insisted upon a more direct tribute of Christian praise and thanksgiving in the songs of the Church, it came to be fed with a pasture not wholesome nor satisfying, in a modern hymnody too often of doubtful orthodoxy and of undoubted sickliness. The music of these metrical Psalms and Hymns (with the exception of those melodies which have come down to our times from more Catholic sources, and a few which have been composed in a similar tone of masculine grandeur) has grown from year to year more and more secular and effeminate; while, from the neglect of vocal music, as an element in clerical and general education, the actual singing of them has ceased to be what it was originally, a national accomplishment in which all the people could and did join. So that the very means taken in an uncatholic spirit to secure the greatest amount of congregational singing has been one of the chief causes of the entire loss, speaking generally, of this essential feature of Catholic worship.

Looking at the history and present condition of music in the Church of England, it would seem that what is required whenever it may be attained is a full Choral Service of the Plain Song order.*

Easy Anthems or Hymns should be sung in the appointed places in Matins and Evensong, and also immediately before them (see Par. 122, note *), and Hymns may also be added at the close of one Service when followed immediately by another or by a Sermon.†

It is to be observed that there is not the least warrant in the Prayer Book

---

* Full directions for which are given in the Rev. Thomas Helmore's Manual of Plain Song, and the Accompanying Harmonies, founded upon Marbeck's Book before mentioned.

† For Anthems, see Boyce's Cathedral Music, "*Anthems* and Services," (printed originally by J. Burns; sold by R. Cox and Co.) The Parish Choir (Ollivier; Pall Mall,) and the Motett Society's Collection of Ancient Music. For Translations of the Ancient Catholic Hymns in like

for the too common diſtinction drawn between the cathedral and parochial Service. The rubrics are alike for both. Nor is the difference of congregations ſuch as to warrant any material difference. What is edifying in the country cathedral is equally ſo in moſt large towns; nor is it at all true that the poor in villages and hamlets are leſs ſuſceptible of the hallowed influence of ſacred muſic properly introduced in the Service of the Church than their more wealthy and urbane fellow countrymen. In large manufacturing diſtricts the taſte for Choral harmony is generally very ſtrong, and ought not to be deprived of its due gratification in the higheſt of all human employments.

The rule to be followed is, that "all things ſhould be done to edification;" and this involves the proper uſe of all available means, and lawful appliances—the only bar to the uſe of the higheſt ſtyle of Choral Service properly regulated in every Church is the inability to perform it. In proportion as zeal for the honour and glory of GOD's worſhip inſpires the miniſters and people of any particular Church, ſo will their worſhip riſe in the ſcale of muſical grandeur and choral dignity.

All the inſtrumental aid which can be made ſubſervient to general devotion and that of the performers themſelves, ought by inference to be conſidered *lawful*, though perhaps a good organ and a competent organiſt are all that will be found in general *deſirable*.

---

metre ſet to their original tunes as preſerved in the Sarum Breviary, Hymnal and Gradual. See Hymnal Noted under the ſanction of the Eccleſiological Society with Accompanying Harmonies (J. A. Novello).

Glossary.

BLUTION. The wine poured into the chalice, and also the wine and water poured into the same and over the Priest's fingers, after the consumption of the Blessed Sacrament. The water should exceed the wine in quantity. It is drunk by the celebrant, and called the Ablution. There are always two Ablutions. See *Purification*.

ACOLYTES. Servers or assistants at Solemn Service to the Sacred Ministers; their special office being to bear the cruets containing the wine and water for the celebration of the Holy Eucharist. In the Latin Church they are the fourth or highest of the minor Orders.

ACOLYTES' CANDLESTICKS should have a round, or, more correctly, a triangular base; they should be smaller than those on the altar.

ALB. The lawn or linen vestment worn by the Priest and Sacred Ministers at the celebration of the Holy Eucharist.

ALLELUIA in the Roman Missal is sung after the gradual at Easter, on those Sundays when the Church *especially* commemorates the Resurrection, and on other Festivals.

ALMS-BASIN. A dish, generally of metal, in which to "present and place" the offertory on the altar according to the rubric.

ALMUCE. See *Amyss*.

ALTAR CARD. (1.) A tablet containing certain parts of the Communion Office; (2.) the square covering of linen, stiffened with card, more commonly called the pall.

ALTAR CARPET. (1.) The pede-cloth on the floor before the altar; (2.) the altar-cloth is so called in Canon LXXXII.

ALTAR CURTAINS. Drapery about the reredos, or dossal, varying with proper colour of the season.

ALTAR, PORTABLE. A small slab of wood or stone, which can be carried about for private celebrations.

AMICE. The vestment which is worn on the shoulders over the cassock and covers the neck —turning over the Alb.

AMPULLA. See *Stock*.

AMYSS. A cape lined with fur.

ANAPHORA. The part of the Liturgy of the East, beginning at the "*Sursum corda*," including the solemn prayer of Consecration, to the end.

ANTEPENDIUM. See *Frontal*.

ANTHEM. The variable Antiphon after the Third Collect at Matins and Evensong.

Glossary

APPAREL. A square or oblong ornament richly embroidered, stitched on the collar of the amice, and at the bottom of the alb before and behind, and on the wrists, and also on the Deacon's dalmatic.

ASPERGILLUM. The sprinkler for Holy Water, originally made of the herb hyssop. Cf. Numbers xix. 18, and Exod. xii. 22.

ASPERSORIUM. A Holy Water brush.

AUMBRYE. A recess for the preservation of the Sacred Vessels, and for the Holy Oil Stock.

BENATURA. A Holy Water stoup.

BIER. A portable carriage for the dead.

BIRRETTA. The square cap worn by clerics over the zucchetto.

BOAT. The vessel that holds the Incense before it is put with a spoon into the censer or thurible.

BUGIA. A hand candle. It is only used in Pontifical Offices, when it is placed on the altar near the Service-book, and at other times held for the Bishop by an assistant Priest.

BURSE. The case for the corporal.

CEREMONIARIUS. The officer whose duty it is to attend to the ecclesiastical order and arrangement in all functions. A director of the ceremonies is as frequently a cleric as a lay person.

CANISTER. The metal case in which altar breads are kept—so called in the old inventories.

CANON. The Prayer of Consecration. In the West that part of the Mass beginning with "*Te igitur*" and finishing with the "*Pater Noster.*" So called because it is the Rule to be rigidly followed.

CANTICLES. The *Benedicite, Benedictus, Jubilate, Magnificat, Cantate Domino, Nunc dimittis, Te Deum,* and *Deus misereatur*.

CANTORIS STALL. The first *return* stall on the left on entering the choir. The Precentor's stall.

CAPPA. A rich dress worn in the Latin Communion by Bishops, &c.

CAPPA MAGNA. A cope with richer orphreys than the ferial one. It is authorized by the old English Canons and Provincial Constitutions.

CASSOCK. The garment worn by ecclesiastics under their official vestments; usually black, and for Bishops purple.

CAUTEL. A caution or direction, as to rightly and duly administering the Sacraments, especially the Sacrament of the Altar, to which alone it is applied in the mediæval Service-books.

CELEBRANT. The Priest who celebrates the Holy Eucharist.

CELEBRATION. The administration of the Sacrament of the Altar. In the Latin Communion the term is also applied to the singing of solemn Vespers.

CENSER. The vessel in which incense is burned.

CHALICE COVER. "The fair linen cloth" with which the Blessed Sacrament is covered after communion of the faithful.

CHALICE VEIL. The silk cover of the chalice when it is first put on the altar.

CHASUBLE OR CHESIBLE. The sacrificial vestment worn by the Priest at the Holy Eucharist. Hence called emphatically "*the* Vestment."

CHIMERE. The Bishop's ordinary dress, worn over the rochet. It is now made of black satin—its colour was formerly scarlet.

CHOIR. The Chancel.

CHRISM. A mixture of balsam and oil, used in the Latin Church in baptisms, confirmation, orders, consecration of churches, &c. We do not use it except for the sick, unless it be ordered by the Bishop in the last-named rite.

CHRISMATORY. A Holy Oil ſtock or caſe, containing three bottles of ſacred oils; for baptiſm, confirmation, and unction of the ſick.

CHRISOM. Sometimes incorrectly ſpelled Chriſm as in the Firſt Book of Edw. VI. the white veſture formerly put upon a child at baptiſm.

CIBORIUM. The veſſel in which the LORD'S BODY is placed inſtead of on a paten when many are to be communicated. Where a Pyx has been preſerved, it is proper to uſe it for this purpoſe.

CINCTURE. The girdle of a caſſock, &c.

COMMUNION. The receptionary part of the Sacrament of the Euchariſt.

COMMUNION or HOUSELLING CLOTH is a white linen cloth ſpread over the rails at the time of the Communion, or is held for the communicants by acolytes or other miniſters.

COMPLINE FUNCTION. See *Prime Function*.

COPE. The veſtment uſed at Solemn Veſpers, proceſſions, litany, &c. &c.

CORNER. The technical term for the extremities of the weſt ſide of the altar.

CORONA. A crown or circlet ſuſpended from the roof or vaulting of a church to hold tapers or gas jets—*corona lucis*.

CORPORAL. The white linen cloth on which the Bleſſed Sacrament is laid. It is ſpread at the oblation of the elements over the "fair white linen cloth" which covers the ſuperfrontal at a celebration.

COTTA. A ſhort ſurplice.

CREATURES. The "matter" of the Sacrament (ſee *Elements*). So called from being compacted of created things.

CRUETS. Small flagons to contain wine and water for the Euchariſt.

DALMATIC. The veſtment of the Deacon at the Holy Euchariſt.

DECANI STALL. The firſt *return* ſtall on the right upon entering the choir. The *Dean's* ſtall.

DESK. The ſtand placed on an altar for ſupporting the Service-book.

DIPTYCH. In the ancient Liturgies tablets containing the names of the dead for whoſe ſouls the Prieſt was to pray. The modern altar-piece is derived from theſe folding tablets. See *Triptych*.

DIVINE SERVICE. The ordinary and ſpecially the Euchariſtic Service of the Church.

DOSSEL. A piece of embroidered needle-work, ſtuff, ſilk, or cloth of gold, hung at the back of a throne or altar, but more particularly the latter.

DUPLICATION. A ſecond celebration by the ſame Prieſt on the ſame day.

ELEMENTS. The materials (*materies*) uſed in the Sacraments, appointed for that purpoſe by our LORD Himſelf—technically called the "matter."

ELEVATION. The lifting up of the Bleſſed Sacrament after conſecration.

EPISTOLER. The cleric who reads the Epiſtle and fulfils the function formerly performed by the Sub-deacon of the celebration. In ſome cathedral ſtatutes the Epiſtoler and Goſpeller are called Sub-deacon and Deacon.

EVE. The day before a Feſtival when not faſted. It is alſo uſed for its Evenſong, viz. its firſt veſpers.

FALDSTOOL. A moveable ſtool. It is uſed particularly as the Biſhop's "chair" of the rubric.

FANON. See *Maniple*.

FERIA. A week-day on which no holiday falls. Monday is of courſe Feria ii. Sunday has its proper Dominical Service.

FLAGON. The veſſel in which the wine for the Holy Euchariſt is brought to the credence-table.

FOOT-PACE. See *Platform*.

Glossary.

FORM. The Sacramental words. Form is also used for "matter" or the outward part of the Sacrament in the doctrinal statement at the end of the first Book of Homilies. "Of the due receiving of his (CHRIST'S) Blessed BODY and BLOOD under the form of Bread and Wine." "Form" is usually the matter together with the words.

FRACTION. The breaking of the Priest's own Bread.

FRONTAL. The vestment hung in front of the altar, called also the *antependium*.

GIRDLE. The cord that girds the alb, usually made of white cotton, about three yards long.

GOSPELLER. The cleric who reads the Gospel and performs the function of the Deacon of the celebration; the name is given to the Deacon, because in the Ordering of Deacons, authority is given to them "*to read the Gospel in the Church of* GOD."

GRADUAL. In the Roman Missal the psalm or part of a psalm that is sung after the Epistle.

GREMIAL. A silken apron placed on the lap of a Bishop, when sitting, during certain parts of the Celebration of the Holy Eucharist.

HOLY WATER VESSEL, THE. This should be an earthen vessel with a cover, from which the vessels and stoups of the church are supplied. It should be emptied and wiped out immediately after use.

HOUSEL. A Saxon word, meaning the Blessed Eucharist. "He (the Priest) halloweth GOD'S Housel, as our SAVIOUR commanded." Elfric's Canons, A.S. 957. Johnson derives it from the Gothic *bunsel*, a sacrifice, or *hostia*, dim. *hostiola*, Latin.

INTROIT. The psalm sung before the celebration of the Holy Eucharist, when the Priest stands at the altar.

INVITATORY. A passage of Scripture, proper for the day, used in ancient times before the "*Venite.*" Our *V*. "Praise ye the LORD," with the *R*. is our present unvarying Invitatory. In the Communion Service the second Exhortation is the Invitatory.

LAVABO. The *secreta oratio* of the Priest when water is poured on his fingers before the Prayer of Oblation.

LAVATORY. A water-drain in the sacristy, where the Priest washes his hands before vesting.

LECTERN. A moveable desk from which the Lessons are read. The Epistle and Gospel are also sometimes read from a lectern. In reading from a lectern the hands should touch the sides thereof.

LESSER LITANY. "The LORD have mercy," &c. ushering in the LORD'S Prayer in the Prime and Compline functions.

LITANY DESK. A low moveable desk at which the Litany is sung.

LITURGY. The celebration of the Holy Eucharist.

LORD'S SUPPER. The last meal of our LORD, when He instituted the Holy Eucharist.

LOW MASS. The plain celebration of the Holy Eucharist, which is simply said; there is no choir, and the Priest is attended by a single assistant called a server, vested in cassock and *cotta*.

MANIPLE. The vestment worn on the left arm of the Priest, Deacon, and Sub-deacon at the Holy Eucharist. This word is also used for any kind of napkin, as that used to wipe the Priest's fingers at Holy Baptism.

MANTELLETUM. A habit used in the Latin Communion by Bishops on ordinary occasions; the chimere is worn in its place with us.

MASS. The name of the office for the Holy Eucharist in the Western Church.

MATERIES. See *Elements*.

MEMORIAL COLLECT. When two holydays fall together, the service of the superior one is used, and the collect of the inferior day is said after that of the Office of the Feast, as its *memorial*.

MENSA. The top or table of the altar.
MILITANT CHURCH PRAYER. See *Oblation*.
MINISTER. One who ministers before GOD in a great action as the Priest in the Holy Eucharist, who is thence called "the principal Minister;" those who minister or serve the Priest as the Gospeller and Epistoler (Deacon and Sub-deacon)—Sacred Ministers; acolytes as ministering to the Sacred Ministers. The Officiant at Matins and Evensong is also so called, as ministering in Divine offices; a layman acting as server, or as Epistoler, or as a reader of the Lessons is also a "Minister."
MINISTERIUM. The Epistle corner of the altar. So called from the Sacred Ministers preparing the chalice, &c. there when the elements are removed from the credence.
MISSA SICCA. The Dry Service—neither Communion nor Consecration, but a sham rite, unfortunately peculiar to the modern Church of England. It includes the Prayer of Oblation, with the oblations omitted, and concludes with one or more of the post-Communion Collects, and the Blessing.
MONSTRANCE. A transparent pyx for processions, or when the Host is exhibited; a casket for the exhibition of the Sacrament.
MORSE. The clasp of the cope.
MOZZETTA. A cape with a small hood worn by canons and others in the Latin Communion.
MUNDATORY. See *Purificator*.
NAVICULA. See *Boat*.
NORTH-SIDE. The part of the altar to the left of the Midst as the Priest stands in front facing the east.
OBLATION, Prayer of. The prayer for the whole state of CHRIST's Church, after the elements are placed upon the altar, and during which the Oblation of them is made.
OCTAVE. The eighth day after any principal Feast of the Church. The intervening days are technically called "of," or "within the octave."
OFFERTORIUM, OFFERTORY. That part of the Liturgy where the lesser oblation is made.
OFFICE. Matins and Evensong.
OFFICIANT. The Priest who sings the Divine Office, &c.
OILS. There are three sorts, viz. the Chrism, the Holy Oil of the sick, and Holy oil.
OIL (Holy). Used now in the Coronation Service instead of Chrism. It was formerly used in baptisms, and thence called holy oil of catechumens.
OIL (Holy) of the sick. Oil consecrated by the Bishop or Priest for the anointing of sick persons.
OIL STOCK. The vessel containing consecrated oil.
ORATIONES. The collects.
ORPHREYS. A band or bands of gold or embroidery affixed to vestments.
OSTENSION. The showing of the chalice after consecration by lifting it up above the head of the celebrant, so that it may be visible.
PALL. A small square, of linen on both sides, cardboard in the midst, with which the chalice is covered. It is about eight inches square and should have no fringe.
PALLIUM or PALL. The ensign of jurisdiction worn by Archbishops.
PARTICLES. The wafers or breads used for the communion of the faithful. Particle is also applied to the crumb of bread with which the Priest cleanses his thumb after the anointing of the sick, &c.
PASCHAL. Of or belonging to Easter.
PASCHAL CANDLESTICK, THE—was placed on the Gospel side of the choir, and lighted during

Mafs and Vefpers from Holy Saturday till Afcenfion. The ftaff had formerly a lectern attached, from which was fung the *Exultet*.

PASTORAL STAFF. The crooked ftaff of a Bifhop or Abbot, the former turning outwards as reprefenting external, the latter inwards as fhowing internal authority. It is often, but incorrectly, called crozier.

PATEN. The metal difh ufed for the oblation of bread in the Holy Euchariſt.

PAX. A fmall plate of precious metal, &c. carried round in the Latin Church, having been kiffed by the Prieft, after the *Agnus Dei* in the Mafs, to communicate the Kifs of Peace. The firft claufe of our Bleffing at the end of the celebration, " *The Peace of* GOD," &c. reprefents the Pax in our rite.

PEDE-CLOTH. See *Altar-carpet.*

PISCINA. A water-drain for ablutions, &c. on the fouth fide of the Sanctuary.

PLAIN SERVICE. See *Low Mafs.*

PLAIN SONG. The ecclefiaftical tone.

PLANETA. The folded chafuble, worn inftead of the dalmatic and tunic by the Sacred Minifters during Advent and Lent, except on the Sundays *Gaudete* and *Lætare*, when either purple "tunicles" (dalmatic and tunic) richly embroidered with gold, or elfe *rofe-coloured*, fhould be ufed.

PLATFORM. The raifed dais on which the altar ftands; and alfo that on which the font ftands.

POME. A round ball of filver or other metal; which is filled with hot water, and is placed on the altar in winter months to prevent danger or accident with the chalice, from the hands of the Prieft becoming numb with cold.

PONTIFICAL. Functions peculiar to Bifhops are fo called. When the Bifhop offers the Holy Sacrifice it is a Pontifical celebration.

PONTIFICALLY ASSISTING. When a Bifhop affifts pontifically he fays the *Pater Nofter*, *Collect for Purity*, *Ten Commandments*, and *The Bleffing*. The only two Rubrics in our Service-book on the matter direct the Bifhop to fay the *Abfolution* as well as the *Bleffing*. It is, however, ufual for the Bifhop not to fay the Abfolution, (at moſt only a remiffion for venial fin). The Rubric does not, of courfe, prohibit the Bifhop from directing the celebrant to fay it. When a Bifhop is fimply prefent on his throne the celebrant may give the *Bleffing;* the Rubrics fuppofe the Bifhop to be prefent pontifically affifting.

POST COMMUNION, THE, begins, as its name imports, after the Communion of the Faithful, and includes the LORD'S Prayer, the Prayer, O LORD *and Heavenly* FATHER, or, *Almighty and everliving* GOD, *Gloria in Excelfis*, and *the Collects*, printed at the end of the Service (when faid). The Poſt-Communion fhould be faid *junctis manibus*. In the Roman Rite the "Poft-Communion" confiſts of collects, one or more, according to the number of collects for the day, and immediately follows the "Communion," an anthem, or fhort fentence fo called, becaufe it is recited juft after the Communion.

PRAISE OF THE OFFICE. That portion of Matins and Evenfong from "*Gloria*" inclufive, to the "*Credo*" exclufive.

PRECES. The petitions which follow the Leffer Litany and *Pater Nofters* they are a felection from the *Preces* ufed at Lauds and Prime, and again at Vefpers and Compline.

PREDELLA. See *Platform.*

PRIE DIEU. A kneeling defk to be fuitably covered with fome hanging, and to be placed in a retired part of the inner Sacrifty. The tables of prayers before and after the Celebration of the Holy Euchariſt fhould hang immediately in front of it.

PRIME FUNCTION. From the *Credo* inclufive to the end of the Office.

PROANAPHORAL SERVICE. A name applied by certain writers to the *Missa Sicca* or "Table prayers"—a rite peculiar to the modern Church of England.

PURIFICATION. The wine poured into the chalice after the consumption of the Blessed Sacrament, and drunk by the celebrant. It is sometimes called the *First* Ablution. See *Ablution*.

PURIFICATOR. The napkin used for wiping the chalice at the conclusion of the Service. It is placed on the chalice under the pall before the beginning of the celebration. It is made of linen, neither coarse nor fine, and should be simply hemmed, and not less than six inches square, with a very small cross worked in the centre. Although it is not required to be blessed, yet, when once employed at the Holy Sacrifice, it should not be used for other purposes, nor be handled by laics (not having the requisite permission), until after having been washed by a Clerk in Holy Orders. The same rules for washing purificators are to be observed as for corporals. Before the chalice is offered the Priest wipes the inside with the purificator *down to the surface of the wine*. It used to be customary in the Latin Church, after the communion of the faithful, for a minister to give to each communicant a purification of wine or wine and water from a chalice, and to wipe his lips with a purificator. Each Priest should have his own purificator.

PYX. See *Ciborium*.

PYX CLOTH. A veil for the pyx.

RATIONAL. An ornament borrowed from the Aaronic by the Christian Priesthood, and formerly worn by Bishops on the breast.

REGAL. A small organ.

RELIQUARY. The casket in which reliques are kept.

REQUIEM. An office for the souls of the departed.

REREDOS. A screen or back placed between the altar and the east wall.

RESERVATION. The reserving the Blessed Sacrament for the sick or other purposes.

RETABLE. A shelf, temporary or otherwise, between the altar and the east wall. A series of receding shelves, or *retables*, behind and separate from the altar, is very convenient for vases of flowers and lights.

ROCHET. A short surplice of lawn with tight sleeves, as worn by Bishops. Without sleeves as used by clerics in baptism, &c. In reality the modern English Bishop's rochet is without sleeves, as the sleeves are sewn on to the chimere.

ROOD. A cross with the figure of our LORD upon it.

ROOD LOFT. A gallery running along the top of the rood-screen, which in parish churches should cross the chancel arch on the nave side. The Gospel and Epistle were, in old times, read from it.

ROOD-SCREEN or CHANCEL-SCREEN. A screen separating the chancel from the nave; sometimes surmounted by a figure of our Blessed LORD on the cross, and on either side the Blessed Virgin and S. John.

SACRAMENT, BLESSED, Consumption of what remains of the. The rubric rules that "the Priest and such of the communicants as he shall then call unto him, shall immediately after the Blessing, reverently eat and drink the same." It is to be noted that the faithful are here supposed to be present during the Consumption and Ablutions,—directed to take place "*immediately* after the Blessing" to ensure such presence. To "*reverently* eat" means, of course, *kneeling*. It is usual for the Priest himself to stand at the Consumption, as he does when he communicates himself.

SACRARIUM or SANCTUARY. The most holy place enclosed by the altar rails.

SACRED (OR CANONICAL) COLOURS—are five in number:—1. White; 2. Red; 3. Violet; 4.

Black; 5. Green. Gold is reckoned as white. On the Sundays *Gaudete* and *Lætare* a dalmatic and tunicle of *rose-colour* is used in Rome and elsewhere.

SACRED MINISTERS. Gospeller and Epistoler (the Deacon and Sub-deacon of the celebration).

SACRED VESSELS. The chalice, paten, ciborium (or pyx), and the large paten used instead, none of which may be handled by those not in Holy Orders without special permission.

SACRISTAN. The keeper of the holy things appertaining to Divine Worship.

SACRISTY. A vestry.

SANCTUARY. See *Sacrarium*.

SANCTUARY LAMP. That which burns before the Blessed Sacrament when It is reserved.

SCARF. Worn by chaplains; it is made of silk of the colour of the nobleman's livery to whom the cleric is chaplain; the ends are "pinked," and not fringed like a stole. The *black* scarf is worn over the gown by Doctors in Divinity, cathedral Dignitaries, and Bishops' chaplains. The scarf ought not properly to be worn with the surplice, as it has little to recommend it either in an ecclesiastical or æsthetic point of view.

SEAT COVERS. For the seat of the Sacred Ministers at Solemn Service; some to be of green, others of purple, others square for the stools, which are used on various occasions.

SECRETÆ (orationes). Prayers said *secreto*. Formerly certain prayers were ordered to be said. These *secrets* varied with the day. The term now denotes the short private supplementary devotions of the Priest.

SEDILIA. Seats for the officiating clergy on the south side of the altar—usually three, for Priest, Deacon, and Sub-deacon.

SEQUENCES. Certain rhythms chanted in mediæval times on particular Festivals after the gradual.

SERVER. The assistant of the Priest at Low Mass.

SERVICE. Stated parts of the Ordinary and Eucharistic Service set to music, as distinguished from those anthems, the words of which are not a matter of settled regulation, and *supplemental to the Plain Song of the Church*. The term includes the Versicles before the Psalms, the "*Venite*," one or more chants for the Psalms, the *Te Deum* and Canticles, the *Dominus vobiscum*, *Oremus*, lesser Litany, *Preces*, Amens, Litany, and Order of Holy Communion. The term is, however, sometimes restricted to the *Te Deum*, the Canticles, and in the Communion Service the Responses to the Commandments, Nicene Creed, and *Gloria in Excelsis*.

SOLEMN SERVICE. A choral celebration of the Holy Eucharist; the Priest is assisted by the Sacred Ministers, &c.

SPECIES. The outward and visible part of the Blessed Sacrament. Cf. Rubric before Communion of Priest, "Then shall the Minister first receive the Communion in both *kinds* himself," &c.

STOCK. The vessel in which the Holy Oil is kept, also called an ampulla. It should have a case of purple silk, and should be preserved in the aumbry.

STOLE. The vestment worn over the shoulders by Priests. The very badge of the Priestly office. It is a narrow strip of silk of the colour of the season, and has three crosses, one in the centre and one at each end. The ends are slightly widened, and terminate in a fringe. It is crossed upon the breast of the Priest, when he offers the Holy Sacrifice. At other times it is worn pendent. A Bishop wears the stole pendent when celebrating the Holy Eucharist, *because* he wears the pectoral cross. The stole when crossed is fastened either by a stud, or by a ribbon attached inside.

SUB-DEACON. The name by which the Epistoler is frequently designated.

SUPER-ALTAR. The ledge at the back of the altar on which stand the altar-cross, altar-lights, and flower vases.
SUPER-FRONTAL. The vestment which covers the *mensa* of the altar; it is put next over the cere-cloth.
TABERNACLE. A receptacle for the Blessed Sacrament.
TABLE PRAYERS. A popular name for the Dry Service. See *Missa Sicca.*
THURIBLE. A censer.
THURIFER. The server who carries the thurible and swings it in procession.
TIPPET. The *stuff* cape worn over the *surplice* in lieu of the hood by literates, and the silk cape permitted to be worn by dignitaries and beneficed Clergy over their *cassocks* at such times as they do not wear the hood.
TORCHES. Very suitable ones may be made of wood grooved to resemble four candles, i. e. the section of which should be a quatrefoil. These may be painted white, and hollowed out to receive a large-sized Palmer's candle-spring. They should have a hollow at the top, to retain any wax that may gutter. In these torches, the ends of the larger candles from the altar-candlesticks may be used up; let, however, the socket of the spring have a small aperture near the top, so that without taking out the candle, it may be seen whether there is sufficient for the occasion required. The ends of larger candles are best for this purpose, as the flame of a torch is naturally thought to be larger than that of an ordinary candle. The torches should be kept in a rack, which is either in a cupboard or capable of being covered over.
TRICANALE. A round ball with a screw cover, whereout issue three pipes. It was used by Bp. Andrewes instead of a cruet, for the water of mixture.
TRIPTYCH. A picture over the altar with folding doors, which usually have pictures painted on them inside, or at least are richly diapered.
TUNIC. The vestment of the Epistoler at the Holy Eucharist.
TUNICLES. The technical phrase for dalmatics and tunics, so used in the First Book of Edward VI.
UNCTION. The anointing with oil used in various rites of the Catholic Church.
VESPERS OR EVENSONG. The sixth canonical hour.
VESTMENT, THE. The chasuble. This term includes its appendages, as amice, alb, girdle, maniple, and stole; and even the frontal of the altar. See Lyndwood *in loco.*
VIGIL. The day before a festival when fasted.
VOLUNTARY. A piece of music played on the organ after the Psalms, and before or after Divine Service.
WAFER BREAD. Unleavened bread authorized to be used by the English Church in the Holy Eucharist.
WHITE ALB, PLAIN. An alb of linen, and not of silk with fringes and embroidery, but only with apparels.
YSOPUS OR HYSOPUS. See *Aspergillum.*
ZUCCHETTO. The cleric's round or skull cap worn under the birretta.

Index.

BSOLUTION, the, 117.
    in communion service, 55.
    position of celebrant during, 55.
    of sacred ministers, 198.
    of acolytes, 200.
Absolution, sacrament of, 249.
Abstinence, days of, 100.
Academical square or trencher cap, 15.
Access, prayer of humble, 56.
    position of celebrant during, 56.
    of sacred ministers, 56.
    of acolytes, 56.
Acolytes or lay assistants, directions for, 200.
Advent, greater antiphons of, note *, 138.
Alb, description of, 15.
    apparels of, 15.
Alms, manner of collecting, 48.
Alms-bowl, to be kept on the credence, and not on the altar, 33.
Alms-dish. See Offertory Basin, 9.
Altar, not to be embedded or fixed to the wall, 5.
    to be raised on a platform, 5.
    ascent to by at least two steps, 5.
    slab of, to be covered with a cere-cloth, 6.
    dimensions of, 4.
    the table of the LORD so called for the first five centuries, note §, 3.
    a Scriptural phrase for the LORD's table, note §, 3.
    parts of, 194.
    preparation of, for Holy Communion, 192.

Altar, the, its furniture, 9.
    furniture of, 9-13.
    time of vesting for a festival, 28.
    curtains to be hung at ends of, 7.
Altar-candlesticks, description of, 10, 11.
Altar-card, no mediæval authority for, 12.
Altar-cross, description of, 10.
    mentioned by Bede, note *, 10.
Altar-lights, statutable, pref. xvii.
    what they symbolize, 10.
    used in Queen Elizabeth's chapel, note *, 10.
    their symbolism as interpreted by the first Injunctions of Edw. VI, note †, 11.
    used in the Syriac, the oldest form of the Eastern rite, to this day, note *, 10.
    not to be lighted except at celebrations, note †, subnote [1], 10.
    authorities for, note †, 10.
    time for lighting, 34, 35.
    manner of lighting, 34.
    by whom to be lighted, 34.
    testimony of S. Jerome, note ‡, 34.
    not cæca lumina, testimony of Fuller, note ‡, 34.
    in Queen Elizabeth's chapel, note ‡, 34.
    42nd canon, under King Edgar, on, note ‡, 34.
    14th canon of Elfric on, note ‡, 34.
    testimony of Dr. Donne, note ‡, 34.
    testimony of Gregory (1671), note ‡, 34.
    testimony of S. Isidore of Seville, note ‡, 30.
    statutable, note †, 11.

Index.

Altar-lights, list of churches in which used, note ‡, 34, 35.
 never to be used as mere candles for lighting the sanctuary, 35.
 and other candles, subnote, 10.
Altar-stone, subnote ², 4.
Affusion, 157.
Amice, description of, 19.
Amyss, description of, 24.
 by whom worn, subnote ², 24.
 "tippets" of, subnote ¹, 24.
Andrewes, Bp. on the word altar, subnote ⁵, 3.
Anointing of the sick, 166.
 office from the First Book of Edw. VI, note *, 167.
 proper method of, note *, 167.
Anthem, the, 137.
Athanasius, S., creed of, 147.
Aumbrye, 8.

Banns of marriage, publication of, 43, 44.
Baptism, sacrament of, 152-159.
 things to be secured for, 152.
 the proper vestments for, 153.
 trine immersion, 154.
 sprinkling not recognized by the Church of England, 154.
 heretical or schismatic, 154.
 priest has power to alter improper names, 155.
 private, 155-157.
 method to be adopted when there are children to be simply admitted into the Church, as well as others to be baptized, 157.
 private, vestments for, 156.
 baptismal instrumenta, 156.
 cautions and directions, 158.
 rochet, a convenient vestment for, 159.
 authority for, note *, 159.
 parents not to baptize their own children, 159.
Benedictions, various, 245-247.
Bidding of prayer, form of, 265.
Birretta. See Priest's cap, 25.
Bishop's throne, proper, position of, 9.
Blessing, the, 66.
 position of celebrant, 67.

Blessing, of sacred ministers, 66.
 rationale of, note §, 66.
 manner of, by a bishop and by a priest, note †, 66.
Bowing at the Name of Jesus, enjoined by canon xviii. of 1603, note *, 132.
 at the Name of Jesus, note *, 42.
 at the Gloria Patri, note *, 42.
Bread, for Holy Communion, 69.
 note †, 70.
 priest's own, note †, 60.
 and wine, oblation of, 48-50.
  rationale of, note †, 48.
  the oblations, 48.
Burial, the, of the dead, 168-171.
 proper vestments, 168.
 holy communion at, 169, 170.
Burse, description of, note †, 32.

Calendar, the, 97-108.
Canon, the, 57.
 position of celebrant during, 57-61.
 of sacred ministers, 198.
 of acolytes, 200.
 of servers, 200.
 taken from the Sarum rite, note *, 57.
Canticles, the, 128.
Cassock, description of, 14, 15.
Cautels of the Mass (Cautelæ Missæ), 83-92.
 and directions, 83.
 and directions for officiant in divine office, 145.
Celebrant, directions for, 193-196.
Celebration, hour of, 33.
 afternoon, condemnation of, 33.
Cere-cloth, note ‡, 6.
Chalice, description of, 9.
 and paten, manner of placing upon the altar at the beginning of the celebration, 31, 32.
 at oblation of the elements, 32, 50, 54.
 after the communion of the faithful, 32.
 is placed on the altar without the veil when a bishop celebrates, note *, 50.
Chalices and patens, directions as to, 204.
Chalice cover of linen and lace, dimensions of, note †, 31.

Index.   299

Chalice-veil of silk, dimensions of, note †, 32.
Chancel, to be separated from nave by rood-screen, 110.
    no laymen, save singers, to have their place there, 110.
Chasuble, description of, 18.
    called by way of excellency "the vestment," 18.
Chesible. See Chasuble, 18.
Chimere, subnote ⁂, 95.
Chirothecæ. See Gloves, 20.
Choir, manner of leaving, 142.
    mode of proceeding to, 112.
    tippet. See Amyss, 24.
Chorister, form of admission of, 250.
    prayers for, 29.
Church militant prayer, pre-reformation prayer with same title, note *, 53.
    position of deacon and sub-deacon at, 54.
Churching, the, of women, 171, 172.
    proper vestments, 171.
Churchwardens, duty of, in regard to "ornaments," pref. xix, note *.
    staves, 264.
Ciborium, used instead of the paten in communicating the faithful, note *, 63.
    description of, note *, 63.
Cleansing of church furniture, 260, 261.
Cloak, mentioned in 2 S. Tim. iv. 13, considered to be the Eucharistic vestment, subnote ⁂, 18.
Collects in communion office, number of, to be said, their rationale, 40, 41.
Collect for the Queen, position of priest at, 38.
    position of deacon and sub-deacon at, 197.
    second collect to be preferred, 38.
    head of seasons, 106.
    other collects at Holy Eucharist, 40.
    in commemoration, 40.
    memorial, when Sunday collect is to be added to that of the Saints' day, 104.
    for the day, 38.
    use of, on vigils, eves, and evensong, 102.
    general rule for using of, first evensongs, 103.
    epistles and gospels, 151.
    to be said standing, 146.

Collection, a, after office, 146.
Colours, canonical, 27, 28.
    of the day, to be used on the minor festivals, subnote ¹, 43.
    Sarum use of, note †, 26.
Commandments and Kyrie Eleisons, 37.
    rationale of, note ‡, 37, 38.
Commemoration of the living and the dead, 51.
Commination, a, 173.
    proper vestments, 173.
    "reading-pew," what, 173.
    position of litany-stool during, 173.
Communion, notice of. See Notices.
    warning of, 44.
    of priest, 62.
    position of sacred ministers during, 62, 198.
    of clergy, 62.
    of choir, 62.
    of acolytes, 200.
    of servers, 202.
    of the faithful, 63, 64.
    or houseling cloth, 33.
    holy, signifies the receptionary part of the office, subnote ¹, 26.
    so used in 1547, subnote ¹, 26.
    the, of the sick, 165-168.
    proper vestments, 165.
    instrumenta, 165, 166.
    priest to have a server, note †, 165.
Concurrence of holy days, 101.
    of first and second evensongs of festivals, 102.
Confession, the general, 116.
    in Communion service, 55.
    position of celebrant during, 55, note *, 55, 93.
    of sacred ministers, 55, 93.
Confirmation, the order of, 160, 161.
    proper vestments for bishop, 160.
    for clergy, &c, 160.
    position of episcopal chair, 160.
    dress for females at, 161.
Consecration, prayer of. See Canon, 57.
    in one kind, 64.
    in one kind, rubric concerning, a transcript of the Sarum cautel, 64.

Index

Confecration of churches, form of, according to the use of the Church of Ireland, 206.
Consumption and purification, 71.
Cope, 24.
   used in the University of Cambridge, 25.
   used at solemn vespers, 24.
   at processions and funerals, 14.
   Cambridge, description of, 25.
   to be worn at solemn vespers, 143.
Coronation service, oblation of, elements, note *, 32.
   secreta of, note *, 32.
   Queen's *second oblation*, note *, 32.
Corporals, washing of, 96.
   not to be touched by laics without permission, note *, 96.
   mediæval practice concerning, note †, 96.
Corpus Christi Day, 98.
Cotta. See Surplice, 22.
Cowle. See Academical Hood, 23.
Credence, 7, 8, 28, 32.
   authorized by the Privy Council, 279.
   how vested, 32.
   preparation of, 32, 33.
Creed, Apostles', 131.
   the Nicene, 42.
   position of celebrant at, 42, 195.
      of gospeller and epistoler at, 43.
   to be said with everything after in the midst of the altar, 42.
Cross, sign of, 193.
   note †, 114, 115.
   not included in the order to destroy images, note *, 10.
   in most ancient illuminations of altars is displayed, and not the crucifix, note *, 10.
   the present Roman rule obeyed if a simple cross, and not a crucifix, be placed on the super-altar, note *, 10.
Croyzer, 21.
Crozier, description of, 21.
Crucifix, statutable, pref. xxi, 277, 278.
   on the altar in Queen Elizabeth's chapel, note *, 10.
Cruets, 9.
Curtains. See Altar, 7.

Cushions, not allowed upon the altar. See Desk, 28.

Daily Eucharist, 69.
   those who communicate spiritually to be counted in so as to form a quorum, note *, 69.
   when the oblation is made the service must go on, note *, 69.
Dalmatic, description of, 19, 20.
   symbolism of, subnote *, 19.
   the episcopal, 20.
Deacon, prayers for when vesting, 30.
   vestments of, 14, 273, 275.
   proper place when ministering at the altar, note ‡, 49.
   assistant, vestments of, 29.
   directions for, in office, note *, 117.
Desk, for altar, 28.
Devotion, Feasts of, 259.
Divine service, a direct tradition from the old English term for the "hours," subnote ¹, 16.
   office, to precede holy communion, note †, 2.
Dominus vobiscum, the, 133.
Duplication, 72.

Elements, prayer when they are set apart in the sacristy, subnote ¹, 49.
   the, 189, 190.
   to be placed on *credence* before the celebration begins, note *, 32.
   Sarum (and old French) use *allowed* it till the first collect, note *, 32.
   in the *Syriac*, quite at the beginning, note *, 32.
   strictly speaking should accompany the introit, note *, 32.
   by whom placed on credence, note *, 33.
Elevation of paten, 60.
Ember collects, 150.
Embroidery, definition of, pref. xxvi, note *.
Epistle, note †, 38, 42.
   everything before, to be said at the north-side, 42.
   book of, to be placed on credence, note ‡, 28.

Epistoler or sub-deacon, not to wear the stole, note §, 2.
 prayers for, when vesting, 30.
 vestments of, 14, 273, 275.
Epitrachelion, of the East, answers to the stole of the West, 16.
Eucharist, holy, a term much more frequent in the English than in the Roman use, 1.
Eucharistic vestments, statutable, pref. xviii.
Eves, 102.
Exhortation and invitatory, 54, 55.
 the, 116.
Expiation and illustration of a church *desecrated* or *prophaned*, short office for, 220.

Fair white linen cloth, 28.
 not to cover the antependium, note †, 28.
  the, may be richly worked in scarlet or blue for festivals, so the work be not embroidery (see Embroidery), but must not be fringed with lace, pref. xxvi, 270.
Fastings, days of, 107.
Festivals, subnote ¹, 43.
Flagon. See Cruets, 9.
Floral decoration, 252-257.
Flowers on the altar, 258.
Flower vases, 258.
Fraction of the bread, note †, 57. 60.
 after consecration, note ‡, 60.
Fridays, how to be marked, 108.

Girdle of alb, 19.
Gloria Patri, the, 119.
 in excelsis, 66.
  position of celebrant during, 66.
  of sacred ministers, 66.
  of acolytes, 200.
  of servers, 202.
Gloves, episcopal, description of, 20.
 Wykeham's, subnote ², 20.
 not to be worn by priests with the vestments of the church, subnote ³, 19.
Gospel, 38, note †, 39, 39-42.

Gospels, book of, to be placed on credence, 33.
Gospeller and epistoler stand facing the east, 2.
 parts of service which may be said by them, 2.
 36, and note †.
"Gray Amice," subnote ², 24.
Gray amys, note *, 112.
Gremial, the, 95.

Hands, position of, 116.
Holy days, public notice of, 43.
 which take precedence of other holy days, 105.
 services of, not to be mingled, 106.
Holy Eastern Church, eucharistical vestments of, subnote ⁶, 16.
Hood, academical, proper shape of, 23.
 not to be used together with the ancient vestments, 46.
 not worn with the eucharistic vestments, nor by any assisting at the celebration, 46.
 in the Roman Church, the religious orders who wear them adjust them under the ecclesiastical vestments, note *, 29.
Houselling cloth. See Communion Cloth, 33.
Hymns, 138.

Immersion, 157.
Incense, authorities for, 12, 13.
Incense, directions for the use of at high celebration, 73-75.
Introit and anthem, rationale of, 36.
Inventories of church goods taken in the reign of King Edward VI. in the Record Office, at Carlton Ride, 276-278.
Invocation, supplemental prayer of, note *, 58.

Kneeling, when celebrant kneels in Communion service, note †, 56.

Lesser litany, 133.
 Lord's Prayer after, 134.
Lessons, the, must belong to the same service as epistle and gospel, 106.
 the, 106.
 reading of, 123.

Liripipe, description of, 23.
Litany, the, 148-150.
    proper vestments, 148.
    position of litany desk, 148.
Liturgy, the celebration of the Holy Eucharist, note †, subnote ¹, 2.
Locker. See Aumbrye, 8.
Lord's Prayer in office, 117.
Lord's Supper, term of, first introduced in Edward VI.'s first book, subnote ¹, 26.
    signifies the consecration as distinct from the communion, subnote ¹, 26.
Lotio manuum, 51.
    authorities for, notes *, †, §, 51.

Magnificat, incense formerly used at, 143.
Maniple, description of, 19.
    always worn by celebrant and sacred ministers, 14, 175, 273, 275.
Mass, the common name for the sacrament of the Lord's Supper in the time of Elizabeth, subnote ¹, 1.
    the sacrament of the Lord's Supper so called in the first book of Edward VI, note *, 1.
    has no connection with the doctrine of transubstantiation, subnote ¹, 1.
Master of the Ceremonies, 263.
Matins and evensong, 109-146.
    hour of, note †, 109.
Matrimony, the form of solemnization of, 161-163.
    proper vestments, 161.
        to be used when there is a celebration, 162.
Mensa, 4, 5.
Missa sicca, 67.
    rationale of, note *, 67.
    vestments of priest, 69, 191.
    only allowable on Good Friday, note †, 69.
Mitre, description of the three sorts of, 20.
    manner of serving, note. 97.
Music of the English Church, 284-286.

Non-communicants, presence of, at celebration of Holy Eucharist, 63.
North-side of the altar, rationale of, note *, 38.
North-side of the altar, explained, 194, 195.
Norwegian church, altar-steps, chasuble, &c, used as in the West, subnote ¹, 18.
Notice of minor festivals, note *, 43.
    of Communion, 44.

Oblations, refers exclusively to the elements, note ||, 51.
    manner of making, 52, 54.
    ancient English use of making, note ||, 52.
Oblation of the elements, chalice and paten how placed at, note *, 31.
    the Sarum custom the same, note *, 31.
    the *present* Roman custom the same, though different before the fifteenth century, note *, 31.
    how ordered according to the most ancient rite, viz. the Syriac liturgy of S. James, note *, 31.
Obligation, feasts of, 259.
Occurrence of holy days, 101.
    and memorial collect, 104.
    of eves, 104.
Octaves, 107.
Offertory, 47.
    position of celebrant at, 47.
    rationale of note †, 47.
    sentences of, at solemn and plain service, note ‡, 47.
    basin, 9.
Office for Palm Sunday, 266.
Office, the Roman term for the "hours," subnote ², 16.
Oil of chrism, 248.
    of the sick, 248.
    holy, 248.
    may be consecrated by a priest, 249.
    consecrated by the bishop in mediæval times as a matter only of convenience and discipline, 249.
Orationes, the, 136.
Oremus, the, 133.
Order of the administration of the Lord's Supper, an ellipse for the order of administration of the sacrament of the Lord's Supper, note *, 26.
Ordinal, the, 174, 175.

Ordinal, the, Lutheran and Calvinist ministers being lay are to be ordained, note ‡, 174.
    deacons, form and manner of making, 175-180.
    priests, form and manner of ordering, 181-183.
    archbishop or bishop, form of ordaining or consecrating, 183-186.
Ornaments of the church, 270-273.
    of the ministers, 273-275.
    statutable authority for, pref. xv—xxi.
    of the ministers, statutable authority for, pref. xv—xxi.
    the incumbent concerned in ordering them as well as the churchwardens, pref. xix, note *.
    the liability of the parishioners, pref. xix, note *.
    of the priest, xix, note *.
Orphreys, description of, 18.
Ostension of chalice, note †, 60.

Pall, archiepiscopal, description of, 21, 22.
    for chalice, description of, note †, 31.
Parts of the altar, 194.
Pastoral staff, description of, 20, 21.
    executed by G. E. Street, Esq. for the late Bp. of Graham's Town, 21.
    executed by R. J. Withers, Esq. for the Bishop of Central Africa, 21.
Pater noster and collect for purity, 37.
    position of priest at, 37.
    to be said by the priest alone, 37.
    rubric concerning the LORD's Prayer at matins, does not govern the Communion office, note *, 37.
    position of, in the ancient liturgies, note *, 37.
    still a præparatio ad missam, note †, 37.
    rationale of the "Amen" at the end of the LORD's Prayer and of the collect for purity, note †, 37.
Paten, description of, 9.
Penance, sacrament of. See Absolution, 249.
Phænolion, of the East, answers to the chasuble of the West, 16.
Piscina, 8.
Plain service, 76-83.

Position of celebrants, sacred ministers, and acolytes, at the beginning of the celebration, 36.
    priest with gospeller on his right, and epistoler on his left hand, stands on ascending the platform at first in centre of the altar, 36.
    at singing of the introit priest goes to north-side, the gospeller standing on the second step at his right, the epistoler on the third step on the right of the gospeller, note *, 36.
    normal, of priest, 93.
    of sacred ministers, 93.
    of hands and feet, note †, 36.
Post communion, the, 65, 66.
    position of sacred ministers during, 65, 199.
Post S. Eucharistiam, 31.
Præparatio ad S. Eucharistiam, 31.
Praise of the office, 119-131.
Prayers for celebrant, sacred ministers, choristers, &c. when vesting, 29, 30.
    for the Queen's Majesty, 139.
    for the royal family, 140.
    for the clergy and people, 140.
    for all conditions of men, 140.
    of S. Chrysostom, 141.
    benediction, 141, 142.
    occasional, the, 150.
Preacher in Communion office, 45.
    how vested if the celebrant, 46.
        if deacon or sub-deacon, 46.
        if not one of the sacred ministers, 45, 46.
    not to kneel in pulpit, 47.
    after office, dress of, 146.
Preces, the, 135.
    secretæ from Sarum missal, 61.
Preface, 56.
    position of celebrant at, 56.
    of sacred ministers, 198.
Prefaces, proper, 107.
Preparatio ad chorum, 111.
Priest, prayers for, when vesting, 30.
    position of, at north-side, 2.
    when he reads the epistle and gospel ought to go off the footpace, 2.

Prieft, ought not to leave the footpace as a general rule, 2.
   fulfilling the function of deacon to wear the proper diaconal veftments, note §, 2.
Prime function, the, 106-117.
Privy Council, judgment of, in the cafe of the Knightfbridge churches, 279.
   comment thereon by J. D. Chambers, Efq. M.A. recorder of Salifbury, 280.
Proanaphoral fervice, note *, 68.
Proceffion and introit, 36.
Proceffional banners, 264.
   crofs or crucifix, 265
   in Lent of wood, painted red, note *, 265.
Proceffions, order of, 262.
Pfalms, the, 121.
   the Gloria Patri, in the, 121.
Pyx, ufed inftead of the paten in communicating the faithful, note *, 63.
   defcription of, note *, 63.
   the authorized veffel in the Church of England, note *, 63.

Rational, defcription of, 22.
Reconfecration and reconciling of churches, 248.
Reredos, 7.
   ferved in mediæval times as the fuper-altar of the prefent day, 284.
   fuper-altar to be preferred to the reredos for the crofs and lights, 284.
Reftoration of a church, office to be ufed in, according to the ufe of the Church of Ireland, 218.
Ring, epifcopal, defcription of, 21.
   fymbolifm of, fubnote ², 21.
   Abp. Lee's (of York), fubnote ³, 21.
   not to be worn by priefts with the veftments of the church, fubnote ³, 19.
Rochet, the, 88, 159.
Rogation days, 108.
   banners for perambulation, 108.
Ruff, academical, fubnote ¹, 24.

Sacrament, Bleffed, to be received by the Prieft—celebrant ftanding, 62.

Sacrament, Bleffed, how to receive, note †, 63.
   dropping particles of, facrilege, note, 64.
Sacred minifters (deacon and fub-deacon) additional notes for, 196.
Sacrifty or Veftry, rules for, 260.
Sanctuary, how to be lighted at evenfong, &c, note †, fubnote ¹, 10.
Sanctus, 56.
Sandal, defcription of, 20.
   Bifhop Waneflete's, fubnote ⁴, 20.
Scarf, pref. xxi, 220.
Sedilia, 8.
   not to be ufed during Matins or Evenfong, 114.
Sentences, the Offertory, 47.
   the Introductory, at Matins and Evenfong, 114, 115.
Septum, 9.
Sermon in Communion Office, 45, and note *.
   how to be preceded, 46.
   no prayer before to be ufed, 46.
   doxology at end of, to be faid turning eaftwards, 47.
Service for Laying the Foundation Stone of a Church, 222.
   for the Solemn Opening of a Church, 228.
   for the Benediction of a Dwelling Houfe, 240.
   the old Sarum term for the "hours," fubnote ², 16.
Servers, directions for, 201-203.
Shirt-collars, not to be worn with the veftments of the church, fubnote ³, 19.
Solemn fervice, fung in prefence of a Bifhop affifting pontifically, 205.
   in the abfence of a fub-deacon, 199.
Spiritual communion, 167, 168.
   the fame provifion to be found in the pre-reformation fervice-books, 168.
Sponfor, the father may not be; the mother may, note *, 152.
"Standing before the table," rationale of, note ‡, 57.
Statute, 23 Henry VIII. c. 19, note ‡, 11.
   gives to ancient canon law the force of ftatute law, note ‡, 11.

Index 305

Statute, 23 Hen. VIII, c. 19, with what limitations, note ‡, 11.
Stole, description of, 15.
    spoken of under the name of Orarium at the council of Laodicea, 15.
    not to be worn during Matins or Evensong, 17.
Sub-deacon. See Sacred Ministers and Solemn Service.
    or epistoler, not to wear the stole, note §, 2.
Sudarium, 21.
Sundays before Advent, 151.
    which take precedence of Saints' days, 105.
Surplice, 19.
Super-altar, description of, 6.
    ornaments to be placed on, 6.
Super-frontal, 6.
    to be vested with three linen cloths, which always remain thereon; the whole to be covered with a strip of green silk, except during the celebration of the Holy Eucharist, note ‡, 6, 7.
Sursum corda, 56.
    position of celebrant at, 56.
    of sacred ministers, 198.
    of acolytes, 200.
    of servers, 202.
Swedish churches, vested altars, crosses, altar-lights, and vestments, used therein, as in the West, subnote ¹, 18.

Thanksgiving, general, 140.
Throat, relaxed, Mr. Macready's opinion as to the cause of, note *, 45, 46.
Throne proper, bishop's, position of, 160.
Tippet, description of, 23.
Tippets, canons of 1603 on, 23.
Translation of festivals, 105.
Tunic, description of, 10.
    the episcopal, 10.
Tunicles, subnote ², 10.

Veiling of Blessed Sacrament, 65.
    description of veil, note *, 65.
Venite, the, 119.

Verger's staff, 264.
Versicles, 118.
    and response, 118.
Vestments, description of, 14-25.
    diaconal, 19, 29, 273.
    eucharistic, 14, 20, 274, 275.
    for the celebrant, 14, 18, 19.
    colours of, 26, 28.
    fashion of, 14, 25.
    for the sacred ministers, 14, 25, 273.
    episcopal, 29, 175, 190, 274.
    for daily service, 22, 25, 112.
    for the ordination of Priests and Deacons, 181.
    old, to be burnt, 248.
    for Priest in solemnizing Matrimony, 161.
    for Priest in Communion of the Sick, 165.
    for Priest and Clerks at Burial of the Dead, 168.
    for Priest in Churching of Women, 171.
    for Commination Service, 173.
    for Bishop in Confirmation, 161.
        Ordination, 175.
        Coronation, 24.
    of a chorister, 273.
    of sacristan, 274.
    of choir, 274.
    of first book of Edward VI, 93.
    arrangement of, for solemn Eucharistic service in presence of a Bishop assisting pontifically, 205.
    arrangement of, where there is no sacristy, 96.
    arrangement of vestments for solemn service by a bishop in his own diocese, 94.
    the same, with very insignificant modifications, throughout the universal Church, subnote ⁶, 16.
    not peculiar to the Roman Church, subnote ¹, 18.
    of catholic use, subnote ¹, 18.
Vestry, rules for, 260.
Vexillum, 21.
Vigils, 79.

Visitation of the sick, order for, 164.
    accustomed form of making a confession, 164.
    proper vestments, 164.
    absolution, 164.
Washing of corporals, 96.
White linen cloth, †, 28.
Wine, for holy communion, 189, and note *, 189.

Words, comfortable, 31.
    position of celebrant at, 31.
    of sacred ministers, 198.
    of acolytes at, 200.
    of servers, 201-204.
    of institution, all that is necessary for valid consecration, note *, 64.

Zucchetto. See scull-cap, subnote ¹, 15.

CHISWICK PRESS:—PRINTED BY WHITTINGHAM AND WILKINS,
TOOKS COURT, CHANCERY LANE.

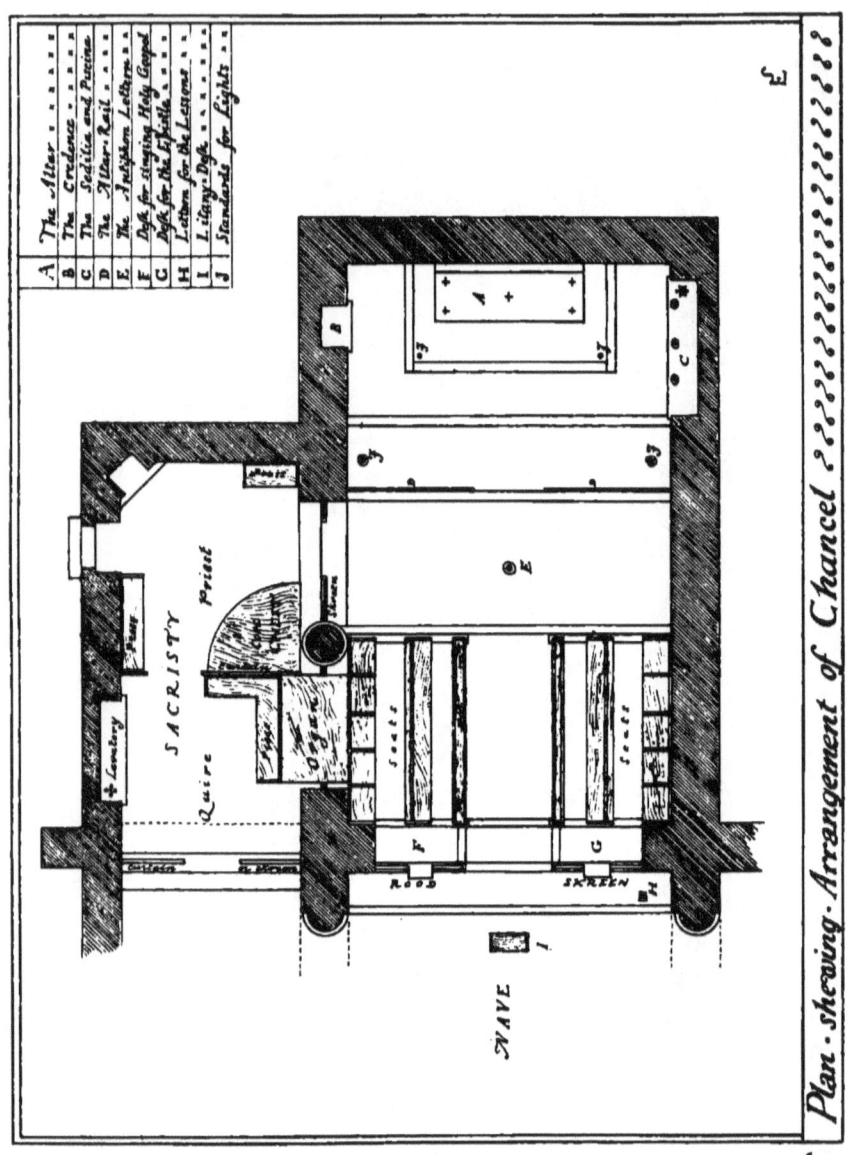

A: Bird's-Eye: view: of: a: Chancel:

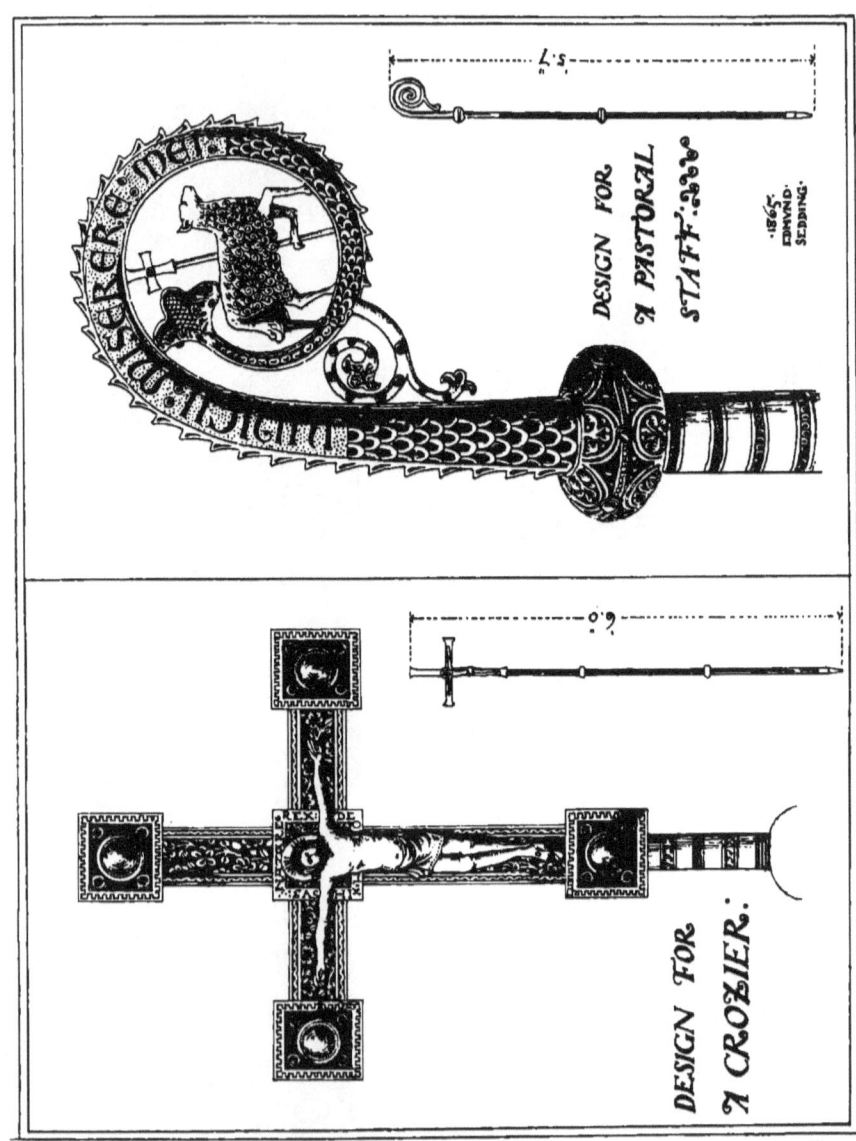

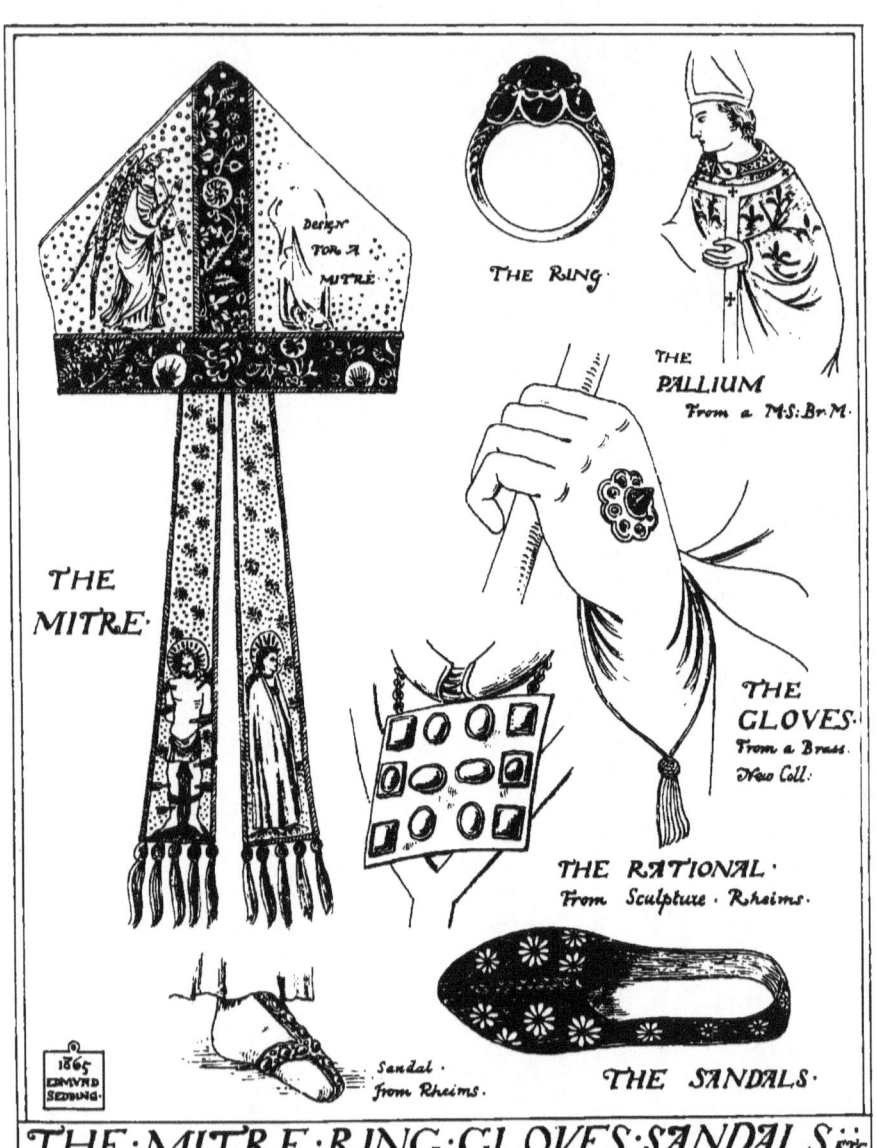

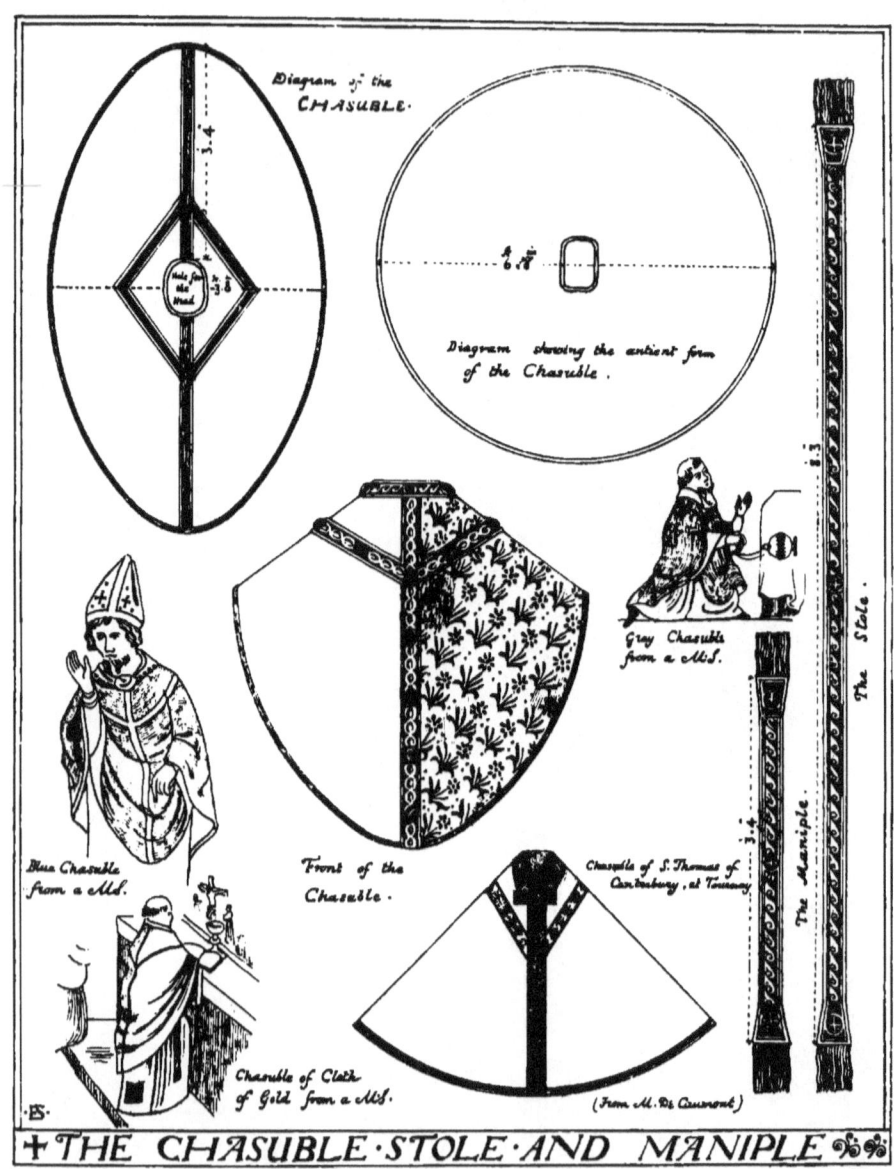

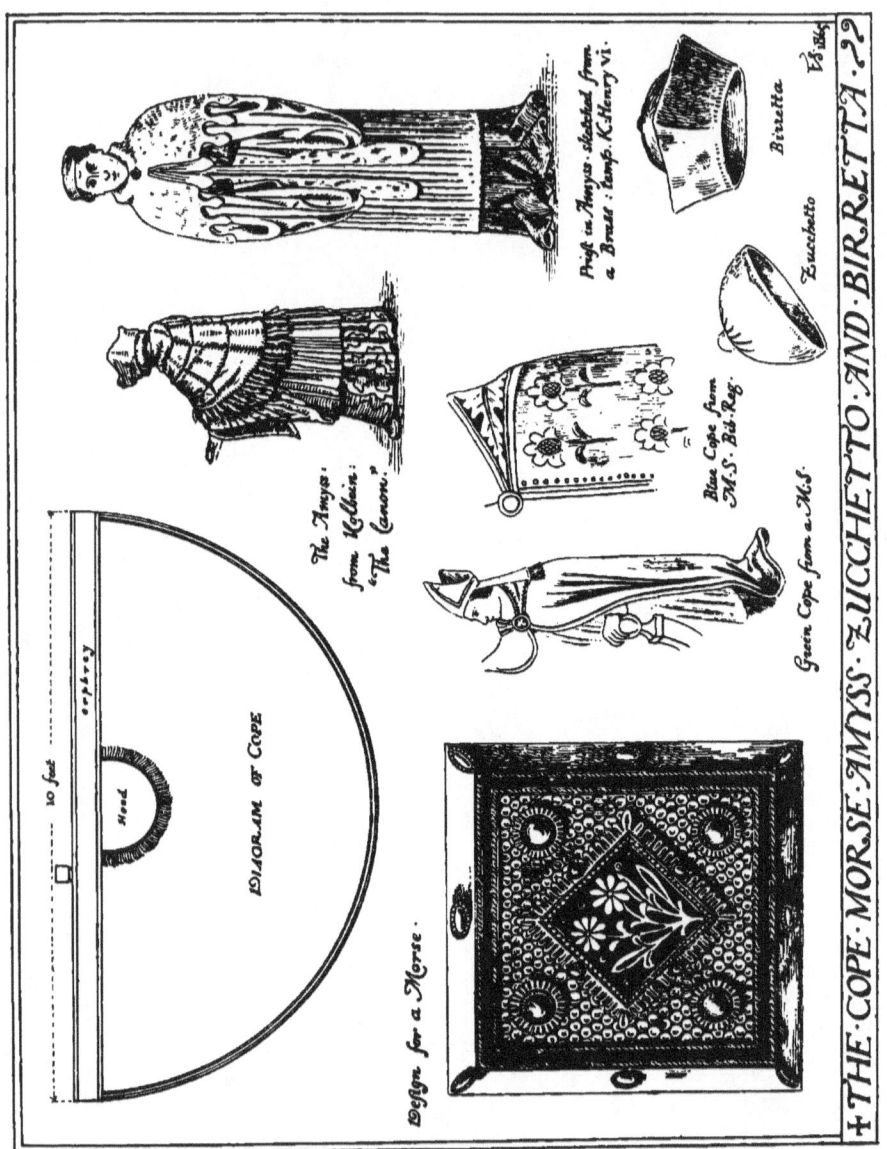

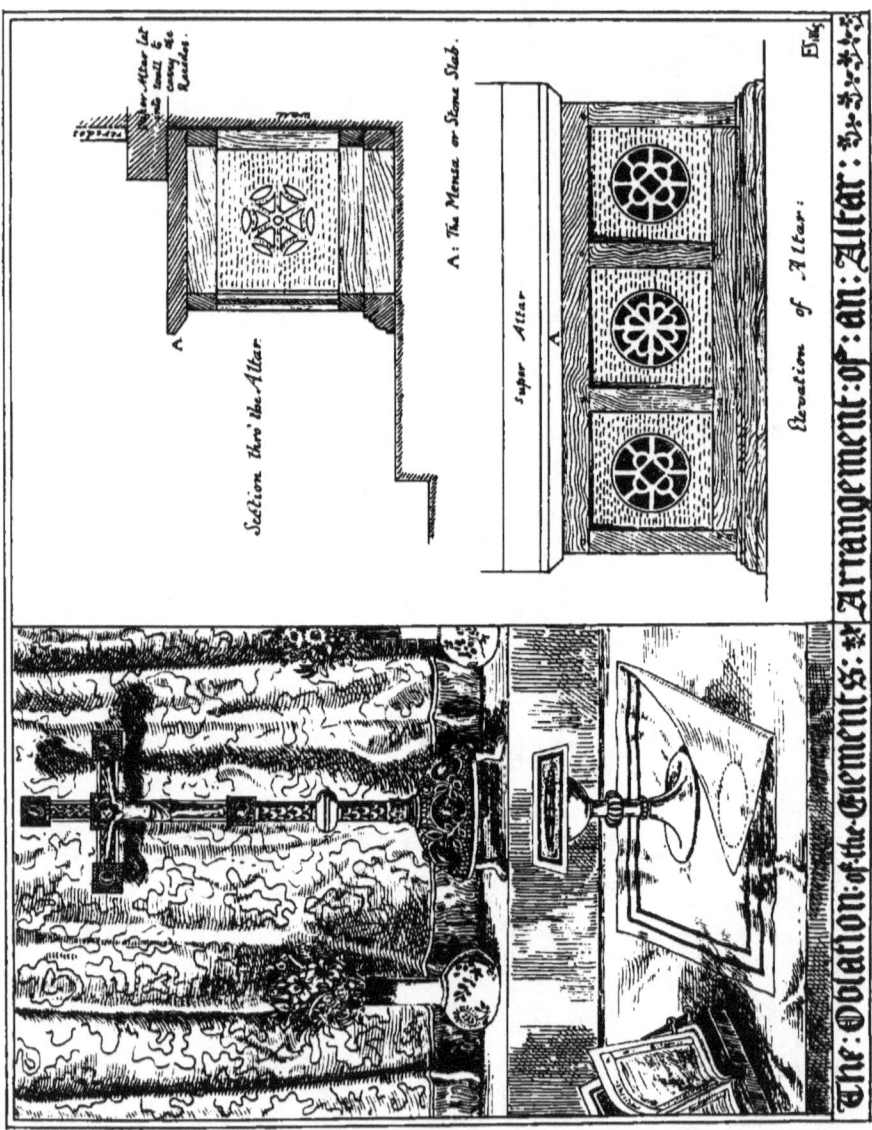

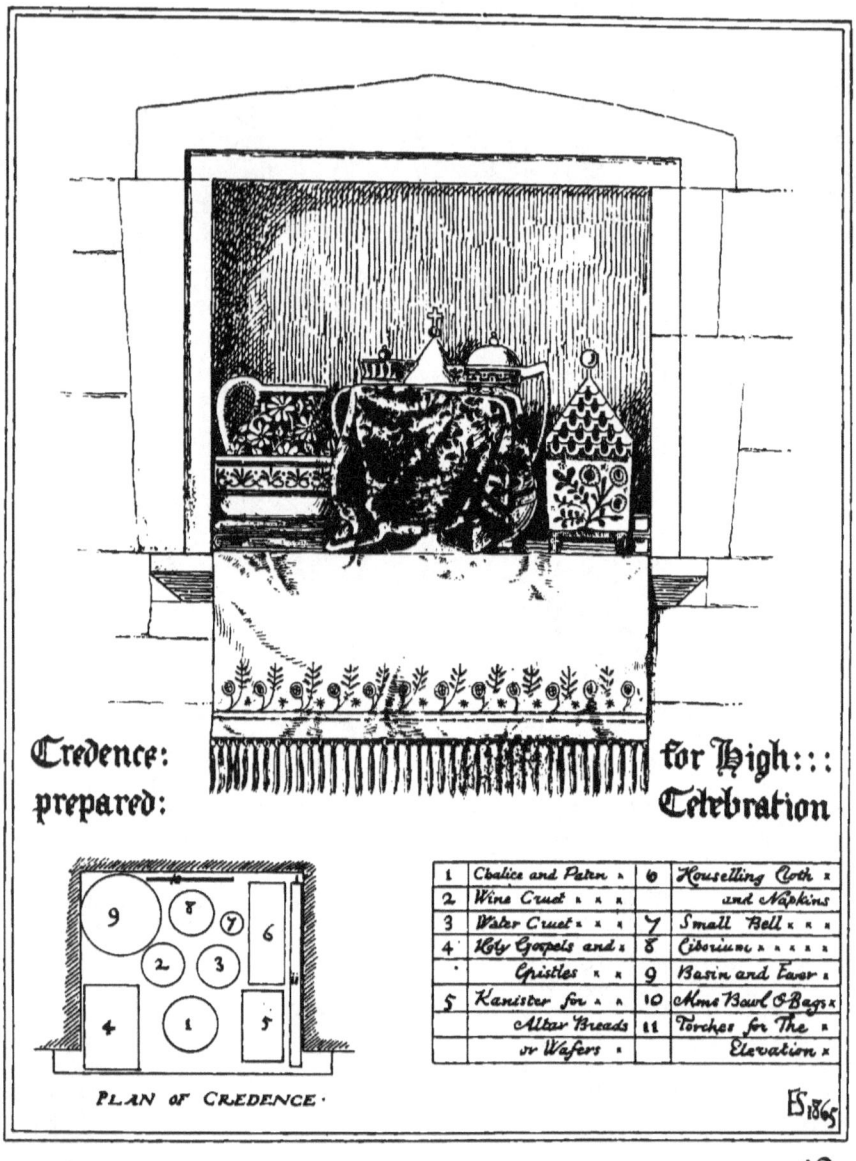

DIAGRAM SHEWING THE DISTINCTION BETWEEN THE NORTH SIDE AND THE NORTH END OF THE ALTAR

| North Corner | North Side | Midst of the Altar | South Side | South Corner |

Diagram shewing the positions of the Ministers at the Altar at the Epistle (High Celebration)

Celebrant
Deacon
Sub-deacon
Acolyte   Acolyte

Diagram shewing the positions of the Ministers at the singing of the Holy Gospel

Celebrant — Step
Deacon — Step
Sub-deacon — Step
(o o Acolytes)

13

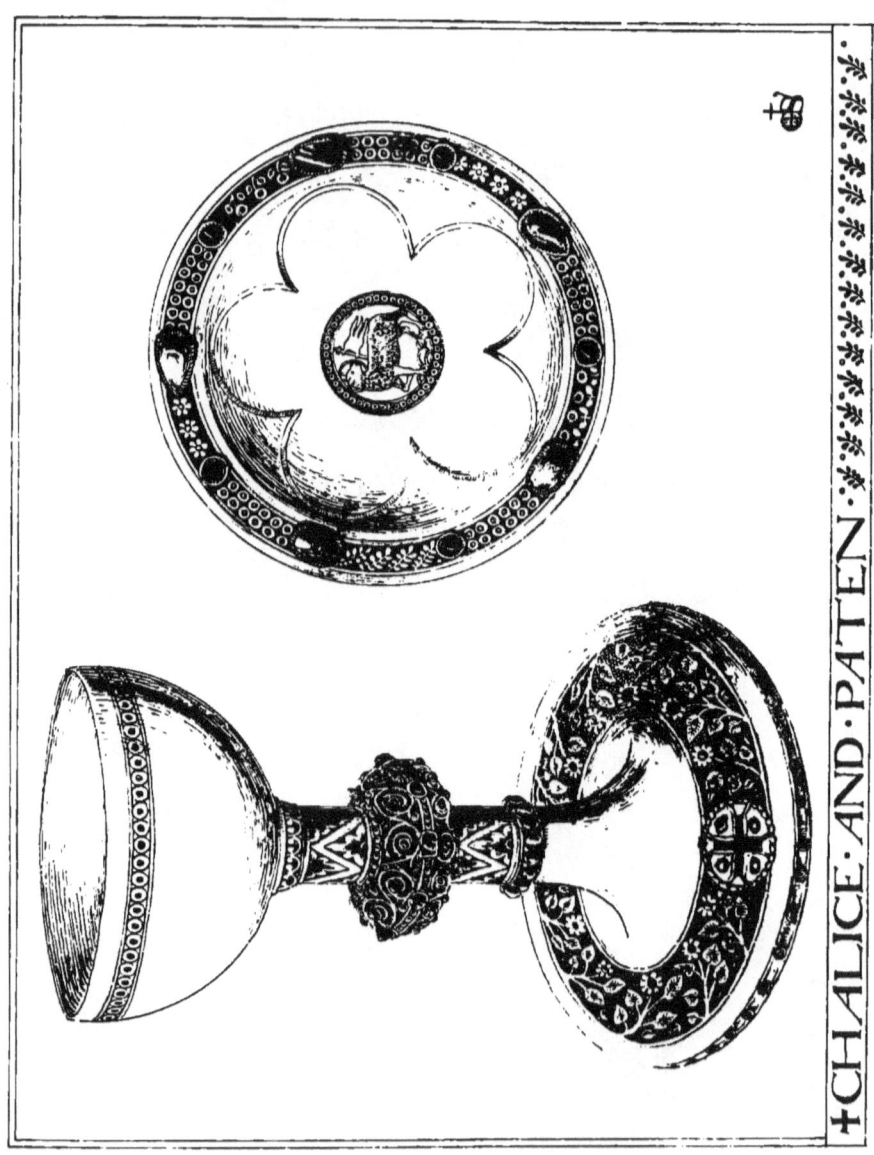

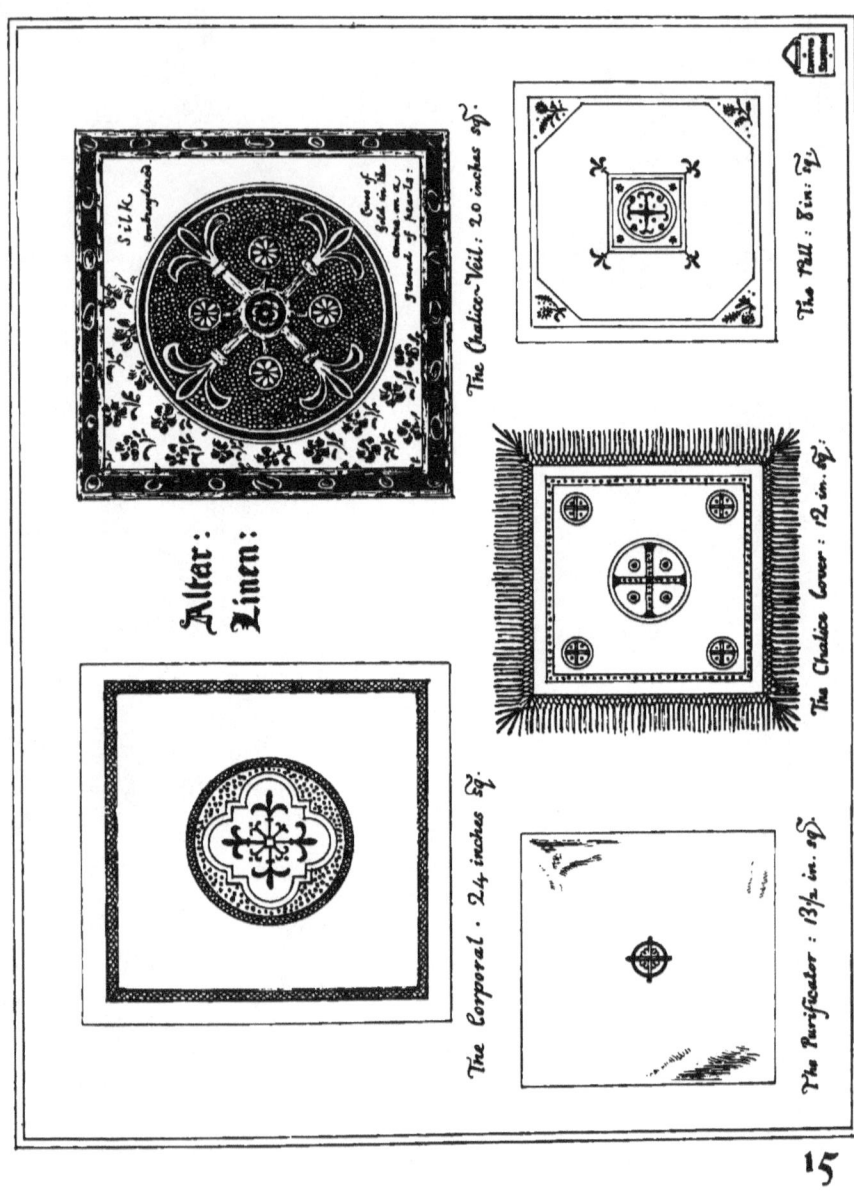

In the Press, being handsomely printed by Whittingham and Wilkins,

Three Altar Service Books,

ACCORDING TO THE PRESENT USE OF THE CHURCH OF ENGLAND.

EDITED BY THE REV. F. G. LEE.

I.

Service Book for the Priest Celebrant.

CONTAINING KALENDAR, COLLECTS, EPISTLES AND GOSPELS, COMMUNION SERVICE, OFFICE FOR CONFIRMATION, Etc.

ARRANGED AFTER THE PLAN OF THE SARUM RITE, WITH THE ANCIENT PLAIN SONG OF THE CHURCH.

II.

Book of Gospels.

III.

Book of Epistles.

LONDON:
THOMAS BOSWORTH, 215, REGENT STREET.

www.ingramcontent.com/pod-product-compliance
Lightning Source LLC
Chambersburg PA
CBHW030347230426
43664CB00007BB/559